THE BRITISH PRESIDENCY

MANCHESTER
UNIVERSITY PRESS

IN MEMORIAM

K

MICHAEL FOLEY

The British presidency

Tony Blair and the politics of public leadership

Manchester University Press
MANCHESTER AND NEW YORK
distributed exclusively in the USA by St. Martin's Press

Published by Manchester University Press
Oxford Road, Manchester M13 9NR, UK
and Room 400, 175 Fifth Avenue, New York, NY 10010, USA
http://www.manchesteruniversitypress.co.uk

Distributed exclusively in the USA by
St. Martin's Press, Inc., 175 Fifth Avenue, New York, NY 10010, USA

Distributed exclusively in Canada by
UBC Press, University of British Columbia, 2029 West Mall,
Vancouver, BC, Canada V6T 1Z2

British Library Cataloguing-in-Publication Data
A catalogue record for this book is available from the British Library

Library of Congress Cataloging-in-Publication Data applied for

ISBN 0 7190 5015 4 *hardback*
0 7190 5016 2 *paperback*

This edition first published 2000

07 06 05 04 03 02 01 00 10 9 8 7 6 5 4 3 2 1

Typeset in Monotype Ehrhardt by Carnegie Publishing, Chatsworth Rd, Lancaster
Printed in Great Britain by Biddles Ltd, Guildford and King's Lynn

Contents

List of figures and tables

Figures

Tables

Acknowledgements

I am indebted to a wide range of individuals for their background briefings, insights and appraisals. Many of them were given to me off the record. Others were not. For the sake of equity, it is appropriate to eschew specific thanks in favour of a general, yet genuine, appreciation to all those who provided me with information and guidance. This work carries their imprint. On a more technical level, I wish to express my gratitude to the editorial and production staff at Manchester University Press. For the prodigious task of turning my research into publishable form, I am particularly thankful to Nicola Viinikka, Pippa Kenyon, Tony Mason, Richard Delahunty, Celia Ashcroft, Rachael Bolden and Diane Jones. In my experience, their professionalism and attention to detail remain unrivalled. I would also like to thank both Jo Foley for her assistance in devising the tables and figures, and Stuart Shields for producing the index. Finally, I must give due recognition to the support of my colleagues in the Department of International Politics at the University of Wales, Aberystwyth. Under the stewardship of Steve Smith and Ken Booth, the department has become a first-rate centre for research. This project has benefited enormously from the intellectual stimulus of open frontiers and critical inquiry. Nevertheless, I cannot attribute everything to such a culture. All errors and omissions are entirely my own responsibility.

Aberystwyth
June 2000

CHAPTER 1

The Blair revolution and the presidential standard

Political commentators are rarely lost for words but they can struggle with superlatives. From the inception of Tony Blair's leadership of the Labour party, and especially his accession to the premiership, it quickly became commonplace for him to be described as a pre-eminent and dominant leader. His position was seen to be so unassailable that the customary language of British politics had to be reformulated to accommodate the phenomenon. It was the sheer scale and penetration of Blair's personal authority that confounded convention and defied traditional analysis. Just as Blair appeared to surpass his predecessors, so he also seemed to supersede the normal methods of characterising party leaders and prime ministers. References to his extraordinary command of the Labour party became legion soon after he secured the leadership in 1994. Blair's commitment to modernising the party by democratising the organisation, by distancing himself from the trade unions and by abandoning Clause Four in favour of a more centrist agenda, generated an electoral strategy that was dependent upon the leadership for its identity and direction. The emphasis upon organisation, discipline and cohesion from the top of a party that had not previously been noted for its ability to control division and dissidence, provoked widespread recognition at Blair's personal achievement in transforming Labour into a formidable electoral machine.

The 'Blair revolution' had created a governing coalition within Labour that transcended its traditional power bases and offered personal vision as well as managerial competence. The asset that Blair had become to his party was best expressed in the disquiet registered in the more conservative sectors of the press, where commentators issued repeated warnings to the Major administration. Simon Jenkins, for example, affirmed that in being 'tough on old Labour and tough on the causes of old Labour', Blair had 'stripped away coat after coat of old paint and damp wallpaper from his party's image'.[1] As a consequence, 'the Moderniser [had] become the Enforcer'.[2] Michael Jones concluded that 'Blair's success in transforming his party's prospects ... depended critically on his personal arrogation of power. Old Labour's ceaseless struggles about who ran the show [had] been replaced by new Labour's adherence to the very Tory principle that policies are best evolved on a strictly need-to-know basis.'[3] To Robert Harris, it was clear that Blair had 'snatched the leadership from under the nose of a better-qualified rival [i.e. Gordon Brown] and did so, in large part, through sheer will power, born of an almost messianic belief that he alone knew what had had to be done'. Since his accession to the leadership, he emerged as the 'most clear-sighted, determined and ruthless leader Labour has ever had'.[4] The substantive character and historical magnitude of Blair's pre-eminence were also underlined by William Rees-Mogg, who by January 1997 was left in no doubt as to the threat posed to the Conservative government by the Labour leadership:

> Tony Blair will himself be one of the main issues of the general election and rightly so ... [H]e has done something that none of his seven predecessors achieved, and only Hugh Gaitskell even attempted. He has changed Labour from being a democratic socialist party to being a social democrat party. He has done that without splitting his party, though old Labour deeply resents the change, and he has established a personal control that none of his predecessors enjoyed. If he wins the election, even narrowly, that will confirm the judgement that Tony Blair is the strongest leader the Labour Party has had in opposition since the war.[5]

The reconfiguration of Labour under Blair created a model of regeneration that was offered to the voting public in the 1997 general election as a project of national renewal. Blair's visible detachment from his party had become accepted as both a technique and an affirmation of a leadership that could be extended to a wider national context and employed as an instrument of social purpose.

After the election, the same depiction of a decisive and conclusive break with the past was evident with Blair's elevation to the premiership. After the divisions and disintegration of the Major administration, when the 'machinery of the state had ceased to function', Blair had ensured that 'the nation [was] being governed again'.[6] Furthermore, this coincided with the 're-emergence of politics as a force and focus'[7] in the life and culture of British society. The new prime minister was said to have inspired and energised the government to such an extent that he had eclipsed the cabinet and parliament as emphatically as New Labour had marginalised the Conservative party after the 1997 general election. Blair did not simply epitomise and symbolise the new government. He was its central organising power and guiding material force. Descriptive inhibitions accordingly fell away:

> From afar, Mr Blair looks the impregnable master of the universe, enthroned on that vast and compliant majority, feared by all of his colleagues, loved by opinion polls, almost certainly guaranteed at least 10 years in office.[8]

> 'All roads lead to Tony' in the words of one Cabinet minister. All the power of the British state has drained to the small office in Downing Street in which Mr Blair works. And when the Government has found itself in difficulties ... it is the PM who has had to stake his personal authority on the matter. *L'etat, c'est Tony.*[9]

> The whole thing falls apart without the supreme leader. Policies and direction, appeal and cohesion, would simply disintegrate if Tony wasn't there to tell the party what to think. Imagine further what Britain would be like if Tony wasn't around to tell us how we feel ... That is the more startling conjecture because in the five months since the election the Prime Minister has come to represent and draw on the mood of the country in a way that no other post-war leader has managed. He has become a kind of emotional and aspirational facilitator, the conductor to a powerful and often barely articulated neediness, which has planted him firmly at the centre of the nation's life.[10]

Given the sweep and authoritarian undertones of Blair's personal, popular and political leadership, in combination with his project to transform the British constitution, commentators have been prompted to extend their analytical speculations to the point of suggesting the existence of a *de facto* constitutional change in the position and role of the premiership. In seeking to convey the extraordinary centrality of Tony Blair both to New Labour and to the Labour government, the term 'presidential' has become an established feature of contemporary political discourse. In an effort to explain a premiership which apparently cannot be adequately accounted for by conventional means, observers have been compelled to employ a term that is especially alien to the British system of government. The prolific references to 'presidential style', 'presidential supremacy' and 'presidential approach' in relation to the Blair premiership satisfies two discernible requirements in the usage of such a characterisation. First, it is a way of giving dramatic emphasis to what is taken to be the exceptional magnitude of Blair's hegemony. Secondly, by deliberately opting for a term that is conspicuously at variance with the standard rationale of British government, it becomes a way of expressing a qualitative shift in the political process. In other words, the prominent deployment of 'presidential' as an instrument of description is seen as warranted by the idiosyncratic properties of the Blair premiership.

Blair and the American connection

In reaching out for an alternative construction of contemporary development at the level of national leadership in Britain, only one feature remains constant. The analogies between Tony Blair and a presidential style, and even a component of presidential power, are rooted overwhelmingly in the American model. It is the United States which provides both the general frame of reference and the specific point of comparability that is used to support the claim of a progression towards a presidential premier. But if the presidential analogy is uniform in this way, it is wholly diverse in every other way. The analogy comes in a variety of guises and contexts that are differently motivated, have different sources and implications, and are differently weighted in explanatory value.

First, are those references which are essentially circumstantial in nature. A comparison between the British premiership and the American presidency is prompted either by the introduction, or by the rising incidence in this country, of phenomena closely associated with presidential politics in the United States. Included in this category would be the enhanced emphasis upon individual leadership, personal communications and presentational style in the conduct of British politics. Allusions to the United States are further fuelled by the concerted use of focus groups and opinion polling in calibrating policy positions with current public attitudes, and by the increasing professionalisation of New Labour's relationships with the media through the use of spin doctors and public relations consultants. A strong body of opinion recognises 'that American influence on political campaigning is considerable in Britain'.[11] 'As other societies become more "American", in terms of levels of affluence, life-style and communication technologies, so there is a growing similarity in campaigning techniques adopted.'[12] Working on this basis, it is possible to extrapolate that the increasing Americanisation of the broadcasting media, together with the associated adoption of cognate campaigning methods, will lead by a process of osmosis to the emergence of American political forms and conditions. Whether it is the purported transition to an American media environment, or the growing significance of personal vision and millennial rhetoric in the propagation of populist projects, or the references to a White House staff structure in Downing Street, or the move to transform Labour party conferences into American-style party conventions, the effect has been to generate a host of impressionistic parallels between London and Washington.

These impressions are strengthened by a *second* dimension of comparison, which is based more specifically upon the close ties between Bill Clinton and Tony Blair. Apart from the fact that they are both comparable in age, that they are both lawyers and that their wives are also lawyers and similarly successful career women who are thought to be more gifted, ambitious and radical than their husbands, Clinton and Blair shared a common predicament. They had both been engaged in making their respective centre-left parties electable after a sustained period in the political wilderness. Both men became close associates in confronting similar problems of trying to change their party images and to redefine the centre-left in an era of established conservative priorities and impulses. By repositioning their parties into the centre-ground without alienating their traditional support base on the left, Clinton's New Democrats and Blair's New Labour project both succeeded in modernising their party structures and in achieving national electoral success for a marketable agenda of cautious reform. As Sidney Blumenthal notes, the similarities between the two were more than coincidental:

> The making of the President has also been the making of the Prime Minister. Their rises are more than accidentally alike ... Since 1992, their campaigns have cross-pollinated. Initially, Clinton benefited from lessons of Labour. Once he assumed office, Blair learned from Clinton's experiences – both victories and setbacks. Clinton has been a paramount subject of study for Blair. Within Blair's political high command, it is agreed that without Clinton, Blair's win would have been exceedingly difficult. Every shift in Clinton's fortunes was closely watched and analysed. Not only did Clinton prove that he could triumph, but his adversaries provided an invaluable education.[13]

Just as New Labour strategists (e.g. Philip Gould) travelled to the United States to observe and also to advise the Clinton campaign in 1992 and 1996, so prominent Democratic consultants (e.g. Paul Begala, James Carville, Stanley Greenburg, George Stephanopoulos) made active contributions to the New Labour campaign, both in the planning and operational phases.[14] This material support was complemented by a profusion of other ties with the United States, ranging from the past employment experiences in America on the part of senior New Labour figures (e.g. Ed Balls, David Miliband, Jonathan Powell) to the personal contributions made to New Labour by prominent individuals on the American centre-left (e.g. E. J. Dionne, Ronald Dworkin, Michael Walzer, John Rawls) and the links between New Labour and progressive US think-tanks such as the Progressive Policy Network and the Institute for Family Values.

As a consequence of this active collaboration, Tony Blair and Bill Clinton assumed a close resemblance to one another in their choice of electoral strategies, in the adoption of policies in areas such as welfare reform, taxation and crime, and in the pursuit of a 'third way' towards a pragmatic synthesis of ideas and approaches that would supersede the outmoded fixtures of left and right ideologies. The myriad effects of this personal and political intimacy were judged in many quarters to have been so extensive as to have led to the effective 'Clintonisation' of the Labour party in that it had 'imported most of its policies and all of its campaign techniques from the United States'.[15] These associations do not in their own right prove the existence of either a dominant American influence or a deliberate attempt on the part of the Blair leadership to emulate Democratic party strategies and positions. For example, according to the prime minister's biographer, John Rentoul, 'Blair did not simply transplant an ideology from America. He used the similarities between the ideas of the modernisers on both sides of the Atlantic in order to apply some of the Democrats' vivid language to a body of ideas which he had already largely developed.'[16] By the same token, Rentoul states that the 1992 presidential campaign constituted 'an important model'[17] for Labour which was made evident in the New Labour campaign: 'Not just the catchphrases ... but the core social moralist philosophy [were] the same.'[18]

By the 1996 presidential election, the convergence of the two parties had been completed, leading Peter Mandelson to celebrate Clinton's re-election as a vindication of New Labour's strategy and an indication of future electoral success: 'Clinton and Blair have each refashioned their parties and driven out the pessimism that had taken root after a succession of defeats ... [Clinton] was voted back because he is a charismatic leader with forward-looking policies ... That is exactly the appeal of Labour under Tony Blair.'[19] Mandelson called upon his party to 'emulate Clinton and achieve what Labour has never managed before: two successive terms of office'.[20] By the time New Labour had achieved office, the parallels between Blair and Clinton had become sufficiently established to lead to speculation on the comparability of their respective positions. This impulse to fuse the British premiership and the American presidency into a common identity was exemplified by Dan Balz of the *Washington Post*. During a visit to Britain to cover the Labour party conference in 1997, Balz was immediately struck by the similarities in national and political roles between Tony Blair and the president of the United States:

> Tony Blair has adopted many personas as Britain's leader: political reformer, griever in chief, genial host of Friday night town meetings, relentless enforcer of a disciplined message. He is called prime minister, but he plays a role more familiar to Americans – the role of president. Both as a candidate and as prime minister, Blair has embraced a presidential style of leadership geared for the age of television and the era of declining faith in political parties. He knows well how to manipulate the levers of party politics, but his soaring popularity

> has grown more out of his ability to tap the public mood and often define it first, unencumbered by party and cabinet.[21]

If the causal dynamics of these comparable outcomes remain open to doubt, there are features of New Labour's strategy for campaigning and governing that seem much more open to the construction of emulation by conscious design. This feature of direct derivation represents the *third* element of comparability. It should be stated at the outset that real intentions are rarely possible to ascertain, and that the precise relationship between outcomes and intentions always remains indistinct. Many of the examples referred to in the first type of prime minister–president comparison may have possessed an active ingredient of conscious intent to replicate American properties. Nevertheless, they are categorised as circumstantial because the American link is one primarily of generalised effect and characterisation rather than that of specific cause. But some features of the Blair leadership are clearly suggestive of a more direct effort to introduce American conditions and methods into the British system.

The establishment of Millbank as New Labour's command and control centre, for example, owed much to the design and rationale of the Democrats' 'war room' in the 1992 and 1996 presidential elections. The same emphasis was given to the co-ordination of collective strategy, opinion poll and focus group intelligence, and media relations that had given the Clinton campaign such a cutting edge. Even the Democrats' 'instant rebuttal unit', which was designed to counteract the negative campaigning of opponents, was replicated by the New Labour leadership. The open-plan design of Clinton's 'war room' was also reproduced at Millbank, with the intention of allowing greater ease of communications and the building of a collaborative *esprit de corps* among the staff. Another example of openly drawing upon American conditions is provided by the Labour government's decision to transfer the control of interest rates to the Monetary Policy Committee of the Bank of England. This was a direct attempt to emulate both the machinery and the stability of monetary policy established by the Federal Reserve Bank in the United States. The American linkage was unmistakable, given that the choice undertaken by the Blair administration in May 1997 'owed much to advice Mr Brown [Gordon Brown] had received from Mr Alan Greenspan, the chairman of the US Federal Reserve',[22] two months prior to New Labour's victory in the general election. By March 1999, the attachment to the American model had become even more evident. In a meeting of European socialist leaders, Blair emphasised the need for the EU to emulate the United States in its social and economic policies. The prime minister stated that 'Europe should recognise that we can learn from the United States'.[23] The

European model needed to be modernised by employing the United States as the chief criterion of modernisation. Blair went on to assert that it was essential for the EU to become more like the United States in order to ensure the success of the single currency project and to enable Europe to compete effectively in the global economy. Other clear derivatives of the American experience include Blair's fascination with the Clinton strategy of 'triangulation', in which a radical centre is thought capable of superseding traditional left and right categories; the usage of American populist devices where leaders establish contracts and covenants with the general public; and the establishment of an annual report on the government's performance given by the prime minister, not to parliament but to an audience of ministers and civil servants 'in Downing Street's Rose Garden, in scenes reminiscent of the US President's State of the Union address'.[24]

The *fourth* and final type of common cross-reference between the Blair premiership and the American presidency lies in the field of interpretation. In this dimension, it is the construction placed upon a series of events and developments by observers which is the controlling value. Individual parallels may be the products of descriptive licence, close observation or substantive insight. They may be circumstantial in nature or the consequence of an intention to emulate American features. Notwithstanding these distinctions, this kind of comparison asserts the existence of an aggregate effect of the multiple references to a presidential dimension in contemporary British politics. Instead of relying upon individual and discrete points of resemblance, this more measured approach posits the need for more systemic conclusions to be drawn from the fragmentary nature of the available evidence. No single feature of the Blair premiership provides a clinching argument in support of a process towards a presidential identity. But by giving careful consideration to the host of surface features that resonate with American properties, another form of comparison is possible. This relates more to the underlying dynamics and collective effects of presidential phenomena that are discernible in the Blair premiership. The characteristic device in this comparison is to move from similes and metaphors to conclusive statements relating to the existence of a presidential dimension as an empirical fact from which value judgements can be drawn.

The Blair premiership has offered considerable scope for the development of interpretive generalisations. It is possible, for example, to point to Mr Blair's success in creating a coalition of power bases and to his actions in seeking to subject the departments of state to greater central control and co-ordination. Reference can be made to his effective presumption of speaking on behalf of the British people and nation, his success in personalising the authority and meaning of his government's programme, and his detachment not only from the Labour party but from cabinet and parliament. From these observations, a case can be made for the presence of forces and dynamics responsible for a premiership with actual presidential properties. After a year in office, the allusions to a presidential style turned increasingly to assertions of presidential substance. In April 1998, the *Sunday Times* concluded that the prime minister stood at an 'unparalleled apex of power'. As a consequence, 'Britain [was] as close to having a presidential system as is possible'.[25] Andrew Rawnsley in *The Observer* also detected a metamorphosis towards presidential government. That a shift had occurred was not in doubt. What was in question were the relative merits of such a change. Rawnsley believed that there were demonstrable 'advantages to the presidentialism of the Blair regime'. Even though the British were usually 'chary of charisma in political leaders', Blair had successfully deployed his own 'personal authority to enormous effect' and nowhere more productively than in Northern Ireland. By the same token, Rawnsley thought there was a down side to such a palpable move towards presidential leadership:

> The defects of presidentialism have also been exposed. Ministers with misgivings about the direction of policy are leery of ventilating their concerns ... His government has started to go down with 'departmentalitis' earlier than most because the way it is constructed tends to encourage Ministers to put their own egos and interests before those of the whole administration. The trend is set from the very top: the most vigorous and vicious turf and spin wars have been between Number 10 and the Treasury. The Cabinet has largely ceased to function as a forum for meaningful decision-making.[26]

But it was perhaps Peter Riddell in *The Times* who was most emphatic in his analysis of Blair's presidential tendencies and most insistent in his efforts to warn the government of the consequences of the development. Riddell conceded that the 'presidential ... approach [had] of course got him a long way'[27] as a national leader able to give expression to popular moods, national ideals and collective aspirations. To Riddell, these were 'great strengths' but a 'presidential style [would] not be enough for lasting success and results'.[28] Blair's New Labour team had effectively translated the centralised command and control of the election campaign to government but, in Riddell's view, experience demonstrated that such an opposition approach could not be sustained in government. What was apparent was not just 'Mr Blair's presidential style, being deliberately above the fray and detached, but also its corollary, the downgrading of the collective and parliamentary aspects'.[29] It was precisely these elements of mutual support and organisational integration which were being eroded by Blair's presidential dispositions and had, as a result, 'exposed the political flaws of being too presidential'.[30]

The significance of these four variants of comparison is one of attributing a set of properties to the Blair premiership that underlines its apparent exceptionalism. The allusions to a presidential dimension are in some instances fuelled by a poverty of political vocabulary. On other occasions, the presidential references are politically motivated either to embarrass or to criticise the prime minister. But even these cases of descriptive licence and partisan mischief reveal a need to employ such a term of reference to convey something seen to be extraordinary. They also reveal that the term has an extensive contemporary currency as an evaluative category. Many other references to the United States comparison are driven by a more analytically rigorous perspective and by a more considered view of the overall configuration of the Blair premiership. But what they all feed off is a drive to explain the first Labour prime minister of an incoming administration for over twenty years in a way that conveys the modernity, change and innovation of the shift from a Conservative hegemony to the establishment of Blair's New Labour project. The extraordinary achievement of Blair, both as a party leader and as a prime minister, called for a commensurately extraordinary form of description. In British political culture, no other term of reference is better equipped to relate contrast and transformation than the American presidency. Because the United States constitutes the best known point of comparison with the United Kingdom in the field of advanced democratic systems, and one that typifies the presidential variant in relation to the parliamentary form of the British structure, the usage of the terms 'president' and 'presidential' in relation to Blair engenders a sense of exceptionalism and dramatic change. Whether the presidential analogy was used as a premise or as a conclusion, the repetitive location of Blair in a presidential context became a familiar feature of British political life after the 1997 general election. The attribution of presidential characteristics satisfactorily fulfilled a widespread need to depict Blair as a conspicuously novel, but also thoroughly atypical and aberrant, figure in British politics.

Disputing the presidential analogy

Dramatic though such assertions are designed to be, the customary subtext to the usage of the presidential analogy in respect to Tony Blair has been that of self-restraint. References to a presidential dimension are almost invariably held at the level of individual idiosyncrasy on the part of the Blair leadership. Accordingly, the reasons, implications and significance of such claims remain largely unexamined, confined as they are to the self-contained features of a premiership allegedly so atypical as to warrant the presidential sobriquet. The usage of the presidential terms of reference in contemporary politics, therefore, tends to be two-edged: radical and alarmist in one sense but theatrical and cautious in another. It gives the impression of confronting conventional arrangements and perspectives. Yet it remains only an impression because the assault is one of innuendoes and associations suggesting change but without giving it an identifying coherence or definition. In seeking to convey something of a transposed identity, the presidential analogy tends to be used to register the presence of changed conditions but without providing a comprehensible account of the substance and sources of such a reconfiguration of authority. As a consequence, the analogy is left vulnerable to four main types of reaction that have served to diminish its value as a serious instrument of analysis.

First, the allusions to a presidential dimension are simply refuted on the formal and structural grounds of the British constitution's governing arrangements. References to a process of 'presidentialisation' in this context are taken literally and, as such, can be summarily dismissed because it can be shown conclusively that the United Kingdom and the United States possess two quite different superstructures of institutional, electoral and party organisation. The American presidency can be shown to operate in a palpably dissimilar system. The strict separation of powers in the United States allows for a chief executive with a national constituency, a fixed term of office, and an electoral and political independence from the legislature. Given this configuration, it can be claimed that there could, in effect, be no substantial points of comparison whatsoever. According to this perspective, references to the presidential properties of the Blair premiership can be safely disregarded as pieces of alliterative exotica and rhetorical excess. The species barrier has not been crossed and neither would it ever be. As a consequence, 'the thesis that a British Prime Minister is really a president, and should be treated as such, is clichéd nonsense'.[31]

A *second* type of reaction to the attachment of presidential properties to the Blair administration is built upon the proposition that such attributions are politically motivated criticisms of the premier and, by extension, of the New Labour government and its policies. In the tradition of Britain's 'political constitution', in which the government and law are assumed to be reducible to the content and effects of contemporary power relationships, any references to an entity like a British presidency can always be interpreted as a set of spuriously contrived attacks upon a government and its programme of policies. Given the centrality of Tony Blair to the identity and project of New Labour, together with the security of his party's large parliamentary majority, the presidential analogy can provide a welcome source of political leverage for a demoralised opposition. On the other side, any attempt to equate Blair with a design to arrogate himself to the overreach of an American president can be seen as a device by which to delegitimise the government through smearing it with constitutional impropriety.

Cultural prejudice and intellectual tradition fuel a *third* reaction against this Anglo-American comparison. Attempts to infer the existence of another constitutional order within the British system of government, or to claim that a particular prime minister has personally transmuted the British constitution into a different entity, are seen as inflammatory allegations of an alien intrusion into the British style of politics. Inflammatory because they are seen to be false allegations, and false because it is an alien construct that is being imputed into the equation. Charges of a presidential presence also suffer from the British disposition towards a conception of politics based upon historical experience and unconscious evolution. Questions on the relative power of cabinets and prime ministers, and the extent to which they conform either to some underlying pattern of relationships or to some anchorage of constitutional principles, are not matters that sober-minded British citizens normally feel the need to dwell upon. They are usually jettisoned accordingly as abstract 'meta-questions (almost metaphysical questions)'[32] that have no place in the British study of British politics. Anthony King's comments illustrate this outlook:

> Much of the academic writing about the cabinet is woolly and confused. Some writers chase constitutional will-o'-the-wisps and others search for 'inner cabinets' like small boys searching for mealie-worms. Since they never specify in advance what an 'inner cabinet' would look like if they found one, they tend to find them everywhere or, alternatively, cannot find them at all.[33]

According to this view, it is much better simply to study what cabinets and prime ministers actually do than worry about what they are or what they are supposed to be. This is especially so given the British system's mutability, in which a new prime minister can supposedly transform any previous pattern of conventions surrounding the office at a single stroke. Accordingly, generalisations are seen as being more appropriate to the United States, with its written constitution and its related preoccupations with textual meanings, constructions of intent, and interpretations of institutional forms and balances.

The *fourth* and final type of reaction perceives elements of a presidential form in the Blair premiership but disregards them as inevitably temporary aberrations based upon an idiosyncratic mix of personality and conditions. Accepting that peculiar circumstances can generate a premiership of exceptional pre-eminence and central power, this acknowledgement is qualified by a core subtext that such a position cannot last. Given the gravitational force of the corporate ethos and the organised collective in British politics, any conspicuously autonomous prime minister is in reality a chimera because power is ultimately and inevitably dependent upon the integrated support of cabinet and party. A prime minister floating free of either may give the brief appearance of presidential independence. But the suggestion of pre-eminence will be merely a prelude to a rapid and painful return to the normality of prime ministerial power contingent upon political interdependence, extended negotiation and multiple accommodation.

The chief problem with a contentious issue of this nature is that both those who deploy the presidential analogy and those who find it objectionable suffer from a lack of perspective. The former are inclined to overlook the past, while the latter tend to ignore the underlying parallels between different systems. The disposition to interpret the contemporary premiership in terms of a presidential dimension is invariably prompted by the need to convey a sense of novelty based upon, and expressed through, the individual ascendancy of the prime minister. The emphasis upon the personal and the immediacy of the present tends to displace the consideration of prior developments and historical experience. It is this limited temporal perspective of the presidential references to Tony Blair that precludes any serious consideration of a debate that has had a long pedigree in British political analysis. It is a dispute which has prepared the ground for the attribution of presidential properties not merely to the leader of New Labour but to the position of any modern British prime minister.

The grand old debate

The classic dispute between cabinet government and prime ministerial government has provided the context for the study of executive power in Britain since the early 1960s. It was initiated in the main by John P. Mackintosh and Richard Crossman,[34] who both asserted the existence of long-term trends that had progressively inflated the power of the prime minister and correspondingly diminished the position of the cabinet as the supreme agent of government in the British constitution. They drew attention to the growth of prime ministerial authority over the cabinet by virtue of his or her capacity to choose its members, to allocate portfolios, to alter jurisdictions, to determine the cabinet's agenda, to chair meetings, to select the subject matter and composition of cabinet committees, and to interpret and declare cabinet decisions. The prime minister had developed other overwhelming advantages. The office allowed its occupants to control government and party patronage; to have first access to the formidable network of government information, political intelligence and administrative direction embodied in the Cabinet Secretariat; to have the prior claim to speak for the government; and to represent government to the public and through the mass media. The prime minister's strategic position, set amid the protective monoliths of a parliamentary party machine and a centralised civil service, was thought to have provided the office with a structural pre-eminence and compelling political superiority. It was no longer feasible to expect the cabinet to deliberate and to decide upon the weighty matters of the day. It had become a panel providing political clearance and official sanction for decisions taken elsewhere. Although cabinets still provided the arena where serious disputes were raised and settled, it was no longer a governing body. In Mackintosh's view, 'the role of the cabinet and the way decisions were taken had changed and changed in a manner which left more influence and power of initiative with the prime minister'.[35] He went on to conclude that the lines of political development had undergone such changes that they had 'led contemporary British government to be described as prime ministerial rather than cabinet government'.[36]

Richard Crossman sought to press the point home in his celebrated introduction to the 1963 edition of Walter Bagehot's *The English Constitution.* He adopted Bagehot's terminology to demonstrate that the 'immense accretion of power to the prime minister'[37] was the consequence of those self-same modern conditions that had changed the cabinet from one of the 'efficient' elements of the constitution into one of its 'dignified' parts like the monarchy and the House of Lords. The change towards 'prime ministerial government'[38] had been so dramatic that Crossman felt there was no alternative but to resort to presidential allusion. This would convey 'the magnitude of power that was now lodged in the prime minister's position'.[39] The modern prime minister was now at 'the apex not only of a highly centralised political machine, but also of an equally centralised and vastly more powerful administrative machine'.[40] The 'voluntary totalitarianism'[41] of British society in World War II had been retained with dramatic consequences that could only be adequately conveyed through the use of the presidential analogy. 'If we mean by presidential government, government by an elective first magistrate then', Crossman declared, 'we in England have a president as truly as the Americans.'[42]

Although Mackintosh felt that to compare the British prime minister directly to the American presidency was an overstatement, both books were responsible for disseminating the idea that prime ministerial power had become so prodigious that it could only be satisfactorily grasped by reference to some feature lying beyond the scope of the traditional framework of the British constitution. The association of the personal authority of the prime minister as the 'focal point of the modern cabinet'[43] and the evident individual stature of an American president proved too close and too appealing a linkage to ignore. In many respects, there appeared to be no other way of adequately assessing and accounting for the process by which 'British government had become more and more a matter of a prime minister governing absolutely'.[44] As a result, the comparability of the prime minister and the presidency became a regular feature of political analysis.

As the political developments originally described by Mackintosh and Crossman appeared to intensify during the 1960s and 1970s, the presidential analogy accordingly became more common. Whether it was used merely as a figure of speech or as an analytical statement, its usage appeared to be logically commensurate with the further development of governmental centralisation. By the late 1970s, the comparison had achieved a resonance in the wider sphere of public discussion. Even James Callaghan, who cut a genial and avuncular figure among the general public, was accused by members of his own party and his own cabinet of diminishing parliamentary democracy and collegiate government in favour of enhancing his own personal authority within government. With such enhancement came the need for protection on the self-same grounds of personal position. James Callaghan was no exception to the habit of regarding criticism of the prime minister as an attack on him as a person and, therefore, as a direct challenge to his personal power base.[45]

During the same period, Tony Benn attempted to generate interest in the presidential dimension of prime ministerial power. In a controversial lecture entitled 'The Case for a Constitutional Premiership' (1979), he sought to use the issue of prime ministerial power in the British system to lever open to public scrutiny the secrecy and unaccountability of Whitehall, and especially the sweeping national security powers afforded by crown prerogative to the highest levels of the British executive. To Benn, the confidentiality and private coercion of government were embodied by the prime minister whose 'centralisation of power' amounted to a 'system of personal rule in the very heart of our parliamentary democracy'.[46] The theme of the progressive enlargement of prime ministerial power also began to picked up by thoughtful journalists such as James Margach. His book, *The Anatomy of Power* (1979), traced the transfer of power from Westminster to the 'secret corridors of Whitehall'[47] during the twentieth century. Margach acknowledged the recent academic debate on prime ministerial and cabinet power, and was convinced that the dispute signified a deep underlying acceleration in the distribution of political resources:

> There has been much speculation among academics who study such developments from the outside about whether prime ministers have become more presidential in style. Those whose job it has been to report at first hand contemporary events as they unfold every day in Washington and London are

> under no illusions. Prime ministers have in fact become more powerful than even Presidents.[48]

The modern thesis of prime ministerial power, therefore, is not new. Prompted initially by the public appeal and political style of Harold Macmillan, and developed subsequently with the careers of Alec Douglas-Home, Harold Wilson, Edward Heath and James Callaghan, the issue of prime ministerial government had percolated into the attentive margins of political reflection well before Margaret Thatcher's accession to the premiership. It may not have been a live political issue or a serious political debate but the question of prime ministerial power had been raised. There was an increased awareness that an alternative frame of reference was available for an understanding of the modern British executive. Moreover, there was a growing susceptibility towards regarding the American presidency not only as directly comparable to the British premiership, but as the plausible end point of its development. The debate generated equally emphatic assertions of the essential continuity of the British constitution. Centralisation could not, and should not, be equated with 'presidentialisation'. Assumptions that it did so provoked the corrective that 'unlike an American president, a prime minister could not make decisions by himself'.[49] As a consequence, 'a prime minister was not a chief executive of government'[50] and, therefore, could not be approximated in any way to a president.

The academic most scornful of the prime ministerial government argument and most active in the attempt to demolish it was George Jones. He it was who originally challenged Mackintosh's work when it was first published and he it was who continued to attack the thesis relentlessly, thereby ensuring that the 'cabinet versus prime ministerial government' argument remained a live dispute in constitutional circles. Jones argued that the 'prime minister's power had been exaggerated and that the restraints on his ascendancy were as strong as ever, and in some ways even stronger'.[51] Jones believed that for every interpretation supporting the thesis of prime ministerial dominance, there was a contrary interpretation denying the validity of such a thesis. The prime minister was not the symbol of his party in the country so much as the 'prisoner of the image of his party'.[52] Television did not help the prime minister to retain his prominence as much as it helped his opponents to become public figures and potential challengers to his position. What might appear to be an exercise of prime ministerial authority over the cabinet was in reality a demonstration of the fact that a prime minister can only be 'as strong as his party, and in particular his chief colleagues, let him be'.[53] Jones believed that many of the assertions of prime ministerial power were not only politically motivated, but were based upon a fundamental misunderstanding of political reality. It required the horse sense of a practising politician such as Ian Macleod to correct such lavish misconceptions.

> Mr Macmillan set a new standard of competence in the business of forming, controlling and guiding a cabinet. It was because the whole Cabinet worked so well and so smoothly that people formed the impression of an absolute personal ascendancy, and the notion grew up that we were changing from a cabinet to a presidential system of Government. In fact the reverse was happening. Mr Macmillan by his skill, restored a great deal of vitality to the cabinet as a body.[54]

Prime ministerial or presidential government, therefore, was a fabrication of the mind, or rather of overactive minds. As an intellectual construction, it failed to take account of the solid realism of internal conflict, of leadership rivals, of possible revolts and of prime ministerial consensus building. Accordingly, presidential pre-eminence in Number 10 was dismissed by Simon James as a 'simplistic allegation'.[55] It served only to demonstrate that a 'simple distortion is easier to popularize than a complex truth'.[56]

The Thatcher effect

By the time Margaret Thatcher moved into Downing Street, the arguments about cabinet government, prime ministerial power and the onset of presidentialism had become an established feature of critical analysis to those observers and analysts who thought about such things. In many respects it had become too established and too esoteric in the process. It was difficult to ascertain whether the respective proponents of cabinet and prime ministerial government were talking about two forms of the same phenomenon, or two reference points that between them could embrace a full range of different variants. It was argued on the one hand that cabinet government represented the base norm of the British system. Prime ministers could come and go but the varied characteristics of their administrations were ultimately reducible, to the limits imposed by the cabinet. On the other hand, it was asserted that individual prime ministers could, and had, exerted such force from the centre that their activities had led to a fundamental change in the balance of power within the British government. The debate went on and on, and round and round. A fatigued Anthony King provided a succinct summary of its main points: 'The two sides contend furiously (and interminably); but it is rather like the old argument about whether the bottle is half full or half empty. The evidence is there to support either contention.'[57]

It might be thought that given the evident nature of Margaret Thatcher's influence upon government, the ground rules of the debate would have changed to accommodate such an iconoclastic figure. She might have been expected to have precipitated a break with the past and to have stimulated the use of a range of more appropriate categories of analysis and evaluation that would transcend the old framework of cabinet claim and prime ministerial/presidential counterclaim. Dramatic and controversial though Margaret Thatcher's administrations were, they did not produce any thorough revision of perspective. They did not lead to any recognition that she may have represented some deep qualitative change in British executive power that might require different ways of looking at it and of seeking to understand it. Even though it is true that Margaret Thatcher ignited public interest over the nature and scale of her office in government, and made the British executive a live political issue, the vocabulary and concepts used in the revived debate were drawn almost exclusively from the old debate. It was as if the question of Thatcher's power had slipped through a grill and fallen into the old channels of dispute.

During her premiership, the manner of Thatcher's leadership was seen as being dramatically different to that of her predecessors in that it was highly substantive in content and directly confrontational in approach. Margaret Thatcher not only had an agenda of her own, she had one that was not shared by most of her party – let alone by much of the country. While other prime ministers may have concerned themselves with keeping the cabinet united at all costs and with maintaining the electoral appeal of an integrated party, Thatcher had to impose herself and her agenda upon the party and the government. Tough, relentless and even inspirational leadership was actually required for Thatcher to remain prime minister, given that she was committed to a programme designed to produce a radical change in political attitudes. It was the radicalism of Thatcher's programme and leadership that essentially radicalised perspectives on the relationships between the state and society, and between government and its own inner hierarchy. For good or ill, therefore, Thatcher's administrations were seen as governments that necessarily had Thatcherite policies, which in their turn were building a Thatcherite society. The interconnections appeared so close and durable that the conclusions drawn from them seemed irrefutable. In the same way that Margaret Thatcher's pervasive influence in government characterised her administration as Thatcherite, so government policy and social change were reduced as a matter of course to derivatives of Thatcherism. As a result, the authority of what was after all only a prime minister, in the context of the British constitution, appeared to be prodigious.

At the very least, Margaret Thatcher was seen to be engaged in 'a gradual strengthening and accretion of prime ministerial influence over and against the cabinet'.[58] As a consequence she gave the impression of being 'an exponent more of presidential than cabinet government'.[59] This view intensified and hardened during her premiership. It became thoroughly conventional to declare that Britain was 'moving towards a presidential system';[60] that the prime minister had acquired a 'quasi-presidential role'[61] in the British constitution; that her cabinet reshuffles were 'a powerful demonstration of presidential government';[62] and even that the powers of the British prime minister had come to 'exceed those of an American president'.[63] George Jones himself, who had always defended the interpretation of British government as cabinet government against such fanciful neologisms as presidential style leadership, was forced to concede that Margaret Thatcher had tipped the balance from 'collective to presidential government'.[64] Simon James also recognised that Mrs Thatcher had 'abetted and exploited an existing trend, driving it further than it would have gone under another premier, perhaps driving it as far as it could go without making the Cabinet vestigial'.[65]

If Thatcher's opponents could rarely agree on which aspects of her programme or personality they deplored most, they were at least united on the magnitude of her influence upon government and society. It was clear to Joe Rogaly, for example, that for eleven years Britain had been

> governed by a prime minister who, whatever her faults, had been infused with a vision. She had been a driven woman, always urging ministers forward, terrifying them, tiring them out one by one, disposing of them, nagging them, politicising their senior officials, popping in on this or that issue, scrawling her comments on everything, vetoing this, insisting on that, overshadowing all.[66]

Hugo Young concluded that Margaret Thatcher had given 'her name to the age in which we live'.[67] None of her predecessors 'more voraciously dominated a peacetime government with their personal impact and commitment than Margaret Thatcher'. He continued: 'She was a leader of lurid style and risky habits, especially in the field of personal relations. Aggressive to a fault, she spent years scorning not only consensual policies but the consensual demeanour.'[68] In Young's view, the Thatcher era was different and 'nowhere more so than in the evidence it offer[ed] that personality can be the single most potent contributor to the pattern of events'.[69]

The Thatcher era generated a renewed interest in the nature of individual leadership and in the relationship between personality, government and history. Margaret Thatcher had broken down many of the barriers to such considerations in the normal run of British politics. With her record in mind, it suddenly became so much easier to conclude that only her government would have undertaken certain policies; and without Margaret Thatcher as prime minister, the government's agenda and performance would have been radically different. Dennis Kavanagh recognised that a leadership role now existed in British politics and that Margaret Thatcher could be said to have successfully fulfilled the potential for such a role. She offered 'to successors, and to students of British government, a model of what was probably the most successful peacetime premiership this century, measured in electoral success and policy initiatives'.[70]

These 'allegations' brought in their wake a set of equally forceful counter-arguments. They led to an instinctive reiteration of the formal principle that 'government decisions in Britain are made in the name of the cabinet, in contrast to the United States where they are made in the name of the president'.[71] Others pointed out that Margaret Thatcher had been 'an imperial prime minister', but had done 'little to increase the power of her office'.[72] Writing in February 1989, Peter Jenkins came to the following conclusion:

> She has shown not the slightest interest in constitution mongering and very little in tinkering with the machinery of government. Since her re-election in June 1987 her manner of governing has become more intensely personal than ever. Yet, as far as I can judge, or discover from the people close to her, there has been no lasting development in prime ministerial government and no reason why, when she eventually goes, Cabinet government – such as it was – will not take up again where she left off. In that sense, 'Thatcherism' will have been a personal *tour de force* which will end with her.[73]

The old faith still held. It was apparently clear that the office was 'like an elastic band'. Margaret Thatcher had 'stretched the elastic' and had 'established her ascendancy',[74] but even she could not defy the physical properties of rubber. In April 1990, Jones concluded that 'as long as her style brings success to her party it will be accepted, but if her luck runs out and she appears a liability, she will be dropped. The elastic will snap back on her.'[75] What appeared to be a visionary and prophetic statement was in reality nothing more than a fatalistic declaration of cabinet predestination. If Margaret Thatcher was a temporary aberration, then she could only be seen as such against the permanent ground rules ascribed to cabinet government, and in terms of her necessary and inevitable return to base. A comet is not a star, but it can only be confirmed as a comet when it starts to come back.

When Margaret Thatcher unexpectedly fell from power in November 1990, the presidential analogy suddenly seemed to fall with her. In a variety of ways, senior ministers had moved individually against her to the extent that she herself believed that she had been the victim of a cabinet coup. Cecil Parkinson alludes to an episode just after Thatcher's decision to stand down, when a colleague placed the blame for her abrupt departure upon the leadership challenge of Michael Heseltine. 'Oh no', she replied, 'it wasn't Heseltine, it was the Cabinet.'[76] To her, it was a 'simple statement of fact'.[77]

But the cabinet as a collective body had not been instrumental in her dramatic downfall. Nevertheless, the fact of her enforced resignation was taken to represent a restoration of cabinet government. This impression was strengthened by the apparently collegiate inclinations of her successor and by his explicit avowal of cabinet decision making. As George Jones took comfort in the fact that 'the elastic snapped back on her',[78] British politics appeared to return to a more 'normal' course of party politics and policy debates. In this atmosphere of practical realism, uncluttered by constitutional self-consciousness, the allusions to presidentialism seemed peculiarly inappropriate; merely part and parcel of the Thatcher *divertissement*. Given the fact that even 'cabinet government' was to many 'a term of art belonging to the textbooks of political science',[79] the notions of 'presidential government' had been quite an intolerable affront to the British way of politics.

This reaction was quite evident in many of the post-mortems of the Thatcher years, but nowhere more so than in an article by Frank Johnson suggestively entitled 'The Cabinet was in charge all along'. In it, Johnson makes it quite clear that rule by cabinet ministers was the satisfactory norm until the early 1960s when 'something ominous happened: political scientists, a new profession, got control of the subject'.[80] Johnson had very little time for the breed:

> They persuade education ministers to give them large sums of our money in order – deep in their sinister plate-glass universities – to lock themselves into their equivalent of the laboratory, brood over their equivalent of the Bunsen burner, and conjure up clouds of hot-air and noxious gases, to the terror of the civilian population.[81]

In the early 1960s, political scientists released the vapour of prime ministerial power. They were joined by Crossman, who also 'liked things to be not as they seemed',[82] and together they popularised the idea of the prime minister possessing a presidential pre-eminence. To Johnson, the theory, for such it was, 'fell with Thatcher ... disproved by events'.[83] With the benefit of hindsight it was crystal clear to Johnson that Margaret Thatcher had been 'constantly outwitted or forced to change her mind, or go against her natural inclinations, by crafty ministers or officials'.[84] With this 'fact' solidly re-established, it was evident that Johnson hoped that normal British politics could be resumed and that mischievous questions over the distribution of power at the highest levels could satisfactorily be left to the dynamic interplay of cabinet ministers.

The point was not to prove or to disprove the arguments over prime ministerial power, so much as to suspend them and, thereby, to prevent the needless disturbance to government and public confidence occasioned by them. But as this study will demonstrate, the Thatcher phenomenon proved to be a precedent of exceptional potency. It could not be dismissed as readily as its originator. In fact, it continued to dog her successor's administration right up until its demise in 1997. John Major was persistently criticised for adopting a more collegiate and inclusive style of decision making. As a consequence, he was subjected to a succession of leadership crises as his actions were continually appraised in relation to the very criteria of vigorous Thatcherite and presidential pretensions that he had originally sought to alleviate. He promoted himself, and was portrayed, as a conciliator dedicated to the corporate ethos of cabinet government. Nevertheless, even the self-effacing John Major found it necessary to defer to the increasingly evident disciplines of individual assertion and conspicuous personal projection in the public conduct of politics.

The American presidency and the politics of British leadership

The discomfiture of Major's interregnum between Margaret Thatcher and Tony Blair bore witness to the continuities of contemporary drives and impulses towards centralised leadership. These forces not only confront the norms of the cabinet model, but challenge the notion that such a model constitutes the only sustainable context in which a prime minister can effectively operate within the British system. Those who adopt the presidential analogy to convey the notion of an unprecedented condition tend to dismiss the extensive precedents for their case. By the same token, those who deny any substantive point of comparison between the British premiership and the United States presidency tend to do so on the basis of a misunderstanding of both the presidential position in the American system and the nature of its contemporary development. One of the chief consequences of the debate over the position of the British premiership is that the attribution of a presidential element to an individual prime minister is almost invariably based upon a caricature of the presidential office. The institution is equated with personal dominion and pre-eminent power. Because the president is formally accorded the status of chief executive, and because the executive department of the United States controls the immense resources of the positive state and the national security apparatus, the president's notional power is merged with the actual power of the federal government. The adoption of such a literal frame of reference, compounded by the evident differences in electoral arrangements, institutional structures and constitutional principles, can result in contrived comparisons. The combination ensures that any similarities between the two offices can be minimised to circumstantial and superficial factors that have no basis in the substantive properties of the respective positions. Such a summary dismissal of even a *prima facia* comparison, however, rests upon a gross distortion of the interior dynamics of the presidency.

Contrary to an impression prevalent in the UK, the American presidency, like the British premiership, is in reality noted for the elasticity of its power, for its numerous constraints, for its dependence upon social conditions and political issues, for its transformation with different incumbents and for the contingent nature of its authority. Those seeking to use the presidency to rebut the charges of prime ministerial power, therefore, often come perilously close to refuting their own arguments. Inaccurate though these comparisons may be, they nevertheless have the effect of reinforcing and perpetrating this country's misreading of American government. As a consequence, they help to close off many potentially valuable avenues of analysis that could be provided by a more sensitive and realistic perspective of the modern presidency.

The misconceptions surrounding this area of analysis are further exacerbated by the motives of those who seek to force a direct comparison as a prelude to political condemnation. This compulsion to smear a prime minister with the terminology of presidential excess was particularly conspicuous during the 1980s, when the comparison was used to suggest a condition of cultural corruption and political mutation. The word 'presidential' was openly used as a polemical device in the Thatcher years. The worst that could be said of Thatcher was that she had become as powerful as a president. Some of this usage of the presidency as the hallmark of personal power was drawn from the anti-Americanism of the 1980s and, in particular, from President Reagan's restrictive social policies and virulent anti-communism. But much of the usage of the presidential analogy came from the same misreading of American politics that afflicted those opposed to attaching the presidential label to Margaret Thatcher. Presidentialism implied supreme power and that in turn implied the potential for, and the probability of, its abuse. Presidentialism, therefore, offered the opportunity to turn policy issues and political argument into a personalised debate about the individual usage of governmental authority. The presidential analogy made governmental power and policies altogether more accessible to political argument by transforming the perspective into *her* policies, *her* power and *her* government.

Despite the widespread currency that the term 'presidential' enjoyed at the time, the circumstances of its usage served to undermine still further the analytical potential of comparing the British premiership with the American presidency. As Margaret Thatcher was elevated into a personal phenomenon unrepresentative of anything other than herself and her government, then her departure was seen as marking both the abandonment of the presidential government allegation and the consequent reinstatement of cabinet government. Even if the allegation could ever be proved true, therefore, Thatcher's fall from government rendered it meaningless as an instrument of analysis. Nothing could be drawn from it since it had been based wholly on the notion of the abnormality of Thatcher's leadership. When she returned home to Dulwich, it was assumed that British government had returned to normal, leaving presidentialism in British politics as a freakish idea connected to a freakish woman in freakish times.

Elements of a similar process were already in evidence during the opening years of Blair's premiership. Notwithstanding New Labour's public policy objectives of greater pluralism, more inclusiveness and an emphasis on devolved decision making, the Blair administration quickly acquired a reputation of extending excessive central control. As Blair himself increasingly attracted presidential epithets which provided purchase for efforts to depict him as a 'control freak', the language of political critique once again began to distort and devalue the presidential analogy. The generally inaccurate view of the American presidency, combined with the rhetorical designs of its British usage, served to re-create the fusion of presidential identity, power and personality that had characterised the Thatcher era. In the same manner, the Blair premiership was increasingly depicted as exceptional and, therefore, unsustainable. The implication was that, like Margaret Thatcher, Blair was predetermined to return to the conventional processes of cabinet government which would once again derogate presidential analogies to the status of aberrational delusions, fit only for the most impressionable or most partisan of commentators.

The present study draws on the proposition originally employed in an earlier version of this work.[85] It asserts the utility of the presidential analogy in reaching a better understanding of the political forces and dynamics shaping the contemporary British premiership. It acknowledges that the office of the prime minister is not, and never can be, the same as that of the American presidency. It also recognises that the presidential analogy is often used in this country in exaggerated and polemical ways to make political capital. But notwithstanding the scale and significance of the structural differences between the American and British systems, or the gratuitous nature of many of the British allusions to the United States presidency, the claim here is that the comparison is not only helpful, but essential, in comprehending the shifting properties of the British premiership. By taking the comparison seriously, it is possible to draw out the interpretive and explanatory potential of a phenomenon that normally remains concealed by the careless use of categories or by a cultural prejudice against anything that is apparently alien to the British system. A careful examination of the

American presidency can yield valuable insights into the British premiership. It can alert us to the existence of the general trends in the underlying patterns of political leadership and to the existence of new resources and strategies of leadership that demonstrate significant areas of comparable development in two ostensibly different systems.

The position informing this study is that through employing perspectives drawn from the American presidency, it becomes clear that prime ministerial leadership has undergone changes of such profundity that they amount to a qualitative shift in the type of leadership which is now viable in British government. These changes are far deeper in substance than the personality and temporary circumstances of any one incumbent. They refer to a systemic shift in the motive forces, structural outlets, political strategies, defining conventions and public expectations of political leadership in this country. As a consequence, the British public has become increasingly exposed to, and conditioned by, a form of presidential politics which thrives on the expectations of leadership, on the components of leadership, and on the attributes of individual leaders in performing a leadership role in British society. The importance of the mass media in leadership projection, the usage of opinion polling and market research to promote leaders, and the deployment of leaders by their respective parties into public settings of individual display and even spectacle, have contributed towards a leadership dimension in contemporary British politics. It is a dimension which not only draws ostensibly unrelated issues into its orbit, but has established the meaning and value of leadership as a political issue in its own right. As a consequence, the significance of such formidable figures as Margaret Thatcher and Tony Blair in the premiership rests less with their particular qualities as individual leaders and more in the way they bring to the surface a set of underlying and irreversible dynamics in the character of the British political system. The similarities between Margaret Thatcher and Tony Blair, therefore, depend not so much upon the latter's conscious evocation of the former's leadership style, as on the existence of deep-set continuities and compulsive drives within what has become a highly advanced and sophisticated politics of national leadership.

The contention of this book is that it is only by understanding the inner properties of the contemporary presidency and by assimilating the analytical perspectives generated by the office that it becomes possible to gauge the impact and implications of the recent changes to political leadership in Britain. By being sensitised to developments in the American presidency, it becomes possible to discern the trends and patterns in the recent evolution of the British premiership. The acceleration of a *de facto* scheme of presidential politics in this country is altering the structure and conduct of

British political life. It is exerting a profound influence upon the forms of political leadership and on the sources and usages of political authority. As a consequence, it is altering the position of prime minister within the system of government to the point where the old conventions of prime ministerial leadership have been stretched out of recognition. It is in this context that the Blair premiership exerts its greatest influence. In responding to the contemporary drives of British leadership politics, it not only reaffirms the deepening resonance of the presidential analogy, but intensifies the dynamics of the process so as to tie his successors ever more tightly to the cumulative norms of strong leadership.

Although the subtlety, profundity and ramifications of these myriad changes can be illuminated by references to the American presidency, it would be a mistake to conclude that the British premiership is converging to a point of equivalence with the United States presidency. It is more accurate to say that the British premiership has begun to move along parallel lines of development. The premiership has evolved out of the British political structure and in response to British political conditions and traditions. In fact, its development has been actively encouraged by the self-interest of political parties and of cabinets and shadow cabinets. Even though the British premiership is the product of indigenous dynamics, it is nevertheless the case that the office is not a pure derivative of institutional authority or established arrangements of power. What is discernible is not a set of extensions or a settled order of growth. It is a qualitative shift in form and interior substance, drawn from a profusion of political developments that have transcended the formal infrastructure of Britain's political system. The British prime minister has evolved, and is evolving away from what a prime minister used to be. The innovative and rapidly changing politics that now surrounds the premiership has moved the office away from the customary patterns of political exchange and evaluation. Indeed, given the scale, depth and implications of these largely unacknowledged changes, it is no exaggeration to declare that the British premiership has to all intents and purposes turned, not into a British version of the American presidency, but into an authentic British presidency.

Notes

1 Simon Jenkins, 'Labour man and Tory measures', *The Times*, 2 October 1996.
2 Jenkins, 'Labour man and Tory measures'.
3 Michael Jones, 'Labour rolls over for the supreme leader', *Sunday Times*, 21 April 1996.
4 Robert Harris, 'Blair takes the wraps off his revolution', *Sunday Times*, 31 March 1996.
5 William Rees-Mogg, 'Blair is remarkable but not invincible', *The Times*, 6 January 1997.
6 Philip Stephens, 'Rip it up and start again', *Financial Times*, 25/26 April 1998.

7 Stephens, 'Rip it up and start again'.
8 Andrew Rawnsley, 'Question: who reckons he's the most radical in the Government? Have a look inside No. 10', *The Observer*, 26 April 1998.
9 'The great performer', *Sunday Telegraph*, 21 December 1997.
10 Henry Porter, 'Tried but still untested', *Independent on Sunday*, 28 September 1997.
11 Margaret Scammell, *Designer Politics: How Elections are Won* (Basingstoke, Macmillan, 1995), p. 291.
12 Dennis Kavanagh, *Election Campaigning: The New Marketing of Politics* (Oxford, Blackwell, 1995), p. 226. See also Ralph Negrine, *The Communication of Politics* (London, Sage, 1996), ch. 7.
13 Sidney Blumenthal, 'Along the Clinton–Blair axis', *The Times*, 5 May 1997.
14 See Patricia Hewitt and Philip Gould, 'Learning from success – Labour and Clinton's New Democrats', *Renewal*, 1 no. 1 (1993), pp. 45–51.
15 'One hundred days', *The Times*, 9 August 1997. See also Stephen Driver and Luke Martell, *New Labour: Politics After Thatcherism* (Cambridge, Polity, 1998), pp. 109–13, 169–73.
16 John Rentoul, *Tony Blair*, rev. edn (London, Warner, 1996), p. 285.
17 Rentoul, *Tony Blair*, p. 285.
18 Rentoul, *Tony Blair*, p. 286.
19 Peter Mandelson, 'We will emulate Clinton', *The Times*, 7 November 1996.
20 Mandelson, 'We will emulate Clinton'.
21 Dan Balz, 'Britain's prime minister assumes presidential air', *Washington Post*, 2 October 1997.
22 Gerard Baker, 'Something new, something borrowed', *Financial Times*, 29 May 1997.
23 Quoted in Andrew Grice, 'Blair: Europe should emulate US', *The Independent*, 3 March 1999.
24 Ewan MacAskill, 'Rivals discuss "radical" Blair', *The Guardian*, 31 July 1998.
25 'President Blair', *Sunday Times*, 26 April 1998.
26 Andrew Rawnsley, 'From novices to natural rulers', *The Observer*, 26 April 1998.
27 Peter Riddell, 'RIP, Cabinet government', *The Times*, 5 January 1998.
28 Riddell, 'RIP, Cabinet government'.
29 Peter Riddell, 'We're missing you Mr Blair', *The Times*, 8 June 1998.
30 Riddell, 'RIP, Cabinet government'.
31 Simon Jenkins, 'Power that will be', *The Times*, 29 July 1998.
32 Anthony King, 'The Prime Minister and Cabinet', *Contemporary Record*, 4, no. 1 (September 1990), p. 22.
33 Anthony King, 'Political Masters' (Review of Valentine Herman and James E. Alt (eds), *Cabinet Studies: A Reader*), *New Society*, 14 August 1975.
34 John P. Mackintosh, *The British Cabinet*, 2nd edn (London, Methuen, 1968), chs 1, 18, 24; Intro. by R. H. S. Crossman to Walter Bagehot, *The English Constitution* (London, Fontana, 1963), pp. 1–57.
35 Mackintosh, *The British Cabinet*, p. 624.
36 Mackintosh, *The British Cabinet*, p. 627.
37 Crossman, Intro. to *The English Constitution*, p. 51.
38 Crossman, Intro. to *The English Constitution*, p. 54.
39 See John Hart, 'President and Prime Minister: Convergence or Divergence?', *Parliamentary Affairs*, 44, no. 2 (April 1991), pp. 209–12.
40 Crossman, Intro. to *The English Constitution*, p. 51.
41 Crossman, Intro. to *The English Constitution*, p. 56.

42 Crossman, Intro. to *The English Constitution*, p. 56.
43 Mackintosh, *The British Cabinet*, p. 428.
44 Bernard Crick, *The Reform of Parliament*, 2nd edn (London, Weidenfeld and Nicolson, 1968), p. 25.
45 Brian Sedgemore, *The Secret Constitution: An Analysis of the Political Establishment* (London, Hodder and Stoughton, 1980), p. 66.
46 Tony Benn, 'Curbing the power of PMs', *The Observer*, 15 July 1979.
47 James Margach, *The Anatomy of Power: An Enquiry into the Personality of Leadership* (London, W. H. Allen, 1979), p. 78.
48 Margach, *The Anatomy of Power*, p. 77.
49 Richard Rose, 'British Government: The Job at the Top', in Richard Rose and Ezra N. Suleiman (eds), *Presidents and Prime Ministers* (Washington, DC, American Enterprise Institute, 1980), p. 25.
50 Rose, 'British Government', p. 32.
51 G. W. Jones, 'The Prime Minister's Power', in Anthony King (ed.), *The British Prime Minister*, 2nd edn (Basingstoke, Macmillan, 1985), p. 196.
52 Jones, 'The Prime Minister's Power', p. 204.
53 G. W. Jones, 'The Prime Minister's Power', *Parliamentary Affairs*, 18, no. 2 (Spring 1965), p. 178.
54 Quoted in Jones, 'The Prime Minister's Power', p. 213.
55 Simon James, *British Cabinet Government* (London, Routledge, 1992), p. 92.
56 James, *British Cabinet Government*, p. 92.
57 Anthony King, 'Men on the Job' (Review of John P. Mackintosh (ed.), *British Prime Ministers in the Twentieth Century: Vol. 1, Balfour to Chamberlain*), *New Society*, 11 (August 1977).
58 Martin Burch, 'The British Cabinet: A Residual Executive', *Parliamentary Affairs*, 41, no. 1 (January 1988), pp. 4–48.
59 John Vincent, 'The Thatcher Governments, 1979–1987', in Peter Hennessy and Anthony Seldon (eds), *Ruling Performance: British Governments from Attlee to Thatcher* (Oxford, Basil Blackwell, 1987), p. 288.
60 Bob Jessop, Kevin Bonnett, Simon Bromley and Tom Ling, *Thatcherism: A Tale of Two Nations* (Oxford, Polity, 1988), p. 83.
61 Richard Holme, *The People's Kingdom* (London, Bodley Head, 1987), p. 115.
62 Ian Gilmour, 'The false doctrine of "Thatchocracy"', *The Observer*, 30 July 1989.
63 Tony Benn, 'Power, Parliament and the People', *New Socialist*, September/October 1982.
64 G. W. Jones, 'Cabinet Government and Mrs Thatcher', *Contemporary Record*, 1, no. 3 (Autumn 1987), p. 8.
65 James, *British Cabinet Government*, pp. 183–4.
66 Joe Rogaly, 'Will the real Mr Major stand up?', *Financial Times*, 28 November 1990.
67 Hugo Young, 'To the Manner Born', in Hugo Young and Anne Sloman, *The Thatcher Phenomenon* (London, British Broadcasting Corporation, 1986), p. 12.
68 Hugo Young, 'Rough justice for a leader born to battle', *The Guardian*, 23 November 1990.
69 Young, 'Rough justice for a leader born to battle'.
70 Dennis Kavanagh, 'Prime Ministerial Power Revisited', *Social Studies Review*, 6, no. 4 (March 1991), p. 132.
71 Dennis Kavanagh, *Thatcherism and British Politics: The End of Consensus?*, 2nd edn (Oxford, Oxford University Press, 1990), p. 254. See also R. M. Punnett, *British Government and Politics*, 5th edn (Aldershot, Dartmouth, 1987), pp. 246–7.

72 Peter Jenkins, *Mrs Thatcher's Revolution: The Ending of the Socialist Era* (London, Pan Books, 1989), p. 185.
73 Jenkins, *Mrs Thatcher's Revolution*, p. xvii.
74 G. W. Jones, 'Prime Minister and the Cabinet', *Wroxton Papers in Politics* (Wroxton College, 1990), pp. 5, 13.
75 G. W. Jones, 'Mrs Thatcher and the Power of the Prime Minister', *Contemporary Record*, 3, no. 4 (April 1990), p. 6.
76 Cecil Parkinson, *Right at the Centre* (London, Weidenfeld and Nicolson, 1992), p. 4. See also Margaret Thatcher, *The Downing Street Years* (London, HarperCollins, 1993), pp. 850–5.
77 Parkinson, *Right at the Centre*, p. 4.
78 Jones, 'Prime Minister and the Cabinet', p. 13.
79 Peter Jenkins, 'The real rebel of cabinet government', *Independent on Sunday*, 22 July 1990.
80 Frank Johnson, 'The Cabinet was in charge all along', *Sunday Telegraph*, 16 December 1990.
81 Johnson, 'The Cabinet was in charge all along'.
82 Johnson, 'The Cabinet was in charge all along'.
83 Johnson, 'The Cabinet was in charge all along'.
84 Johnson, 'The Cabinet was in charge all along'. For a similarly jaundiced view of what academics can contribute to the debate over prime ministerial power, see Alan Watkins, 'It's no good trying to be like Mrs Thatcher', *The Observer*, 9 June 1991. Watkins refers to the way that 'several academics, whose closest acquaintance with Whitehall and Westminster was from the top deck of a number 11 bus, popularised the notion that we are living under a presidential system of government'. The most prominent had been John Mackintosh, who 'had worked out his views at the Universities of Edinburgh and Ibadan, Nigeria'.
85 Michael Foley, *The Rise of the British Presidency* (Manchester, Manchester University Press, 1993).

CHAPTER 2

Outsiders and spatial leadership in modern American politics

In order to grasp the case for a substantive comparison between the American presidency and the British premiership, it is necessary to look away from those features that are usually employed to characterise political systems. Comparisons normally dwell upon such factors as institutional structures, operational procedures, relationships between the constituent parts of governmental systems, and established conceptions of authority, control and consent. Nevertheless, it is often more revealing to examine the less explicit and often obscure elements of government which provide evidence of underlying forces at work within a political system. It is these deeper developments which not only provide insights into the American presidency, but also into the development of the British prime minister's office. In this way the American presidency can be used as a lever to open up some of the less visible, but arguably more important, properties and dynamics of the British premiership. In doing so, it will become clear that a number of features central to the American presidency are now shared by the premiership in this country. These features are highly significant, for they can illustrate the scale and substance of the changes occurring behind the apparently imperturbable edifice of British cabinet government. They can also draw attention to the full implications of such changes and, in particular, to the way that *de facto* presidential politics has been altering British perspectives of parties and elections, and British evaluations of public authority and political performance.

This chapter will examine one of the key features of modern presidential politics in the United States. It is not a single phenomenon so much as an assemblage of trends and developments. They relate to the methods and opportunities by which presidents have sought to remain at the centre of government, while at the same time removing themselves from the negative connotations of Washington in a political culture that is increasingly sceptical of any government. The need to occupy the president's position of national leadership at the core of the federal government, while at the same time retaining an intimacy with the citizenry and a responsiveness to its populist prejudices, has given rise to a set of strategies geared to squaring the circle – i.e. being in government but not of it. The contemporary requirement of maintaining and cultivating a sense of space between the White House and the apparently systemic afflictions of an otherwise inert and ingrown government has given rise to a peculiar type of leadership. For the purposes of this study, the term 'spatial leadership' has been adopted to convey the way in which political authority is protected and cultivated by the creation of a sense of distance, and, occasionally, detachment, from government. In this form of leadership, physical distance and political distance are intended to become synonymous with one another. The strategy of spatial leadership allows a president to remain an integral part of government, while at the same time affording opportunities to disengage selectively from many of its actual and reputed defects. Leadership of this kind can appear to be counter-intuitive and even paradoxical in nature. It seeks to reconstitute a president's status as the ultimate Washington insider to that of a persistent outsider and heroic victim of a conspiracy of dynamics against the public interest. And yet, spatial leadership possesses an interior logic that draws upon many of the dichotomies of American government and that, far from undermining a president, can provide the office-holder with one of the most effective ways of maintaining a central position in government.

Past masters: Nixon, Carter, Reagan, Clinton

RICHARD NIXON

Richard Nixon was probably the first president to be aware of the contemporary dynamics of big government and anti-politics. He sensed the political potential of tapping the impulses of American individualism and using them to construct a dual identity that allowed him to condemn the Washington establishment at the very same time that he sought to monopolise its power centres. Nixon's belief in being an outsider led him to identify his presidency with what he called the 'silent majority', i.e. those whom he thought shared his resentments against the 'liberal establishment' in Washington. Through this device, Nixon wanted to appeal to those who were not vociferous and militant minorities and who were not publicly critical of American values and commitments. Nixon surmised that there was a vast untapped source of forgotten people who could be encouraged to see Nixon as one of their own. He hoped to arouse a populist movement, centred on 'middle America', that would accept Nixon as its natural leader and support him in a patriotic confrontation against the critics and innovators that appeared to occupy the commanding heights of Washington.[1]

Although Nixon had touched upon a rich vein of popular resentment, he was not really the person to mobilise and translate it into a movement. In winning the presidency, Nixon had failed to secure the silent majority. What should have been the culmination of a long political career was marred by the challenge of a powerful third party, which denied Nixon a majority of the popular vote. The intervention of George Wallace into the election had disrupted the political landscape and damaged the electoral performance of the two main parties. Nixon won only 43 per cent of the popular vote. This was the lowest proportion of the vote to be acquired by a winning candidate since 1912. It was a salutary warning to Nixon that a notorious outsider like Wallace could inflict serious damage, not just on his own Democratic party but on the Republicans' populist crusade against the liberalism of the Kennedy–Johnson period. To make matters worse, Nixon became the first president since 1848 to enter the White House without a Congress controlled by his own party. Large numbers of voters had split their preferences by opting for a Republican president but balancing it with a Democratic Congress. Furthermore, Nixon's level of public approval was significantly lower than the norm for incoming presidents. The politician who won the presidency under the banner of the ordinary person's champion had to adjust to the fact that he was not held in great affection or trust by the silent majority.[2]

Nixon's period of office was characterised by frustration. Much of this was caused by the fact that he was a radical in a minority party surrounded by entrenched political interests. Nixon felt himself to be an outsider, not just politically but by birth and background and also by personality and temperament:

> Nixon the politician ... concealed Nixon the man and the man was, even to some of his close friends, an unbelievably complex, shy, remote and tense figure whose iron control seldom permitted anyone to glimpse the tumult inside ... At the root of this incapacity was his loneliness, and the loneliness was partly an inheritance of birth in a poor and undistinguished family, partly his environment as a poor boy, partly the harsh way politics had dealt with him.[3]

It was difficult for Nixon to be a champion of the middle-class outsiders of America if he could not communicate with them. It was even more difficult when it became clear that Nixon's main objective was to gain admittance to Washington's 'inside'. Nixon had grown up with the modern presidency. He had observed the office at close quarters as vice-president in the 1950s. He remained a zealous defender of vigorous presidential leadership and its role in purposefully directing the nation. He now wished to claim his Rooseveltian inheritance. But times had changed. Nixon's personality seemed quite unable to cope with the fact that presidential power, which had always been provisional in nature, was now highly contentious and more dependent than ever upon the skills and subtlety of the man in the White House. Nixon's political frustrations, together with his propensity for self-pity and for feeling the subject of unwarranted victimisation, led him to resort more to private means to confront government. He found the 'silent majority' too shapeless and self-limiting a weapon to use effectively in his drive to make government come to heel.

As the Nixon administration became increasingly insular and ingrown, its resentments and aggression also became more conspicuous. Nixon's relationship with the media – his lifeline to what fashionable Washingtonians referred to disdainfully as 'out there' – suffered accordingly. To the Nixon White House, the media were not merely uncooperative in their manner, they were the leading element of the resistance movement confronting the government itself. As Pat Buchanan, one of Nixon's White House staff, explained:

> This hasn't been our town. They live in Georgetown, with their parties; they never invited us, they ignored us. We were the vanguard of Middle America and they were the liberal elite. It's a schism that's cultural, political, social, emotional. When we came in 1968, they dominated all American society – the media, the Supreme Court, the bureaucracy, the foundations. They left us with our cities burning, and inflation going, our students rioting on the campus. And Nixon challenged all this.[4]

The Nixon team operated on the premise that there was a 'counter-government' at work in American society and that its purpose was 'clearly aimed at the destruction of our traditional institutions' which it 'could not hope to eliminate through the elective process'.[5] This subversion justified exceptional forms of 'hardball' infighting. Tragically for Nixon, soon after winning the 1972 presidential election, his authority crumbled away in the Watergate scandal. His proposed campaign against government was undermined by charges that he had himself already usurped and corrupted government. Nixon's remoteness as a figure left his supporters surviving on the belief in his good faith, but as one revelation of duplicity and intrigue followed another, Nixon finally lost the respect of his silent constituency. He had lost touch with his public and, ultimately, betrayed them by being seen to be at the epicentre of 'Washington corruption'.[6] To the silent majority, Nixon had reached the heights of high government and the depths of depravity in the 'imperial presidency' – positionally and morally he was not one of them after all.[7]

JIMMY CARTER

Nixon's excesses ultimately brought Jimmy Carter to Washington. Carter's whole campaign had been based on the proposition that he could provide a moral antidote to the power politics and duplicitous statecraft that had discredited Nixon's administration. To Carter, the answer to the 'imperial presidency' was to elect an individual so totally divorced from Washington that he could be regarded as its personal antithesis. On the basis of background, character and experience, Carter presented himself as the ideal candidate to correct America's disenchantment with itself and its government. Carter relished and cultivated the role of outsider. He would revive and redeem American government. To a secure and confident figure like Carter, being an outsider was a virtue and a mark of distinction to be exploited to maximum political effect.

In many respects, Carter's attachment to the role of outsider was dictated to him by the circumstances of his election. He had begun his campaign as an ex-governor of Georgia, with no experience of Washington, no real links with the major elements of the Democratic party, and no opportunity to impress the party cadres in any national arena. As a consequence, it is true to say that 'Jimmy Carter could only have won the Democratic Party's nomination and the ensuing general election by pursuing as he did the strategy of an "outsider"'.[8] In a brilliant primary election campaign that was a model exercise in how an obscure politician could use the new channels of public participation to impose his candidature on the national party, Carter defeated his more illustrious rivals for the nomination. His direct appeal to the rank and file was based upon a visceral attack upon Washington and the need for the 'chasm between the people and government to be bridged'.[9] Carter openly deployed his outsider status to lend weight to his concept of an isolated and unresponsive government in Washington. Public confidence in the integrity and competence of government could only be renewed by wide-ranging reforms, through which the public might penetrate the edifice of a private state. In Carter's words:

> The natural opposition of special interests, selfish bureaucrats, and hidebound elected officials must be overcome. This is not so difficult as it might seem. These opponents simply cannot prevail against the truth and an aroused and determined public. I have often seen them retreat into their dark corners when exposed to public scrutiny and debate.[10]

This was an effective message and a successful electoral strategy. But it was more than this. To Carter, the veracity of the message was reaffirmed by the manner of his own rise to office. His self-image of a morally scrupulous outsider acting as an agent of the people against its own government was vindicated in his eyes by his popular passage to the White House against all the odds.

The odds had indeed been considerable. Carter had no experience of the federal government or of international affairs. He was even an outsider in his own party. He depicted himself as someone outside the normally expedient character of American politics and, in particular, outside the wheeler-dealer character of congressional decision making. Furthermore, he was from the South – America's outsider region. This was the area of the United States traditionally most hostile to the federal government and traditionally the subject of prejudice and ridicule from other parts of the union. Being a Southerner had long been thought to be a disqualification for the White House. Carter had overcome this disadvantage, but he was well aware of the disparagement that remained.

> The local cartoonists had a field day characterizing us as barefoot country hicks with straw sticking out of our ears, dad in overalls, and unfamiliar with the proper use of indoor plumbing ... Although many Southerners were angry at the regional ridicule, our family was too exuberant to have our spirits dampened. We were able to laugh at these articles and political cartoons.[11]

To Carter, and the 'Georgian Mafia' he brought with him to Washington, the laughter was founded on the self-confidence that they had succeeded in reaching Washington in spite of the establishment who lived and worked there.

Carter tried to maintain that combination of moralism and populism which had been the hallmarks of his rise to power. This was always going to be a difficult strategy because it entailed the president seeking to remain an outsider while situated inside the centre of Washington. Carter saw the potential for using the sense of distance between himself and the rest of Washington as an effective strategy for maintaining the lustre of public contact and trust that had accompanied his election. Unfortunately for Carter and his presidency, he was unable to convert that potential into the desired effect.

Carter aggravated political leaders in Washington by his sense of moral superiority and intellectual detachment, and by his insistence that he owed nothing to anyone as he had secured the presidency through his own direct relationship with 'the people'. The cost of Carter's attachment with the public came to be measured by a commensurate deterioration in his links with the party, with Congress and with the rest of the Washington 'insiders'. Carter might have done better if he had not made it quite so obvious that he preferred an abstract affinity to the public rather than any tangible engagements with the public's other representatives. The president was poor at consulting with members of Congress and at giving adequate notification of his legislative proposals.[12] He vetoed their pork barrel projects and was uninterested in their claims for patronage. He often refused to compromise and had a habit of publicly disclosing the contents of political negotiations while they were still under discussion.

Carter himself made no apologies for these failings:

> I was not part of the Wall Street business Establishment, the Washington political Establishment or the Hollywood entertainment Establishment in any way. I was a Southern peanut farmer populist type. That was fine with me ... We were alien in some ways. There were ways I could have reached out. It was not an antagonistic attitude. It is just not part of my personality. I do not condemn the cocktail circuit. It is just not natural for me to be part of it.[13]

The unconventional nature of Carter's leadership mixed high intelligence with political amateurism; religious humility with personal disdain. It led to charges of arrogance. David Broder's accusation was typical of the genre:

> As an outsider, he often has failed to recognize the legitimacy of the complex system of constituency representation, reflected in Congress, the bureaucracy and the interest groups. He often has failed to involve other leaders, with constituencies of their own, in the common tasks of governing or to give them a substantial stake in the success of his policies ... Too often in this term, Carter has been captured by the conceit that his own mystique and communion with the 'People' could substitute for the daily drudgery of coalition-building in Congress and the political realm.[14]

Carter's evocation of Thomas Jefferson's ideal of wise innocence paled into public fatigue for a range of reasons. In one sense, it would have been difficult for any president to survive the body blows of continued stagflation, rising energy costs, high interest rates, budget deficits, pressure on the dollar and a full-blown hostage crisis in Iran. But probably more critical to his presidency were two factors that disoriented and, ultimately, undermined his outsider status in Washington. First, as a 'populist who tried to run the U.S., [he] learnt to his sorrow that Washington politics is a complex profession'.[15] His attempts to master the administration almost single-handedly as a public champion of good government led him to be buried in detail and, as a result, to appear indecisive and even incompetent. As Carter became enveloped in government problems, he lost that sense of space between himself and the government that signified his attachment to the public.

Secondly, Carter used his own licence as an outsider to take upon himself the task of informing the American people about subjects that no previous president had ever dared to raise. Carter's candour, and his special relationship with the public, led him to tell his fellow citizens that America's social and economic problems were intractable; that there were many problems which government simply could not solve; and that there were even problems to which no solutions existed at all. He urged Americans to face the truth that there were limits to economic growth, limits to higher standards of living and limits to energy provision. Expectations had to be lowered.[16] America's relative economic and military decline had to be accepted. Americans in effect had to accustom themselves to painful changes. Apart from the message itself being unpalatable, and apart from the economic crises that plagued Carter's administration and gave credence to his warnings, the fact remains that Carter mishandled his own populist resources. He made the mistake of using his public position to tell Americans that they themselves were the problem – thereby turning populism on its head. He compounded this mistake with another by informing them that there were even more severe problems looming on the horizon and that no one could do anything about them apart from accepting their existence. Carter overplayed his outsider role to such an extent that he ended up outside the public itself.

RONALD REAGAN

It was Ronald Reagan who provided the master's touch to the strategy of spatial leadership. He it was who demonstrated its exceptional properties and the extraordinary uses to which it could be put. Like Carter, Reagan entered the White House by virtue of a campaign against government in Washington. But unlike Carter, Reagan insisted upon retaining his public distance from Washington in spite of his central position within it. Reagan was also exceptional in respect to the 'energy with which he campaigned against government even when he *was* the government'.[17] Reagan refused to become entangled in complex issues or in the grind of government management. What Reagan did take very seriously were the links with his public constituency outside Washington. This was where his chief political resource lay and he knew it could best be tapped by persistent and broad-based ideological assertions of social optimism, national pride and a healthy scepticism of Washington politics.

Instead of Carter's intellectual and fatalistic diagnoses of America's problems, Reagan offered the prospect of dramatic escapes through the sheer exertion of American will. The war for national self-belief was more important than lost battles over policy and administration. Reagan was another self-proclaimed outsider. It was from such a vantage point that Reagan intended to engage in a fundamentalist crusade to release America from excessive government dependency and regulation. His whole career had been dominated by the desire to challenge the federal government. He was committed to a frontal assault upon the 'smothering hand'[18] of Washington. His campaign was unequivocally designed to undermine the federal government's legitimacy and to reverse the scale of its operations in American society. Reagan's presidency would continue the mission. He had to lead, but he also had to symbolise the office's own emancipation from governing structures.

At the beginning of his administration, when he was seeking to install the main framework of his economic reform programme, Reagan extended the confrontational and plebiscitary approach to the presidency that his recent predecessors had begun. When he encountered stiff opposition in Congress, Reagan recalled his time as governor of California: 'In Sacramento, the most important lesson I learned was the value of making an end run around the legislature by going directly to the people; on television or radio, I'd lay out the problems we faced and ask their help to persuade the legislators to vote as they wanted, not in the way special-interest groups did.'[19] This became the Reagan way in Washington. To Reagan, the New Deal liberals in Congress constantly sought to frustrate his plans and then to pin the blame for the subsequent deadlock on to the president. He would always refute the allegation. In his view, Congress was especially susceptible to special interests and not to what he regarded as being the public will. To strengthen his identity with the public, and thereby substantiate his assumption that 'Reaganomics' reflected popular demand, the president regularly plunged himself into the American populace in order 'to keep the heat on Congress'.[20] Trips, speeches, radio interviews and televised broadcasts were all directed to the objective of asking 'the people to make their views known to their elected representatives'.[21] His early efforts were successful and the reform package secured congressional approval in July 1981. Reagan felt vindicated on all fronts. In his view, he had turned the tide of government by taking himself to the people and instilling in them a renewed sense of their own autonomy.

Following this high-water mark, Reagan found the forces deployed against him too formidable to engage in any further exercises of mass mobilisation directed to the theme of budgetary counter-revolution. In the years of attrition that ensued, the Reagan administration and the Democratic Congress battled over the budget on a yearly basis. Confronted with the intractable nature of the process, Reagan increasingly shifted the focus of his leadership to a position of detachment from the negotiating framework of the budget. After 1982, the public was regularly presented with the sight of a president who, while formally responsible for the federal government's budget, openly dissociated himself from the discussions over its substance. After reiterating his original principles of reduced taxation, diminished social spending and increased military expenditure, and offering a budget that was usually ignored by an incredulous Congress, Reagan would then bathe publicly in his own intransigence. He would affect not to negotiate on the key issues; he would threaten to take parts of the budget to the people through televised addresses; he would promise vetoes; and he would dissociate himself from the final outcome. In the judgement of Louis Fisher, 'Reagan was content to sit on the sidelines and tell Congress: "You figure it out." In matters of budgeting, it is difficult to find a more irresponsible President in the twentieth century.'[22] Behind the scenes, Reagan would make compromises and reach accommodations to facilitate the budget's passage into law. In public, the impression was quite different. It was of a feisty man of principle cowed only by the greater force of lesser men. As responsibility was offloaded, either on to Congress for budgetary priorities or on to members of his cabinet for unpopular decisions, Reagan was able to preserve his standing as a crusader committed to internal exile.

President Reagan would always allocate culpability for the conditions of the government's finances to the Democratic Congress. In doing so, he appeared to absolve himself from even partial blame. He reached out to the public by distancing himself from the ascribed myopia and self-seeking of ordinary politicians in Washington who were necessarily misrepresenting the public. Reagan's exemplary command of spatial leadership was based essentially upon acts of defiance. Instead of Carter's gloomy realism, Reagan had always preached a gospel of defiance against economic limits, intractable problems and national decline. As his presidency developed, Reagan extended this defiance to his own record. He defied the failures of his programme, the severity of its effects, the significance of the deficits, the divisiveness of his policies and the retreats from his stated positions. As a result, the Reagan years were marked by policy failures, U-turns, internal dissension and administrative disarray.

In spite of these apparent setbacks, President Reagan's stature with the public remained undiminished. His verbal gaffes, his intellectual deficiencies, his inattentiveness and even his indolence were celebrated as acts of defiance against the protocol of government. He was termed the 'Teflon' president to whom no charge ever stuck. This was mainly because he had developed an identity separate from that of the government. In fact, as John Sloan explains, he remained a constant campaigner whose natural habitat was one that lay outside of, and was external to, Washington:

> One intriguing aspect of Reagan as campaigner was his continuing role identification as an 'outsider', challenging the pathologies of the federal government even *after* he was elected to office. By playing the role of crusading outsider

> who had heeded his country's patriotic call to clean up the stable, Reagan often succeeded in avoiding the disadvantages of a president in office while, at the same time, exploiting the powers that the office afforded him. He handled the logical inconsistency of this position by defining government as Congress and the bureaucracy.[23]

Reagan's public popularity for being both public and popular gave him an extraordinary dispensation from critical scrutiny. His ability to dissociate himself from his own administration baffled analysts and journalists alike. It was said that Reagan possessed 'formidable powers of denial',[24] even to the point of disputing the existence of evident failures and the validity of factual knowledge. To Garry Wills, American politics under President Reagan were 'shot through with unreality'.[25]

Reagan's formidable powers of disengagement allowed him to build up a dichotomy in the public's mind between on the one hand the leadership, and on the other the president's own policy proposals and political conduct. The period of the Reagan administration, therefore, was marked by an extraordinary disjunction between a high public approval of his presidency and majority disapproval of his policies. Reagan's visceral relationship with the American public was witnessed at first hand and graphically conveyed by Jane Mayer and Doyle McManus: 'Reagan seemed to share a strange kind of alchemy with the American public ... They were inspired by his optimism ... They felt he was more trustworthy than other politicians. They thought he had backbone – whether they approved of his programs or not.'[26] This is precisely the point. While Reagan regularly received strong public approval ratings for his presidency, more people consistently disapproved of his policies than approved them. In 1985, Louis Harris observed that Reagan had 'never been so popular personally and his programs so little supported by the public'.[27] Reagan may have been able to draw on the public's negative disposition towards government in general terms, but he was quite unable to disturb the public's attachment to the tangible benefits, and even the ideals, of the New Deal's positive state. But to a politician so adept at spatial leadership, this did not seem to matter. In many respects, Reagan seemed to thrive on public setbacks. Conspicuous defeats on politically untenable causes (e.g. abortion reform, school prayer amendments, progressive tax reduction, increased assistance to the contra rebels in Nicaragua and a constitutional amendment mandating a balanced federal budget) seemed only to enhance his reputation. They embodied social frustration over government in general and maintained the satisfying imagery of earnest confrontation against the impersonal forces of governmental power.

It is a tribute to the remarkable qualities of Reagan's engagement with the public as an endearingly tough outsider that he was able to survive the Iran-contra scandal of 1987. The deceiving, and even self-deluding, properties of Reagan's emphasis upon appearance and presentation were painfully exposed in this episode. The Reagan White House was seen to be in open disarray and guilty of breaking not only its own publicly declared policies, but also the rule of law. Reagan himself was revealed to be ill informed, negligent, evasive and remote. It was a particularly serious crisis for the Reagan presidency because it threatened his public standing with the potentially deadly condition of hard realism and critical inquiry. Reagan's popularity never recovered to the levels he had achieved in the mid 1980s. Nevertheless, he did regain enough of his rapport with the public to leave office in a surge of national fervour. Astonishingly, he was still as popular at the end of his presidency as he was at the beginning. He had played the role of outsider successfully for eight years.

While confounded commentators and political opponents complained that Reagan and his public had been outside of reality itself, Reagan had shown that by playing to the public a president need not become tainted by Washington and could avoid failure by converting leadership into an effect on public spirits. Reagan had always insisted that the victories and successes ascribed to him were not his at all. In his final address to the nation, he reiterated this theme of the president as the people's agent: 'I've had my share of victories in the Congress, but what few people noticed is that I never won anything you didn't win for me. They never saw my troops, they never saw Reagan's regiments, the American people. You won every battle with every call you made and letter you wrote demanding action.'[28] The corollary to this proposition was that, while Reagan accepted little of the credit for his reforms, he similarly accepted little of the blame for their effects. His message had been one of affirming his confidence in the people and of returning power back to the public domain. It was difficult to criticise the 'feel good' messages of a president who not only placed his trust in the audience's own view of American values and traditions, but who seemed able to situate himself at the centre of the auditorium as he did so.

BILL CLINTON

Clinton's passage to the presidency was in many ways born out of a reaction to George Bush's failure in emulating the spatial leadership of his patron Ronald Reagan. The most extraordinary feature of Bush's period in the White House was the way he had actually attempted to repeat Reagan's virtuoso performance in outsider politics. It was remarkable because George Bush had never been an outsider in his life. He was in fact the living epitome of America's East Coast establishment. Coming from a highly privileged background and educated at Andover and Yale, Bush had followed his father in dedicating himself to the obligations of public service. As a consummate insider, and vice-president for eight years, the metamorphosis into an exponent of outsider politics was no easy task. Stung by the criticism coming from Republican rivals for the nomination, Bush's image had had to be hastily reconstructed. His managers distracted attention away from his New England patrician background by playing up his connections to Texas and his early career as an oilman. The candidate toughened up his language, became more aggressive and made every effort to accommodate himself to the legendary outsider perspectives of the Republican right wing.

George Bush's discomfort in the presidency was in many respects a consequence of the political imperatives of having to follow the populist impulses of the 'silent majority'. It was a measure of the contemporary pressures exerted upon presidents that Bush was continually placed in the position of having to act out of character. Bush's disposition towards government had always been based upon the ethos of public obligation. He was temperamentally attached to its institutional values and *esprit de corps*. It is, therefore, highly significant that Bush of all people felt constrained to resort to populist rhetoric and to distance himself conspicuously from government wherever this was possible. It was Bush, the archetypal Ivy League insider, who felt compelled to be an outsider and publicly exploit government as a term of abuse. It can, of course, be argued that Bush was never particularly convincing as an outsider and largely failed to translate the space he created for himself into a form of public leadership. Nevertheless, what is significant is that Bush – even Bush – evidently felt that there was no alternative but to try and change his image from that of progressive Republican and team player to one of a maverick figure quietly preserving public services while loudly running down the 'government'.

The election year of 1992 was a vintage period of outsider politics. To Bush, 1992 was a 'weird year' with a 'lot of crazy people running around'. It was, he said, a 'funny season where everyone wants to have the most populist appeal'.[29] The president was confronted by the visceral blue-collar populism of Pat Buchanan on the Republican right and by the startling surge in public support for the anti-politics ticket of Ross Perot. More critically, Bush was faced with an array of outsiders from the Democratic party, intent upon exploiting every variant of outsider politics in an effort to distance themselves from Washington's political culture, in an effort to acquire legitimacy for their respective campaigns for the party leadership. It would be no exaggeration to say that the Democratic party in 1992 achieved a truly exotic level of outsider competition. Six minor runners contended the nomination after the party's heavyweight figures (e.g. Mario Cuomo, Al Gore,

Lloyd Bentsen, George Mitchell) had earlier refused to enter the race. They had been deterred from doing so when Bush's popularity in the afterglow of the Gulf War had given every indication that he could be assured of re-election to a second term of office.

After a series of setbacks caused in the main by revelations of his marital infidelities, Bill Clinton managed to prevail and become the first Democrat to win a presidential election for sixteen years. He had defeated an incumbent president, yet he had secured only 43 per cent of the popular vote in a three-way contest. The nature of his mandate was questionable. The ambiguity was compounded by Clinton's own opaqueness on policy. In some respects he was a New Democrat, committed to the centre ground and to the need to retain something of the Reaganite scepticism of big government. Accordingly, Clinton sought to distance himself from the bureaucratic negatives of government. He drew attention to the achievements of the National Performance Review in eliminating 16,000 pages of federal regulation and in cutting federal employment by over 200,000 jobs, thereby reducing the bureaucracy to the smallest percentage of the civilian workforce since 1933.[30] On the other hand, Clinton was suspected of being a closet liberal whose underlying inclination was to the tax-and-spend drives of the New Deal and the Great Society.

These suspicions rose exponentially when Clinton made his hugely complex measure of healthcare reform the top priority measure of his administration. Although Clinton tried to sell the reform as a cost-neutral policy, it succeeded only in generating intense partisan conflict within Congress. The president was widely regarded as having exceeded both his mandate and his support base. Clinton was accused of being disingenuous and of moving to the left once in office, in order to satisfy the vested interests and old policy paradigms of the congressional Democrats. Clinton became smeared with the disgrace of 'big government' by a rampant Republican party that was now released from the constraints of the presidency and intent upon deepening the Reagan crusade against the state. Clinton's flagship policy slowly sank beneath him. The episode damaged his reputation for competence and undermined his presidency.

Within two years of taking office, Clinton was perceived to be a Washington insider and therefore out of contact with public sentiment. His party lost control of Congress in the 1994 mid-term elections. The House of Representatives was taken over by the Republicans for the first time in forty-two years. Moreover, Clinton was confronted by a resurgent opposition party which had been galvanised into action by a radical leadership dedicated to assault upon the federal government even more severe than that instituted by President Reagan in the 1980–81 period. Newt Gingrich, the pugnacious

Republican leader and now Speaker of the House of Representatives, claimed a national mandate on the basis that, after having publicly endorsed the Contract With America (CWA), enough Republican candidates had subsequently achieved electoral success to assume control of Congress. The CWA not only included public policy commitments but also incorporated a set of pledges to reform Congress, thereby linking the need for political change with structural transformation.

After 1994, Bill Clinton was placed in the unconventional position of a president seeking to use the office to curtail a Republican programme of administrative and budgetary reform, to limit the inventiveness of the Republican agenda, and to steer the Republican engine of change away from the social dangers of its own indiscriminate appetite for cuts.[31] The 'Republican revolution' and its revolutionary leadership inadvertently provided Clinton with the opportunity to reposition himself in the political centre as the public's expression of anxiety over the projected sweep of Republican cuts in social provision. Clinton had come to understand the hybrid nature of the government issue. The theme had genuine properties of dissent that drew upon public hostility against government in an abstract sense. But it was also a theme that was heavily conditioned by factors of therapeutic complaint and measured invective. The Republican leadership in Congress threatened to take the rhetoric of anti-statism literally and to engage in a socially disruptive assault upon programmes and subsidies that would threaten middle-class Americans as much as the undeserving poor. In these circumstances, Clinton moved to a strategy of 'triangulation' by which he sought 'not just to blend the best of each party's positions, but to transcend the traditional continuum and create a genuinely third force'.[32] Whether it is seen as Clinton being marginalised by the congressional Republicans, or the president ceding initiative and space in the public arena, the net effect was to enable Clinton to reinvent his presidency as a rearguard defence against the political overreach of Newt Gingrich and his supporters.

President Clinton played on the inexperience and immaturity of the Republican ascendancy in Congress. By ceding the initiative to the Republicans, Clinton was able to recapture some of the outsider resonance that had characterised his 1992 presidential campaign. His political isolation gave him the opportunity to develop the Reaganite role of president as 'dissenter in chief' within government. His involuntary disjunction from those centres of power that were now setting the domestic agenda enabled Clinton to distance himself from the negative connotations of Washington and to amend the reputation he had acquired during the 1992–94 period as a promoter of 'big government'. The partisan attempts to make political capital out of various scandals surrounding the Clintons contributed towards a public perception of a president besieged by the ingrown preoccupations of Washington elites. President Clinton's rehabilitation as a candidate for re-election in 1996 was given a powerful boost by the upturn in the economy. But equally significant was the selection of the archetypal Washingtonian, Bob Dole, as the Republican candidate. The Senate Majority Leader's age (seventy-three) and his reputation as the Washington 'fixer' of his generation constituted a highly suggestive counterpoint to the relatively young and dislocated president. Clinton was quick to exploit the contrast to maximum symbolic effect.

Minding the gap

It should be pointed out that spatial leadership is quite at variance with the customary conception of leadership in the modern presidency. The central theme in the development of the office has traditionally been seen as one of inspired leadership forcefully and skilfully imposing itself upon a congenitally fragmented system of entrenched interests, political enclaves and dispersed authority. The character of presidential activism has been dominated by the simple imperative of a need being met. It was Franklin Roosevelt's New Deal programme in the 1930s and his leadership in World War II that set the precedent that subsequently provided the standard upon which succeeding presidents would be judged. After Roosevelt, it was not merely a hope that presidents would counteract the dissonance of America's government and provide a central form of public purpose. It was an expectation. The modern presidency emerged as a formidable office built upon the achievements, precedents and *de facto* powers of an exceptional leader. The model role of the presidential office was accordingly transformed into one of necessary activism that propelled Roosevelt's successors into positions of conspicuous centrality.

The structure and role of the presidency became progressively institutionalised in the period following Roosevelt's term of office. The American system became dependent upon presidential leadership for direction, co-ordination, decisiveness and a sense of national vision. It was widely recognised that 'the contributions that a president could make to government were indispensable'.[33] In Thomas Cronin's words, 'only the president could be the genuine architect of US public policy, and only he, by attacking problems frontally and aggressively and by interpreting his power expansively, could slay the dragon of crisis and be the engine of change to move this nation forward'.[34] As a result, the modern presidency was acknowledged to be '*the* strategic catalyst for progress in the American system'.[35] In this guise, the presidency was America's 'instrument of twentieth century government'[36] –

an instrument that had facilitated the full and irreversible establishment of both the 'positive state' and the 'national security state' in the ostensibly anti-statist culture of the American republic. Accordingly, the presidency came to be considered 'the nearest thing to a concrete embodiment of the state'[37] in the scheme of American politics.

Notwithstanding the fact that the assertions made on behalf of the modern presidency were overdrawn, the model's historical and normative elements have remained a key reference point, both for the occupants of the White House and for the legions of observers who subject the presidency to critical appraisal. Presidents continue to extend and develop their bureaucratic structures and managerial techniques to optimise the level of central control over the legislative, administrative and budgetary dimensions of the executive branch of the federal government. Presidents are still required to show competence in the conduct of government. They will be judged on it and held to account for their record in meeting public expectations in the field of administrative and decisional performance. Nevertheless, within the limits of such standards, presidents have been able to generate a defiant disjunction between themselves and the claims and mechanics of government. This disjunction gives expression both to an abstract disaffection towards big organisations in general and to a set of specific irritants associated with allegations of federal extravagance and systemic corruption. President Reagan exemplified this dialectic of running with the hare by running with the hounds. He successfully dramatised the normally private struggle between the chief executive and the federal executive into a public spectacle of ideological confrontation between presidential populism and the state.

It is often remarked that Ronald Reagan began his term of office as president and head of the administration with the disclaimer that he was against government: 'Government is not the solution to our problems. Government is the problem.'[38] What is overlooked is the fact that he was still convincingly claiming this to be true eight years later, and without a hint of self-contradiction. President Reagan exploited to the full those opportunities that had grown up over the previous twenty-five years for leadership to become detached from government. Reagan revealed the extent to which it had become possible to open up space between the presidency and the branch of executive government over which he was expected to preside. He managed to retain and to develop throughout his two full terms of office the role of outsider that he had so assiduously cultivated as a candidate before his election. The extent of his popularity at the end of his administration represented a triumphant affirmation not merely of Reagan himself, but of the extraordinary potential of a leadership style that was at one and the same time both self-denying and self-promoting in nature.

By the mid 1990s, the congressional Republicans had succeeded in shifting Clinton to the right on a series of key issues (e.g. welfare reform, tax cuts and a commitment to a balanced budget by 2002). After a year of working with the Republican leadership in Congress, Clinton was willing to defer to the change in public philosophy. A Democratic president in the mould of Roosevelt and Kennedy had to concede that the time when Democratic presidents personified a philosophy of government and were instrumental in a progressive advance of federal intervention was at an end. Clinton conceded that the 'era of big government is over'.[39] In his 1996 State of the Union Address, Clinton set out to distance himself from Washington: 'We know big government does not have all the answers. There is not a program for every problem. We know we need a smaller, less bureaucratic government in Washington – one that lives within its means.'[40] Far from acclaiming the progressive advance of enlightened government, the president celebrated its contraction. 'The federal government is the smallest it has been in 30 years, and it is getting smaller every day.'[41]

The examples of Reagan and Clinton have been not isolated incidents in the development of the contemporary presidency. Their positions on 'big government' and on the need to work towards the displacement of the presidency away from presumptions and connotations of its existence were not simply driven by personal idiosyncrasies or political persuasion. The disavowal of the modern presidency, and its operating ethos of utilising the federal government as the engine of socio-economic change, are the product of several underlying influences. These include:

- The growth of partisan dealignment and voter volatility.
- The increased incidence of 'ticket splitting' and the normalisation of 'divided government' in which control of Congress and the presidency is split between the main parties.
- The rise of candidate-based campaigns and personalised mandates.
- The disaggregation of voting blocks and power centres.
- Public concern over the abuse of central power and the onset of legal measures to prevent it.
- Declining public trust in the integrity and competence of the federal government.

The convergence of such factors over the previous twenty years has formed a syndrome of conditions to which presidents have been driven to respond in terms of spatial leadership. These influences have created a political context in which presidents have been able to retain their prominence by developing a dual existence which simultaneously locates the office at the centre of government while allowing the office-holder to devise new relationships with a public increasingly disenchanted with the federal government.

The device of spatial leadership is in essence a reaction to the contemporary political weaknesses and eroded power bases of the presidency. Presidents as much as voters are set adrift in the cross-currents of electoral volatility and eroded partisanship. Given that elections in themselves have become 'less effective as ways of resolving political conflicts in the United States', and given that 'political struggles ... and crucial policy choices tend to be made outside the electoral realm'[42] (e.g. institutional conflict, congressional investigations, judicial review, media revelations), presidential hopes of reaching the dry land of a party-based mandate for an effective party-based government are invariably seen as unrealistic. The cumulative effect of these several political and institutional trends, set as they are in a context of neo-liberal drives towards deregulation, down-sizing and devolution, has been to isolate presidents in a deepening disjunction of 'increased demands of political leadership and diminishing resources available for its support'.[43] The theme that characterises almost every study of the contemporary American presidency is this contradiction between the persistent allocation of responsibilities and the deficit in power to make a satisfactory response to them. In analysing the state of the presidency, it has become customary for observers to make references to the 'beleaguered presidency', the 'no win presidency' and the 'impossible Presidency'. In the view of Michael Genovese, presidential scholars have been compelled to be more 'sensitive to the weakness of presidential power and to the limitations, checks, and constraints placed on it; so many checks, so few balances; so many roadblocks, so few resources; so much separation, so little power. Institutional impotence, not power, has become part of the new textbook presidency.'[44]

The problem of insufficient resources is seen as the defining condition of the 'postmodern presidency'. The issue extends beyond domestic policy to the foreign policy and national security enclaves of executive prerogative where, in an increasingly interdependent world, a postmodern president 'soon recognizes that there are few problems of significance to him that can be resolved by unilateral American action'.[45] The office-holder is constrained by the multiplying volume of presidential responsibilities and by the contingent nature of a president's capacity to exert leadership and assume an authoritative presence at the centre of government. It is only to be expected, therefore, that besieged incumbents will renegotiate the public relationship between their own conspicuous positions in the government hierarchy and the impersonal machinery of the federal bureaucracy. The declining legitimacy of government, combined with the increasing personalisation of presidential politics, makes spatial leadership an effective confection of formal responsibility and symbolic, and even substantive, disengagement. Presidents increasingly seek to combine their formal role as exponents of responsible government with the equally conspicuous role of providing high profile expressions of political responsiveness to public dissent concerning the performance and remit of the federal government. This exotic hybrid allows chief executives selectively to distance themselves from the originating and functioning philosophy of the federal bureaucracy. At the same time, it allows them to engage in innovative leadership strategies that seek to demonstrate political autonomy, self-assertion, radical vision and a commitment to change through dramatised campaigns to dismantle the infrastructure of the Washington bureaucracy.

Leadership against Washington

Presidents and presidential candidates have little alternative other than to exploit the popular resentments against Washington. They have become part of a syndrome that produces critical constructions of individual phenomena and systematises specific conclusions into general indictments of American politics. This jaundiced outlook fuels a perception of policy and budgetary inertia in which pluralist competition has broken down in favour of a generalised satisfaction of group demands through the aggregate resources of the public treasury. Subsidies, tax breaks, immunities and pork projects persist, not just because of the defensive resources of their individual political sponsors, but because of the mutual protection afforded by the pack instinct of all the participating interests. The system of concentrated benefits and dispersed costs is seen as operating in a framework that maximises group claims through the centralisation of power. But this can only remain operational as long as the costs are manageable and do not become an issue that arouses the public to think of itself as a corporate interest, whose welfare and rights are being overridden in favour of vested minority interests, uncapped spending and successive deficits.[46]

According to this perspective, the constitutional checks and balances, which were originally designed to defend the public interest against the abuse of governmental power, are now seen as having been perverted into perpetuating abuses through the prevention of any serious challenge to the multiplicity of interests incorporated into the budget. Over the past twenty years, the issue of the federal budget has centred upon the need to curtail expenditure, reduce taxation and balance the budget, while at the same time fostering ever more intensive defences of programmes and subsidies in the ideological and cultural squeeze on the positive state. The result has been an increasingly rancorous politics in which public cynicism has been activated into populist assaults upon what is depicted as the entire culture of Washington.

The capital city is now commonly depicted as a citadel of vested interest, inefficiency and parochialism that is chronically insulated from the rest of the United States. In his study of the imperial pretensions and decadence of Washington, Kevin Phillips uses the metaphor of a hothouse which provides the perfect conditions for the 'orchids of power, hubris and remoteness from ordinary people'[47] to flourish to the exclusion of all other species. The implications and associations of such an apparently impregnable power centre draw freely upon the populist impulses of American political culture and, in particular, upon the concept of an entrenched political class whose interests and activities amount to a conspiracy against the public. This jaundiced and indiscriminate outlook feeds as readily upon the implicit scandals of 'soft money' contributions, 'independent expenditures', corporate tax breaks and the bankrolling of congressional candidates by political action committees as it does upon the explicit scandals, such as the Savings and Loan bailout, the Iran-contra affair and the succession of accusations surrounding the Clinton presidency.[48]

Legislative–executive confrontation in this interpretive context is easily characterised as gridlock. This in turn is widely suspected to be the result, not of an accidental outcome or a principled impasse, but of a deliberate device for securing the status quo. This allows political representatives to avoid taking any decisive action in response to the nation's problems and to evade any individual responsibility for the consequences of a politically beneficial immobilism. As a consequence, gridlock is seen to have little relationship to any notion of electoral choice or voter responsibility. This constantly negative depiction of Washington has helped to fuel a public discourse on the state of American governance which is dominated by the themes of alienation, powerlessness, expropriation and the moral degradation of public service.

Fired by the legitimacy and moral superiority of the people's will, and by the need for it to be directly and forcibly expressed, political leaders and presidential aspirants in particular have been forced to create campaigns that underline the virtues of being outside the Washington establishment and even outside the customary pool of potential leadership. Paradoxically, those elements in a candidate's *curriculum vitae* that would once have disqualified a person from serious consideration are now considered to be virtues that are seen to qualify an individual for office. Political bureaucratic inexperience of Washington in particular has become an integral feature of campaigns intent upon exploiting the current populist appetites for amateur politicians who claim they are not only anti-government but anti-politics in their convictions.

The Perot phenomenon

The candidacy demonstrating the rich potential of this outsider genre and which revealed the scale of voter volatility in response to the issue of Washington government was provided by Ross Perot's campaign for the presidency in 1992. Perot's drive for the presidency was based upon a highly publicised attack upon the imagery of Washington and upon his own self-appointed role as a redemptive figure who wanted to act as the people's champion. The problems of the nation to Perot were not attributable to the people but to the deficiencies of their agents in government. Washington was only nominally based upon consent. In reality, Perot claimed, it had been subverted from its democratic roots by the penetration of lobbyists and political action committees and by the self-serving agendas of professionalised incumbents, by the remoteness and inertial forces of the bureaucracy and by the redundancy of the two-party system. Perot presented himself as the consummate outsider, with no party organisation, media managers or public financing to support his candidacy. His credentials were limited to his vaunted independence, his success as a businessman, his billionaire self-sufficiency and his stated vision of a mission to fix the system. In his view, Washington had become 'a town filled with sound bites, shell games, handlers and media stunt-men who posture, create images, talk and shoot off Roman candles but who don't ever accomplish anything.'[49] To Perot, the 'entire political system [was] broken' because it was operated by politicians who had different agendas to that of the citizenry: 'It is run by insiders who do not listen to working people and are incapable of solving our problems.'[50] As a consequence, it was 'time to take out the trash and clean out the barn'.[51]

Perot's simplistic messages of empathy, rage and available solutions resonated with the electorate. They demonstrated the level of voter dissatisfaction and alienation, and reflected the extent to which it could be mobilised by a leader that could offer something different by being seen to be different from other politicians. Perot made Bill Clinton and President Bush look like typical politicians. He made other solutions look like part of the problem. This was because he could claim to have the perspective and the independence of an outsider to convey not merely citizen dissatisfaction but a technical proficiency to provide imaginative correctives to national problems. Perot sought to win votes by repudiating the need to run a professional campaign and by condemning the conduct of contemporary electoral politics. His very amateurism and his against-all-odds challenge fitted the explanatory logic of his message. Perot's presumption to condemn and to lead was rooted in his reputed humility in seeking a direct alliance with the rest of society's outsiders that would allow the people to reclaim their government. He defined his message in the following terms:

> The government should come from the people, and we should have a government that gives people an effective voice. The people feel very strongly that they have no voice in their government ... Running up and down the halls of Congress all day, every day, are the organized special interests who have the money to make it possible to buy television time to campaign to get re-elected ... Now make the Congress – make the White House – sensitive to the owners of the country again. That's very important to me.[52]

Perot's message generated an immediate response. Within weeks of openly considering whether even to be a candidate, Perot had moved by the end of April 1992 to a position in the polls where he was within five points of Bill Clinton, the front-runner. By the middle of May, Perot had hit the lead with 34 per cent. This was the first time in American history that a third-party candidate had ever led a national opinion poll. Without entering a single primary election and without a nationwide political organisation to support him, Perot threatened to derail the campaign of both the major parties. Ultimately, he was not able to sustain the momentum, but even though he could not break the duopoly of the two-party system he 'demonstrated the openness, even the vulnerable porousness, of the American political system'[53] by securing 19 per cent of the popular vote in the best performance by a third-party candidate for eighty years. Perot's achievement also revealed the volatile state of an electorate high on citizen dissatisfaction and one in which weak party attachment and self-styled independent behaviour made nearly a fifth of the voters opt for 'a previously unknown candidate with no experience in elected office'.[54]

Even though Perot gave special emphasis to the federal deficit as a defining issue, his campaign was, for the most part, based upon generalised protest and an appeal to temperament, rather than a specific programme of policies. His campaign gave graphic illustration of the susceptibility of the electorate to the generic theme of government irrespective of party control. Notwithstanding the revelations and speculations surrounding his autocratic character, his paranoid behaviour and his political insensitivity, Perot succeeded in showing the effectiveness of an appeal to replace a discredited system with a new framework that would provide systemic solutions to current problems. To Gwen Brown, Perot personified a process by which 'politics and government were inextricably linked and ... made indistinguishable from one another to become politics/government, the new enemy'.[55] As the 'only legitimate outsider who could successfully overcome that enemy', Perot proposed to 'replace the power and decision-making abilities of politics/ government with the power and decision-making abilities of the people'.[56] Perot's simple prescription was for a plebiscitary democracy based upon referenda, town meetings and the imperative drives of popular sovereignty. In effect, he offered the prospect of an outsider who could, by establishing a nexus between himself and the people, effectively relocate the standards, conventions and institutions of representative democracy to the margins of governance.[57]

Distance learning

The aggregate effect of these factors and precedents has been to make the idea and practice of spatial leadership not merely an option but a necessity for presidents discomforted both by the high expectations of government and by the accentuated public mistrust of its practitioners. Government is now seen as crippling presidencies instead of empowering them.[58] Presidents are deemed to be in a 'no win' situation.[59] The presidency has become 'impossible because the gap between public illusions and reality as well as between expectations and performance [is] so massive that no one [can] bridge it any longer'.[60] According to this view, presidential government has become a nullity because the problems of government are intractable, the interests served by government are unassailable, the political structures capable of exerting control are lying broken in pieces, and the public's interest in political issues is narrow, unstable and unpredictable.

It is in response to this syndrome that presidents have increasingly felt their way towards a leadership strategy that seeks to cultivate an outsider image over and against a Washington portrayed – by the presidency's own insistence upon distance – as an unresponsive fortress of insider exclusiveness and privilege. Spatial leadership has become a device by which presidents can turn the vice of multiple weaknesses into the benefit of a collective strength by positioning themselves at the pressure points of public dissent and acting as expressions of citizen anxiety over government. Presidents have built upon the constitution's *prima facia* separation of the chief executive as a single entity distinct from the institutionalised nature of the rest of the federal government. They have also capitalised upon America's ever-available tradition of popular sovereignty, which emphasises the primacy of a participant political culture, arouses a concomitant suspicion of government, and translates democracy primarily into a device for preventing the abuse of power. Furthermore, presidents have been able to use the very prominence of their public position to attract attention to themselves as outsiders whenever it has been in their interests to convey this impression.

The substantive and symbolic payoffs of spatial leadership are considerable, but the strategy does carry political risks. While political defeats can be an effective way of generating public sympathy for a president's construction of reality in Washington, a president runs the risk of detachment being confused with weakness or incompetence. In such circumstances, a president can be made to seem out of touch with government and with his responsibilities as chief executive. A president has to judge when appearing to be out of touch with Washington government puts him in touch with the broader constituency of public views and impulses. Defeats have to be chosen with care, in order to ride the wave of such self-inflicted populism. What is significant is that the incentives and opportunities for such leadership clearly exist and are regularly tapped by besieged presidents. They provide welcome means to maintain the chief source of presidential authority – namely the electoral process during which a president's original appeal was formed. Most contemporary presidents start as outsiders in a pack of party hopefuls. They win their party's nomination by a series of public appeals and, subsequently, secure the presidency in an extended campaign outside Washington and against Washington. Spatial leadership, therefore, becomes a way of retaining in government – albeit in diminished form – the drama of popular acclamation that accompanied the original elevation of inexperience and public contact to the presidential office.

Spatial leadership can be protective and purposive, especially for a radical right president such as Ronald Reagan. More often it is reactive and negative in nature. On either count, it is deeply problematic as a political device. The role of the outsider, for example, is a difficult one for a president to sustain without being denounced as a failure in the role of chief executive. The logic that impels a president to maintain his outsider credentials in order to assume insider leverage within Washington is the very same logic which will render an incumbent president liable to assault as an insider by challengers necessarily more on the outside than the office-holder. The transmutation of an outsider into an insider is an evolutionary process which every president is committed to resist but which they can never overcome. The ideas, symbols and prejudices mobilised by presidents to highlight the division between government and civil society further deepen the issue of responsiveness and prepare the ground for fresh outsider insurgents to undermine the presidency by repeating the process. Another cyclical dynamic is evident in the nature of outsider campaigns pitted against the political system. These raise public cynicism to a level where the projected solution of an alternative leadership creates greater impatience for results because of the anti-politics message of the original campaign. The problem is exacerbated by the emphasis that is given to refracting complex issues through appealing and marketable simplicities. Almost invariably this can only work within a limited timeframe and in relation to prospective action. Given time and the practical experience of government, the complexities reassert themselves and submerge the clarity and rhetoric of tangible solutions into the obscurity of remote possibilities and long-term objectives:

> Government has become a harder and harder thing to do . . . This puts politicians in a bind. They earn much of their living by exploiting anxieties, encouraging people to feel more than they should about the state of their country, and then promising panaceas for ailments they cannot cure. When they fail to cure them, they are blamed.[61]

Insiders who had originally run for office as conspicuous outsiders can exacerbate the resultant injection of cynicism by seeking to melt away from their promises and performance, and to assign responsibility for government inaction or insufficient action to structural rather than to individual factors. But the public has been encouraged by the established discourse of repeated election campaigns to think in terms of personal remedies in the form of new leadership – preferably from outside Washington and even from outside the ranks of professional politicians.

Spatial leadership is a strategy designed to prevent, or at least contain, these cyclical pressures of presidential displacement by outsider challenges feeding off the populist and rejectionist impulses of a volatile electorate aroused by images of a government acting against the public interest. In reality, the message is more complex than a simple reaction against government and carries a host of often contradictory themes related to preserving the benefits of the positive state while condemning its aggregate costs and excesses, its inertia and its outreach. The angst of contemporary citizen dissatisfaction is drawn from the apparent permanence and intractable nature of so many social and economic problems at a time when the simple polarities of liberal and conservative alternatives are no longer available. Very often the solution to these chronic afflictions is seen to be the act of mobilisation itself. In a period of dealigning party organisation and diminishing partisan attachment, effective citizen-based politics can suddenly break through the conventional framework of representative government's intermediary channels. The language of disaffection and the devices of mobilisation in a more open textured format of political exchange can lead to sudden surges of support for figures and ideas connected with the themes of anti-government and anti-politics. Their detractors may point out that such self-professed political leaders are neither leaders nor politicians. They may claim with some justification that they have no substantive rallying points and no solutions other than the expression of popular responses to a set of grievances. In many respects, it can be said that what they offer is in effect a vacuous protest against the perceived vacuousness of government. Nonetheless, the sheer presence of a large pool of voters who are independent or have weak partisan attachment, together with the precedents of outsider success (e.g. Ronald Reagan, Ross Perot) and the defeat of incumbent presidents (e.g. Jimmy Carter, George Bush), provide an ever present warning to the occupants of the White House.

Even if the defining purpose of populist mobilisation fades with the act of mobilisation itself, it carries the threat of a sudden disorientation in the configuration of public opinion and electoral strategy. Presidents can quickly be made to look isolated, remote and out of touch with the tidal forces of public concerns. Dissidence is less constrained by party loyalty, or cold war discipline, or presidential respect than it used to be. As a result, presidents have to market themselves as the equivalents of the public's own mixed reactions to government. They have to prevent themselves from being seen to be detached from the public by being publicly attached to the government *in toto*. Presidents, therefore, display the symbolic resources of their office to suggest a series of confections. These are designed to demonstrate the way in which professional competence can be fused to amateur insurgency; executive authority can be joined to popular sovereignty; tough anti-statism can be combined with targeted investment; ideological conservatism can co-exist with pragmatic liberalism; and the ceremonial distance of statesmanship can be joined to the visceral intimacy of the personalised presidency. By opening up, and effectively occupying, a sense of space between the individual and the material, polemical and mass aspects of Washington, a president can draw on, and engage in, the public's own ambivalence over the role of the federal government in American society. Spatial leadership in effect is a reflection of a wider condition of equivocation in the body politic. 'Divided government' is in many respects an expression of the cognitive dissonance and disjunctive values present in the American electorate. Similarly, a president's spatial leadership is a response in microcosm to the same concurrent and unresolved dualities that pivot upon the issue of political responsiveness and trust in a fractured and suspicious democracy.

Notes

1 Theodore H. White, *The Making of the President, 1968* (London, Jonathan Cape, 1969); Richard Nixon, *The Memoirs of Richard Nixon* (London, Sidgwick and Jackson, 1978), pp. 295–414.

2 Philip E. Converse, Warren E. Miller, Jerrold G. Rusk and Arthur C. Wolfe, 'Continuity and Change in American Politics: Parties and Issues in the 1968 Election', *American Political Science Review*, 63, no. 4 (December 1969), pp. 1083–1105.
3 Rowland Evans, Jr and Robert D. Novak, *Nixon in the White House: The Frustration of Power* (New York, Vintage, 1972), p. 4.
4 Quoted in Theodore H. White, *The Making of the President, 1972* (New York, Bantam, 1973), pp. 292–3.
5 E. Howard Hunt, *Undercover: Memoirs of an American Secret Agent* (London, W. H. Allen, 1975), p. 156.
6 See Theodore H. White, *Breach of Faith: The Fall of Richard Nixon* (London, Jonathan Cape, 1975); J. Anthony Lukas, *Nightmare: The Underside of the Nixon Years* (New York, Viking, 1976).
7 See Fred Emery, *Watergate: The Corruption and Fall of Richard Nixon* (London, Pimlico, 1994).
8 Clifton McCleskey and Pierce McCleskey, 'Jimmy Carter and the Democratic Party', in M. Glenn Abernathy, Dilys M. Hill and Phil Williams (eds), *The Carter Years: The President and Policy Making* (London, Frances Pinter, 1984), p. 128.
9 Jimmy Carter, *Why Not The Best?* (New York, Bantam, 1976), p. 168.
10 Evans and Novak, *Nixon in the White House*, p. 4.
11 Jimmy Carter, *Keeping Faith: Memoirs of a President* (London, Collins, 1982), p. 23.
12 Gaddis Smith, *Morality, Reason and Power: American Diplomacy in the Carter Years* (New York, Hill and Wang, 1986).
13 Quoted in an interview with Ronald Kriss and Christopher Ogden, *Time*, 11 October 1982.
14 David S. Broder, 'Paradox in Carter's future', *Washington Post Supplement* in *Guardian Weekly*, 1 December 1979.
15 George F. Will, *Statecraft as Soulcraft: What Government Does* (London, Weidenfeld and Nicolson, 1984), p. 16.
16 'Crisis of Confidence televised address, July 15, 1979', in *Congressional Quarterly Almanac*, 97th Congress, 1st Session 1981, Volume XXXV (Washington, DC, Congressional Quarterly Inc., 1980), p. 46E.
17 Garry Wills, *Reagan's America: Innocents Abroad* (London, Heinemann, 1988), p. 357.
18 Ronald Reagan, *Speaking My Mind: Selected Speeches* (London, Hutchinson, 1989), p. 98.
19 Ronald Reagan, *An American Life* (London, Hutchinson, 1990), p. 234.
20 Reagan, *An American Life*, p. 286.
21 Reagan, *An American Life*, p. 287.
22 Louis Fisher, 'Reagan's Relations with Congress', in Dilys M. Hill, Raymond A. Moore and Phil Williams (eds), *The Reagan Presidency: An Incomplete Revolution?* (Houndmills, Macmillan, 1990), p. 98.
23 John W. Sloan, 'Meeting the Leadership Challenges of the Modern Presidency: The Political Skills and Leadership of Ronald Reagan', *Presidential Studies Quarterly*, 26, no. 3 (Summer 1996), p. 797.
24 Robert G. Kaiser, 'Ronald Reagan's America: an intoxicating myth for our time', *Washington Post Supplement* in *Guardian Weekly*, 4 November 1984.
25 Garry Wills, 'What happened?', *Time*, 9 March 1987.
26 Jane Mayer and Doyle McManus, *Landslide: The Unmaking of the President, 1984–1988* (London, Fontana, 1989), p. 31.
27 Quoted in Seymour M. Lipset, 'Beyond 1984: The Anomalies of American Politics', *PS* (Spring 1986), p. 228. See also Everett C. Ladd, 'The Reagan Phenomenon and Public

Attitudes Toward Government', in Lester M. Salamon and Michael Lund (eds), *The Reagan Presidency and the Governing of America* (Washington, DC, Urban Institute Press, 1984), p. 255.

28 Reagan, *Speaking My Mind*, pp. 415–16.

29 Quoted in Joe Klein, 'Goofy Bush chases rainbow in downpour', *Sunday Times*, 19 January 1992.

30 See Donald F. Kettle and John J. Dilulio, Jr (eds), *Inside the Reinvention Machine: Appraising Governmental Reform* (Washington, DC, Brookings Institution, 1995).

31 See Elizabeth Drew, *Showdown: The Struggle Between the Gingrich Congress and the Clinton White House* (New York, Simon and Schuster, 1996); Dan Balz and Ronald Brownstein, *Storming the Gates: Protest Politics and the Republican Revival* (Boston, Little Brown, 1996).

32 See Dick Morris, *Behind the Oval Office: Winning the Presidency in the Nineties* (New York, Random House, 1997), p. 80.

33 Richard E. Neustadt, *Presidential Power: The Politics of Leadership* (New York, John Wiley, 1960), p. 185.

34 Thomas E. Cronin, *The State of the Presidency*, 2nd edn (Boston, Little Brown, 1975), p. 84.

35 Cronin, *The State of the Presidency*, p. 84.

36 Clinton Rossiter, quoted in Neustadt, *Presidential Power*, p. 152.

37 Bert A. Rockman, *The Leadership Question: The Presidency and the American System* (New York, Praeger, 1984), p. xvi.

38 Taken from 'President Reagan's Inaugural Address, January 20, 1981', in *Congressional Quarterly Almanac*, 97th Congress, 1st Session, 1981, Volume XXXVII (Washington, DC, Congressional Quarterly Inc. 1982), p. 1E.

39 The President's State of the Union Address, 23 January 1996, distributed by The White House <Publications-Admin@WhiteHouse.Gov>, 23 January 1996.

40 The President's State of the Union Address.

41 The President's State of the Union Address.

42 Theodore Lowi and Benjamin Ginsberg, *American Government: Freedom and Power*, 5th edn (New York, Norton, 1998), p. 264.

43 Rockman, *The Leadership Question*, p. 223.

44 Michael A. Genovese, *The Presidential Dilemma: Leadership in the American System* (New York, HarperCollins, 1995), p. 20. See also Thomas E. Cronin and Michael A. Genovese, *The Paradoxes of the American Presidency* (New York, Oxford University Press, 1998), ch. 1.

45 Richard Rose, *The Postmodern President: The White House Meets the World* (Chatham, Chatham House, 1988), p. 28.

46 See Jonathan Rauch, *Demosclerosis: The Silent Killer of American Government* (New York, Times Books, 1994); Gary Orren, 'Fall from Grace: The Public's Loss of Faith in Government', in Joseph S. Nye, Philip D. Zelikow and David C. King (eds), *Why People Don't Trust Government* (Cambridge, MA, Harvard University Press, 1997), pp. 79–83.

47 Kevin Phillips, 'Fat city', *Time*, 26 September 1994.

48 See Kevin Phillips, *Arrogant Capital: Washington, Wall Street and the Frustration of American Politics* (Boston, Little Brown, 1994); Susan J. Tolchin, *The Angry American: How Voter Rage is Changing the Nation* (Boulder, Westview, 1998); Joseph N. Cappella and Kathleen H. Jamieson, *Spiral of Cynicism* (New York, Oxford University Press, 1997).

49 Quoted in Ian Brodie, 'A Texas folk-hero aims to join race', *Daily Telegraph*, 23 March 1992.

50 Quoted in Martin Walker, 'The postmodernist saviour of America', *Guardian Weekly*, 7 June 1992.
51 Quoted in Walker, 'The postmodernist saviour of America'.
52 H. Ross Perot quoted in an interview with Henry Muller and Richard Woodbury, *Time*, 25 May 1992.
53 Gerald M. Pomper, 'The Presidential Election', in Gerald M. Pomper *et al.*, *The Election of 1992* (Chatham, Chatham House, 1993), p. 133.
54 Martin P. Wattenberg, *The Decline of American Political Parties, 1952–1994* (Cambridge, Harvard University Press, 1996), p. 183.
55 Gwen Brown, 'Deliberation and its Discontents: H. Ross Perot's Antipolitical Populism', in Andreas Schedler (ed.), *The End of Politics: Explorations into Modern Antipolitics* (Houndmills, Macmillan, 1997), p. 140.
56 Brown, 'Deliberation and its Discontents', p. 143.
57 Jack W. Germond and Jules Witcover, *Mad as Hell: Revolt at the Ballot Box, 1992* (New York, Warner, 1993).
58 Harold M. Barger, *The Impossible Presidency: Illusions and Realities of Executive Power* (Glenview, Scott Foresman, 1984); Godfrey Hodgson, *All Things To All Men: The False Promise of the Modern Presidency*, rev. edn (Harmondsworth, Penguin, 1984); Hugh Heclo, 'The Presidential Illusion', in Hugh Heclo and Lester M. Salamon (eds), *The Illusion of Presidential Government* (Boulder, Westview, 1981).
59 Paul Light, *The President's Agenda* (Baltimore, Johns Hopkins University Press, 1982).
60 Barger, *The Impossible Presidency*, p. 7.
61 'Voters, blame thyselves', *The Economist*, 29 October 1994.

CHAPTER 3

Moving in from the outside: the Thatcher precedent

At first sight, the perversities of spatial leadership are peculiarly American in nature. They seem perfectly consistent with a political culture that evidently possesses a state but has 'no acceptable tradition of one'.[1] As a consequence, it is possible to turn political scepticism into a political conviction and to use it to compete for high political office. In the United States, a politician can run against government itself, in order to become not merely part of the offending structure, but its most central and active part. Once there, he or she can exploit America's populist anxieties, dissenting traditions and libertarian temperament to maintain a position inside government by being seen to be conspicuously outside of it and unaccountable for it. To many, this bizarre dissociation is unique to the United States. It is seen to be a derivative of America's own constitutional development, its characteristically fragmented system of government, its idiosyncratic forms of political mobilisation and the unique ancestry of its republican attachment to limited government. Plenty of arguments can be marshalled along these lines but they begin to look less secure when Margaret Thatcher's premiership is taken into account. Indeed, many parallels can be drawn between the nature of her leadership and the motives, objectives and strategies of recent presidential leadership. And in the same way that presidential leadership can reveal deep-seated and long-term developments in the American polity, so the changes in the British premiership during the 1980s also signify the existence of political developments which would make spatial leadership, in one form or another, a permanent feature of the British political landscape.

The rank outsider

Three factors stand out as being instrumental in the development of Margaret Thatcher's reputation, not only as an outsider but as an outsider who could exploit her weaknesses and disadvantages, and translate them into formidable political strengths.

First, were the circumstances surrounding her elevation to the party leadership in 1975. After two general election defeats in 1974 and a series of earlier policy reversals in government, there was a groundswell of opinion in the Conservative parliamentary party in favour of a leadership election. At the very least, it was thought that an election would help to re-establish Edward Heath's authority. Although Heath's aloof and even arrogant style of leadership had embittered a large proportion of the party, it was assumed that he would prevail in any first election. It was thought that no one outside the cabinet had the requisite weight to displace him and that no one inside the cabinet would dare be so disloyal as to challenge him. Speculation surrounded Sir Keith Joseph, the maverick right-winger who had been Heath's minister for social services. But after being rash enough to make a number of inflammatory speeches about social and economic policy, Joseph refused to let his name go forward. Edward du Cann, chairman of the 1922 Committee, was another who had flirted with the idea of challenging Heath, but who subsequently refused to declare himself a candidate.

These wilting violets forced the dissidents to look elsewhere. Eventually, they came up with Margaret Thatcher, a middle-ranking member of the shadow cabinet. According to James Prior,

> I don't think anyone at that time really thought that Margaret was a serious contender. After all it was quite clear that Airey Neave and a number of others were determined to get rid of Ted, and they were going to try to find almost anyone to take on, and that's why they first of all went to Keith Joseph, and when he dropped out for some reason or other, then they actually approached Edward du Cann and he dropped out for some reason or other, so they were getting pretty desperate by then. There was literally no one else within the Cabinet or anywhere near the Cabinet who was prepared to stand against Ted Heath, unless Ted Heath said he was going to go.[2]

Prior did not believe that even Thatcher 'thought of herself as a candidate for the leadership'.[3] The dissidents, however, needed her to test the waters and measure the vulnerability of Heath. They knew that if Heath could be sufficiently embarrassed in the first ballot to stand down as a candidate, then the rules allowed other candidates to enter for a second ballot. A heavyweight like Willie Whitelaw would no longer feel confined by his loyalty to Heath. Once the initial breach was made, he could step in and cruise to the leadership that many believed was his rightful inheritance.

Margaret Thatcher's position was a very exposed one. 'I know', she said, 'that if I lose, my political career is over.'[4] For her, it was the gambler's throw of an outsider who was no part of the inner club of senior Conservatives and Tory grandees. 'Questions were raised about the desirability of the party being led by a Grantham grocer's daughter with a second-class degree in

Chemistry, only able to be in politics because she had a rich husband, and totally ignorant of foreign affairs.'[5] To Airey Neave, her own campaign manager, Thatcher was a stalking horse capable only of inflicting damage on Heath. In some respects, she was even limited as a stalking horse. She was a woman in a male-dominated profession and seeking to lead a notoriously hierarchical party. As Secretary of State for Education, she had also been associated with small but politically damaging issues such as her widely condemned ending of free milk to primary school children between the ages of eight and eleven. On the credit side, 'Neave had two things going for him. First, probably more than two-thirds of the parliamentary party wanted Edward Heath out. Second, his candidate was a conceivable, if not yet credible leader.'[6]

The antipathy towards Heath was evident in the shock result of the first ballot. Thatcher defeated Heath by 130 votes to 119. Heath promptly withdrew. Others rushed in to fill his place (Willie Whitelaw, Geoffrey Howe, James Prior, John Peyton) but the momentum behind Thatcher was too great. She won the second ballot easily. The party had rallied to its new leader. To most Conservatives, it was enough that 'she offered something different'[7] – different, that is, from Heath. 'Her supporters could hardly believe it and her critics within the Party reacted by speaking of her as a stop-gap or a temporary aberration which in due course would be corrected. That the Party had chosen such a dissident and outsider was phenomenon enough. But this outsider was a woman.'[8] Margaret Thatcher had become leader of a party that hardly knew her. She had toppled an incumbent party leader and former prime minister, but she was still an outsider. That was seen by many of her supporters and detractors as a handicap. It was seen by Margaret Thatcher as an opportunity to be exploited.

A personal manifesto

The second factor in the development of Margaret Thatcher's version of spatial leadership centred upon the content of her personal manifesto for the party. She not only stood outside the mainstream conventions on public policy to which Conservatives had adhered since World War II, but wished to use her position to challenge the premises and principles of that orthodoxy. The 'post-war settlement' represented an intuitive agreement between the two main parties on the basic ground rules for managing the political economy. It was rooted in the Conservative party's recognition of the welfare state and in its acceptance of the central objective of full employment, together with the need for Keynesian techniques of macro-economic management to finance these twin pillars of social stability. The Conservatives had no wish to risk the social upheaval of attempting to dismantle all the innovations of the 1945–51 Labour government. In their desire to bury the party's association with the mass unemployment of the 1930s, the Conservatives accommodated themselves to the principle of a permanent managerial state. As a result, Conservative governments in the 1950s and early 1960s were politically attuned to the need to co-operate with the trade unions; to intervene in the economy through planning, subsidies and incentives; to maintain a high level of public expenditure on social welfare programmes; and to exploit deficit financing in order to maintain demand in the economy, even if this was at the price of mild inflation.

By 1970, this pattern of consensus politics had become ossified into a controlling orthodoxy. Its effects on the size, the role and the responsibilities of the state were the cause of increasing concern to a large section of the Conservative party. It was troubled by what appeared to be the self-propelling dynamics of state intervention in which government action and provision led ineluctably to more and more of the same. The state had already become the largest single employer, spender and consumer in the economy – and the pace of its advance showed no signs of deceleration. Intervention was increasingly seen to be not merely a requisite response to an economy declining in productivity and competition, but also a direct material cause of the economy's poor performance. As the private sector diminished in relative size and wealth, the standard circular response was to increase state intervention even more, in order to correct for the lack of economic growth.

The incoming Heath government of 1970 was pledged to radical change that would break this circle of rising public expenditure and diminishing economic performance. Heath intended to reduce government spending, to curb trade union power and to restore competition. He wanted to dispense with prices and incomes policy. His intention of injecting the economy with the incentives and disciplines of the free market meant that the government would no longer bail out 'lame duck' companies. But within two years, the Heath government had had to engage in a series of humiliating U-turns. The *force majeure* of established political forces and expectations was too great even for the government to resist.

As the Labour government (1974–79) also proceeded to sink into double-digit inflation, industrial strife and rising demands on public expenditure, the defeated Conservative party began a critical review, not just of the Heath government but of the entire nature of the post-war settlement. Margaret Thatcher was part of a group of Conservatives who wanted the most thorough and comprehensive reconsideration of the assumptions that lay behind this political orthodoxy. She joined the charge against the excessive state and the high tax economy that ignored not just the productive, but also the moral elements of human motivations in working for personal advancement and self-esteem. She drew attention to the 'noble ideals of personal responsibility' and to the fact that 'in some respects the concepts of social responsibility had turned sour'.[9] At the risk of increasing inequality and even unemployment, Margaret Thatcher believed it was necessary to release human and social energies by relating rewards to effort, risk and wealth creation. Her economic vision, therefore, included

> the promotion of thrift, the defence of 'sound' rather than 'suitcase' money, the matching of effort to appetite, the provision of positive incentives rather than of negative cushioning, the privatization of state-owned industries, the encouragement of calculated risk-taking within the context of a market freely responsive to patterns of individual choice, and an increase in the number of those with a propertied stake in social order.[10]

These principles, unequivocally stated and proposed in deadly earnest irrespective of the consequences, were sweeping and highly controversial in nature. To many, they were positively inflammatory and quite contrary to the governing ethos of the post-war settlement. It was thought that Thatcher, and people like her, were intent upon marshalling popular support against the progressive achievements and civilising traditions of that settlement. They acquired the reputation of being 'less concerned simply to shift the balance between capital and labour within the crumbling framework of the "post-war settlement" than to abandon the whole project in favour of a new edifice more favourable to capital'.[11]

Such an indictment would not have perturbed an individual like Mrs Thatcher. This is because she not only had an outsider's flair for the unconventional, but possessed that element of moral certainty and inner righteousness that thrives in such a self-conscious outsider. To Margaret Thatcher, being an outsider was synonymous with being right, and to sustain that certainty it was necessary to remain an outsider. One of Mrs Thatcher's central convictions was that the rest of her convictions were dependent upon a zeal and passionate intransigence that were warranted in her eyes by the moral integrity of her outlook. Bearing in mind the compromises, reversals and defeats of the Heath government, the idea of a true faith and an unshakeable attachment to it, together with an absolute commitment to defend it, was part and parcel of her programme. It was integral to her *raison d'être* as a politician and to her style of leadership. In this respect, Margaret Thatcher was doubly exceptional. She was outside the conventional mainstream of the party in terms of her policy positions. But she was also outside the party's traditions of pragmatism and aversion to philosophical speculation. She openly adhered to a set of iconoclastic economic principles and, to make matters worse, she did so with an intransigence that seemed to be as challenging to the Conservative party as it was to the Labour party.

A populist insurgent

The two elements of Margaret Thatcher's leadership mentioned so far – her outsider status and her unconventional proposals – were both instrumental in generating a third component. This was Mrs Thatcher's populist appeal to those who had come to feel marginalised by the convulsive events of the 1970s. To those who could only look upon the period with a mixture of anxiety, resentment and incomprehension, Mrs Thatcher offered the prospect of a tangible expression of private grievance and inner outrage. Whether it was an old-age pensioner whose savings had been eaten up by inflation, or families reduced to candlelight by industrial action, or skilled workers humbled by unskilled workers, Mrs Thatcher's sentiments and style evoked a widespread murmuring of acknowledgement. Her outsider status, her pugnacious temperament and her tough message of old economic disciplines, individual responsibility and social obligations aroused interest in her as an individual emblem of social unrest. Margaret Thatcher for her part saw the political advantages to be accrued from reciprocating the interest. In the highly volatile political conditions of the 1970s and early 1980s, when political allegiances were weakening and third parties could prompt sudden changes in electoral behaviour, Mrs Thatcher sought to establish her own direct links to the electorate. Like Richard Nixon, she wanted to identify with society's 'silent majority'.

Many of Margaret Thatcher's parliamentary colleagues in the Conservative party were very wary about her avowed rejection of the 'post-war settlement'. They approved of her performance as a blistering and unremitting critic of the Labour government. They condoned her crusade against socialism as a national disease, even though the tone of her attacks was strident and the possible repercussions of her ideas on social stability were serious. But many senior Conservatives proceeded on the assumption that she would inevitably have to accommodate the starker qualities of her vision to the prevailing forces and traditions of British politics. It was believed that she was enough of a politician to realise that persuasion, conciliation and concession were necessary to make any headway with a radical reform programme. Even one of her staunchest critics, Francis Pym, saw that 'although a populist by nature, she recognised the need to change the climate of intellectual opinion in the country'.[12] But this could only be done gradually and pragmatically.

Margaret Thatcher was certainly a politician and a far more adept one than her outspoken mentor, Sir Keith Joseph. But her political sense led her to appreciate the advantages of cultivating a public constituency. Negotiations could be reached discreetly. What was important was that they should not be seen to characterise her administration or to compromise the integrity of her public connections. Appearance was of central importance. The public image of a public leader, directly implicated in popular issues, could generate its own material benefits of enhanced influence and leverage inside the party and the government. For Margaret Thatcher, it was better to be up-front and calculatedly headstrong rather than to be collegiate, measured and impotent. Like Ronald Reagan's, the strategy was one of defiance and theatrical bluff. Thatcher would seek the centre stage and ignore protocol and convention in pursuit of her radical ambitions. By conveying a picture of political determination and conspicuous personal resolve, the bluff could pay off with compromises overlooked, the programme advanced and her leadership secured.

There are many facets to, and interpretations of, Margaret Thatcher's populism. To some, it was confined to her new style or methods of political communication. This could include her positive ability to translate the intellectual critiques of the New Right into the easy accessibility of simple moral axioms, gut reactions and housewifely economies. It could also include her negative 'streetfighter' or 'fishwife' performances in the House of Commons or the hustings. The combination could generate mixed feelings from even her admirers. Her biographer, Kenneth Harris, for example, recalls that she could engage with political opponents at

> the level of everyday argument, deliver personal attacks in the language of the market place and more than hold her own if a shouting match began. Her voice was refined, her appearance was elegant, her manner cool and calm, but the commonsense and basic values she expressed came from the grocer's daughter. Among the other qualities she now displayed was that of being the nearest thing to a demagogue the leaders of the Conservative Party had ever produced. She bid fair to become the first Conservative populist.[13]

Others give emphasis to the policy components of Thatcher's populism. They point to her continual public support of such right-wing back-bench issues as capital punishment and immigration control, even after her election as party leader and her subsequent rise to the premiership. Julian Critchley observed at the time that 'her popularity increases the further down the party structure one goes'.[14] In many respects, this was because she remained one of the rank and file. Edward Pearce described her affinity with the party workers in terms of physical and emotional compulsion: 'Mrs Thatcher – a lady in a petal hat made queen – genuinely loved her party, breathed in and out with it, and shared its hates and loves, especially its instincts for class war, for which members of a higher social class felt fastidious distaste. It was not nice to watch but it was authentic.' [15]

In another sense, her populism could be seen as discreet rather than explicit – a conclusion drawn from her economic programme. John Vincent, for example, believed that her market economics appealed to the skilled working class, whose position in the industrial hierarchy had been eroded during the 1970s: 'Thatcherism resembles trade unionism in that both are about differentials. The need which Mrs Thatcher intuited in 1975–80 was to give a moral meaning to latent anti-egalitarian feeling among those who had seen their differentials eroded.' [16] In yet another dimension, Thatcher's populism was interpreted as indicative of a major sociological change. Opinions vary on the nature of the change. One view sees Thatcherism as representing a conscious mobilisation of the British people against the social democratic state, in which political differences and identities were submerged into a more consensual and neutral polity. Another perspective sees Thatcher's populism as an 'authoritarian populism', which was essentially manipulative in its intentions and divisive in its nature:

> It is not concerned with an active populist mobilization – which would be threatening to the decisional autonomy of Thatcherism. Instead it is concerned to outflank organized opposition from government backbenches (especially the so-called wets) as well as from the labour movement. For, if Thatcher represents the people directly, opposition can be presented as undemocratic.[17]

Whatever the relative merits of these various perspectives of Thatcher's populism, they all serve to substantiate the close relationship between the style of her leadership and the nature of her personal background and rise to prominence. Her position outside the mainstream of the party and outside the governing orthodoxies of post-war government lent weight to the radical credentials of her economic programme. Her conspicuous independence and her iconoclastic aims reflected and illuminated each other to the extent that they appeared, ultimately, to be analogous in nature. The dogmatic and populist style of her leadership was also closely interconnected with her policy objectives and outsider status. As an outsider, Margaret Thatcher was especially adept at risking the unconventional and circumventing the traditional intermediary structures that lay between government and the public. As an outsider and a populist politician, she was able to use intransigence not just as a means to acquire her policy aims, but as a functional objective in its own right. Through the spectacle of her intransigence, she sought to direct the force of public protest, to appeal to popular temperament and to rally a change in social attitudes.

Obduracy served Mrs Thatcher's interests because it inferred the existence of a cause that was simply too profound and indispensable to warrant even the consideration of compromise. The revolution and revival, of course, were as much to do with radicalising public impulses as they were with government deregulation and reduced public expenditure. And to complete the circle, it was the visceral nature of the issues raised by Thatcher's leadership which helped in turn to serve that leadership – firstly by highlighting the importance of a leader's public prominence to radical change and, secondly, by legitimising the outsider qualities appropriate to providing such novel direction.

Thatcher in space

Margaret Thatcher's outsider origins, her radical programme and her populism were the key ingredients in her development of spatial leadership in British policies. Her premiership exhibited the full potential that existed for this type of leadership in a system which appeared to be quite unamenable to such a form of high level dissociation. Although the story of Margaret Thatcher's period in office is a familiar one, it frequently overlooks the significance of her ability to occupy the centre of power while simultaneously distancing herself from it.

The conventional account of Margaret Thatcher's rise to power plots her progress from the periphery to the centre; from a flamboyant outsider to an apparently immovable insider. And yet, in spite of the increased security of her position, Margaret Thatcher's outlook and leadership style did not change. It was neither to her taste nor to her advantage to be regarded as an established figure in the established streets of Whitehall and Westminster. To a populist politician who had benefited from and encouraged populist politics in Britain, Margaret Thatcher was keen to play down her position and to preserve that distance from government by which she could exert pressure upon it. Thatcher's *raison d'être* as a leader continued to be based upon the notion that government itself was the overriding issue in contemporary politics. This outlook was rooted in her self-image as an outsider standing apart from prevailing political ideas and practices. But it was also a direct consequence of her political instincts. Far from feeling dominant, Thatcher was more aware of the severity of the political constraints surrounding her, and the need to resort to negotiations and accommodation with other centres of political power. Even in her own cabinet, she was regularly in a minority position and frequently defeated. The feeling that she was nowhere near to being dominant could lead to an over-reaction. In Peter Jenkins's words: 'Her outsider mentality led her to regard government as a personal conspiracy against her. Her technique was to conspire against it. This she did by bringing in outsiders, by dealing directly with officials who took her fancy, by operating a network of trusties strategically placed in the departments.'[18]

More important, though, than not feeling dominant was the need not to convey the impression of dominance. In other words, Thatcher's political instincts drove her to try and retain her initial outsider status in government, even during the very period when the force and centrality of her power were at their most formidable. To a remarkable extent, and for an extraordinary length of time, Margaret Thatcher was effective in preserving that original sense of space between herself and the government which characterised her rise to office. 'Government' could then remain the issue, with Thatcher located some distance away from its most negative associations of high taxation, wasteful spending and mass regulation. Accordingly, Thatcher could revel in her cabinet defeats, maintain her reputation as a non-appeaser and engage in highly publicised interventions into government departments, even to the extent of claiming individual policy areas (e.g. the national curriculum, local government finance, football supporters' identity cards) as her own. 'I am the cabinet rebel',[19] she once remarked with pride. It was important to her personally to be a rebel. But it was even more important for her political position and leadership style to be *seen* as a rebel.

Behaving as an outsider was a natural precondition to being seen and understood as an outsider. And being an outsider gave her the licence to engage in that form of leadership which suited her best. Her favoured role was that of beleaguered enlightenment facing dark forces of restrictive practices, moribund immunities and impregnable privileges. This was a conflict where righteousness was always viewed to be inversely proportional to size. Such leadership made her curiously dependent upon the existence of forces that were both plausible and threatening. She battled against inflation, taxation, government expenditure and public ownership in her crusade to rid the country of the scourge of socialism. She 'stood up' to Arthur Scargill and the National Union of Mineworkers, to General Galtieri and the Argentinean military in the South Atlantic, and to Jacques Delors and his sovereignty-sapping proposals for European union and social reform. Most of all, she tested her mettle, and that of her mission, against the public sector forces of the British establishment. By choice and temperament, hers was 'punctuated by set battles, sometimes broken off, but always resumed, against all those forces which, in her view, had brought, or were bringing

Britain low'.[20] Battling drew attention to her leadership, but it also highlighted what it was she could not control and why she needed such a belligerent approach.

Despite her reputed dominance of government, therefore, Thatcher was still dependent upon its reputed autonomy and inertia for her primary *raison d'être*. Her spiritual detachment from government allowed her to engage in a publicly fought holy war against government and to maintain the paradoxical position of increasing state powers, in order to decentralise government control. This form of detachment was not the same sort that had crippled Heath's premiership. His detachment denoted arrogance, isolation and weakness. Margaret Thatcher's detachment was consciously planned and founded securely on close ties with Conservative back-benchers and popular opinion. Margaret Thatcher, like Ronald Reagan, was often described as having the ability to give expression to the anxieties and prejudices of the lower middle class and, in particular, to the upper working class. Thatcher's tough confrontational approach to issues was often deplored by professional people and by traditional Tory gentlemen, but it found approval among many in the C2 (skilled workers) stratum of society. To Peregrine Worsthorne, Thatcher's style 'conformed with much of their own experience; rang true to the realities of their own lives. On this point there is really no doubt about what C2s believe. They believe that it is a rough old world in which only the strong and bloody-minded have a chance of surviving.'[21] Worsthorne went on to add that 'the political class had no faith in Britain: disapproved of the bourgeoisie and sniffed at the working class. Mrs Thatcher attached legendary qualities to both.'[22]

Thatcher's was a high risk strategy, but it did possess the public glamour of high risk. It kept her both centre stage and peculiarly off-stage for eleven years. It produced charges of her being an imperious prime minister at the same time that it revealed her weaknesses, exposed her cabinet defeats and aroused concern over government disunity. The mixture of an apparently raw appetite for personal power and a public facility for melting away from the appearance of its possession baffled fellow politicians and political observers alike:

> This insistence on being the active leader of the government – on leading it, as it were, from outside rather than inside – manifests itself in another, rather curious way: in the prime minister's penchant for talking about the government as though she were not a member of it. The customary pronoun used by prime ministers when speaking about their own government is we; Thatcher's pronoun is usually 'we', but often 'they'. 'They' are making life difficult for her; 'they' are having to be persuaded; 'they' are too concerned with defending the interests

of their own departments. The language is not typically British. It is more like that used by American presidents when speaking about Congress. It is significant that the prime minister thinks in this way of her own cabinet as being, in effect, another branch of government. And, just as American presidents have to put up with hostility from Congress, so Thatcher has to put up with her not always amenable cabinet colleagues. (Anthony King)[23]

I'm sure that loyalty matters enormously to her. I think 'Is he one of us?' is one of the most remarkable phrases that has ever come out of a prime minister in Britain. In a sense it's almost as though she thought of herself as being one of a small band of pioneers and conspirators that found themselves in a kind of minority, an exposed position in Whitehall and Westminster, and that they had to stick together as a club in order to get the great machinery of state to be responsive to their new and radical approach. (Peter Shore)[24]

Her persona is, in part, that of the ordinary person: the tradesman's daughter, the person who talks of 'little' issues, housekeeping for example, expresses 'little' emotions, perpetually giving voice to the desires and anxieties of 'ordinary people', often to the point where she conveys the notion that she, like them, is not interested in politics, but is simply the woman we see bustling about with her handbag on her arm. (John Gaffney)[25]

What I think is her peculiar quality is that she manages at once to be a powerful leader of her government and to detach herself from her government – to be in a sense leader of the government and leader of the opposition at one and the same time. I was very struck, watching her dedicating the memorial in St James's Square to that poor policewoman who was shot in that terrible terrorist incident when she said, 'These incidents must stop.' Now this was very interesting. It was detaching herself from the government, because if anybody can stop it ... it's the government who can, not the county council or the opposition or whatever. It's the government who can do it, and yet she was saying, 'It's intolerable that this goes on. It ought to be stopped. It ought to be stopped by, not my government then, but the government. Why doesn't the government stop it?' She does have this curious capacity, which is clever. (Roy Jenkins)[26]

The oddity of Mrs Thatcher's position, is that she both is and is not the Government. Her personal brand of populism enables her to detach herself from government actions whenever it suits her to do so. Usually it is the Government's inactions from which she distances herself, so that when ministries actually do anything she can take the credit. In 1984 she said that she hoped that she had 'shattered the illusion that government could somehow substitute for individual performance'. Populism is thus identified with being anti-

> government. This means that it is ideally suited to radical Conservatives when they are in opposition. But what are they to do when they are the Government? The answer, for Mrs Thatcher, is all too easy: she can disown the lot of them whenever it suits her. (Noel Malcolm)[27]

> Cabinet discussions were kept to a minimum, whilst she reserved the right to make public her disagreements with her own ministers ... [She] was notorious for keeping up a private running commentary on the failings of her ministers and their policies, as if the Government was in some way nothing to do with her. Stevas has described how she once stood on a chair during a party in Downing Street and announced herself to be 'the rebel head of an establishment government'. (Robert Harris)[28]

Coinciding with Margaret Thatcher's remarkable distance from the government that she purportedly dominated was the emergence of an American-style distinction between leadership and policy. The differentiation in question is that between the public's assessment of a leader, based on the possession of various personal traits thought to be essential to leadership, and the public's disapproval of many of the policy objectives associated with that leadership. Survey evidence suggests that Mrs Thatcher's 'New Right' strictures on moral standards, censorship, tax cuts, free enterprise, market discipline, individual responsibility, privatisation and government dependency were not shared by a majority of respondents – even at the height of Mrs Thatcher's popularity. Attitudes on issues such as health, housing, education and unemployment demonstrated that 'the public remained wedded to the collective, welfare ethic of social democracy'.[29] And yet, in spite of 'the failure of Thatcher's cultural crusade',[30] she was 'widely if grudgingly respected as a leader'.[31] She translated government and its role in British society into a full-blown political issue. In doing so, she was able to compensate for her poor showing on social and economic issues by attracting widespread affirmation of her 'fitness to govern', exemplified more than anything else by Mrs Thatcher's own leadership. In the opinion of Ivor Crewe it was Thatcherism's statecraft which was 'at least as distinctive as its economic and cultural prejudices' and which represented the 'neglected element of its electoral success'.[32]

Like President Reagan, Margaret Thatcher was a highly prominent and successful leader whose policy programme was firmly rejected by the public. Nevertheless, they both won re-election by large margins. Mrs Thatcher did so on two occasions, in 1983 and 1987. President Reagan regularly enjoyed a high public approval rating in *spite* of his political proposals. It is often pointed out that Mrs Thatcher was different in so far as she never achieved the public approval levels of either Reagan or any other post-war prime minister, apart, that is, from Edward Heath, whose government collapsed in 1974. Her average approval between 1979 and 1987 was only 39 per cent compared, for example, with Harold Macmillan (1957–63) with 51 per cent, Harold Wilson (1964–70, 1974–76) with 59 per cent and 41 per cent, and James Callaghan (1976–79) with 46 per cent.[33] However, what has to be borne in mind is that such leaders embodied the programmatic and collegiate basis of their respective parties and drew support to themselves accordingly. Margaret Thatcher, by contrast, received an approval rating on the basis of her performance as Margaret Thatcher. Given the high level of public dissatisfaction with Thatcher's policies (average of 67 per cent), reflecting the broadscale contempt in which her objectives were held, the figure of 39 per cent for the public's satisfaction with Thatcher herself was a substantial one.[34] It denoted the capacity of a leader to transcend her own widely declared aims and to appeal to the electorate on grounds that were not solely confined to, or reducible to, social and economic policy.

In a parliamentary system whose chief characteristic is the fusion of the legislature and the executive through party discipline and collective responsibility, Margaret Thatcher's leadership was remarkable for the way that it allowed her to escape from her government's own record and to be judged on alternative criteria. It was itself a mark of her leadership that government management and style became as important as what a government did or intended to do. Reminiscent of the traditions and impulses of America's separation of powers system, 'leadership' under Thatcher had become a political issue in its own right. In effect, leadership had been translated into an objective function of government and, thereby, into a distinct object of political evaluation.

Thatcher's understudies: (1) David Steel, David Owen, Paddy Ashdown

It is commonly asserted that Margaret Thatcher acquired an extraordinary pre-eminence over her cabinet and, to all intents and purposes, 'presided' over government. Just as common is the proposition that her leadership was wholly exceptional and peculiar to herself and to the particular circumstances that gave rise to her premiership. In one sense this is irrefutably self-evident and something of a truism. No prime minister is exactly the same as another prime minister. Nevertheless, in a different and more important sense such a proposition is needlessly self-limiting. In seeking to account for Thatcher's leadership by recourse to exceptionalism, it not only fails to offer any real explanation, but jeopardises the potentially deeper insights and generalisations that can be drawn from Thatcher's premiership. As has already been made clear, this study is predicated on the conviction that Thatcher's period in office is just as significant for what it discloses about underlying political pressures and developments as it is for what it reveals about a singular woman.

Margaret Thatcher may have been an exceptional prime minister but in many respects the forces to which she was responding and the techniques she employed in her leadership were not confined to her alone. On the contrary, they were and have been apparent in other guises, in other parties, in other leaders. The public cultivation of public space between a leader and the party, and its usage to make leaders look more like leaders so that they can participate more effectively in the contemporary forum of leadership, has become a conspicuous feature of party competition. The success of third parties over recent years, for example, has been due in no small part to their capacity for producing leaders with a built-in licence to compete politically at some distance from their party structures. Leaders from minor parties have been able to acquire a degree of public exposure for their political views and personal attributes that has been quite out of proportion to the scale of their organisational base. In many ways, such leaders have been able to compensate for the weaknesses of their own parties by developing the appearance of comparability with the major parties at the leadership level. This has entailed a widening of the gap between such leaders and their parties. It is a gap that parties have had to condone, and even to encourage, in order to compete at the high table and to maximise their political influence.

The modern conditions of political competition have progressively stretched the space between a leader and the party from an initial licence to engage other leaders on an equal footing to an altogether more marked and public detachment. Once leaders begin to compete with one another in public arenas they quickly find that they need more and more discretion to cultivate their standing outside the party and to attend to political strategies that have become increasingly leadership oriented in nature. Leaders in this position will insist upon the widening of space between themselves and the party's decision-making structures, in fact as well as in appearance. They will insist that such space is essential to pursuing the party's interests. The process continues, with leaders finding that in order to compete effectively they have to spend more and more time away from the party, thereby strengthening the appearance of space and enhancing the impression of effective leadership. Leadership in these conditions is characterised by a leader who has been leader enough to detach him- or herself from the party, whose nominal unity in allowing such distance rests upon the benefits expected or imagined by way of such high ranking political licence.

The Liberal party has traditionally been the home of protest politics and selected anti-statism. Its ancient heartlands in the West Country and on the Celtic periphery have always given it an iconoclastic and radical edge. In many ways, it has been the archetypal outsider organisation and doomed to remain outside government.[35] This has often made it an undisciplined, and arguably an unmanageable, party. But starting with Jeremy Thorpe and continuing with David Steel and Paddy Ashdown, the party has risen to become a genuine third force in British politics.[36] Steel steered the party away from its traditional preoccupations with community politics and protest voting with the aim of competing for national power at Westminster. To do this, Steel had increasingly to detach himself from the party's internal disputes, its multiple policy positions and its libertarian outlooks. He had to portray himself as a leader separate from the incipient disorganisation of his party and with the freedom to manoeuvre for leverage in the context of leadership politics.

The Social Democratic party displayed a similar process of accelerated development in leadership politics. Its original conception of a collective leadership in which the various skills and power sources of Roy Jenkins, Shirley Williams, David Owen and William Rodgers were pooled together, quickly gave way to the norm of a single leader (i.e. Roy Jenkins). The nature of party competition at the national level had made a single identifiable leader, who could personify and publicise the party, into an indispensable requirement. After the 1983 general election, a considerable body of opinion in the new party felt that it was important not just to have a single spokesman or -woman, but a dynamic individual leader. This being so, Roy Jenkins, the founding father of the party, felt obliged to resign and make way for David Owen.

With David Owen's reputation for urbane self-possession and forthright political judgement, the party was made to appear distant and even superfluous to its own chances of success. To all intents and purposes, sheer leadership had displaced party in image and policy substance. The party had knowingly selected as leader a domineering individual, who was described by a fellow founder of the SDP, William Rodgers, as 'not a man who works with a team ... or who likes listening to his equals in politics'.[37] When David Steel's Liberal party and David Owen's Social Democratic party came together to form the Alliance to fight the 1987 general election, the combination exposed the perils of spatial leadership. The two parties wished to maximise their electoral advantages by joining forces but, in doing so, they inadvertently jeopardised their most valuable assets. The sense of space around each leader was hopelessly compromised. As the 'two Davids' attempted to conduct a joint election campaign, each unavoidably undermined the position of the other.

The Alliance campaign rotted from the head down because the 'two Davids' approach to leadership was wholly incompatible with the basic requirements of political competition at the leadership level. Loner leaders on licence to cultivate spatial leadership were much more likely to be distrusted when placed together in a partnership of 'co-leadership'. They exposed, and even exaggerated, the lack of unity beneath. David Steel found it all so intolerable that he launched his plan for a full merger of the two parties only days after their failure to gain a breakthrough in the 1987 general election. David Owen sensed a takeover by the Liberals and refused to jeopardise his position by even contemplating union. As a result, he was left in the end with a small rump of zealous Social Democrats who refused to join the new Social and Liberal Democrat party. It was a mark of Owen's extraordinary leadership skills that he was able to command a high profile leadership position even with a visibly decaying party base.

Steel's successor, Paddy Ashdown, continued the campaign to maintain the third party's positional advantages in the recognition and deployment of political leaders on the national stage. He drew openly upon the outsider ethos of the party's culture and extended it to an open hostility to the rituals of Westminster and conventional party politics. He made a point of travelling extensively around Britain, in order to break out of the metropolitan myopia of London and to receive an education in the diversity of life experiences and cultural traditions in the UK. He took his message of a new pluralist and participatory politics directly to the communities of Britain. His constant indictment of the two-party system and his championing of constitutional reform and enhanced citizenship were the animating themes of what was a permanent campaign. It struck a chord with that dimension of public opinion that was fatigued with the tribalism and theatricality of the mainstream parties' duopoly. Ashdown's flamboyance was able to attract public attention far in excess of that warranted by the level of support for his party. He consistently outranked one or more of his rivals for the premiership in opinion polls on who would make the best prime minister. The culmination of his leadership was to come in 1997 when the Lib Dems won forty-six seats and a place in cabinet government. It was seen very much as his personal achievement. It was a testament to a political design that placed spatial leadership not merely as a strategy but as an objective in its own right.

Thatcher's understudies: (2) Neil Kinnock

The Labour party has long been considered immune from the sort of free-wheeling improvisation that has traditionally marked the Conservative party and led to the idiosyncratic individualism of its leaders. Labour leaders, by contrast, are seen to be set firmly in a matrix of party organisation built layer by layer according to formal rules and procedures designed to produce a democratically constituted hierarchy. Tensions between the leadership and the rank and file have always existed in the Labour movement. While the leadership customarily presses the case for discretion and patronage, the party adheres to its organisational principles of sustained participation and accountability. The leadership's need for the support of party solidarity is met by the party's traditions of democratic dispute and open debate. Labour leaders are almost invariably placed in a predicament where they have to reconcile the requirements to compete with the Conservative party's traditions of strong leadership and loyal followership, and the need to accommodate Labour's roots as a participatory organisation originally developed outside parliament. Throughout the history of the Labour party, these tensions have only ever been temporarily suspended. In the late 1970s and early 1980s, they once again rose to the surface. They were to produce a paradoxical outcome of an increase in democratic participation combined with an enriched potential for leadership authority.

Following the defeat of the Callaghan government in 1979, the party embarked upon a bitter internal power struggle in which all these tensions surfaced amid recriminations and allegations of betrayal. As part of a general reform thrust designed to democratise the party and limit the power of the leadership, the right to choose the party leader was stripped from the Parliamentary Labour Party (PLP) and lodged instead in a new electoral college specifically constituted to select the leader. The trade unions possessed 40 per cent of the electoral college votes, the Constituency Labour Parties (CLPs) had 30 per cent and the once dominant PLP was left with 30 per cent. The first beneficiary of the new system was Neil Kinnock, but he had to wait until 1983 for the opportunity to exploit the possibilities of rapid promotion that the electoral college offered to leadership aspirants. Prior to the passage of the reforms in 1981, Michael Foot had replaced James Callaghan in 1980. He had won the party leadership under the old PLP system and in many ways embodied the traditional framework of parliamentary hierarchy. He had been an eminent backbencher and had had direct experience of government as a minister. But within a year, Foot's influence in the fracturing party was minimal. According to Gallup, his standing as leader of the opposition was the lowest on record. Foot appeared old, weak, indecisive and out of touch. His personal eccentricities were cruelly exposed by television. Just as it was a reflection of Michael Foot that he did not see the need to tailor his appearance or speaking style to television, so it was also a reflection of the Labour party's complacency over the public's perception of leadership that it persevered with Foot for as long as it did.

As the party stumbled towards, and finally succumbed to, an emphatic election defeat in 1983, it became clear that Foot would have to be replaced by a younger and altogether more modern politician. Foot stood down in October 1983 and effectively ended his generation's presence in the party leadership.

Under the old leadership selection system, it is generally agreed that Roy Hattersley would have been the choice of the PLP. Hattersley himself believed that his chances of securing the leadership even in the electoral college were still good. But he reckoned without Neil Kinnock. Kinnock had been cultivating the trade unions and constituency parties for years. While Hattersley had been serving in government during the 1970s, Kinnock had declined office and used the time instead to build up a formidable network of support and alliances that had secured him a strong place on the National Executive Committee (NEC) of the party. Kinnock 'simply neglected parliament in favour of political activity outside and had failed, as a result, to build up a base of support in Westminster'.[38] He even told his local party in 1980 that he would attend outside political engagements even if it meant defying three-line whips. Between November 1981 and October 1982, for example,

> he did not ask a single oral question in Parliament, put down only twenty-eight written questions and voted in just seventy-nine out of a total of 332 divisions. Excluding those who died during the session or who represented Northern Irish seats, this gave Kinnock the tenth worst attendance record in the entire House of Commons – an astonishing performance for a Shadow Cabinet spokesman.[39]

Kinnock had been strongly in favour of the electoral college and in 1983 he became the first leader to benefit from the reform. With the unions and CLPs already sewn up, the PLP bowed to the inevitable and took the outsider as its leader with prudent good grace.

Kinnock had been a very young outsider and an unlikely candidate for the party leadership. He won it by successfully converting his outsider status into political advantage. After his accession to the leadership, he managed to retain a reputation for being his own man. He often jeopardised his party position and risked party splits by confronting the 'hard left' on the grounds of the public damage it was inflicting on the party's image and on Kinnock's own authority as leader. The division between Kinnock and the Militant Tendency even worked to his advantage. It allowed him openly to demonstrate his capacity to distance himself from a wing of the party and still remain effective as leader. Arguably, it made him more effective because it improved his public standing and with it his position over the party as a whole.

Kinnock was as much an exemplar of leadership-centred politics as Margaret Thatcher was in the Conservative party. He not only changed his party into a formidable electoral organisation but he was *seen* to have renovated and reformed it. In October 1989, *The Observer* gave recognition to Kinnock's achievements: 'Without the charisma of Gaitskell, or the intelligence of Wilson, Neil Kinnock has done more than either to march Labour, often backwards, to change. Unsaleable commitments shed, the Left neutralised, the party moved to the centre and all done democratically. A huge achievement.'[40] By May 1991, even a senior Conservative such as John Biffen was prepared to concede that Kinnock had successfully led his party into a position of electoral contention:

> He has done more to bring the Labour party back to the centre ground of British politics than Hugh Gaitskell ever was able to succeed in doing, notwithstanding the intellectual brilliance of Gaitskell ... When it came to sheer political sensitivity, knowing where to apply the pressures, Neil Kinnock has been quite outstanding in putting the Labour party into a better position politically than it has been in for decades. After so many years in the margins Labour now looks distinctly electable.[41]

Although Kinnock had taken care to carry his party with him,[42] the achievement was seen to have been Kinnock's in design and execution. He had made the party look as leader-led as the Conservative party. He had changed the party's style to conform to modern electioneering conditions. He had also been instrumental in turning its programme into a marketable centre-based socialism that was compatible both with the state of popular preferences and with the modern electoral imperative of protecting the party leader's claims to exterior public leadership.

Even the Labour party, therefore, had found it prudent to give its leader the level of discretion required to compete with other leaders and to enhance the party's appeal beyond Labour's contracting natural constituency and out towards an increasingly dealigned and independent electorate. Kinnock's style certainly produced criticism that he had betrayed socialist principles for the slick presentation of centrist policies, in support of a market economy and individual freedoms. On the other hand, he was also condemned for not being enough of an outsider in what has been described as 'the world's supreme insider culture'.[43] He was criticised for being too entrenched in a diminishing Labour heartland of big factories, large housing estates and old allegiances to state action. To a critic such as Martin Jacques, Kinnock mobilised an outsider campaign from outside parliament, but it did not go far enough because Kinnock was not a true outsider. As a result, he was never able to compete with the spatial leadership of other outsiders. He was still locked firmly in 'the highly introverted and self-absorbed' characteristics of Labour's 'ghetto culture and its fixation with the mass production society' [44] of 1945.

In spite of the rumbling debate about the nature of Kinnock's leadership, he succeeded in making his leadership, and the policy revision associated with it, into the focal point of unity for the party in its approach to the 1992 general election. Astonishingly for the Labour party, Kinnock had acquired a position in 1990 where, after seven years as leader, he could 'set his agenda ... without looking permanently over his shoulder'.[45] Not only had the party's electoral college given a formal and unambiguous recognition of the office of Labour leader for the first time in its history, it had afforded it unprecedented authority and discretion.[46] Party traditions were cast aside in the face of the overriding need to compete effectively in the rapidly developing arena of leadership politics. Kinnock, for his part, took full advantage of his position.[47] It was a measure of the Labour party's desperation to challenge its opponents on the grounds of political leadership that it was prepared to condone such a sweeping transfer of initiative to the leader's office. Even though the party had a long tradition of animosity towards the 'cult of the individual',[48] it buried such ambivalence in the overriding need to elevate its leader's public standing and to convey the impression that the party was effectively organised for government through the authority of its leader.

The leaders of the 1980s busied themselves in creating as much distance as possible between their leadership and the stereotypical images of their respective parties. Some, like Roy Jenkins and David Owen, felt compelled to form an entirely new party in order to escape from the traditional culture of the old. All the leaders in the 1980s advanced the trend in leadership towards a middle-class professionalism based upon socially mobile and often self-made individuals who were attuned to the nature of social change and to the need for political adaptation.[49] These leaders had to carve out their own identities and, in doing so, they refashioned the identities of their parties, allowing them to appeal to an ever more fluid and unpredictable public. In order to achieve this flexibility of purpose, these individuals exploited the growing opportunities to engage in spatial leadership. They all distanced themselves from the organisation they purported to lead. They all, either implicitly or explicitly, turned on parts of their own organisation. And they all cultivated an outsider position in their own parties so that they could enhance their personal claims of public attention and popular representation.

Thatcher's understudies: (3) John Major

Leadership politics in the 1990s drew heavily upon the Thatcher precedent. This was particularly noticeable with her successor, John Major. Major's initial appeal was based upon the impression that he was the antithesis of his predecessor. His reputation was as an archetypal 'organisation man', whose experience in banking and the Treasury and capacity for smooth conciliation offered a recuperative period of self-effacing tranquillity in the after-shock of Thatcher's fall from power. But even John Major soon discovered that Thatcher had brought to the surface, and subsequently developed, an array of leadership dynamics, strategies and disciplines that no leader could afford to ignore, let alone to dismiss. Measured consultation and collegiate decision making had to be tempered by more flamboyant expressions of individuality. In Major's case, he took his cue from the master.

In accordance with the Thatcher model, Major strove not merely to remind his party and the public of his meagre background, but to elevate it to the defining characteristic of his premiership and his political significance. A private man with a reputation for wishing to remain private, Major abandoned his privacy and began to exploit every opportunity for using the office to publicise himself as an ordinary person and to establish an identity with those like himself who were outsiders in established hierarchies. Major used his own ordinariness as a weapon in a much larger conflict. To Major, his own rise from the lower middle classes was the decisive affirmation of his own principles in the importance of opportunities and choice in individual advance. In a quite unselfconscious way, Major was his own walking ideal and the validation of his conception of an open society. He was a social outsider in the blue-chip society of the Conservative party. And yet he had made it to the top. At the same time, he retained his lack of pretension and his open adherence to middle-brow tastes and interests (e.g. C&A suits, Happy Eater meals, Chelsea Football Club).

John Major appealed to a vast constituency of aspiration. Major had had direct experience of hard times. He had painful memories of his father's bankruptcy and of having to live on the fourth floor of a Brixton boarding house. The two-room flat had a gas ring on the landing and a shared toilet on the ground floor. Major himself had been unemployed in his youth. His sympathy for those suffering from deprivation, therefore, seemed genuine and caring. He held high office, but in every other respect he appeared to remain an outsider, linked to that wider public which could identify closely with him and his principles. Major had shown in the past that he knew how to make 'skilful political use of this "ordinariness" on Labour's own class ground'.[50] His outsider appeal was so strong that it offered the prospect of providing the governing party with a distractive property that could turn attention away from its failures and mistakes. If Major was not exactly an anti-hero, he did provide an invaluable image that ran counter to much of his own party and the government.

Such were the motive forces of contemporary leadership that Major was compelled to extend the logic of his outsider position to create a sense of space between himself and the government. For a man whose political life had been one dedicated to the virtues of discreet accommodation, Major began to make public incursions into the government machine. His interventions were usually well publicised and designed to give the impression of an attentive prime minister breaking free from collective restraints and personally turning on some aspect of government policy or government machinery on behalf of the public.

His first venture in this role of 'prime minister as defender of the public' came in December 1990, when he announced a £42 million settlement for 1,200 haemophiliacs who had contracted the HIV virus through blood transfusions. The government's settled policy up to that point had been that no public money would be made available to such sufferers, as liability and compensation would have to be determined by the courts. In February 1991, Major played benefactor again by distancing himself from another set of government rules that threatened to produce charges of an unrepresentative government. Major stepped in to relax the rules on cold weather payments when severe weather conditions hit the country. Major waived the rules for two successive weeks.

Major's free-wheeling interventions became commonplace and spread to the outer limits of prime ministerial influence. Its wide-ranging character can be gauged by the headlines they generated in the press:

> Major tells CBI wage increases must be earned (*The Times*, 25 May 1991)
>
> Major overturns plans for testing in schools (*The Guardian*, 4 July 1991)
>
> Major cuts BR fares rise (*Daily Mail*, 14 October 1991)
>
> Major orders action to halt homes crisis (*Sunday Telegraph*, 15 December 1991)
>
> Major questions high food prices (*Sunday Times*, 2 February 1992)
>
> Major boost for gay rights (*Sunday Telegraph*, 1 March 1992)

This was not the same sort of interventionism as that practised in the past by premiers such as Harold Wilson. It was different in scale but, more importantly, it was different in nature. Wilson intervened to act for, or on behalf of, the government. He acted to protect the political reputation of his administration by intervening to preserve and defend the government under Labour. Major, on the other hand, acted more as a guerrilla commander against the impersonalism and unresponsiveness of contemporary institutions. In his adopted role as the personal representative of broad public concerns, Major intervened as much to provide demonstrable evidence of his empathy with the ordinary person as to produce action. The act of intervention was important in its own right, irrespective of effect. It protected Major, and by extension his administration, because it allowed him to distance himself from the negative aspects of modern government and in the process to melt himself more into the public's own conception of its condition.

Major's most ambitious plan to act as an agent of popular complaint and as an instrument of redress was the Citizen's Charter. This was his flagship policy not just because it matched so closely his outlook as prime minister, but because it was a way of patenting his interventionism on a mass basis. Its aim was to return power to the consumer by establishing performance standards, laying down more effective complaint procedures and giving various rights of redress when public services broke their obligations. Major described it as the 'widest ranging and most comprehensive'[51] initiative ever undertaken by government to raise quality, increase choice, secure better value and extend accountability of public services. Its target was the mass public and its intention was avowedly populist in character. Major was intent upon opening up some space between himself and 'government', thereby identifying his leadership with the common good. This was made transparently clear in his televised address to the nation on the Citizen's Charter: 'I called it the Citizen's Charter because quite simply it's on your side – not on the side of the state, the politicians, the bureaucrats or the union bosses – on your side, the citizen's side.'[52]

Major's attempt to fuse his outsider persona with his imitation of Thatcher's spatial leadership was revealed in its starkest form in the final Conservative party conference before the 1992 general election. In his speech to a party still in shock over the vacuum left by Thatcher's removal, Major made it clear that she had been replaced by an equally remarkable individual. The new prime minister announced that the party's post-Thatcherite theme for the election would be based not so much on policy as on 'Reaganesque self-exposure'.[53] Major offered himself for re-election to the premiership. 'He invited people to identify in his personal mythology and to follow in his footsteps from Coldharbour Lane, Brixton to Number 10 Downing Street.'[54] He explicitly linked his present principles and programme to his own underprivileged background and his rise to prominence as an outsider. Because of his experience, the party – his party – was not indifferent to the plight of the unemployed: 'I know how they feel – I know what it's like for a family when a business collapses. What it's like when you're unemployed and when you have to search for the next job. I haven't forgotten – and I never will.' [55] Because of these hard knocks, he would 'never play fast and loose with the economy'.[56] His private difficulties in the past were now not only publicly aired by Major himself, but openly deployed to justify his occupancy of Number 10 and to vindicate the values of his party. Although he acknowledged that the cabinet was a form of collective leadership, Major gave emphasis to his own power. It was he who could be entrusted with its usage because of who he was and what he had been through. It was precisely his background and character that would prevent his incumbency from becoming one of detachment and insensitivity. His memory of being just one of a crowd would always ensure a genuine, and electorally attractive, identity with the average person. For a modest man, Major's exploitation of his personality had been extraordinary. In Hugo Young's view, the speech

> made clear that the Conservatives' visionary appeal is built, to a startling extent, around one model: himself. This was the unexpected coda to the Thatcher era. Mrs Thatcher was often charged with hubristic domination, and her conference speech was delivered and received as an annual consummation of one-woman government. But she was never so shameless in representing her own life as the proof of all she had to say.[57]

After John Major was able to establish the claim that he had personally plucked victory from the jaws of defeat in the 1992 general election, the prime minister went on to make spatial leadership the chief property of his premiership. Soon after the election victory, Major was faced with a chronic syndrome of a rapidly disintegrating party and a government increasingly mired in sleaze and the problems of longevity. Even though the affliction persisted throughout the course of the government, it was Major's image as a man apart from the pack that for long periods provided the Conservatives not only with a form of redemption but with the only strategy for survival. But what Major was not able to foresee in his calculations was the sudden appearance of a figure whose natural talent, personal appetite and political opportunity for spatial leadership far exceeded those of the prime minister. Major was not so much challenged as eclipsed by a leader who was able to realise the full potential of the next generation of spatial leadership available within the British system.

Notes

1 Bert A. Rockman, *The Leadership Question: The Presidency and the American System* (New York, Praeger, 1984), p. 41.

2 Quoted in Hugo Young and Anne Sloman, *The Thatcher Phenomenon* (London, British Broadcasting Corporation, 1986), p. 30.

3 Jim Prior, *A Balance of Power* (London, Hamish Hamilton, 1986), p. 99.

4 Quoted in Patrick Cosgrave, 'The stalking horse who romped home', *The Independent*, 30 November 1989.

5 Kenneth Harris, *Thatcher* (London, Weidenfeld and Nicolson, 1988), p. 31.

6 Cosgrave, 'The stalking horse who romped home'.

7 Francis Pym, *The Politics of Consent* (London, Hamish Hamilton, 1984), p. 5.

8 Harris, *Thatcher*, p. 32.

9 Margaret Thatcher, *The Revival of Britain: Speeches on Home and European Affairs, 1975–1988*, compiled by Alistair B. Cooke (London, Aurum, 1989), p. 3.

10 Michael Biddiss, 'Thatcherism: Concept and Interpretations', in Kenneth Minogue and Michael Biddiss (eds), *Thatcherism: Personality and Politics* (Basingstoke, Macmillan, 1987), p. 2.

11 Bob Jessop, Kevin Bonnett, Simon Bromley and Tom Ling, *Thatcherism: A Tale of Two Nations* (Oxford, Polity, 1988), p. 61.

12 Pym, *The Politics of Consent*, p. 5.

13 Harris, *Thatcher*, p. 62.

14 Julian Critchley, 'Mrs Thatcher's Tory Party', *The Listener*, 9 October 1990.

15 Edward Pearce, 'Fighter with a golden tongue', *The Guardian*, 26 November 1990.

16 John Vincent, 'The Thatcher Governments, 1979–87', in Peter Hennessy and Anthony Seldon (eds), *Ruling Performance: British Governments from Attlee to Thatcher* (Oxford, Basil Blackwell, 1987), p. 279.

17 Jessop, Bonnett, Bromley and Ling, *Thatcherism*, p. 82.

18 Peter Jenkins, *Mrs Thatcher's Revolution: The Ending of the Socialist Era* (London, Pan, 1989), p. 184.

19 Quoted in Peter Jenkins, 'The real rebel of cabinet government', *Independent on Sunday*, 22 July 1990.

20 Robert Skidelsky, 'The pride and the fall', *The Guardian*, 21 November 1990.

21 Peregrine Worsthorne, 'Whose party is it now?', *Sunday Telegraph*, 16 June 1991.

22 Peregrine Worsthorne, 'Who'll speak for England?', *Sunday Telegraph*, 25 November 1990. For more on Mrs Thatcher's overtly populist approach to politics and policy, see Vemon Bogdanor, 'Democracy is dying: long live democracy!', *Listener*, 17 April 1986; Desmond King, *The New Right: Politics, Markets and Citizenship* (Basingstoke, Macmillan, 1987).

23 Anthony King, 'Margaret Thatcher: The Style of a Prime Minister', in Anthony King (ed.), *The British Prime Minister*, 2nd edn (Basingstoke, Macmillan, 1985), pp. 117–18.

24 Quoted in Young and Sloman, *The Thatcher Phenomenon*, pp. 53–4.

25 John Gaffney, *The Language of Political Leadership in Contemporary Britain* (Basingstoke, Macmillan, 1991), p. 158.

26 Quoted in Young and Sloman, *The Thatcher Phenomenon*, pp. 95–6.

27 Noel Malcolm, 'Mrs Thatcher: housewife superstar', *Spectator*, 25 February 1989.

28 Robert Harris, *Good and Faithful Servant: The Unauthorised Biography of Bernard Ingham* (London, Faber, 1991), pp. 150, 93.

29 Ivor Crewe, 'The Policy Agenda: A New Thatcherite Consensus', *Contemporary Record*, 3, no. 3 (February 1990), p. 5.

30 Ivor Crewe, 'Values: The Crusade that Failed', in Dennis Kavanagh and Anthony Seldon (eds), *The Thatcher Effect* (Oxford, Oxford University Press, 1989), p. 250.

31 Ivor Crewe, 'Has the Electorate become more Thatcherite?', in Robert Skidelsky (ed.), *Thatcherism* (London, Chatto and Windus, 1988), p. 45.
32 Crewe, 'Has the Electorate become more Thatcherite?', p. 45.
33 Crewe, 'Has the Electorate become more Thatcherite?', p. 44.
34 The average of 67 per cent for Margaret Thatcher's policies was derived from the responses to a series of questions on 'specifically Thatcherite policies and decisions' presented in Crewe's article [Crewe, 'Has the Electorate become more Thatcherite?', p. 41]. The average of 39 per cent for Margaret Thatcher's leadership is the figure given by Crewe (*ibid.*, p. 44). The differences between the public's view of Mrs Thatcher and her policies was also evident in Gallup's regular monthly questions of 'which party has the best leader?' and 'which party has the best policies?'. For much of the Thatcher period, there was often a clear discrepancy in preferences favouring Conservative leadership over Conservative policies. Although the response to leadership must have been based upon Mrs Thatcher's reputation for ascendancy, the public's favourable outlook was not extended to what were logically her policies. This disjunction was even present during the nadir of the Thatcher era. In September 1990, for example, only 30 per cent believed that the Conservatives had the best policies, while 39 per cent thought Labour had the best policies. What was a -9 per cent net rating on policy, however, turned into a +11 per cent rating when the question changed to leadership, with 42 per cent believing that the Conservatives had the best leader and only 31 per cent regarding Labour as the party with the best leader *Gallup Political Index*, Report No. 361, September 1990.
35 James Alt, Ivor Crewe and Bo Sarlvik, 'Angels in Plastic: The Liberal Surge in 1974', *Political Studies*, 25, no. 3 (September 1977), pp. 343–68.
36 The party changed its name to the Social and Liberal Democrat party following a merger with the majority faction of the Social Democratic Party in 1987. It is now known simply as the Liberal Democrat party.
37 Quoted in BBC Radio 3, *The Gang That Fell Apart*, Part 4, broadcast on 18 September 1991.
38 Robert Harris, *The Making of Neil Kinnock* (London, Faber, 1984), p. 138.
39 Harris, *The Making of Neil Kinnock*, p. 184.
40 'Neil's niceness isn't enough', *The Observer*, 1 October 1989.
41 Quoted in Richard Ford, 'Tory praises "outstanding" Kinnock revival', *The Times*, 27 May 1991.
42 Peter Kellner, 'Labour annuls its loveless marriage', *The Independent*, 25 May 1990.
43 Tom Nairn, 'The future according to Benn' (Review of Tony Benn, *Parliament, People and Power: Agenda for a Free Society*), *Guardian Weekly*, 23 January 1983.
44 Martin Jacques, 'Labour needs to shed its old clothes', *Sunday Times*, 14 August 1988.
45 Peter Kellner, 'A party no longer hounded by the left' *The Independent*, 5 October 1990.
46 R. M. Punnett, 'Selecting the Leader and the Deputy Leader of the Labour Party: The Future of the Electoral College', *Parliamentary Affairs*, 43, no. 3 (April 1990), pp. 179–95.
47 See Eileen Jones, *Neil Kinnock* (London, Robert Hale, 1994).
48 Barrie Axford, 'Leaders, Elections and Television', *Politics Review*, 1, no. 3 (February 1992), p. 20.
49 Dennis Kavanagh, 'From Gentlemen to Players: Changes in Political Leadership', in William B. Gwyn and Richard Rose (eds), *Britain: Progress and Decline* (London, Macmillan, 1980), pp. 73–93; Anthony King, 'The Rise of the Career Politician in Britain – And its Consequences', *British Journal of Political Science*, 11, no. 3 (July 1981), pp. 249–85; Anthony King, 'The British Prime Ministership in the Age of the Career Politician', *West European Politics*, 14, no. 2 (April 1991), pp. 25–47.

50 David Selbourne, 'Left, right, here comes the all-purpose Major', *Sunday Times*, 13 March 1992.
51 Quoted in George Jones, 'Major pledges power for the consumer', *Daily Telegraph*, 23 July 1991.
52 Party political broadcast, 25 July 1991.
53 Harvey Thomas, 'Hero of suburbia', *The Guardian*, 12 October 1991.
54 Peter Jenkins, 'Just a Brixton boy made man of the people', *The Independent*, 12 October 1991.
55 Leader's speech to the Conservative party conference 1991, *The Independent*, 12 October 1991.
56 Leader's speech to the Conservative party conference 1991.
57 Hugo Young, 'Surprising egotist proves he is more equal than others', *The Guardian*, 12 October 1991.

CHAPTER 4

Moving in from the outside: the Blair phenomenon

Labour had been engaged in a process of progressive readjustment for much of the 1980s but the drive to modernise the party under the leadership of Neil Kinnock had only succeeded at the level of presentation and projection. Kinnock had been effective in preventing the party from sliding into the status of a third force. He had openly confronted the Militant Tendency and other elements of the hard left in an effort to marginalise them in the public's perception of the Labour party. He had also set in motion a full-scale policy review of the party's attachment and priorities in an effort to shift the movement into a more marketable resource. The culmination of this prodigious exercise was to have been the 1992 general election. But in spite of having had a clear lead in the polls since July 1992, and despite leading the Conservatives during the election campaign, Labour could not prevent John Major from securing an unexpected working majority in the House of Commons.

Enormous efforts had been made to ameliorate the party's hybrid reputation for political extremism and institutional conservatism. And yet, notwithstanding the movement towards modernisation, the party could not free itself from the public perception of distrust and disaffection. Its 'negatives' remained as strong as ever. It was seen to be an organisation geared not only to trade union power, but to a tax-and-spend culture of redistribution and to public ownership. Its attachments to the positive state, to macro demand management, to a public sector devoid of cost consciousness and to a class-based ideology of social thought and historic mission were perceptions that further diminished its political reputation. Even after eleven years of Conservative government and an economic recession, Labour failed to secure as many votes as it had done in 1987. In some quarters, it was seen as a failure of leadership. The party had not been convincingly supportive of the leadership-induced change of identity which led inevitably to disjunction, confusion and distrust. In other quarters, blame was attached to the party itself, which was seen to be locked into a historic purposelessness because of its intrinsic inability to adapt to changing conditions. According to this view, '[no] policy initiatives or presentational improvements could touch the party's basic problems, for these were rooted in its culture and identity. There was no quick fix possible when the issue was one of trust, feeling and perception.'[1]

When Kinnock's heir apparent, John Smith, took the leadership he was confronted by the claims of both camps. The traditionalists believed that with a little fine tuning it was inevitable that Labour's electoral machine would win the next general election, if only because the Conservatives would by then have become unelectable. The modernisers disputed the feasibility of victory by default and claimed that without radical change Labour would consign the country to a permanent one-party Conservative state. John Smith moved cautiously on the issue of reform, believing that the party could only be politically effective when its explosive energies were kept in a quiescent condition. He was prepared to engage in reform but only through external consultation and consensus. Smith saw his leadership role primarily as one of holding the party together through Wilsonian techniques of balancing interests and policies. Smith's evident middle-class status and his capacity to portray personal probity and trust were assets to a party that needed to appeal to middle England. And yet, Smith remained a figure deeply embedded in Labour party culture and in the labyrinthine complexities of its bureaucracy, language and rituals. This was widely interpreted at the time as a source of weakness:

> The greatest blow to his reputation has ... been the speed with which trade union leaders announced their support for his candidature. This made him look an old style Labour apparatchik, the creature of the block vote, the favourite son of Labour's own old Magic Circle. Since the close connection with the unions remains Labour's albatross, his leadership is tainted. How can he offer Labour a new beginning when he has got to the top without debate and without a programme for renewal?[2]

Smith was duly criticised for his 'organisation man' outlook and his brokerage style of leadership that aimed at closing the party's ranks and minimising conflict. Simon Jenkins in *The Times* typified the common view that Smith's incremental adjustments towards making Labour into a more electable organisation were largely negative achievements. He thought that Smith embodied Labour's dominant problem that it had 'lost an empire and not found a novel role'. Jenkins continued:

> Mr Smith has not achieved the Wilsonian coup and made the Tories look like the old Britain and Labour the new ... What Mr Smith's speeches do suggest is that he is content to have the old cabals around him. His instincts are deeply

> conservative. He nod[s] towards the need to arrest the Tories' drift to centralism, to reassert local democracy. But he is basically happy with the cosy corporatism of the post-1945 settlement.[3]

Nevertheless, by the time of his death in May 1994, John Smith had acquired the reputation of a leader who had consolidated the marginal changes to the party and reduced the controversy levels in the organisation to a minimum. In doing so, he had succeeded in giving at least the appearance of making Old Labour into an electable alternative to a chronically discredited Conservative government.

Spatial leadership and New Labour

It was John Smith's successor who provided a quite different form of leadership and one that by comparison made Smith look like an introverted leader of an ingrown party. Tony Blair's leadership style and purpose were just as much a response to John Smith as they were to John Major. In changing the emphasis away from party equilibrium and in openly resisting the gravitational force of the party itself, Blair responded to the underlying pressures and incentives of contemporary leadership politics. He provided the most dramatic affirmation of spatial leadership since Margaret Thatcher.

Blair was able to benefit from the collective shock of John Smith's sudden death and from the public interest it generated in the circumstances of a leaderless party. He also acquired an advantage from the full activation of Labour's recently reformed leadership selection system, which lent itself to comparisons with an American primary election. In what was the largest democratic exercise ever organised by a British political party, the contenders for the leadership (Tony Blair, John Prescott and Margaret Beckett) engaged in a public process of appealing for the 4.5 million available votes in Labour's electoral college. Given the size of the electorate, the intense media attention and the popular interest in the race, the winner was in a position to claim that the leadership selection had taken place in the public domain. As a result, it could be construed as a popular choice rather than as merely a party decision. Blair certainly took it as read that a victory in these circumstances signified something more than the outcome of an internal process. He had secured decisive majorities in the three elements of the college (i.e. trade unions, MPs and constituency parties). These components amounted in their own right to a large sample of the electorate and a representative section of influential opinion formers. Furthermore, he had done so in a process observed, appraised and in many ways driven by the media and public opinion. Blair was therefore placed in a position where he was able to assert that his leadership reflected a process sanctioned by the public. He was able to invoke public concerns and popular authority in his contact with the party. And he was able to use the outcome of such a vast participatory exercise to exert his leadership upon the party in an emphatic move to transform Labour into an organisation capable of sustaining not merely public interest but popular support.

Blair exploited the public and popular nature of the leadership election to propel the modernisation of the party in a squeeze strategy involving leadership vision at the top and populist pressure from below. To Blair, relying upon the unpopularity of the Conservative government and the inflated opinion poll leads for Labour constituted dangerous complacency for a party that had a known capacity for losing soft support at critical periods. In the view of Blair and his fellow modernisers, the Labour party was an ingrown and backward-looking organisation locked into an outdated set of dogmas related to a socio-economic system that had been superseded by new and rapidly changing cultural and global conditions. Labour did not just require some of its old eyesores to be removed for the sake of social acceptability. It needed a complete transformation in the form of a new identity and a fresh appeal. In an increasingly market-based society, the party needed to be made aware of its potential client base and then to be professionally marketed. With two to three years before a general election and with a new leader commanding unprecedented authority, Blair had a unique opportunity in 1994 to confront the party and challenge it to break with its traditions in order to widen its appeal.

Blair had always been a stranger to Labour's traditional union culture and to the ideological dogmas of the party's activists. He had not been born and bred into the party. On the contrary, he was thoroughly middle class. His father was a self-made businessman and a Conservative councillor who had harboured ambitions to become an MP and ultimately a Conservative prime minister. After attending Fettes and St John's College Oxford, Tony Blair had practised law before becoming an MP in 1983. In addition to his atypical social background, it was clear that he was not temperamentally at one with the visceral nature of his party. Blair's outsider status was observed at close quarters by Philip Stephens:

> Mr Blair comes as a stranger to the culture of activism. Despite his overwhelming leadership victory over Mr John Prescott and Mrs Margaret Beckett, he is better known in the media than within his own party ... [U]nlike Mr Neil Kinnock or Mr John Smith, he has never been a party insider, a politician at home in the smoke-filled rooms in which Labour has traditionally done its business. Even among many Labour MPs the unclubbable Mr Blair is an unknown

> quantity. More than one shadow spokesman has sought the advice of journalists at Westminster on how they should approach the new leader.[4]

Blair, however, made a virtue of such distance. It gave him critical perspective and a grasp of what lay outside the organisation. Blair himself was acutely aware of his own vantage point: 'There is a sense in which I really almost stood outside the Labour party and looked at it and said, if you were an ordinary person looking at British politics, how would you want to see it develop, how should it develop. And ever since I have been in it, I've thought we have to change.'[5] To Blair, his own party was as much of a problem as the Conservative government. Enormous reserves of social resentment and alienation had been built up over the Thatcher–Major period. And yet the rigidities and suspicions associated with Labour meant that the main opposition party could not be relied upon to tap these insurgent energies and channel them into an effective challenge to the Conservative hegemony. Labour needed to adapt to what was a changing constituency. The modernisers' view was that because Labour had delayed and postponed change for so long, the need was now for a genuine transformation that would enable the party to respond and react to the currents of political dissent that would otherwise pass it by. Blair's position was that Labour's renewal would be both a model and an instrument of national renewal. His objective was to use the distance between the leadership and the movement to push the party *to* the people, rather than pushing the people into the party.

Blair's strategy was to arouse the idea of a silent majority that had been marginalised by successive Conservative governments and effectively disenfranchised by Labour opposition. He sought to remove the popular suspicions and antagonisms connected with Labour by openly and explicitly transforming the party. He wanted to make Labour into a more accessible organisation with altered agendas and priorities, a newly enlarged membership, and a greatly diminished attachment to traditional dogmas and historic norms. Blair's intentions were made evident from his first speech as Labour leader to the party conference in 1994. In private discussions with his advisors, Blair had made it clear that he would not be content with merely leading the party. He wished to reinvent it on behalf of the wider public. 'Past Labour leaders lost because they compromised', he confided to Philip Gould. 'I will never compromise. I would rather be beaten and leave politics than bend to the party. I am going to take the party on ... Conference must build New Labour. It is time we gave the party some electric shock treatment.'[6]

Blair *v.* Clause Four

In his speech, Blair first set out the populist position that Labour had become the 'mainstream voice in politics today'.[7] By referring to the ordinary fears that plagued everyday life, Blair identified himself and his party with majority resentments:

> The Tories have failed you. We are on your side. Your ambitions are our ambitions. To men and women who get up in the morning and find the kitchen door smashed in again, the video gone again; to pensioners who fear to go out of their homes, let us say: The Tories have abused your trust. We are on your side. Your concerns are our concerns ... The Tories have forgotten you again. Your anxieties are our anxieties.[8]

Labour could once again lay claim to being the people's party because it was able to articulate the concerns of the forgotten majority. Blair sought to shift the party's traditional emphasis away from trade union concerns, class politics and state-based socialist prescriptions by stressing the importance of community, partnership, co-operation and mutual responsibility.

The leader then went on to urge the party to redefine itself in order to make itself electable. The party had to allow itself to become openly responsive to changing conditions and to place the leadership in a position to be more proactive and pragmatic without being continually undermined by sectarianism and ideological distractions. Blair wanted a 'new politics – a politics of courage, honesty and trust'. It would be an emancipation for the party and a rededication of public purpose: 'Those most in need of hope deserve the truth ... They are tired of dogma. They are tired of politicians pretending to have a monopoly on the answers. They are tired of glib promises broken as readily in office as they were made on the soapbox.'[9] This was as much an indictment of Labour as it was of contemporary Conservative governments. Accordingly, Blair gave an undertaking: 'When we make a promise, we must be sure we can keep it. That is page 1, line 1 of a new contract between government and citizen.'[10]

At this point, Blair challenged the party to make a thorough revision of its objectives and to produce a new constitution that reflected more closely the prevailing conditions of the 1990s:

> It is time we had a clear, up-to-date statement of the objects and objectives of our party ... This is a modern party in an age of change. It requires a modern constitution that says what we are in terms the public cannot misunderstand and the Tories cannot misrepresent. We are proud of our beliefs, so let's state them – and in terms that people will identify with in every workplace, every home, every family, every community in our country.[11]

The encoded references for constitutional change meant an attack on Clause Four,[12] which was not only regarded as the animating principle of socialist philosophy but the core objective of the socialist march through history. In many parts of the party, an attack on Clause Four was tantamount to an attack upon the Labour party's soul. Clause Four had acquired almost mythical status in the movement, not simply on account of its content but because of the influence it had had upon the language, strategies and calculations of Labour party politics. Blair had deliberately engaged in a 'transgression of Labour's unwritten law that no one touches Clause Four'.[13]

Blair's disruptive intervention into the subtle protocols of Clause Four proved to many that he was an outsider who was utterly devoid of any understanding as to how the Labour party operated in practice. Party members who were repulsed by such iconoclasm denounced it as an exercise in heretical overreach that would lead to civil war within the party. In his desire to market New Labour, Blair seemed to be dislodging the party's historical anchorage points and identifying his opponents as not merely old Labourites but the 'Old Labour' party – i.e. the party left behind and marginalised by New Labour. Clause Four had been a problem for the leadership of the party since the 1930s but it was always deemed too sensitive a subject for political capital to be expended in changing it. Blair's assault upon Clause Four typified his approach of making the party more outwardly understandable even if this did risk internal disruption and division. The outsider position and perspective of Blair fostered a Thatcherite outlook of 'them' and 'us'. Like Thatcher, Blair placed value on the idea of an uncompromising thrust that would widen the space between leader and organisation and allow the leadership to drive the party to change by driving almost recklessly at the party itself.

Blair's public challenge on Clause Four came as a complete surprise both to the assembled delegates and to the numerous broadcast journalists observing the new leader's first major occasion since the leadership election. Even though the conference approved a motion affirming Clause Four two days after Blair's speech, the leader had set in motion an extensive exercise in highly publicised consultation and debate. This culminated in April 1995 with 85 per cent of party members giving their approval to the leadership's new statement of aims and values. Blair had risked his entire leadership and dared the party to undermine its key electoral asset in the Clause Four debate. It was a clear sign that Blair was intent upon transcending the party in order to widen and to deepen its public appeal. It was also clear that the party had come to acknowledge the imperatives and disciplines of leadership politics in contemporary political engagement.

The contrast between Tony Blair and John Smith on the subject reflected entirely different approaches to the party. Smith believed that to raise the ghost of Clause Four would be detrimental to party unity and, as such, it was better to treat it as a historical anachronism whose meaning, significance and usage could be safely accommodated within the party's own conventions. Blair, by comparison, had a more fundamentalist approach in which the anomaly had to be confronted and resolved, even at the cost of party unity and his own leadership. To John Rentoul, the contrast was stark and highly significant:

> John Smith's view ... had been that if the only thing people heard about the party was that it was repudiating its past, it would betray a lack of self-confidence – people would distrust the party's motives and be ready to believe the worst about what it really intended ... Smith's approach to Clause IV was symptomatic of his wider strategy, to put the Left to sleep and allow people to forget about them, whereas Blair was deliberately to open Pandora's box to let out more dragons to slay.[14]

The turmoil over Clause Four set a general pattern in which the Blair leadership sought to reposition the party away from the negatives of the past. Blair regarded Labour's unrepresentative radicalism of the 1970s as the antithesis of his vision. He recalled that during that period, 'there was a huge mismatch between activists and leaders, and a perpetual tension between what leaders had to say to the public and what they had to say to the party'.[15] In respect to the trade unions, Blair claimed that the 'old relationship didn't do either of us much good' and that it was important for New Labour to make clear it 'represent[ed] the governing interests of the whole country'.[16] Far from having preferential treatment, the unions would have the 'same access as the other side of industry'.[17] A New Labour government would not be the 'political arm of anyone today other than the British people'.[18] Instead of past dogmas based upon class strife, Blair pressed for a partnership of mutual benefit: 'Let us settle these arguments about industrial laws once and for good. There will be no return to the 70's ... Forget the past. No more bosses versus workers. You are on the same side. The same team.'[19] Blair pointed to the gains to be made from 'public and private finance working together in transport, in housing, in capital projects, in health and in education'.[20] It became evident that Blair's vision of a renewed community-conscious Britain drew its inspiration as much from the business and private sector as it did from the trade union and public sectors.[21] In his speech to the 1994 Labour party conference, Blair referred to the way in which some companies could provide a model of a stakeholder society based upon a commonality of interests and motivations: 'Go and look at a company that is succeeding. It will treat its workforce not as servants but as partners. They will be motivated and trained and given a common purpose.'[22]

The populist counterpoint

Blair's interest in business extended far further than the desire to apply best business practice on a wider scale. He wanted business to have confidence in New Labour as a governing party. The best method of optimising the party's chance of achieving that confidence was an offer to return the compliment. In his interview with the *Financial Times*, Blair went further than any previous Labour leader in closing the historical divide between business and labour:

> In the end there is no escaping from the fact that businesses run business. And the best thing government can do is set a framework within which business has the stability to plan and invest in the future ... I want a situation more like the Democrats and the Republicans in the US. People don't even question for a single moment that the Democrats are a pro-business party. They should not be asking the question about New Labour ... New Labour is pro-business, pro-enterprise, and we believe there is nothing inconsistent between that and a decent and just society.[23]

No other Labour leader would, or could, have given such assurances. No other Labour leader would have had the authority to make such statements or to have had them received as credible assertions. They were symptomatic of a grand design to reinvent not just the party but its relationships with society. The new solutions would not be taken from the past but would be reached pragmatically on the basis of current conditions and a sense of social justice. Blair wished to distance himself from big government and from corporatist strategies. He advocated a thorough overhaul of the welfare state that would break the cycle of dependence and provide 'not more benefits, but help in getting off benefits ... helping people to move on and move up'.[24] Blair proposed a revival of local communities that would in the process cut crime, delinquency, family breakups and insecurity: 'We have to have the courage to build a new civic society, a new social order, where everyone has a stake and everyone plays a part.'[25] New Labour would be the leading expression and chief instrument of a project that would constitute a genuine third way as equally divorced from neo-liberal dogmas as it was from traditional socialist nostrums. In declaring New Labour's emancipation from the heavy industry of Old Labour's state intervention, Blair claimed the discretionary space to devise cleaner, leaner and more 'high-tech' and selective solutions to social problems.

The subtext of Blair's leadership and his drive for New Labour was populist in design. He continually restated the need for the party to connect with the British people and to reflect not just their interests in a global abstract sense but to demonstrate an understanding of the daily impulses and fears experienced by individual citizens. In his memorandum to the leadership, Philip Gould stressed the importance of recognising that what most voters wanted was 'to advance and improve their lives. In short to become better off.'[26] Gould's instincts were suburban in nature. He believed that Labour had to show it understood the legitimacy of people who wished to advance their position. To Gould, the 'ultimate foundation of the Labour party [was] not dogma, or even values' so much as the 'hopes and aspirations of ordinary people. My instincts are populist', he declared, 'I put people first.'[27] As a consequence, his advice to Blair was unequivocal: 'This is absolutely critical. The progress and well-being of individuals and their families [should be] our central reference point in making sense of politics. It allows Labour to respect the value of work, which is, after all, the original reason for its existence.'[28]

The requirement to use the leadership to connect Labour with the tangible immediacy of 'people' issues was demonstrated not merely by the party's repudiation of corporatism or the block vote, but by an active concern to register the everyday irritations of the silent majority. Prompted by opinion poll tracking, focus groups and market testing, New Labour further enhanced its appeal by its capacity to respond to a stream of gut issues. Blair slammed into the 'excess profits of the new robber barons'.[29] He promised to levy a windfall profits tax on the privatised utilities and to spend it on extensive work and education programmes. He tore into the Tories for wasting £1.6 million of the National Health Service budget on 'bureaucracy, accountants and company cars' that could have been 'spent on beds and patients and nurses'.[30] The National Lottery was also highlighted as a suitable case for reforming treatment. It was the 'people's lottery. The people should get more out of it.'[31] Blair declared: 'I want the people's money to go on the people's priorities.'[32] He turned his fire on education and condemned not just run-down schools but poor teachers: 'if teachers can't teach properly they shouldn't be teaching at all.'[33]

The leader touched upon many other popular themes, ranging from a conspicuous championing of family values to the need to change the welfare state. He took particular pride in Labour's success at addressing the gut issue of crime. He was not prepared to allow the left's associations with tolerance and social understanding to impede his campaign to establish New Labour as the party of law and order. At the 1996 party conference, Blair was unambiguous in his populist position on the issue: 'I say to the people who tell us it's wrong to want to crack down on violent crime, drug pushers, anti-social neighbours or hooligans: Try living next door to them.'[34] While the Major government prevaricated on the issue of gun control following the Dunblane tragedy, Blair made a point of cutting through all the counter-arguments and difficulties. He gave voice to a common impulse: 'I believe we should ban the private ownership and possession of hand-guns.'[35]

Perhaps most startling of all was New Labour's commitment to economic caution and financial prudence. Blair was determined that the party would not be made vulnerable to Tory charges of economic incompetence and 'tax bombshells'. Labour's new leader gave voice to those alienated by the sharp rises in taxation under the Major government. Families and family structures, he believed, had been secretly hit by tax increases. 'We all want ordinary hard-working families to pay less tax.'[36] What made matters worse was that additional money had been required to fund the failures of Conservative policies. 'I don't mind paying taxes for education and health and the police', said Blair. 'What I mind is paying them for unemployment, crime and social squalor.'[37] Blair was determined to establish New Labour as the party of sound finance and budgetary competence. As a result, the leadership announced that for the lifetime of a first Labour parliament, the government would not only refrain from any increases in income tax, but adhere to the spending targets of the previous Conservative administration.

Daring to be Thatcher

In making Labour electable, Blair was variously accused of engaging in social democratic revisionism, of being a liberal and even of being a closet Tory. Blair professed himself to be thoroughly indifferent to such charges and believed that they were merely signs of Old Labour's preoccupation with dogma and history. He did not object to parallels being drawn between him and Margaret Thatcher. On the contrary, he even encouraged such references. Blair was prepared to draw parallels between himself and Margaret Thatcher not merely as a standard of political leadership, but as an expression of Blair's iconoclasm towards his own party.

To most inside his own party, Margaret Thatcher remained an anti-Christ figure that personified every social and economic affliction that had disfigured the country for a generation. Blair, by contrast, believed that the Labour movement and its identity had to move on from the past. The party had to give recognition not just to the failures of Thatcherism, but also to its achievements in trade union reform, privatisation, deregulation and in 'destroying outdated attitudes'.[38] In a speech to the News Corporation Leadership Conference in 1995, Blair conceded that the New Right leadership of Margaret Thatcher had 'got certain things right'.[39] He alluded to the placing of a greater emphasis upon enterprise and to the rewarding rather than the penalising of success. He approved of the way that Thatcherism had led to the 'breaking up of some vested interests'.[40] Blair concluded from this record that 'Mrs Thatcher was a radical, not a Tory'.[41] This was the critical judgement because Thatcher had shown that the political system was susceptible to radical leadership and that a radical programme could succeed in transforming policy and society if it were pursued with Thatcherite conviction.

To Blair, New Labour could not only complete Thatcher's economic and social revolution, but improve it to take account of the problems of social cohesion and institutional decay. The centre-left could only generate an alternative through the drive and direction of a radicalising force. If the left 'remained mired in the past', it would not be able to 'offer political leadership in providing security through change'.[42] The model and inspiration would be that of Margaret Thatcher. Her methods and her style were endorsed in Peter Mandelson and Roger Liddle's *The Blair Revolution*, which was the nearest approximation to a manifesto of New Labour's modernisation programme. 'Margaret Thatcher's success lay in her ability to focus on a set of clear goals and make everything (and everyone) conform to these priorities.' In government, Blair's aim would be to 'achieve a similar level of policy fulfilment' but 'without the accompanying costs'.[43] Blair would need to 'have an equally clear and bold personal agenda'.[44] To Mandelson and Liddle, Blair had the temperament to match the Thatcherite requirements of the premiership: '[L]ike Mrs Thatcher, Blair always has a clear idea of what he wants, he is impatient when others do not have the courage or imagination to go along with him, and he does not let up when he has resolved on a way forward. Muddling through is an anathema to him.'[45]

Others agreed that Blair was following in the Thatcherite mould of a personal crusade conducted as much against his own party and its traditional constituencies as against the Conservatives. Matthew Symonds noted that Margaret Thatcher had been able to 'launch her coup against the Tory establishment because its nerve was shattered after the digressions and disasters of the Heath government'.[46] In similar manner, Blair was able to launch a comparable coup because the 'old establishment of the Labour movement ha[d] been shredded of confidence and legitimacy by four successive election defeats and the terminal decline of labourist collectivism'.[47] To David Marquand, it was this freedom of manoeuvre within his own party that afforded Blair the opportunity to build a coalition comparable with that formed by Mrs Thatcher. He did so by 'detaching crucial elements from his predecessor's constituency and annexing them to his own'.[48]

Marquand drew important parallels between the Thatcher coalition that had dominated the 1980s and the Blair coalition that created such a threat to the Conservative hegemony in the 1990s:

> Each was assembled by a politician of genius, with a capacity to reach out, across familiar ideological boundaries, to the core constituency of the opposing party. Both the politicians concerned were curiously rootless figures, cut off – in one case by gender and in the other by upbringing – from the cultures of their respective parties. Above all, each coalition owed as much to a revulsion from old attachments as the attractions of new ones.[49]

Blair was able to use his Thatcherite credentials to create further embarrassment to the Major administration that was already languishing in an apparent vacuum of political leadership. Peter Mandelson and Roger Liddle were able to imply that Blair, rather than Major, was the natural successor to Margaret Thatcher on the grounds of conviction and drive: 'Despite their different temperaments, Blair shares Margaret Thatcher's resolve – more so than does John Major ... Not surprisingly, by behaving as if he was one among equals in his cabinet, Major shows a lack of authority and drive that has contributed substantially to his government's unpopularity – a lesson for Tony Blair.'[50] Given this context, it was unsurprising that Thatcherite discipline and strength should become a characteristic property of Blair's modernisation project. It became a 'guiding precept of New Labour that no act should be undertaken that smacks of weakness when tested against the Thatcherite norm'.[51]

Blair's was a defiant and irreverent leadership. Hugo Young noted Blair's 'refusal to succumb with the slightest tremor of caution to the sacred cows of old socialist argument ... What agonises the Labour Party – what would startle all his predecessors living and dead – appears barely to touch him.'[52] To Young, Blair was genuinely different from his immediate predecessors because of the nature and clarity of his convictions:

> The danger Labour runs with Blair seems to me close to the opposite of the one usually identified. It is not that he is all things to all men, a pliant ingenue sounding good on television, but that he has exceptionally clear ideas, painful to many sentimentalists, about how the Labour Party should deal with its past, and make itself a new future ... While Kinnock and Smith made indispensable contributions to the Labour Party's renewal, neither managed to transcend the impression that they were doing what they did for reasons of expediency. They were painted, sometimes unfairly, as men defining their party to comply with opinion polls. The role of Mr Blair is critically different ... It is to complete the process by converting Labour's talk of markets and opportunity, of

community and competence, into language from the heart of socialism not just from its manipulative and sound-biting head.[53]

Blair relished his outsider credentials and his cultivated licence to go against the grain of the party. To Sarah Baxter, Blair was only able to lead the modernisation project because of his position in relation to the party: 'Blair believes in administering shocks to the party to prove to voters that Labour has changed. It is a fundamental part of his project, not a sideshow ... [H]e looks at Labour from the point of view of an outsider ... [It] has been one of his great strengths.'[54] To those who complained that he had not captured the heart of the party, Blair would respond that his heart was not in that particular construction of the party: 'I was not born in the party. I chose it' was a frequent rejoinder used by Blair in support of his claims to lead the party away from its redundant past. 'The true emotional attachment to the Labour party is not to cling on to something long past its sell-by date', he claimed. 'It is not a question of ... not changing the emotional baggage of the Labour party. It is that my emotions are grounded in something different.'[55] Blair was not prepared to lead the party as a middle-class figurehead, or as an intellectual trustee for trade union vested interests or socialist ideology. He wanted a genuine synergy between the leadership, the membership and the electorate. His role would be to provide a recognisable expression of views and beliefs with which large sections of the public could identify.

To an increasingly atomised and individuated electorate, Blair offered a popular immediacy with Labour. The leader provided the prospect of a fast track and direct connection to a party that was now an outwardly porous and malleable entity. He had worked to diminish the old deterrents of inverted snobbery, sectional favouritism, genetic selection, intrinsic folklore and insider exclusiveness. The leader had explicitly bypassed the National Executive Committee (NEC) and the party conference on the Clause Four issue (1995) and the draft manifesto (1996) by appealing directly to the membership, which itself had been inflated through Blair's own personalised publicity campaign. The level of trade union influence in the party had been significantly diminished in the areas of parliamentary candidate selection, conference leverage, NEC representation and party funding. The role of the NEC itself had been altered to make it into more of a support structure for the leadership, and less of an alternative power base. Blair's own conspicuous rootlessness in the Labour party was now a key factor in the strategy of offering voters a new home that they had purportedly already helped to design. He personified his own message of a new Labour party that could appeal across class and social barriers. His acquisition of the leadership, together with his conspicuous detachment from Old Labour, was intended to signify the sheer responsiveness of New Labour. The logic ran as follows. If someone with the views and background of Tony Blair could not only be in the Labour party but actually lead it, then it must have changed enough to offer a home to a wide spectrum of society. In many respects, therefore, the space revealed and underlined between the leader and the traditional structures of the Labour party was more than consistent with Blair's strategy. It was an indispensable element of his leadership.

A personal contract with Britain

Blair knew the vulnerability of Labour to the negative imagery of its traditional deficiencies that had damaged the party so severely in previous election campaigns. Accordingly, Blair concentrated on the distinctive properties of spatial leadership. It was in this sphere that the party's identity could be continually refracted through the personal vision and individual manifesto of the very figure most palpably detached from the organisation and its past. The party remained an expression of the public interest, but almost by not being Labour, or at least by not appearing to be Old Labour or, indeed, any old-style party. New Labour would literally reflect public opinion by being the register of popular demands, choices and anxieties conveyed through new or reformed channels to a responsive leadership. New Labour was also more direct in the sense of subordinating doctrinal and ideological constructions of the public interest to the more immediate expression of interests by the public. Labour would remain the people's party but the emphasis was now given to the people positioned outside the party as the active and originating element in the relationship.

Blair sought to substantiate New Labour's claims to be a defining centre of populist expression through a variety of means. He spearheaded the party's shift to the centre and the establishment of policy initiatives designed to optimise Labour's appeal. He championed the recruitment drive in party membership to widen the party's political base and to provide a counterweight to the trade unions and Labour's traditional activists. He sought to relocate Labour activism back into the community from which it had drifted into sectarian detachment during the 1970s and 1980s. Blair also endorsed constitutional reform as part of his project to transform the nature of British politics. He wanted a Labour victory to produce 'not just a new set of politicians but a new politics ... that [would] alter the relationship between the people and the Government'. This would be an evangelising campaign beyond party and traditional attachments: 'Power to the people is not a slogan but a necessity if we are to reconnect politics with the majority and create the new politics on which a new Britain will, in part, be built.'[56]

But in spite of all these initiatives on policy and party reform, Blair was aware of Labour's persistent problem with the issue of public trust. He was also conscious of the charge that there could appear to be a leader–party disjunction in interests and identity that could generate as much distrust as before. In September 1996, *The Economist* reported that 'the one-man-band question [was] still the one the leader's intimates fear[ed] most' because it could 'cost them the election'.[57] The following month, at the final party conference before the long-awaited general election, Blair decided once again to go for broke. He would make the possible vice of isolation into a virtue. He would use his public position to enter into a personal contract with the British people in which he would be the personal guarantor of Labour's promises and political conduct in government. Blair referred to a personal 'performance contract'[58] between himself and the British people. With clear parallels to Newt Gingrich's 'Contract With America' and President Clinton's 'New Covenant', he gave ten vows on New Labour policy relating to such issues as education, welfare, devolution, the NHS and taxation. He conspicuously established himself at the centre of government responsibility and accountability: 'That is my covenant with the British people. Judge me upon it. The buck stops here.'[59] This represented another extraordinary episode in leadership presumption in a party previously noted for its bureaucratic culture, its layering of policy construction, and its collective and democratic ethos.

The New Labour compound of populist themes and subtexts, together with a leadership providing an explicit antidote both to Old Labour and to public suspicions of Labour in general, was conveyed repeatedly in the 1997 general election campaign. Blair used his assault upon the party as the model for his attack on the Conservatives. New Labour had been market tested. It was now prepared for a national sales launch. Old Labour had been depicted in Washingtonian images of impregnable culture and dogged inertia. The idea of a citadel that had succumbed to the firepower of New Labour's popular mobilisation was now recast in the form of the Conservative government. For Blair, this second Washington was also characterised by a congenital immobility and unresponsiveness. Like his battle with Old Labour, he saw the challenge as one of confronting an establishment of vested interests, ideological fatalism and institutional torpor. The Conservative government was portrayed as having become detached from contemporary social change and needs. It required an organised political will to break down the barriers between the citizenry and their notional representatives. Blair declared the existence of an alternative to the neo-liberal postulate of there being no alternative to a market-driven society. The answer lay in a leadership-centred array of nuanced policy shifts that would be pragmatic and effective. At the same time, Blair believed in the need to reform the political culture to give greater expression to the social values of community, obligation, participation and responsibility.

Inherent in Blair's repositioning of Labour was his own relocation as leader in relation to the party. His visible distance from the organisation was publicly equated with a proximity to public concerns and to public trust. Dave Hill observed how the 'Tories would ... love to demonstrate a wider cleavage between leadership and rank-and-file'. Hill sensed the achievement of Blair's spatial leadership and the massive potential it had to secure an electoral breakthrough:

> [T]he perception of Blair as a man free to plough his own furrow, no longer harassed by wild red devils or union 'dinosaurs', as being wholly in command of the party underneath him, is considered a priceless asset. In these terms, the credibility of the New Labour project depends heavily on Blair's ability to persuade voters to trust him personally, to believe that he personifies the principles he preaches, that there is something in the values he promotes in which they can share and [from] which they can profit, too ... And every opinion poll suggests that trust is there.[60]

Blair's contract with the people was a corollary of Labour's own contract with him to secure victory. The party had ceded him discretionary licence to contest power at the level of national leadership. Whether or not the exact terms of this implicit pact were ever consciously understood, the consequences of the arrangement very quickly became evident following Labour's triumph on 1 May 1997.

The prime minister and 'the people'

On his accession to government, Blair lost no time in lecturing the inflated contingent of MPs on the reasons for their presence in Westminster and the role they were expected to fulfil:

> Be under no illusion. It was New Labour wot won it. Let us learn that lesson well. We ran for office as New Labour. We govern as New Labour. Remember, you are not here to enjoy the trappings of power but to do a job ... We are not the masters. The people are the masters. We are the servants of the people. We will never forget that.[61]

This became a recurrent theme of the New Labour administration. The retained linkage between the electorate and the government was expressed in a variety of guises. References were made to the New Labour government's insistence upon governing in the interests of the people. The 'people's priorities' and the 'people's concerns' were incessantly claimed to animate the Blair administration. The National Lottery was metamorphosed into the 'People's Lottery'[62] that dealt with the people's money. It needed to reflect popular causes more accurately and to ensure that 'the people ... get more out of it'.[63] Similarly, Blair's prospectus for EU reform would be instrumental in creating a more responsive and democratic 'people's Europe'. In an interview for *The Mirror*,[64] for example, the new prime minister used the term 'people' on no fewer than twenty-seven occasions.

New Labour's mandate was explicitly equated with the project's declared rationale of a non-class-based and non-adversarial politics, that would be geared to an all-inclusive pluralism. Sometimes, the term 'people' would denote a sense of immediacy and accessibility. 'People come through my door from all walks of life', claimed Blair. 'The difference between this Government and the last is that we see all the people, not just a section, and we make decisions in the national rather than a sectional interest.'[65] Blair felt 'humility at people's trust in me'[66] and asserted the need to sustain the public's confidence in his premiership. 'I should always remember people regard the Prime Minister as their person.'[67] At other times, the 'people' word was used to provide 'a favourably populist cloak over any Government idea'.[68] New Labour conspicuously sought to pursue people-based policies that reflected popular values and beliefs. It also tried to fuse content with method by opening up important constitutional change to referendums, by endorsing devolution and by establishing a more rights-based culture through the incorporation of the European Convention on Human Rights into British law. Such aims could be construed not only as being populist in substance but also as involving a 'transfer of power away from the political and civil service elite to the people themselves'.[69]

The repeated invocation of the people continued to be a distinguishing characteristic of the Blair premiership. The modernisation project of New Labour had been based upon infusing the party with a populist frame of reference. Now Blair continually reminded the party of its instrumental role and the need to condition its formal electoral legitimacy with a *de facto* nexus between the leadership and its defining conception of public choice and popular values. The Labour party was the beneficiary of a landslide victory. It had achieved the largest majority of seats since 1935. And yet, many questions remained unanswered. How decisive had the win been? What mandate had been secured? Which ideas and convictions had been endorsed by the electorate? For Blair, the victory was only a provisional one. The battle with the party and its past, together with the battle for the definition of Labour values, would continue after the amnesty of the pre-election period. It was necessary for the leadership to prolong the discipline of the election and to extend its extra-curricular cultivation of populist politics – i.e. to keep reminding the party of the people and of the leadership's proven proximity to them.

The priority for Blair was that the 'advice I shall try to follow is the advice most in tune with [the] instincts of the people'.[70] The space created by Blair between the leadership and the party, which had served the public consumption of New Labour so effectively, was extended into government. The dynamic became increasingly conspicuous, both because of the intense publicity generated by the new regime and because of the leadership's determination not to become sucked into the internal obscurities of party management at the expense of his public credentials. Blair's view of the party was that of a supportive structure for the New Labour mandate. It was not accepted as having an independent public legitimacy separate from that of the leadership. As a result, the space between the leadership and the mass of the parliamentary party which had been evident to those in the Labour party during the 1994–97 period of opposition now became clear to a much wider audience as it was transposed into government. 'For someone so attuned to the nation', Blair remained conspicuously and 'strangely isolated within his own party.'[71] One of Blair's close associates encapsulated the relationship: 'he is *leader* of his party, but not *of* it.'[72] Blair had 'none of the tribal instincts of a party born of an earlier struggle between working and capitalist classes'. Consequently, he 'project[ed] himself as a national rather than a partisan leader'.[73] After a year in office, Steve Richards concluded: 'Blair is above party because he chooses to be so.'[74]

A premier apart

The premium placed upon radical change and proactive government by Labour's prime minister led to a discernible impatience with the established institutions of political intermediation, collective decision making and consensus building. For a prime minister with a large parliamentary majority, high public approval ratings and a discredited opposition, the incentive was to attend to the immediate needs of the modernisation programme for Britain. Blair believed that his populist politics accounted for Labour's victory and defined the nature of both the mandate and the party's right to govern. Blair's outsider status and his remoteness from the party's instincts and traditions, therefore, were not seen as a problem requiring action so much as an operational concomitant of the New Labour project. The unconventional and iconoclastic nature of Blair's reconfiguration of the party in opposition was sustained in government. He made it clear at the outset that he would not rely upon the parliamentary party for information on New Labour's constituency. He not only took the political risk of proposing the establishment of a 5,000-strong focus group (the 'people's panel') to gauge public reaction to Labour policy proposals and government performance, but had the political strength to secure it. The party's traditional machinery for policy formulation was largely disengaged. While the party's NEC sought to tighten party management by restricting dissent and preventing any resumption of open textured policy schisms, the leadership announced plans to transform the party conference into a more leadership-conscious event by reducing its scope to make a public exhibition of internal party dissent.

At the same time, Blair established a profusion of task forces and advisory groups to provide policy reviews and to prepare the ground for policy innovations. Many of them were conspicuous for the inclusion of representatives of the business sector. The drive to employ the best and brightest in the style of a US administration led to a series of controversial appointments in which businessmen were allocated senior posts in the government. For example, Sir David Simon[75] became Minister for Trade and Competitiveness in Europe and David Sainsbury[76] was appointed Parliamentary Under-Secretary of State at the Department of Trade and Industry. Most controversially, Gus Macdonald,[77] who was chairman of the Scottish Media Group and not even a member of the Labour party, was made Minister for Industry at the Scottish Office. Transfers from industry and commerce to government had not been unknown in previous administrations. But with the admission into government of such high profile figures from the private sector, combined with the estimated infusion of 350 business leaders into Labour's advisory structure,[78] it was evident that 'the scale [was] wholly different'[79] to past practice. It suggested an outsider prime minister deliberately going outside the customary patterns of recruitment to nominate outsider ministers. The leadership appeared wholly disinterested in the constitutional argument that by 'looking outside parliament for ministers, Labour [was] telling the nation that the body to whom they send their representatives no longer matters'.[80] The underlying subtext to the large pool of Labour MPs who were available for executive work was that as politics had become a professionalised career, few could be regarded as having the requisite background or experience in management to be considered serious candidates for departmental posts. Blair appeared on the one hand to boost their careers through the establishment of a New Labour government with an intake of 262 new MPs. At the same time, his selection priorities to the executive demonstrated that, for most Labour members, their political careers had reached a dead end in respect to any foreseeable transition to ministerial status.

The sidelining of the PLP was made even more painfully evident in the prime minister's cultivation of a working partnership with the Liberal party. The suspicion that Blair was working towards a realignment of the centre-left in which New Labour would effectively fuse with the Lib Dems was further fuelled by Paddy Ashdown and other senior figures in his party regularly entering Number 10 to attend cabinet committee meetings on constitutional reform. On 11 November 1998, the two leaders pledged even further co-operation by disclosing that the merits of the cabinet committee on constitutional reform would be extended to cover other policy areas, including education, health, welfare and Europe. The joint statement referred to the move as 'an important step in challenging the destructive tribalism that can afflict British politics'.[81] To many Labour MPs, it was precisely Blair's lack of tribalism that distinguished him from the mass of his party colleagues and which to them constituted a serious problem. Like Margaret Thatcher, Tony Blair was not temperamentally disposed to the requirements and accoutrements of party contact.

> Mr Blair, for his part, is known to loathe party business, which he delegates to Margaret McDonagh [General Secretary of the Labour party] and to Sally Morgan [Blair's political secretary]. His attention span for party matters is famously short – so much so that there are stories of him whispering to Ms Morgan every five minutes at meetings on internal matters, 'Can I go yet?'[82]

Aware of the prime minister's remoteness from the party and conscious of Blair's belief in its marginal significance in relation to the 'big picture', many MPs from the Old Labour heartlands in Scotland and Wales came to the conclusion that their political futures lay in the devolved bodies of the Scottish parliament and the Welsh assembly.

The ramifications of Blair's spatial leadership were not limited to the PLP. The prime minister was regularly accused of treating the House of Commons with contempt. At a general level, the case was built upon a series of charges. These included the reduction of Prime Minister's Questions from two sessions to one; the breach in the convention that Budget details should not be leaked prior to their announcement in the House of Commons; the use of referendums as 'part of the legitimisation of change',[83] determining in effect the political outcome of key policy issues; the administration's intolerance towards the House of Lords' powers of obstruction; and the infusion of unelected advisors into government. At a personal level, Blair was criticised for not taking his prime ministerial duties to parliament as seriously as he should have done. To Peter Riddell, it was clear that Blair and his followers operated on the assumption that parliament was no longer a central force of political significance: 'The Blairites ... tend to be dismissive of Parliament, for which most have little feel or liking. They see all its many weaknesses and view it as incidental to the project.'[84] As a consequence, Riddell observed that '[m]any ministers, particularly younger Blairites, spend little time in the House'.[85] Blair himself was a conspicuously infrequent attender in the chamber. In the first 15 months of his administration, for example, the prime minister voted in only 19 of 353 House of Commons votes. Between 20 May 1997 and 1 December 1997, he did not record a single vote. Furthermore, Blair was absent on almost every key vote pertaining to key government policy pledges (e.g. NHS reforms, school standards legislation, the Bills authorising referendums on Scottish and Welsh devolution, the crime and disorder enactment,[86] and the ban on hand guns). His low profile extended to other areas of House of Commons activity. It was very rare for the prime minister to open a major debate in the House or even to sit on the front bench in support of ministerial colleagues. His interest in policy did not extend to engaging in its promotion in the parliamentary arena.

Similar complaints relating to prime ministerial detachment were made in reference to the cabinet. It was common knowledge that cabinet meetings would often last for no longer than half an hour, and even then they would deviate from the agenda. The widespread view was that the Blairites believed the cabinet to be an inadequate and superfluous decision-making body. Peter Riddell observed the changes at close hand:

> [Blair] has little contact with most ministers, either socially or politically ... Cabinet meetings rarely have even a marginal political significance: some meetings chaired by him meet infrequently and much business is done in informal groups, or via messengers from the Downing Street Policy Unit. Consequently, there is little sense of the collective, or any collegial spirit.[87]

Dennis Kavanagh and Anthony Seldon draw attention to Blair's early dependence upon a personal team of advisors. 'There was something akin to a US presidency in the importation of his own staff'[88] at Number 10. This reliance upon a corps of trusted advisors and the corresponding 'neglect of the cabinet' promoted concerns at the very outset that the prime minister was 'in danger of becoming isolated from his senior colleagues'.[89] If such isolation was deemed to be a problem to analysts, commentators and political participants, it did not appear to constitute a source of the slightest anxiety to the prime minister. This attitude on the part of Blair towards his cabinet, his party and the House of Commons was highly revealing. It betrayed an underlying conviction that the New Labour project needed not merely to facilitate the normal political and party structures but, wherever possible, to transcend them. They were to be supplemented and at times superseded by alternative sources of mobilisation, communication and authority based upon the leadership's cultivation of a direct and extra-institutional dimension of public representation.

Blair at a distance

Tony Blair raised the concept and application of spatial leadership to unprecedented levels of development and sophistication. He equated space with the existence of a functioning nexus linking the leadership with the public's needs, impulses and values. The public display of such space was a necessary expression of its presence and significance. It also constituted an instrument that provided him both with discretionary licence to exercise leadership and an exterior constituency affording leverage upon party organisations and government institutions. Blair needed the leadership's dimension of public engagement to remain idiosyncratic and peculiar to him. He could not allow it to become subsumed or assimilated into the party's sources of authority or even made reducible to his own government's mandate. Blair was an outsider as opposition leader. He remained an outsider as prime minister. In many ways, New Labour opposition and New Labour government became indistinguishable from one another. Blair aimed to provide a continuity of populist energy and irreverence, in which the leader's role of receptor and expositor of public concerns, anxieties and irritations over imposing structures would remain intact.

Given the inclination of previous Labour governments to disintegrate into internecine conflict and sectional division, and given the inconclusive nature of New Labour's victory over Old Labour, Blair was committed to keeping the party in a heightened state of mobilisation. The prime minister was intent upon maintaining the same level of discipline that he had secured during the pre-election campaign when he had been leader of the opposition. Blair resisted any reduction in his campaigning distance from the party. He refused to become embroiled in party management and was committed to avoiding public rows over party rebellions. Always mindful of the cautionary tale of John Major's torrid experiences of chronic party disorder and debilitating leadership crises, Blair stood firm for the 'millions of people who depend upon our party to protect them and to promote their interests'.[90] He would not 'return to the factionalism, navel-gazing or feuding of the Seventies and Eighties'.[91] The requirement was for a 'modern disciplined party with a strong centre'.[92] The responsibility of government was a challenge, which Blair was determined New Labour would meet by giving him the room to provide a public exercise of leadership. 'It takes resolve, determination and real grip and a sense of purpose and direction. That is what New Labour offers. That is what I offer. Strong leadership. Real leadership. Leadership the country wants and deserves.'[93] Blair repeatedly drew attention to the existence of hard choices requiring tough decisions by a strong leader.

Old Labour values were acceptable, albeit in an interpretive framework determined by the prime minister. But, as Blair made clear, Old Labour policies would not be on the agenda: 'Much of the deregulation and privatisation that took place in the 1980s was necessary ... Big government is dead. The days of tax and spend are gone.'[94] For the benefit of his own leadership, Blair required the kind of party support that rendered the party anonymous and which did not disturb his capacity to provide a personal and largely non-partisan appeal on behalf of his party. Public trust in New Labour was based upon the trust in the leadership's construction of the party and government, and ultimately in the leadership's power to give material effect to its own construction. Party unity needed to be maintained, therefore, in order to sustain the leadership's working principle that it was dedicated to a unified public interest. By making the stated necessity of re-election and a second term of office the overriding objective of his administration at the very outset of his premiership, Blair established a state of permanent election that would maximise his chances of maintaining the effectiveness of his brand of spatial leadership.

The Blair premiership occasioned change but by the same token it also signified change. It revealed the capacity of the British system to accommodate a leadership that relied so explicitly upon a public dimension. The range and penetration of Blair's spatial leadership were built upon the precedents established by his immediate predecessors and especially those provided by Margaret Thatcher. However, unlike Thatcher, whose ideological zeal and confrontational style made her iconoclasm seem direct and institutional, Blair gave the appearance of breaking the rules inadvertently, as if they were no longer relevant. His emphasis upon pluralism, inclusiveness and necessary modernisation gave the impression that previous traditions and conventions had simply been supplanted. His engaging style effectively disarmed the opposition against constitutional reform. His public trustworthiness lowered resistance to regarding change as nothing other than inevitable. As Blair confounded, or rather transcended, the rules, he baffled observers and participants alike. To Peter Riddell, for example, it was beyond anything he had experienced before as a political analyst:

> Tony Blair has become the most unusual Prime Minister this century. He makes Margaret Thatcher look almost conventional. Mr Blair is undoubtedly a subtle and effective politician, able to sense and articulate the public mood. But his

> successes have been despite a lack of interest in many of the political arts that Prime Ministers have regarded as essential. It is almost as if Mr Blair exists outside normal politics. He has little contact with most ministers.[95]

On occasions, the confusion and incomprehension would only be resolved through criticism and complaint. Blair was accused of attempting to depoliticise politics, to inaugurate a government by rolling referendum, and to using the people as a political device that ran 'against the grain of British life and the British constitution'.[96] Dangers were alluded to; and claims were made concerning the aberrational nature of Blair's departures from standard political practices. But Blair remained elusive. The leadership's view was that after eighteen years of one-party rule, and with Britain approaching the end of the century, some reconfiguration of political institutions and activity was to be expected.

In devising New Labour and transposing its properties into government, Tony Blair had developed and refined the politics of public identity to new levels of sophistication and political leverage. In doing so, he underlined the presence of structural forces, political dynamics and currents of opinion that supported the projection of such leadership. The style of these developments has threatened, and continues to threaten, the settled order of political relationships. In this respect, critics are right to be alert to the problems of the unknown because it is the normal frames of reference that have been so decisively and irreverently disturbed. The nature and implications of this disturbance will be the subject of further analysis in due course, but at this point it is necessary to change the focus of inquiry. This study has examined the incentives, techniques and styles of outsider politics and spatial leadership, which are predominantly bottom up in character and where the emphasis is on the receptivity to, and usage of, public opinion. It is now time to turn to the other half of the relationship. Namely, the essentially top-down nature of those leadership strategies associated with the active projection of leaders into the public sphere, where the emphasis lay with the construction and maintenance of a tangible connection rather than with abstract claims.

Notes

1 David Marquand and Anthony Wright, 'The Euro-option', *New Statesman and Society*, 1 September 1995.
2 'A mandarin for all seasons', *Sunday Telegraph*, 19 July 1992.
3 Simon Jenkins, 'The conservative party', *The Times*, 29 September 1993.
4 Philip Stephens, 'Testing journey to the party's roots', *Financial Times*, 1–2 October 1994.
5 BBC Radio 4, *Desert Island Discs*, 24 November 1996.

6 Philp Gould, *The Unfinished Revolution: How the Modernisers Saved the Labour Party* (London, Little Brown, 1998), pp. 216, 218.
7 'New Labour, New Britain', leader's speech to the Labour party conference 1994, in Tony Blair, *New Britain: My Vision of a Young Country* (London, Fourth Estate, 1996), p. 35.
8 'New Labour, New Britain', p. 35.
9 'New Labour, New Britain', pp. 46–7.
10 'New Labour, New Britain', p. 47.
11 'New Labour, new Britain', p. 49.
12 Clause Four of the Labour party constitution states the following as an aim: 'To secure for workers by hand and brain the fruits of their labour by the common ownership of the means of production, distribution and exchange.'
13 'Blair triumphant', *New Statesman and Society*, 28 April 1995.
14 John Rentoul, *Tony Blair*, rev. edn (London, Warner, 1996), pp. 408–9.
15 Tony Blair, 'True story of the wilderness years', *The Observer*, 17 December 1995.
16 Interview with Tony Blair, *New Statesman and Society*, 15 July 1994.
17 Quoted in Rentoul, *Tony Blair*, p. 401.
18 Speech to the Labour party conference 1996, *The Independent*, 2 October 1996.
19 Speech to the Labour party conference 1996, *The Independent*, 2 October 1996.
20 'New Labour, New Britain', p. 40.
21 Paul Anderson and Nyta Mann, *Safety First: The Making of New Labour* (London, Granta, 1997), pp. 36–45.
22 'New Labour, New Britain', p. 36.
23 'Hopes of winning friends', Tony Blair interview with Richard Lambert, Philip Stephens and Robert Preston, *Financial Times*, 16 January 1997.
24 'New Labour, New Britain', p. 45.
25 'The Young Country', leader's speech to the Labour party conference 1995, in Blair, *New Britain*, p. 68.
26 Gould, *The Unfinished Revolution*, p. 212.
27 Gould, *The Unfinished Revolution*, p. 212.
28 Gould, *The Unfinished Revolution*, p. 212.
29 'The Young Country', p. 68.
30 'The Young Country', p. 69.
31 'The Young Country', p. 70.
32 Speech to the Labour party conference 1996, *The Times*, 2 October 1996.
33 'New Labour, New Britain', p. 40.
34 Speech to the Labour party conference 1996, *The Times*, 2 October 1996.
35 Speech to the Labour Party Conference 1996, *The Times*, 2 October 1996.
36 'The Young Country', p. 64.
37 'New Labour, New Britain', p. 37.
38 Tony Blair, 'Is Labour the true heir of Thatcher?', *The Times*, 17 July 1995. See also Tony Blair, 'How I have learnt from Mrs Thatcher', *Daily Telegraph*, 30 August 1996.
39 Blair, 'Is Labour the true heir of Thatcher?'.
40 Blair, 'Is Labour the true heir of Thatcher?'.
41 Blair, 'Is Labour the true heir of Thatcher?'.
42 Blair, 'Is Labour the true heir of Thatcher?'.
43 Peter Mandelson and Roger Liddle, *The Blair Revolution: Can New Labour Deliver?* (London, Faber and Faber, 1996), p. 236.
44 Mandelson and Liddle, *The Blair Revolution*, p. 237.

45 Mandelson and Liddle, *The Blair Revolution*, p. 238.
46 Matthew Symonds, 'The toughness Blair and Thatcher share', *The Independent*, 22 June 1994.
47 Symonds, 'The toughness Blair and Thatcher share'.
48 David Marquand, 'The Blair paradox', *Prospect*, May 1998.
49 Marquand, 'The Blair paradox'.
50 Mandelson and Liddle, *The Blair Revolution*, p. 238.
51 Siôn Simon, 'The party's new battle cry', *Daily Telegraph*, 29 March 1999.
52 Hugo Young, 'A vision for the future', *The Guardian*, 17 January 1998.
53 Hugo Young, 'Only Blair dares to admit that the good old days are gone', *The Guardian*, 16 June 1994.
54 Sarah Baxter, 'Hard lesson for the hard left in Blair's New Labour party', *Sunday Times*, 26 February 1995.
55 BBC Radio 4, *Desert Island Discs*, 24 November 1996.
56 Tony Blair, 'Power to the people must be our aim', *The Independent*, 7 February 1996.
57 'Labour's awkward one-man band', *The Economist*, 28 September 1996.
58 Speech to the Labour party conference 1996, *The Times*, 2 October 1996.
59 Speech to the Labour party conference 1996, *The Times*, 2 October 1996.
60 Dave Hill, 'Action man', *New Statesman*, 29 September 1995.
61 Quoted in Michael White, 'We are servants – Blair', *The Guardian*, 8 May 1997.
62 'The Young Country', p. 70.
63 'The Young Country', p. 70.
64 The Mirror, 29 July 1997.
65 Quoted in Patrick Wintour, 'Tony – spend the money', *The Observer*, 23 November 1997.
66 Quoted in Christopher Howse, 'The people's person', *Daily Telegraph*, 30 July 1997.
67 Quoted in Howse, 'The people's person'.
68 Peter Riddell, 'People who don't need people', *The Times*, 8 December 1997.
69 Vernon Bogdanor, 'Why Fabianism could not survive', *New Statesman*, 7 August 1998.
70 Quoted in Isabel Hilton, 'Beware a leader who talks about the people', *The Guardian*, 30 July 1997.
71 Philip Stephens, 'Rip it up and start again', *Financial Times*, 25–26 April 1998.
72 Quoted in Stephens, 'Rip it up and start again'.
73 Philip Stephens, 'Politician as weather-maker', *Financial Times*, 24 December 1997.
74 Steve Richards, 'You got what you deserve', *New Statesman*, 1 May 1998.
75 Sir David Simon was subsequently ennobled. He took the title Lord Simon of Highbury.
76 David Sainsbury was subsequently ennobled. He took the title Lord Sainsbury of Turville.
77 Gus Macdonald was subsequently ennobled. He took the title Lord Macdonald of Tradeston.
78 The estimate of 350 business leaders was provided by a study issued by Cranfield University. See Donald Dewer, 'The judgements of Scottish business are what matter', *The Independent*, 6 August 1998.
79 Peter Riddell, Non-members welcome', *The Times*, 10 August 1998.
80 Jonathan Freedland, 'We've got Blair and his chums, so we don't need elections anymore', *The Guardian*, 5 August 1998.
81 Quoted in Andrew Grice, 'Lib Dems to make government policy', *The Independent*, 12 November 1998.

82 Anne McElvoy, 'No wonder Tony is a control freak', *The Independent*, 22 November 1998.
83 Peter Riddell, *Parliament Under Pressure* (London, Victor Gollanz, 1998), p. 120.
84 Peter Riddell, 'RIP, Cabinet government', *The Times*, 5 January 1998.
85 Peter Riddell, 'Does anybody listen to MPs?', *The Times*, 23 March 1998.
86 Apart from the clause relating to the age of homosexual age of consent.
87 Peter Riddell, 'We're missing you, Mr Blair', *The Times*, 8 June 1998.
88 Dennis Kavanagh and Anthony Seldon, *The Powers Behind the Prime Minister: The Hidden Influence of Number Ten* (London, HarperCollins, 1999), p. 286.
89 Kavanagh and Seldon, *The Powers Behind the Prime Minister*, p. 289.
90 Tony Blair, 'If control freakery means strong leadership, then I plead guilty', *The Independent*, 20 November 1998.
91 Blair, 'If control freakery means strong leadership, then I plead guilty'.
92 Blair, 'If control freakery means strong leadership, then I plead guilty'.
93 Tony Blair, 'My party is more ideologically united than I've ever known it', *The Independent*, 8 January 1999.
94 Tony Blair, 'Speaking Mandarin', *Prospect*, December 1998.
95 Riddell, 'We're missing you, Mr Blair'.
96 Hugo Young, 'Who governs Britain: parliament or people?', *The Guardian*, 2 October 1997.

CHAPTER 5

Going public and getting personal in the United States

In the United States, commentators have repeatedly drawn attention to the way that presidents have sought to compensate for their weaknesses in Washington by appealing directly to the public for support. Presidents have exploited the individuality of the office to project themselves as the focal embodiments of popular concern and the public interest. In 'going public',[1] it is claimed that presidents generate a personal following in the country which displaces the traditional need for political negotiation and accommodation within Washington. A White House faced with the prospect of fishing for the votes of hundreds of congressional minnows can turn to the publicity resources of the Oval Office to create public support for a proposal before it is discussed with Congress. If successful in this, a president need not bargain for votes; instead, members of Congress are forced to support a White House proposal by the tide of public opinion that the president has created.[2]

The increased incidence of public appearances, televised addresses and political trips has massively enhanced the presidency's centrality in American politics. It has reached the point where it is claimed that presidents are able not just to 'speak directly to voters over the heads of Congress and organised interests' but to 'overrule the influence of these traditional adversaries'.[3] This in turn has projected presidents into 'the limelight of American politics, and citizens come naturally to organise their political thinking and focus their hopes for the future around the White House'.[4] The availability of the means to engage in individual outreach through the mass media, together with the generated imperatives to cultivate public links and maintain a conspicuous pre-eminence to national audiences, have shifted the priorities, objectives and strategies of the contemporary presidency to a point where the office is commonly referred to as the 'public presidency'.

Going public

In the view of Samuel Kernell, the public presidency represents a systemic change in American politics. It marks a transition from a state of 'institutionalised pluralism' to one of 'individualised pluralism'.[5] Presidents used to be in a position to negotiate alliances and build coalitions on the basis of stable power blocs (e.g. the 'conservative coalition', sectional and regional groupings, party leaders, congressional committee 'barons', a manageable media and a limited number of 'big interests'). The position now is far more unstable, fluid and multilateral in nature. With the penetration of the federal government into so many spheres of society and the rise of issues that cross-cut traditional political allegiances – together with the decentralisation of Congress and the erosion of parties – presidents have had to shift the balance of persuasive strategies from private accommodation and more towards public salesmanship. Presidents have increasingly followed this route as a way of countering the smaller but less disciplined and more intransigent power centres that have arisen in Washington. 'Going public' has become a means of assembling temporary coalitions from splintered interests and groupings on an issue-by-issue basis.

As a consequence of this development, presidents are now more actively involved in using their positions to generate support for their political objectives through direct and more undifferentiated appeals to the public. Just as parties have weakened in organisation and support, so politicians run individualised, candidate-centred campaigns and operate within a context of weakened hierarchies and plural networks of political exchange. Kernell points out that it is precisely this sensitivity to public opinion on the part of elected representatives in Washington that makes them vulnerable to changes in popular mood and to presidential influence: 'By campaigning around the country, the president can create uncertainty for them while offering refuge in their support for his policies. By giving up bargaining with individuals and instead working with politicians *en masse*, a president achieves comparative economy.'[6] The scale and depth of this trend towards a 'public presidency' have been so dramatic that it is widely regarded as being one of the most important and revealing developments in recent American politics. In the words of James Pfiffner, 'contemporary presidents have the capacity to reach the public in ways that could not have been imagined by earlier presidents, and they have consciously formed their strategies of governing to exploit that capacity'.[7] Ryan Barilleaux makes the same point but in more unequivocal terms: 'contemporary presidents tend to rely heavily on public politics to govern'.[8]

The 'public presidency' thesis does not claim that 'going public' has replaced the need for bargaining and negotiation, or that good public approval ratings are in themselves sufficient for presidential success in securing legislation. 'Public approval gives the president leverage, not control.'[9] The Reagan presidency, for example, was renowned for its disjunction between high approval ratings for the president and high disapproval ratings for his policy positions. But without leverage and without a capacity to shape the agenda and keep opinion focused upon it, presidents would find their position untenable. Contemporary presidents need to reach out and cultivate an 'interpretive community' in order to marshal the kind of collaborative media support necessary for effective leadership.[10] The resort to public presentation is significant for the extent to which it reveals that presidents no longer have a reliable infrastructure of influence within Washington. In relation to public projection, 'a president may not have a choice, either because of media demands or because he has so few other advantages'.[11] As Charles Jones points out, presidents do not so much go public as simply exist in a concentrated public domain: '[P]residents *are* public. They cannot fail to be the major political figure, given their treatment by modern-day media.'[12] As a consequence, they are constantly watched, measured and appraised.

Successful presidents turn this imposition into a resource to optimise their political position. In this context, 'going public' may not be explicitly related to a political agenda or to a legislative initiative. Instead, it should be seen as a device in maximising the channels of communication and the access points to public exchange. The route-ways have to be maintained for protective and preventative reasons. They afford opportunities for preserving the basis of leadership trust, for limiting the negative effects of critical news comment, and for preventing a loss of political initiative. To a president, 'going public' may not in itself be a solution, but a failure to 'go public' will certainly compound all existing problems. As a result, in spite of the 'history of the failures and frustrations of the public presidency', Bill Clinton epitomised the contemporary presidential predicament by insisting upon assigning 'strategic primacy to communications'.[13]

Presidents use an array of techniques to establish the office in the public realm and to present White House policies, positions and priorities to the wider constituencies outside Washington. Presidential conferences, addresses, interviews, briefings and ceremonial occasions are all established means by which presidents can forge links with national audiences. But presidents are not limited to this stimulus–response dynamic in projecting themselves into the public consciousness. They are assisted by the professional and market-based demands of the mass media that continually gravitate towards the president to provide a focus for national newsgathering. The basis of the connection is one of mutual need and support. The media not only need to report the news, they need news to report and the presidency is in a unique position to satisfy both requirements. The presidency is geared to satisfying the voracious demands for comments, briefings, speeches, interviews and pictures. This helps the presidency to be both the centre of government communications and the most newsworthy subject of popular interest. As a consequence, the White House is used by the media 'almost automatically because the president is looked at as the great explainer and a personified demonstration of today in government'.[14] The president, for his part, is similarly dependent upon the news organisations. They can supply him with information and advice on matters of current public concern. They can inform him about issues and conflicts inside his own administration, the progress or otherwise of his policy proposals, and the condition of his political status in Washington. More significantly, they can provide him with his point of contact with the public. They furnish him with the lines of communication through which he can convey his construction of world events and his interpretation of domestic needs. With the assistance of the electronic media, in particular, the president can carry his own news continuously to the public through the constant public exposure of his activities as president.

The mass media occupy an intermediary and filtering position between government and the citizenry. As a consequence, the relationship between the White House and the channels of political communication is one of paramount importance to any administration. The substance, agenda and tone of information provided by the news services will not only influence the professional standing of the president, but will also affect his public status and political capital. A high public standing can enhance the reputation of the whole administration for political, managerial and administrative competence. By the same token, if the media's disposition becomes critical then the whole process can work in reverse, to the president's detriment. News content or usage is rarely neutral in nature or effect. News coverage of the presidency can reflect and subsequently reinforce a cycle of economic performance or a trend in public opinion. The media can respond to a change in public attitudes and alter the terms of their reporting in such a way as to promote and reaffirm the shift. 'Low approval rating and negative media coverage feed each other, heightening the perception that the president is floundering, deepening the drumbeat of decline – dissolving one of his few persuasive resources, the notion that public opinion is on his side.'[15] It is for this reason that effective media management now ranks as a critical objective for any president. The status and power afforded to the Office of Communications, and to its director within the hierarchy of the White House, reflect the priority given to the cultivation of the media outreach in the contemporary presidency.[16] In effect, the Office of Communications has become the keeper of the presidential image in an environment where public appearance carries a host of political resonances.

'The great communicator'

Presidents have become more inclined and more adept at taking issues directly to arenas of public opinion. The White House has become increasingly dependent upon a climate of favourable public opinion to maximise its influence over the political agenda and to retain its authority in Washington. As a consequence of these developments, television has become an indispensable instrument of presidential politics. The impetus towards 'going public' impels contemporary presidents not merely to influence the editorial selection and treatment of news, but to cut out such filters altogether by expressly creating news events for television in which the imagery is more penetrative than the content. In doing so, they force broadcasting organisations both to prioritise items in their presentations, but more significantly to carry the event in an unmediated form as primarily a visual experience and, therefore, in the way it was designed to be received by the viewing consumer.

The Reagan White House set the standard in the concerted promotion of public image in the pursuit of presidential goals. It was part of an integrated strategy designed to structure the media's access to Reagan and to ensure that Reagan's messages reached the public, irrespective of the press corps' interest in them or its interpretation of their content.[17] The Reagan team was intent upon controlling and structuring media access to the president, in order both to preserve the coherence of the administration in general and to ensure the primacy of the White House's selected news theme for each particular day. The strategy was to gear news coverage of the administration on the president's own terms. In accordance with this strategy, the Reagan White House engaged in an exceptional tightening of the flow of government information. This included strict 'lines of the day' formats, random lie detector tests to counter the problem of leaks and an 'unprecedented degree of censorship on government officials'.[18] But the cornerstone of the White House strategy lay in restricting the media's relationship with the president to one where the emphasis would lay upon set-piece occasions in which the opportunities for unanticipated intrusions or for departures from the script were kept to an absolute minimum.

Television was the most effective medium through which to pursue these objectives.[19] It allowed Reagan to maximise the presidency's visibility and sense of immediacy in relation to the public. Television also commended itself for another reason. It was perfectly suited to Reagan's skills, experience and political predicament. His background in the cinema and visual arts had prepared him for politics in the television age, where complex argument could be displaced by visual associations, graphic assertions and sound bites.[20]

Kathleen Jamieson, in *Eloquence in an Electronic Age* (1988), points out that because 'television is a visual medium whose natural grammar is associative, a person adept at visualizing claims in dramatic capsules will be able to use television to short-circuit the audience's demand that those claims be dignified with evidence'.[21] Reagan had an instinctive grasp of how a leader could use television on its own terms and through its own grammar. The Reagan White House not only produced speeches with the compulsory verbal nuggets for the attention of the media's newscasts, but staged the speeches to provide them with a visual dimension.

Television permitted the Reagan White House to seize the initiative by providing the media with irresistible news events that featured the president engaged in a visual performance staged wherever possible in an evocative setting designed to blend into the substance of the message. This would provide a compounded subtext of competence, authority, history, statesmanship, idealism, patriotism, populism and national well being. The staging was chosen to co-ordinate with the message and to place it in a concentrated context of dramatised images. Such staging was designed to intensify the effect of the words to such an extent that it would supersede their meaning with the comparatively emotional effect of a visual experience. Ronald Reagan was extremely successful at 'synopsizing an important sentiment in memorable visual and verbal form on an appropriate stage so that it could be telegraphed to a national audience by the news media'.[22] For this reason, nationally televised speeches became the Reagan presidency's preferred form of public communication. 'Even if the speech or appearance of the moment did not include a direct appeal to voters to support the president's policies, the very context and structure of presidential appearances on television became a form of public politics.'[23]

The Reagan White House exemplified the importance of the visual element in public politics and the need for it to be cultivated and protected at the expense of other elements. In the words of Michael Deaver, who was President Reagan's senior media advisor and Deputy Chief of Staff in his first administration, 'TV has changed everything so much. The visual image is all important.'[24] It was Deaver who prohibited the distraction of reporters' questions at photo opportunities. It was Deaver who intensified the White House's inclination to favour camera crews over reporters in respect to media access. And it was Deaver who set the standards for the attention to detail in the effective staging of presidential appearances that would stamp the imparted message directly in the minds of the viewing public.[25] Michael Deaver's role in making Reagan into a 'sort of supreme anchorman whose public persona was the most important element of the Presidency'[26] is described by his White House Chief of Staff, Don Regan:

> It was Deaver's job to advise the President on image and image was what he talked about nearly all the time ... He saw – designed – each Presidential action as a one-minute or two-minute spot on the evening network news, or a picture on page one of the *Washington Post* or the *New York Times*, and conceived every Presidential appearance in terms of camera angles ... Every moment of every public appearance was scheduled, every word was scripted, every place where Reagan was expected to stand was chalked with toe marks.[27]

In highlighting the penetrative properties of organised image and word through television in particular, the presidency of Ronald Reagan and the activities of his successors have raised an awareness of the general potential and the underlying implications of the 'public presidency' in the American polity. Scholars and commentators do not question the existence of the phenomenon, so much as raise questions over its significance and express anxiety over its wider consequences. Bruce Miroff, for example, points to the way that presidents have derogated the substance of leadership into a derivative of public spectacle in which actions are meaningful 'not for what they achieve but for what they signify'.[28] To Miroff, spectacles imply a passive audience whose attention is concentrated upon a central character engaged in an emblematic action designed to appeal to the senses of the onlookers rather than to their reason. Because presidents are increasingly the subject of excessive and contradictory expectations, they use their centrality in the political process in order to 'turn to the gestures of spectacle to satisfy their audience'.[29] If the spectacles are correctly orchestrated to magnify the appropriate qualities in the individual president, gesture can be made to supersede fact and accomplishment. Miroff believes that the Reagan administration exemplified the extent to which deliberately crafted symbolism on a mass scale can deflect the critical faculties and suffuse the president in benevolent affection devoid of policy content. Consequently, 'the Reagan presidency largely floated above the consequences of its flawed processes or failed policies, secure in the brilliant glow of its successful spectacles'.[30] As the 'moving synoptic moment ... replaced the eloquent speech'[31] of reason, analysis and argument, Reagan revealed the vulnerability of modern leadership to the sensory effects of television upon the public mind. In the view of Charles Dunn and David Woodward, Reagan's style matched his environment to perfection: 'The political skills of an impressionist painter in the Oval Office beautifully coincided with the dictates of the electronic media that rewards style over substance and symbolic impression over substantive impact.'[32]

Television helps to shape the categories of popular political judgement in accordance with television's own properties as a communications medium.

It encourages people to think not only that they can adjudicate between different candidates, but that they can do so on the basis of the visual impressions conveyed through television. The sober reflection of professional reputations and policy ideas supposedly gives way to personal immediacy and accessibility. Accordingly, 'the gestures of ... spectacle are becoming more prevalent, and are coming to dominate the public's perception of leadership in the White House'.[33] Such assumptions have come to have a material effect in the United States. The emphasis on imagery and on its manipulation for political effect is now central to political leadership. For an aspiring president, 'going public' is therefore something of a honey-trap. In order to reach the public, it is necessary to be a willing captive of television and of what it can communicate to a mass audience. Political leadership has at the very least to be compatible with the disciplines and priorities of television. This means that for leadership to remain viable it must be continuously set in a public context by television and favourably assessed by the public through television.

Television is habituated to the characteristics of its audience and to the properties of its subject matter. For good or ill, it is imprisoned by its own market conditions and by the very nature of the medium in producing news as a visual experience of visual events. 'Whatever the political desires of its producers may be, television is at its best picturing the concrete and at its worst explaining the abstract. Political leaders are much more telegenic as tangible, individual faces, voices, and personalities than as members of abstractions such as political organizations or coalitions.'[34] As a result, leaders are also imprisoned by the need to demonstrate leadership through visual means by satisfying the intrinsic demands of a medium that relies on the depiction of news and events.

Other perspectives locate the influence of television and spectacle as part of a wider development towards the dissemination of presidential thoughts, words and beliefs as guiding points of governing influence. In a seminal article entitled 'The Rise of the Rhetorical Presidency',[35] James Ceaser *et al.* underline the importance, not so much of vision but of hearing in the presidency's penetration into the public's consciousness. They demonstrate that the use of popular rhetoric to attract public attention and to marshal political forces is a relatively recent phenomenon in the United States. It has replaced America's traditional fears of mass oratory and demagoguery, and challenged the country's republican ideal of enlightened reasoning through the medium of the written word. Popular rhetoric had its beginnings with Woodrow Wilson, whose progressivism embraced the idea that political leadership should aim for an activated public opinion in the search for a visionary new order. It gathered pace with advances in communications technology and the democratisation of party structures. By the 1980s, the United States had reached the point where 'popular or mass rhetoric, which presidents once employed only rarely, now serves as one of their principal tools in attempting to govern the nation'.[36]

A president is now expected as a matter of course to move the public, to inspire an allegiance to a common purpose, and to draw the ideals and interests of a mass public to his own person. As a consequence, presidents are increasingly measured by word rather than deed – or, more accurately, by the popular effects of words rather than by serious attempts at concrete achievements. To an increasing degree, presidential speech and action reflect the opinion that 'speaking is governing. Speeches are written to become the events to which people react no less than "real" events themselves.'[37] To James Ceaser *et al.*, the success of presidents in using rhetoric to enhance their own leadership threatens to make the mobilising property of rhetoric into a central objective of political leadership, and even into an end in its own right. In the same vein, they see the prospect of the public being deceived by its own receptivity to presidential rhetoric. In their view, this misplaced 'reliance on inspirational rhetoric to deal with the normal problems of politics ... leads us to neglect our principles for our hopes and to ignore the benefits and needs of our institutions for a fleeting sense of oneness with our leaders'.[38]

Getting personal

According to Samuel Kernell, presidents now *have* to publicise themselves, in order to maintain their public visibility as leaders and, thereby, their influence over other Washington decision makers. The need for personal projection is taken literally by presidents, who have increasingly used public appearances to reaffirm their centrality to government and to attract the news media's attention to presidential agendas (see Figure 5.1). In doing so, however, they risk reducing the skills of governing to the techniques of campaigning, and transforming policy into a device for substantiating the rhetoric of public statements. Moreover, the presidential strategies of public politics contribute further to the highly volatile nature of America's political agenda and its policy-making decisions. In essence, the 'effect of the president's own public standing on his ability to rally public opinion behind his policies exposes policy to extraneous and wholly unrelated events. Whatever affects the president's standing with the public will alter the prospects for those policies he sponsors.'[39] As a consequence, presidents have come to be obsessed not only with how the public view them, but with what can be done to influence still further the popular perceptions and

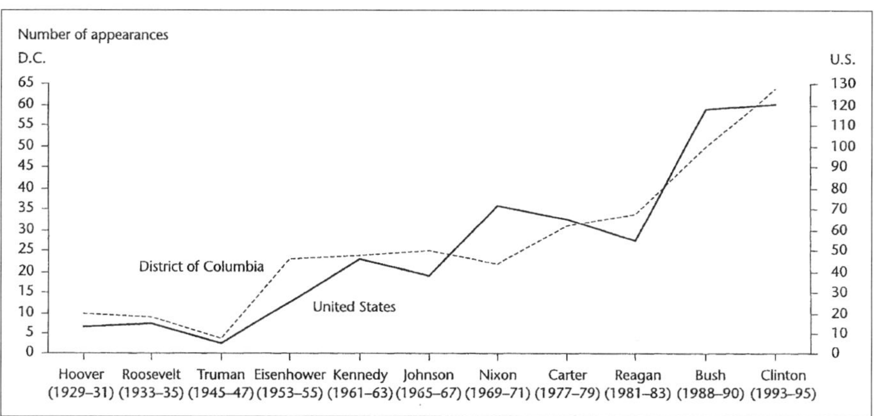

Figure 5.1 Public appearances by presidents, 1929–95 (yearly averages for the first three years of the first term). *Source*: Samuel Kernell, *Going Public: New Strategies of Presidential Leadership*, 3rd edn (Washington, DC, Congressional Quarterly Press, 1997), p. 118.

judgements of their political leadership. These preoccupations have brought in their wake the extensive, and at times exotic, forms of political marketing that have come to characterise presidential politics in the United States. Presidents and presidential candidates now seek first to ascertain the condition of public opinion and then to promote themselves as expressions of popular anxieties and aspirations, and as such the rightful beneficiaries of consumer choice.[40] In Richard Rose's view, as 'personal popularity is now a necessary, and perhaps sufficient condition for running for the presidency',[41] so public exposure between elections has become an integral feature of presidential politics. It can even be claimed that going public has become 'a political objective in itself' in which policies are 'judged, not so much in terms of their intrinsic character, as in terms of their suitability for political marketing'.[42]

It is no longer possible for presidents merely to use the public to complement their other leadership facilities. A president has to be popular. Moreover, he has to be prominently and enduringly popular. It is not enough for presidents simply to resort to the communications media in order to circumvent and weaken Washington's opposition to their policies. Presidents have to be incorporated into the media's handling of the news on a virtually permanent basis simply in order to maintain their position. Neither can presidents any longer merely claim to be the expression of the popular will. They need instead to be seen to be implanted physically within it. With this in mind, each president can do no other than to affirm and to intensify a process that progressively propels presidents into the public eye of television, while at the same time inducing them to adopt a style of leadership that will be amenable to the national networks. As television is such a potent vehicle of popular mobilisation, and as it inevitably defines the required characteristics of leadership in terms of its own visual and personal properties, so presidents are increasingly induced to exploit the mass media in order to cultivate a form of personalised leadership.

It can be argued that leadership is now the only satisfactory way of comprehending the relationship between a prominent politician and his or her public. Leadership is provided by leaders. Moreover, leadership is characterised and defined by the personal qualities of leaders. Television thrives in this logic because as a medium of people it can justify its interest in individuals by reference to 'leadership'. It can also justify its personalised treatment of politics and election campaigns through the same device. As television is people centred, leadership likewise becomes person centred, thereby giving television companies further encouragement to translate politics and government into projections of individual characteristics and personal conflict. The net effect is that presidents not only have to be popular; they have to be popular as highly individualised leaders. To be a leader, it is necessary to be seen first and foremost as an individual. To be solitary is the minimal precondition to being outstanding. Together the effect is to make the personalisation of the office the best, and perhaps the only, way of retaining the presidency's televised access to the public.

The need to attend to the media takes time and resources. For example, according to one of his aides, President Reagan spent two-thirds of his time in the White House on public relations and ceremony, and only a third on policy matters.[43] Much of the White House staff was also geared to what is called 'political outreach', by which the messages and images of the presidency are constantly disseminated to the public. All this effort is partly to ensure that the president's policies and objectives are properly conveyed. But it is also to maintain a high level of public prominence and public recognition for the brand name of the presidency. The accent is upon filling the many pathways to the public on a daily basis, in order to ensure that they are not filled by someone else. Presidents have to cultivate a continuous engagement with the public, which means that they have to maintain a capacity to displace other competitors for public attention. This is not an easy feat to achieve, as the American political system tends to arouse popular interest in potential presidential leaders. The electronic media's own inclination towards personalising political disputes gives particular encouragement to the cultivation of presidential aspirants. As a result, a successful president has to maximise his exposure simply to keep challenges at bay and to prevent the integrity of his administration from being compromised by the appearance of alternative leadership.

One of the most effective strategies employed by presidents, and one that they find growing incentives to use, is based less on content and more on style and suggestion. Because of the media's conjunction of personalisation with publicisation, and because many of the problems faced by presidents can be reduced to a lack of authority over competing power centres, presidents have sought to instil an impression which the media are particularly adept at conveying. The image is that of the man apart from the pack; the individual pitted against impersonal structures and forces; the tangible persona set against anonymous organisations. Presidents use the very intractability of Washington government as a counterpoint to their own individual distinction. This can have the effect of increasing a president's problems by making Washington even more intractable than before. But it can also ease them by confirming his publicly declared indictments of government and further enhancing the personal authority of his public touch.

The drives and disciplines of the presidency in such a media-centred system are often consistent with the incentives of 'spatial leadership'. They can complement and reinforce one another. Every successful contender for the presidency begins as an 'outsider' and knows the importance of protecting himself against the challenge of other potential leaders who, if nothing else, can always make substantial claims to being 'outsiders'. In the American system, the chief opposition to a presidency will come from a pack of prototype leaders competing, or preparing to compete, in a primary election campaign. Each will try to differentiate him- or herself from the others by making the personal and, therefore, televised qualities of leadership the main issue at stake. Each will seek to make a virtue out of the debilitating condition of being an outsider, which all of them emphatically are by the very status of being presidential contenders. In this setting, the president is always at risk of appearing to represent the archetypal Washington insider. It is in the presidential interest, therefore, to protect his personal leadership by flavouring his activities and speeches with a sense of populist distance and aggravation. By going public through television, a president can propagate the suggestion that he is in a sense separate from government. He can sit in the voters' living rooms looking in on government with them. Part of Reagan's genius as a communicator on television was the way he could use the medium to talk to a mass audience as though he were having an intimate conversation with each one of its members. The familiarity of Reagan's speaking style 'identified him with his audience. He could speak for us, in part because he spoke as we did.'[44] This skill made his detachment from government even more credible.

Presidential campaigning and the 'new media'

It was Ross Perot who first demonstrated in 1992 the political potential of new technologies and new media strategies. Perot had no inhibitions in casting the national news media as part of the political establishment which he was dedicated to confront at every level in his populist crusade. Perot explicitly tied the content of his message with the method of conveying it to his audience of disaffected and alienated voters. Instead of relying upon the peer review and editorial selection of the networks and news services, Perot dispensed with the effort of having to negotiate his candidacy through the established intermediary channels. As a consequence, he became the 'first candidate to discover that the structure of the news media had become so fragmented that it was possible to find alternative means of communicating with voters using channels in which he ... would have greater control over the message'.[45]

Perot concentrated upon 'soft format' television – primarily talk shows such as *Larry King Live*, *Good Morning America* and *Today*, where he would be given the maximum opportunity to relay his views and policies without interruption or critical response. It could even be claimed that his candidacy had been conceived in the spontaneity of *Larry King Live*, when the idea of running for president appeared to be implanted by the host during an interview on the country's problems. The bravura of a challenge involving an individual without a party or recognised supportive movement competing for the presidency matched the bravura of the CNN show in taking on the established news processes. Perot responded to the challenge by stating that he would be prepared to run for president if supporters placed his name on the ballot in all fifty states. When the viewers called his bluff and performed the role of a party or social movement in registering him on the ballots of the separate states, then he felt obliged to honour the obligation he established through cable television.

Perot's candidacy continued in the manner of its inception, with news conferences and stump speeches being kept to a minimum. The emphasis remained that of circumventing mainstream political journalism and the mainline news services in favour of purchased television time, talk show appearances, teleconferencing, televised 'town meetings' and presidential debates. Perot's challenge was designed to tap into the groundswell of voter discontent with the two established parties. It expressed a sense of amateur insurgency reflected in Perot's thirty minute 'infomercials' which constituted a conspicuous foil to the 'soundbite' culture and media manipulation that reached such extensive levels in the 1988 Republican presidential campaign. The campaign was also highly professional in identifying databases formed from caller-recognition phone systems and using them to compile demographic profiles by which to organise campaigns of voter mobilisation. This mix allowed Perot to make rapid inroads into the territory of the main parties. Voter volatility was now matched by organisational mutability with the sudden establishment of a viable challenger. 'In the wired nation, Perot did not need a history, a party, a platform or even a record of consistency.'[46] The segmented environment of the new media[47] permitted a disjointed candidacy, run by an 'anti-organization organization',[48] to become a serious force in American politics. Perot pitched himself against government, party and media hierarchies, and used the new media not merely to establish himself as an expression of popular resentment, but to break down the barriers of exclusion by relating his prominence to an active, material and direct process of public participation.

In 1992 the effect of the new media was felt by both mainline candidates, but especially by Bill Clinton. The Democratic front-runner was suddenly introduced to the negative effects of a media environment in which segmented players and satellite technology could lead to dramatic shifts in news agendas. For example, Gennifer Flowers's revelations of a long-standing affair with Clinton were originally published by *The Enquirer*, a down-market supermarket magazine. The story was picked up by *Star*, a tabloid newspaper that sought to move the story along the food chain to the major dailies and to the networks. When mainstream newspapers dismissed the story, Gennifer Flowers's sponsors at *Star* arranged for a news conference to force the pace. The networks agreed to cover it but only on the regular basis of broadcasting edited pieces to local affiliate stations and network bureaus. Unusually, the affiliates demanded the 'raw feed' of unmediated coverage for their own use and, in particular, for full 'real time' transmission. The downloading of the direct feed by satellite on the part of local stations gave the story a huge injection of public interest. It effectively overrode the filtration process of the elite corps of experienced political journalists which had initially sidelined the story as a junk product of the 'trash media'.

In breaking during the critical period of the New Hampshire primary, the Gennifer Flowers story threatened to derail the Clinton campaign. It led in turn to another example of devolved political coverage and diversified political journalism. In order to prevent any further slide in the polls, the Clinton campaign team purchased television time to organise an 'electronic town meeting' that linked radio stations to a direct feed of Clinton responding to unvetted questions from a live audience. The emphasis was on citizen interaction and public participation at the expense of candidate control and cultivated stagecraft. This exercise was backed up by a decision to book the candidate and his wife to appear on CBS's *60 Minutes* and face sustained questioning on his personal behaviour and values, and on the state of his marriage. Apart from being compelling television which helped to develop the character issue as a key category of political analysis and evaluation, the exercise demonstrated the extent to which old distinctions were giving way to a new melange of popular and political journalism. *60 Minutes* was a life-style magazine for CBS. Its methods and audience were not those of standard political programmes which feature hard news and critical analysis. Clinton's main defence, therefore, rested on a confessional performance broadcast on a 'soft format' show that catered for personal exposure and public visibility while allowing the candidate some measure of space and discretion to make his case in a non-adversarial setting. Just as media outlets had responded to a declining interest in news and analysis[49] with an increase in 'infotainment' shows, so the Clinton campaign provided a hybrid of its own. The candidate fused his political message with a format of viewer accessibility and personal revelation.

Initially, George Bush poured scorn on his challengers for resorting to the medium of 'some weird talk show'[50] but ultimately he too succumbed to *Larry King Live* and even to an interview on MTV.[51] The incumbent president had come to realise that talk shows had benefits for the individual voter. They provided an 'injection of spontaneity into the political dialogue' and permitted the electorate to 'examine the candidates for longer than a shrinking soundbite'.[52] By the end of the campaign, Perot, Clinton and Bush had made thirty-nine separate appearances on talk shows such as *Larry King Live*, *CBS This Morning*, *Good Morning America* and *Today*. In addition, the candidates made numerous appearances on cable channels, ranging from the more mainstream outlets such as CNN and C-SPAN to the more specialist series such as MTV, ESPN and the Nashville networks. The combination of politics and soft media formats was thought not only to have made candidates more accessible to the public but to have increased popular interest in the electoral process.

Perot's success in exploiting the non-news formats to make political appeals was copied by Clinton when he too appeared on *Larry King Live* in June 1992 as part of his strategy to project his background and character and to dissociate himself from politicians. Clinton went even further in enlisting what his campaign team termed the 'counterpolitical' media by appearing on MTV in a late night show hosted by the African-American, Arsenio Hall. In what has been described as 'perhaps the most startling iconography of the soft revolution',[53] Clinton wore sunglasses and played the saxophone in a performance that was 'information rich, making generational and racial points simultaneously. It also showed Clinton's clever reading of the subtexts of late-night television: his campaign was demographically sophisticated enough to realize that, for the purposes of its candidate, the middle-brow Jay Leno program would be too square and the ironist David Letterman's program too hip.'[54] Such appearances were widely considered to have had an effect on voter attitudes towards the candidates: 'Nearly half the voters on Election Day said that the candidates' appearances on television talk shows helped them decide how to vote. The talk shows especially influenced less frequent voters.'[55] Whenever a presidential candidate made an appearance on a talk show, there would be a strong public response to the call-in component. Given that participatory viewers tended to be in the younger age range, talk shows could be said to have provided a 'comfortable and hence appealing, sort of socialization to politics and, thereby, a precedent for subsequent forms of political communications'.[56]

Bill Clinton's strategy of combining serious policy discussion with popular culture was part of a highly effective campaign operation that succeeded in securing the presidency. The Clinton campaign managed not only to steer the party to a New Democrat position in the political centre, but also to confront the formidable electoral machine of a Republican party that had won five out of the previous six presidential elections. President Bush had achieved the highest approval levels on record in March 1991. His defeat, therefore, was seen as a testament to the proficiency and refinement of the Clinton campaign organisation, which rapidly acquired the reputation as a model exercise in creating and maintaining public support. It developed the usage of soft format television and radio appearances and engaged in differentiated appeals to strategically selected media markets. It distributed 30,000 videos of the candidate's life story to undecided voters in New Hampshire and pioneered a capacity for the 'instant rebuttal' of any negative claims concerning the candidate. The campaign team exploited the locally segmented nature of the media by providing channels of direct access to Clinton through the use of satellite feeds to local television stations.

As a result of these methods, the Clinton campaign was seen as an exceptional exercise in the marshalling and co-ordination of news, and in the development of alternatives to normal news processes. It had used the new media to cultivate different dimensions of campaigning and to carry the Clinton message to different audiences by different means. The campaign organisation itself benefited from the new technology in communications. Lightweight cameras, portable up-links, satellite feeds, video communication, data exchange and cellular phones permitted the Clinton team to provide a partial imitation of a news network by pooling information from the field and directing its dissemination and usage from the command and control centre at campaign headquarters. This allowed the strategists in the 'war room' at Little Rock not just to maintain their focus on the interrelated elements of the campaign, but to monitor and react to the course of the election through the very medium in which it was being publicly experienced and fought out.

The Clinton campaign in 1992 was effective in winning the Democratic nomination, the assaults on the candidate's character and behaviour, and in negotiating a way through a highly problematic three-way contest. Despite these achievements, President Clinton received only 43 per cent of the popular vote. He had little claim to a decisive mandate for his policy agenda. He remained an object of distrust in a period of chronic cynicism over politicians and the conduct of politics. As the chief expression of the New Democrats' centrist vision for his party, Clinton could not rely on many of the established constituencies of his own party. At the same time, Ross Perot threatened to remain a catalyst and focus for public disaffection. Moreover, the main opposition party would be intent upon defending the Reagan–Bush legacy and on proving that there would be no post-Republican regime. In effect, Clinton's victory was partial, ambiguous and unfinished as a process of public persuasion. Any contemporary president needs to engage in something like a permanent election. With Clinton this requirement was reinforced by the particular conditions of his victory, by the established nature of Clinton's technique in reaching public audiences, and by the prevailing atmosphere of negative politics in Washington. The marginal character of his victory, the hostile context of President Bush's defeat, and the unreliability of the party and other organisational bases prompted Clinton to opt for a continuation of the 'war room' outlook in actively generating and co-ordinating public engagement as a political device.

The permanent campaign

In a concerted effort to project the spirit of the 1992 election into the operation of government, President Clinton combined the resources and prestige of the White House with those techniques of public access that had been effective in the proving ground of a presidential election.[57] For example, Clinton's compulsion for a sense of immediacy with the public led him to adopt the electronic town meeting to take key policy initiatives to the people. The president would have the opportunity of addressing important issues on his terms unmediated by journalistic analysis or by digressive exchanges with professional interviewers. These town meetings would occasion public participation through question-and-answer sessions in which the president could be seen to be instigating a demonstrable form of interaction with the citizenry. Such meetings were employed both to cut out media middlemen in an effort to revive the partnership between 'the rulers and ruled' which

Clinton avowed in the election campaign, and to generate public pressure upon members of Congress and other centres of resistance in Washington. In a town meeting in Detroit in February 1993, for example, the president used the occasion to arouse support for his economic programme. His intention was made quite clear: 'Listen to what I say. Decide whether you think it's fair and tell me and your senators and congressmen whether you think I'm right or wrong.'[58] The subtext was clear: the president as personal confidante and popular tribune juxtaposed against the anonymity and distance of Washington. Clinton would appear to be in physical proximity to the public, trading opinions, conveying ideas, depicting responsiveness and drawing the public into a customised presidential channel of representation, policy and accountability.

President Clinton did not limit his experiments in media populism to town meetings. The president's drive for public immediacy and for greater control over the political agenda led him to continue his appearances on television talk shows and talk radio. He also engaged in live television 'talk-ins' with audiences in the White House Rose Garden and pioneered the use of on-line computer access to White House statements, briefings and speeches. His efforts to marginalise the media establishment of national anchormen and pundits were maintained in the White House with the deployment of audience interactive technology. This gave Clinton the rudiments of creating his own electronic version of a talk show through an email exchange network and computer bulletin board. The Clinton administration introduced the use of email communications direct to the White House and set up a White House computer forum through which views could be registered and exchanged. The latter had an additional advantage of providing an in-house barometer of public opinion to White House actions and positions. Clinton also tried to convey an image of being an ordinary American, whether by reference to his background, family history and interests, or by revealing his weakness for junk food, drive time radio and popular television. For example, he permitted an album of his impromptu saxophone solos to be released under the title *The President Blows*. Moreover, he was not above making an in-flight call to a local radio show from Air Force One in order to participate in a live talk-show.[59] Suspicion of the media elites in Washington prompted the president to invite a profusion of reporters from out of town radio stations to cover the launch of his healthcare reform direct from the grounds of the White House. In similar vein, Vice-President Gore publicised his technical scheme to reinvent the federal bureaucracy through cable channel outlets, network breakfast shows and even the comedy show *Late Night with David Letterman*.

One of the chief problems raised by this kind of concerted public engagement was a deterioration in relations with the White House press corps. Initially, Clinton hoped to bypass the professional White House correspondents in the same way that he had sought to marginalise the network news and upmarket dailies during the election. He doubted the motives of the press in general after the Gennifer Flowers scandal that had almost ended his candidacy in early 1992.

> As president, he wanted to go directly to the people, with the kind of 'town meetings' and talk shows he had successfully used during the campaign. And at first, the president had some luck with this strategy, swatting at softballs tossed by local TV anchorpersons while refusing to grant an interview to White House 'regulars'. But Clinton's press staff made the mistake of not only ignoring White House reporters but actively disdaining them.[60]

In contrast to his role model, John F. Kennedy, who held frequent press conferences in order to exert a measure of co-ordinated control over the distribution of government information, Clinton waited for nearly three months in office before he bowed to pressure for a press conference. It was evident that the priority lay with how the president fared on television news on a daily, and even on an hourly, basis. As president, Clinton could claim news space. It was therefore necessary to maximise the opportunity to fill it to his benefit. Jack Germond and Jules Witcover explain the position from the president's perspective:

> [I]f that perfect soundbite can better be accomplished with a visit to McDonald's or a brief response to a question during a 'photo op', why bother answering 20 questions on topics that may be diversions or booby traps ... [devised] by posturing reporters clamoring for network exposure ... Why put up with some querulous ink-stained wretch when you can spend an hour talking live to Larry King or even answering questions from voters?[61]

Bill Clinton himself was even rash enough to acknowledge the dynamics when addressing the Radio and Television Correspondents' Association in March 1993: 'You know why I can stiff you on the press conferences? ... Because Larry King has liberated me from you by giving me to the American people directly.'[62]

In an interview published in the *New Yorker*, Clinton's press secretary, Mike McCurry, reflected upon what is a characteristically presidential suspicion of the constraining permanence and independence of the generic press corps: 'His [i.e. Clinton's] view of the press is that there is a unique political culture in Washington defined by establishment figures in the press ... and those figures have never been able to accept him for what he is ... That is why from the moment he arrived here they tried to destroy him.'[63] In the

Clinton presidency, it was evident from the start that while the president was concerned over the need to cultivate the public prominence of the office, he was deeply suspicious of the power and status of the established White House press corps and their news organisations. He objected to their intermediary position as Washington regulars and regarded such journalists as part of the generic problem of Washington government. As a result, 'a low priority [was] given to keeping the press corps informed through the formal resources of the Press Office and its press secretary',[64] the president called few press conferences and, whenever possible, bypassed the whole process through the use of alternative media channels.

Clinton came to realise that the Washington community of 17,000 journalists, and especially the 2,200 White House correspondents, were central to the creation of his particular type of 'public presidency'. The eclectic nature of talk radio, electronic town meetings and MTV may have evoked a sense of escapism from Washington politics. Nevertheless, it did so at the price of undermining the president's position in the larger and more integrated structure of opinion formation that dwelt upon such fundamental themes as leadership ability and political competence. The Clinton White House was forced to change its posture towards the press when it came to realise that an alienated group of professional insiders could not only aggravate problems for the administration in Washington but disrupt the White House message and its communications to outside constituencies. Clinton became more conscious that the Washington media are a constituent part of the permanent government. As a result, the White House became increasingly aware of the benefit to be accrued by experienced Washington watchers in establishing political reputations, policy credibility and reserves of public good will. By the same token, Clinton had been made more aware of the negative consequences of sidelining the mainline media in the form of the rising tide of inquiries in the Whitewater affair. The White House began to give more consideration to the press corps. Clinton gave more forceful recognition that the White House was operating a twin-track media strategy of old and new media links.[65]

Bob Dole

In the 1996 presidential election, a reconfigured Bill Clinton faced the Senate Majority Leader, Bob Dole. The Republican leader faced severe difficulties. He had not only been tainted by the publicly perceived extremism of Newt Gingrich but had been out-positioned by a president who had moved to the right prior to the campaign period. In terms of 'going public', Dole had to fight against his own background and rationale as a Washington insider and parliamentary deal maker. His previous point of access to the public had been as Senate leader. Dole's initial plan had been to use his position as Majority Leader to generate publicity for his presidential campaign. This would entail running for the White House from the floor of the Senate. In doing so, Dole attempted to demonstrate his professionalism as a parliamentary politician and his capacity to deliver legislative promises. Nevertheless, Dole found that his campaign was persistently distracted by congressional activities beyond his control. More importantly, the campaign was subverted by the imagery of a candidate who was immersed in Washington politics and therefore could not be seen to be directly engaging with the visceral mass of the American public. In order to revive his campaign, Dole made the dramatic sacrifice of resigning not merely from his leadership position but also from his Senate seat. He felt he had no choice. By freeing himself from an association with the unpopular House Republicans, Dole would be in a better position to create his own message and agenda. Dole had belatedly and regretfully learnt that to defeat a sitting president, even a Senate Majority Leader had to leave Washington behind in order to project himself as a public commodity without privilege or status. On the day of his resignation, Dole announced that he now belonged entirely to the American people: 'I ... stand before you without office or authority, a private citizen, a Kansan, an American, just a man.'[66]

By dramatically resigning from the Senate to take his campaign to the country, Dole acquired enormous publicity. But ironically his resignation set such a high standard in political spectacle that he was never able to match it in the actual election. Furthermore, Dole's newsworthiness had always been converted to his position in the Senate and therefore with legislation. Once Dole left the Senate, he was immediately disconnected from the base of legislative news. He found it difficult to make up the deficiency, especially when journalists began relating his campaign pledges to previous positions taken in the Senate. In reversing his Senate positions on affirmative action and tax cuts, for example, Dole found it difficult to criticise Clinton for moving his own positions on the deficit and welfare reform.

In 'going public', the Republican candidate increasingly found that he had little with which to oppose the president and little to offer in the way of an attention-grabbing agenda. He had tried to float the idea of a 15 per cent tax cut but, given his reputation as a fiscal conservative, this was not seen to be a genuine commitment. Far from boosting his libertarian and populist credentials, it was treated as a contrived piece of insider manoeuvring. Dole suffered grievously in having to engage in such a highly publicised process as a presidential election. He had poor 'candidate skills' in the context of television politics. He was ascerbic, taciturn and not given to taking advice.

He was visually at a severe disadvantage in competing with a candidate who was younger, fitter and altogether more adept at working with television. Although Clinton was vulnerable on the themes of sleaze, land deals, sexual misconduct and the abuse of power, Dole had to constrain his attacks on the character issue because of the electorate's poll-tested distaste for negative campaigning. During the campaign, Dole failed to cut Clinton's lead, which often reached levels of fifteen to twenty points. The effect was to make the media more critical of the Dole organisation for its inability to engage effectively with the public and to retain audience interest in election news and analysis. As a result, the media greatly reduced their coverage of the contest, which further ensured Dole's inevitable eclipse. As an exercise in going public, the Dole campaign had been a model failure. It was accompanied by a decisive electoral defeat. Dole's strengths as a visceral congressional leader, accustomed to the skills of hand-to-hand fighting and to the subtleties of legislative manoeuvre, did not translate well into the paranoid intensity of prolonged personal exposure and cultivated populism required in the publicity blitz of a contemporary presidential election.

Trends

The election witnessed a further intensification of trends in direct access. For example, candidates were given greater amounts of free airtime, which allowed them to address audiences without the intervention and analysis of journalists. More media outlets were influenced by the 'civic journalism' movement, which advocates greater opportunity to the public to establish its own priorities in the construction of news agendas. As the number of households connected to the Internet increased to 11 per cent, the use of web sites became a prominent part of the campaigning landscape. Apart from the ease and economy of communicating with members of the public and disseminating up-to-date information on campaigns, the Web facilitated intensive exercises to exchange views and test public opinion. Some web sites not only became the source of news stories but the subject of regular news coverage. While the 1996 presidential election underlined the continued impact of the new media and the new formats of political television and radio, it was the Monica Lewinsky scandal (1998–99) that provided the most significant insight into the implications of media developments in relation to politics and the presidency. The scandal brought to public attention some of the major changes that had occurred in the ecology of information provision and reception that had been occasioned by technological innovation and altered conventions on news reporting. The significance of political scandal in contemporary leadership will be addressed in other chapters. Nevertheless, it is appropriate at this juncture to acknowledge that the Lewinsky affair, which led to the impeachment of President Clinton, was originally fuelled and sustained to a considerable extent by the Internet and by the activities of several cable channels.

The story was initially publicised by the Matt Drudge Internet gossip site, which leaked allegations that had been under investigation by *Newsweek*. 'Where the Internet dared, the old press followed. Rumour was published before it had been verified.'[67] The libertarian ethos of the Internet that allowed unreviewed and unedited news to be immediately circulated forced the mainstream news organisations into a response that progressively disoriented their normal practices in order to take account of the unfolding drama. The channels best able to assimilate the means of information generated by such a scandal were the cable news organisations, where the viewing figures sharply increased as they reacted to the public demand and provided blanket coverage of the daily developments. For example, MSNBC, the part cable, part web channel, experienced a ratings increase of 109 per cent in July–September 1998 compared with the corresponding period in 1997. The ability of such twenty-four hour channels to sustain public interest on a continual basis, together with the mushrooming of Internet news chat rooms and bulletin boards devoted to Bill Clinton's transgressions, represented an emphatic affirmation of a dramatic change in news processes and values. Ben Bradlee, the celebrated former editor of the *Washington Post*, remarked on the curious nature of a story that was never allowed to die. Whenever signs appeared that it was about to slacken off, a fresh episode provoked sudden bouts of journalistic excitement that generated an insatiable demand for fresh sensation. 'It used to be that there were, maybe, two news cycles in a day … But with this constant television coverage we now have … an endless cycle.'[68]

Aided and abetted by a series of leaks from the Independent Counsel's Office, the presidency became embroiled in a multifaceted drama in which the prodigious news and management resources of the Clinton administration were confronted by a succession of unpredictable revelations, allegations and rumours. For an organisation that was accustomed to preserving the news initiative, the scandal continually outmanoeuvred and wrong-footed the White House because of the sheer speed and immediacy of the exchange of information. When the report of the Independent Counsel, Kenneth Starr, was published on 11 September 1998, it was released simultaneously on the Internet. This effectively stripped the White House of any opportunity to engage in pre-emptive, corrective or distractive exercises in spin control. It also prevented news editors from analysing or prioritising the information before the public had access to Starr's findings. The report was simply deposited in the public domain in a wholly undigested and unrefined form.

By being exempt from the normal news processes, the report highlighted the extent to which they had been superseded by new technology. Clinton sought to outflank the mainstream news networks by directing presidential spokespersons and allies to engage his detractors on those shows and channels that had previously been instrumental in conveying the White House message. In the process, he too was outflanked by the Internet. 'It was truly awful', commented Mike McCurry, the White House press secretary who had to absorb the flow of information as quickly as he could in order to give some impression of control over something that was being broadcast with no reference to news value conventions and traditions. From his perspective, the egalitarianism of the Internet meant that no one had any advantage:

> It was a horrific moment. It was when all of the filters in the world of journalism just evaporated and you had raw information suddenly available in the mainstream and so the American people themselves had to serve the role of the editor sitting at the newsdesk deciding what was worthy to print and not. That is why I think it was a profound moment. It was instantaneous information but without any of the editorial standards and filters that define what we think of as the modern business of journalism.[69]

The problems were compounded by the release on 21 September 1998 of the videotapes of President Clinton's grand jury testimony. Once again, there were no guiding precedents as the news networks followed the cable channels in broadcasting live the president's answers to intimate questions related to his sexual behaviour and moral standards. In what was a voyeuristic television event, the audience was invited to respond to an unmediated feed where body language, intonation and facial expressions were as significant as the content of the president's answers. The usage of both the new media and their conventions by the president's detractors propelled the issue not only into the public domain but also into the institutional apparatus of government, which in turn was prompted into impeachment proceedings and ultimately a Senate trial.

The Starr report and the president's videos epitomised the effects of the disseminating power of the Web and the voracious appetites of the twenty-four hour cable news channels in the progressive 'disintermediation' of information exchange. The experience prompted *Newsweek* to the following sombre self-analysis:

> New technologies are bearing down at high speed on the old engines of information. This scandal may be remembered as the moment at which the status quo in the news business finally crashed and burned. The outlets often associated with the story – Matt Drudge, Salon, MSNBC, Don Imus – all take

> a looser approach to the news, full of argument and attitude. Older, weightier sources are having to adapt. The Lewinsky story saw partisans on both sides mobilize in cyberspace. While Clinton critics lost their struggle in the country as a whole, they won on the Web. If 'old media' were often seen as liberal, 'new media' are materializing as conservative and libertarian. The next big political crisis might see the Internet and cable leading public opinion rather than railing against it.[70]

In making himself so available to the new media, Clinton had been instrumental in making the new media available to the devices and designs of his opponents.

In many respects, Clinton became the victim of his strategy of reconfiguring the public presidency into an altogether more individuated format in which revealed character traits and personal behaviour became the touchstone of public accessibility. Clinton had originally been forced into such a position by having to defend himself on television against the allegations of Gennifer Flowers at the very beginning of his public campaign for the presidency. More significantly, he ran for the White House at a time when populist fervour for government responsiveness and public impatience with the opaqueness and disengagement of Washington culture generated demands for closer and more palpable connections between government and the citizenry. This expression of political populism coincided both with an upsurge in television programmes geared to self-revelation and social transparency, and to the rise of specialist channels devoted to this populist genre. Together they helped to promote the hybridisation of news and entertainment in the mainstream news channels. In the words of one experienced commentator: 'We are witnessing the Oprahfication of the American presidency in a confessional culture which extends from the Oval Office to the tens of millions who watch their daily dose of don't-blame-me television courtesy of Oprah Winfrey and Jerry Springer.'[71] Clinton's emphatic endorsements of 'infotainment' formats rendered him an agent of complicity in the ultimate subversion of his own presidency. He had prepared the ground and cultivated the techniques for the elevation of the 'character issue' as the defining category in a process that culminated in his impeachment and trial.

In a fundamental sense, the drive on the part of presidents to have a more direct relationship with the public means that the relationship will also inevitably become more personal in method, substance and effect. The impulse to locate political responsibility and accountability at a personal level, and to prevent the kind of unwitting disengagement with the public that rapidly corroded the Bush presidency, has led presidents to develop new vulnerabilities that can be exploited by their political opponents. This is a time when the definition and control of news are in disarray, and when the distinction between public knowledge and the private sphere has largely evaporated in the wake of the Clinton scandal. As a result, contenders for the presidency will now have to project their personas still further while at the same time remaining aware of the anti-personnel properties of contemporary leadership. In the immediate aftermath of the scandal, *Time* reported that the campaign trail for 2000 had already been affected by the subversion of the Clinton presidency:

> The early front runners are trying to define an acceptable zone of privacy, but they find themselves in a world in which the only rule is that there are no rules ... Even if mainstream reporters refrain from asking questions about sex and drugs ... no one can stop an old girlfriend or dealer from calling a press conference. And if the Establishment media play these down, there will be the Matt Drudges, Howard Sterns and Flynts to play them up.[72]

Just as Clinton was locked into the dynamic of the public presidency, so his successor will be further subjected to its imperatives. This will be so not least because of the need on the part of any successful campaign to reclaim the public's trust in the institution by demonstrating an even closer proximity to the people in an increasingly unstructured and volatile network of political communications.

The need to establish a palpable and customised linkage with the public prompted Vice-President Al Gore to engage in a ritualistic dissociation from Washington as part of his preparations for the 2000 presidential campaign. In October 1999, he announced to 200 business leaders in New York that he was transferring his headquarters from K Street in Washington to Kmart in Nashville, in his home state of Tennessee. This move was rich in symbolism, for he was shifting 'from the power street of lobbyists and hot lawyers to the people's shopping mall'.[73] This was followed by a televised declaration that his vice-presidential office and status in Washington counted for nothing. The implicit message was that he could identify with average voters, just as they should be able to identify with him in his predicament: 'I am now in effect the underdog and I'm campaigning like the underdog.'[74] Just as Gore had to respond to the challenge of his rival Bill Bradley, so the Republican front-runner, Governor George W. Bush, experienced the same kind of insurgent pressures from populist challengers such as Steve Forbes and Senator John McCain. Both maximised the potential of the Internet to disseminate their message, mobilise public support and raise money in an effort to undermine Bush's claims to a public leadership position built up outside Washington.

The public cultivation of an agenda of popularly based issues and concerns has become a dominant theme of the contemporary presidency. In fact, the very identity of the institution has become fused to that of the public. The office has developed from a position whose influence was ultimately drawn from public support, to one whose influence is now drawn heavily from a continuous and demonstrable relationship with the public. The convergence of the presidency and the public to categories that are extensions of each other reflects a systemic change in the character of politics that has been beyond the ability of any single president to change – let alone to reverse.

Notes

1 Samuel Kernell, *Going Public: New Strategies of Presidential Leadership*, 3rd edn (Washington, DC, Congressional Quarterly Press, 1997).
2 Richard Rose, *The Postmodern President: The White House Meets the World* (Chatham, Chatham House, 1988), p. 35.
3 Rose, *The Postmodern President*, p. 35.
4 George C. Edwards III, *The Public Presidency: The Pursuit of Popular Support* (New York, St Martin's Press, 1983), p. 5.
5 Kernell, *Going Public*, ch. 2.
6 Kernell, *Going Public*, pp. 28–9.
7 James Pfiffner, *The Modern Presidency* (New York, St Martin's Press, 1993), p. 36.
8 Ryan Barilleaux, *The Post-Modern Presidency: The Office after Ronald Reagan* (New York, Praeger, 1988), p. 132. See also Bruce Miroff, 'The Presidency and the Public: Leadership as Spectacle', in Michael Nelson (ed.), *The Presidency and the Political System*, 2nd edn (Washington, DC, Congressional Quarterly Press, 1988), pp. 271–91; Murray Edelman, *Constructing the Political Spectacle* (Chicago, University of Chicago Press, 1988); Jeffrey Tulis, *The Rhetorical Presidency* (Princeton, Princeton University Press, 1987); K. K. Campbell and Kathleen H. Jamieson, *Deeds Done in Words: Presidential Rhetoric and the Genres of Governance* (Chicago, University of Chicago Press, 1990); Barbara Hinckley, *The Symbolic Presidency: How Presidents Portray Themselves* (New York, Routledge, 1990); Theodore J. Lowi, *The Personal President: Power Invested, Promise Unfulfilled* (Ithaca, Cornell University Press, 1985). For an extension of Lowi's thesis into the 1980s and 1990s, see C. A. Rimmerman, *Presidency by Plebiscite: The Reagan–Bush Era in Institutional Perspective* (Boulder, Westview, 1993).
9 George C. Edwards III, 'Frustration and Folly: Bill Clinton and the Public Presidency', in Colin Campbell and Bert A. Rockman (eds), *The Clinton Presidency: First Appraisals* (Chatham, Chatham House, 1996), p. 254. See also Renee M. Smith, 'The Public Presidency Hits the Wall: Clinton's Presidential Initiative on Race', *Presidential Studies Quarterly*, 28, no. 4 (Fall 1998), pp. 780–7.
10 See Craig A. Smith and Kathy B. Smith, *The White House Speaks: Presidential Leadership as Persuasion* (Westport, Praeger, 1994).
11 Charles O. Jones, *The Presidency in a Separated System* (Washington, DC, Brookings Institution, 1994), p. 146.
12 Jones, *The Presidency in a Separated System*, p. 146.

13 Edwards III, 'Frustration and Folly', p. 255.
14 Stephanie G. Larson, 'The President and Congress in the Media', *Annals of the American Academy of Political and Social Science*, 499 (September 1988), p. 66. See also Michael B. Grossman and Martha J. Kumar, *Portraying the President: The White House and the News Media* (Baltimore, Johns Hopkins University Press, 1981); Doris A. Graber, *Mass Media and American Politics*, 3rd edn (Washington, DC, Congressional Quarterly, 1989), pp. 235–54.
15 Robert M. Entman, 'The Imperial Media', in Arnold J. Meltsner (ed.), *Politics and the Oval Office: Towards Presidential Governance* (San Francisco, Institute for Contemporary Studies, 1981), p. 94.
16 See John A. Maltese, *Spin Control: The White House Office of Communications and the Management of Presidential News*, 2nd edn (Chapel Hill, University of North Carolina Press, 1994); Howard Kurtz, *Spin Cycle: Inside the Clinton Propaganda Machine* (London, Pan, 1998).
17 Robert E. DiClerico, 'The Role of Media in Heightened Expectations and Diminished Leadership Capacity', in Richard E. Waterman (ed.), *The Presidency Reconsidered* (Itasca, F. E. Peacock, 1993), pp. 129–35.
18 Maltese, *Spin Control*, p. 197.
19 See Larry Speakes, *Speaking Out: The Reagan Presidency from Inside the White House* (New York, Scribners, 1988).
20 Robert Donovan and J. Ray Scherer, *Unsilent Revolution: Television News and American Public Life, 1948–1991* (Cambridge, Cambridge University Press, 1992), ch. 14.
21 Kathleen H. Jamieson, *Eloquence in an Electronic Age: The Transformation of Political Speechmaking* (Oxford, Oxford University Press, 1988), p. 13.
22 Jamieson, *Eloquence in an Electronic Age*, p. 117.
23 Barilleaux, *The Post-Modern Presidency*, p. 137.
24 Quoted in Michael Cockerell, 'The packaging of the President', *The Listener*, 8 November 1984.
25 See Michael Deaver with Mickey Herskowitz, *Behind the Scenes* (New York, William Morrow, 1987).
26 Donald T. Regan, *For the Record: From Wall Street to Washington* (London, Hutchinson, 1988), p. 246.
27 Regan, *For the Record*, pp. 247–8.
28 Bruce Miroff, 'The Presidency and the Public: Leadership as Spectacle', in Michael Nelson (ed.), *The Presidency and the Political System*, 2nd edn (Washington, DC, Congressional Quarterly, 1988), p. 272. See also Murray Edelman, *Constructing the Political Spectacle* (Chicago, University of Chicago Press, 1988).
29 Miroff, 'The Presidency and the Public', p. 274.
30 Miroff, 'The Presidency and the Public', p. 283.
31 Jamieson, *Eloquence in an Electronic Age*, p. 117.
32 Charles W. Dunn and J. David Woodward, 'Ideological Images for a Television Age: Ronald Reagan as Party Leader', in Dilys M. Hill, Raymond A. Moore and Phil Williams (eds), *The Reagan Presidency: An Incomplete Revolution?* (Basingstoke, Macmillan, 1990), p. 123.
33 Bruce Miroff, 'Secrecy and Spectacle: Reflections on the Dangers of the Presidency', in Paul Brace, Christine B. Harrington and Gary King (eds), *The Presidency in American Politics* (New York, New York University Press, 1989), p. 158.
34 Austin Ranney, 'Broadcasting, Narrowcasting, and Politics', in Anthony King (ed.), *The New American Political System*, second version (Washington, DC, American Enterprise

Institute, 1990), p. 187. See also Robert Schmuhl, *Statecraft and Stagecraft: American Political Life in an Age of Personality* (Notre Dame, University of Notre Dame Press, 1990).

35 James Ceaser, Glen E. Thurow, Jeffrey Tulis and Joseph M. Bessette, 'The Rise of the Rhetorical Presidency', in Thomas E. Cronin (ed.), *Rethinking the Presidency* (Boston, Little Brown, 1982), pp. 233–51.

36 Ceaser, Thurow, Tulis and Bessette, 'The Rise of the Rhetorical Presidency', p. 234.

37 Ceaser, Thurow, Tulis and Bessette, 'The Rise of the Rhetorical Presidency', p. 234.

38 Ceaser, Thurow, Tulis and Bessette, 'The Rise of the Rhetorical Presidency', p. 234. For a full exposition of the thesis, see Tulis, *The Rhetorical Presidency*.

39 Kernell, *Going Public*, p. 259.

40 Joe McGinniss, *The Selling of the President* (Harmondsworth, Penguin, 1970); Nicholas J. O'Shaughnessy, *The Phenomenon of Political Marketing* (Basingstoke, Macmillan, 1990), ch. 9; Frank I. Luntz, *Candidates, Consultants and Campaigns: The Style and Substance of American Electioneering* (Oxford, Basil Blackwell, 1988), chs 3, 5.

41 Rose, *The Postmodern President*, p. 97.

42 Rose, *The Postmodern President*, p. 36.

43 Cockerell, 'The packaging of the President'. For a study of the extraordinary attention given to public image in the Reagan White House, see Lawrence I. Barrett, *Gambling with History: Reagan in the White House* (New York, Penguin, 1983).

44 Jamieson, *Eloquence in an Electronic Age*, p. 175.

45 F. Christopher Arterton, 'Campaign '92: Strategies and Tactics of the Candidates', in Gerald M. Pomper *et al.* (ed.), *The Election of 1992: Reports and Interpretations* (Chatham, Chatham House, 1993), p. 89.

46 Edwin Diamond and Robert A. Silverman, *White House to Your House: Media and Politics in Virtual America* (Cambridge, MIT Press, 1995), p. 78.

47 See Richard Davis and Diane Owen, *New Media and American Politics* (New York, Oxford University Press, 1998).

48 Diamond and Silverman, *White House to Your House*, p. 75.

49 See Godfrey Hodgson, 'The end of the grand narrative', *Prospect*, August/September 1999; James Q. Wilson, *American Government*, 4th edn (Boston, Houghton Mifflin, 1997), pp. 87–92.

50 Quoted in Diamond and Silverman, *White House to Your House*, p. 3.

51 See Dirk Smillie and Martha McKay, 'Talking to America: The Rise of the Talk Shows in the '92 Campaign', in *An Uncertain Season: Reporting in the Postprimary Period* (New York, Freedom Forum Media Studies Center, 1992).

52 James S. Fishkin, 'Talk of the Tube: How to Get Teledemocracy Right', in Walter D. Burnham (ed.), *The American Prospect: Reader in American Politics* (Chatham, Chatham House, 1995), p. 235.

53 Diamond and Silverman, *White House to Your House*, p. 3.

54 Diamond and Silverman, *White House to Your House*, p. 3.

55 Kathleen A. Frankovich, 'Public Opinion in the 1992 Campaign ', in Pomper *et al.*, *The Election of 1992*, pp. 128–9.

56 Frankovich, 'Public Opinion in the 1992 Campaign', p. 129.

57 James A. Barnes, 'The endless campaign', *National Journal*, 20 February 1993.

58 Quoted in Martin Fletcher, 'Clinton preparing bitter medicine to turn round the economy', *The Times*, 15 February 1993.

59 The phone call was made at a height of 30,000 feet to radio station KMOX in St Louis on 24 June 1994.

60 Eleanor Clift and Mark Miller, 'Don't mess with the media', *Newsweek*, 7 June 1993.
61 Jack Germond and Jules Witcover, 'Clinton press policy works – for now', *National Journal*, 20 March 1993.
62 Quoted in Diamond and Silverman, *White House to Your House*, p. 5. See also Howard Kurtz, 'Inaugurating a talk-show presidency', *Washington Post*, 12 February 1993.
63 Ken Auletta, 'Inside story', *New Yorker*, 18 November 1996.
64 Auletta, 'Inside story'.
65 Kurtz, *Spin Cycle*, *passim*.
66 Quoted in Rhodes Cook, 'Dole's gamble gets spotlight, but questions remain', *Congressional Weekly Report*, 18 May 1996.
67 'The end?', *The Economist*, 13 February 1999.
68 Quoted in Deborah McGregor, 'Media may have fanned the flames', *Financial Times*, 12 February 1999.
69 Quoted in BBC 2, *Correspondent: The President's Scorpions*, 9 January 1999.
70 Jonathan Alter, 'The fallout', *Newsweek*, 8 February 1999.
71 Gavin Esler, 'From cowboy to the psychiatrist's couch', *The Independent*, 19 September 1998.
72 Richard Lacayo, 'New rules of the road', *Time*, 22 February 1999.
73 Harold Evans, 'Gore v. Bradley: 'Look mom, I'm losing', *The Guardian*, 4 October 1999.
74 Vice-President Gore, quoted in Evans, 'Gore *v.* Bradley'.

CHAPTER 6

John Major, Tony Blair and the struggle for public outreach

In Britain, references to political leaders going public and to the subsequent 'presidentialisation' of British politics have grown with the rise of the broadcasting media, and especially television, as the pre-eminent vehicle of political information. Like their counterparts in the United States, British premiers have come to recognise the imperative nature of effective and continuous public outreach in the construction and maintenance of political authority. Histories of the origins and development of media-centred and personalised campaigns in Britain have now become an established feature of the literature on political communications in this country.[1] But like the United States, the ramifications of the media's impact upon British political activity are not limited to the dimension of purely electoral competition. Going public has become as much a part of the daily conduct of politics and government in this country as it is in Washington. The impulse to personalise and publicise drives the strategies of the political parties. It dominates their political calculations, their positional manoeuvres and their agenda-setting activities. It provides the measure of their political effectiveness and impels them towards making political leadership both an incessant theme in public discussion and a key criterion of political evaluation. Just as one leader's failure to retain the initiative in favourable public projection can undermine his party's claims to authority, so another's success in establishing forms of effective public outreach can foreshadow the replacement of one regime with another. Nothing illustrates the pivotal significance of this public dimension in contemporary British politics more forcibly than the disintegration of John Major's government and the corresponding rise of Tony Blair and the New Labour project.

The implosion of the Major government

It was with some justification that the Conservative victory in 1992 was characterised as a personal triumph for John Major's public projection of security, continuity and trust against a Labour party presented as slick, superficial and untrustworthy. The prime minister, who in 1990 experienced the greatest injection of popularity since Churchill's accession to power in 1940, had now acquired a legitimacy of his own by being seen to be more than an antidote to Margaret Thatcher. Against the odds and in defiance of opinion poll projections, Major's trust in the mobilising power of the Conservative party had been rewarded by a record fourteen million votes and a working majority in the House of Commons. Unfortunately, it was to be the climax of his leadership, for within months of victory the Major administration suffered the public humiliation of having to suspend Britain's membership of the Exchange Rate Mechanism (ERM).

The appearance of a government that had lost control of its economic policy with successive interest rate increases on the same day, combined with a dishevelled Chancellor announcing an effective devaluation of sterling on the pavement outside the Treasury, had undermined the Conservative government's reputation for economic competence. 'Black Wednesday' was a political and personal disaster from which the Major administration never recovered. Major had not only been a leading proponent of the ERM in the late 1980s, he had been instrumental in pressurising Margaret Thatcher into agreeing to enter the system in 1990. He was also primarily responsible for establishing sterling within the ERM at a deflationary rate of 2.95 marks to the pound. By September 1992, Britain was in the depths of its worst recession since the 1930s.

For the first three years of the parliament the Major administration was besieged by rising unemployment, business closures, falling living standards, budget deficits, internal party divisions, a declining party membership, a collapse in business donations and a public discourse dominated by persistent complaints about Major's leadership. The prime minister was having to manage a party that was not only deeply split over Europe but still in disarray in coming to terms with the achievement of Thatcherism and the challenge of developing a new identity and policy agenda. Many old battles continued to be fought and to be contested increasingly in the public eye. With a working majority of only twenty-one, Tory rebels assumed a pivotal significance in the party and within the political system as a whole. They were highly adept at publicising their positions and were able to cultivate close ties with the conservative press, which was assuming an increasingly jaundiced view of Major and his team. Even though the Conservative party had secured only 42.3 per cent of the popular vote in 1992, it was accustomed to the belief that it represented a diminished hegemony, which provided its own opposition. The Eurosceptics in particular, combined with vociferous anti-European elements in the press, constituted a *de facto* party within a party.

This alliance was able to draw heavily upon the populist antipathies evoked by the prospect of a European superstate.

Major sought to balance the factions in his party and to maximise the level of attainable unity. He defended the principle of the NHS and continued the budgetary commitment to social security spending. He attempted to appease the Eurosceptics by achieving critical opt-outs on the social chapter and the single currency. He extended the 'Thatcher credo into areas where the future baroness had either feared to venture or not been daft enough to try'[2] (e.g. rail privatisation, the HMSO and a failed attempt to privatise the Post Office). Major also strengthened and widened the scope of the Citizen's Charter. His administration developed the internal market in the NHS, introduced the Lottery as a source of alternative public funding, sponsored the publication of attainment levels in schools and other public bodies, and encouraged private finance initiatives in public projects. And yet because of Major's refusal to rule out Britain ever becoming a participant in Economic and Monetary Union, the Thatcherite forces would not regard him as one of their own and, therefore, would not always defer to his calls for party unity.

Major's problems stemmed from the circumstances of his accession to the premiership. Thatcher's credibility as a leader had been damaged by what was seen to be her intransigence towards Europe. Her attitude was suspected of being counter-productive to Britain's position in European Community negotiations. Furthermore, her statements and behaviour had aggravated senior party and cabinet figures, whose accumulated resentments were beginning to find expression. These strains, combined with the widespread conviction that the party would lose the next election, led to Thatcher's fall from office. Major had been the consensus candidate. His fair-minded integrity and civil service attributes of being able to assimilate contrasting positions within a single brief allowed him to preside through ambiguity and nuance. And yet, as Allan Massie observed in August 1993, the tensions implicit in Thatcher's removal had not been resolved. It was because of this impasse that Major's position became so problematic: 'It is difficult to lead people who do not want to be led and the truth is that the Conservative party is now so bitterly divided on Europe that it cannot all be led in the same direction.'[3] As a consequence, Massie concluded, '[f]ew prime ministers have had a harder year; few have had their leadership qualities so persistently questioned'.[4] The prime minister himself was left to ruminate on questions for which he had no answer: 'How had so much bad blood welled up so fast? How had members of what had so recently been a winning team turned against each other, plotted against each other, betrayed each other, careless of the opportunity this was building for the common enemy?'[5]

What was true in 1993 remained equally valid for the remainder of Major's premiership. In many respects the problem for John Major remained one of not being Margaret Thatcher in a party that had become accustomed to vigorous and dogmatic leadership. His position was further exacerbated by the presence of a sub-party grouping of zealots dedicated to resisting what it took to be a progressive dilution of Margaret Thatcher's record and agenda. Four years after Massie's observations, the picture had barely changed. At the outset of the 1997 general election campaign, Michael Jones summarised what had become a familiar set of themes:

> Major was forced into a defensive position that became increasingly difficult to sustain. Tory rightwingers chafed at his 'wait and see' European policy while Tory moderates from the One Nation tradition accused him of selling out to extremists ... No Tory leader in history had to contend with such an adverse parliamentary position. Tory MPs fought amongst themselves with an abandon that invited destruction. Even the very institutions they were pledged to defend trembled as public confidence in them collapsed ... Media coverage alternated between Tory uproar over Europe and popular disenchantment with Major's government for most of its second term.[6]

And yet, Major had survived to become the fourth longest-serving prime minister since World War II. Nevertheless, in doing so he had demonstrated to the full the damage that can be inflicted upon a premiership by its failure to engage effectively in the public dimension of British leadership politics.

Following the debacle of Britain's withdrawal from the ERM and the war of attrition over the Maastricht Treaty, Major's second administration suffered a dramatic decline in its opinion poll ratings. So precipitous was the collapse and so sustained was its effect that the prime minister and the government became demonstrably disconnected from the public. The disjunction between government and people became the subject of continued public debate in which the polls featured significantly as newsworthy stories in their own right. In May 1993, for example, Gallup reported that majorities of over 60 per cent thought that John Major and his government were uncaring (66 per cent), ineffective (68 per cent), shortsighted (72 per cent), incompetent (62 per cent), out of touch with the country (71 per cent), and unable to inspire confidence (81 per cent).[7] In that month, public approval of the government was registered at 16 per cent. Since the war, monthly government ratings had fallen below 20 per cent on only seventeen occasions. Seven of the seventeen had come in seven consecutive months from October 1992 to April 1993.

The historic scale of the public antagonism was underlined in the following month, when Gallup revealed that John Major and the government were 'now held in lower esteem than any other prime minister or government since opinion polling began in Britain in the late 1930s'.[8] As public approval of the government slumped to just 12 per cent, Labour's lead in voting intentions rose to 24 per cent. This represented 'the second highest ever recorded in Gallup's 56-year history'.[9] Although the prime minister had attempted to stamp his authority on the party with a cabinet reshuffle in which he removed Norman Lamont, the Chancellor of the Exchequer, his personal standing declined to 21 per cent. This represented an all-time low for any prime minister recorded by Gallup. Major remained a likeable individual in the public's mind, but he was now increasingly regarded as the personification of an incompetent government: 'His problem seems to be that both he and his Government are seen to be indecisive and ineffective; and because the Government is his Government he inevitably takes much of the blame.'[10] By October 1993, the position had worsened still further. According to Gallup, 88 per cent thought the government did not inspire confidence, 85 per cent believed it was divided and 78 per cent did not think it was in touch with the country. Three-quarters of voters thought the government was ineffective and two-thirds were of the opinion that it was weak and dishonest. Anthony King concluded that it would be 'hard to imagine a more damning indictment of a freely-elected administration by the people of any country'.[11]

Relapse into leadership fever

This association between a failing government and a failing prime minister generated a fevered atmosphere of speculation. Opinion polls were used in publicising the scale of the slump and in directing public opinion ever more explicitly to the problem of leadership and to its possible solution in the form of alternative leadership. For most of the 1993–94 period, the public satisfaction ratings for John Major hovered around the 20 per cent mark, while the dissatisfaction ratings remained in the region of 70 per cent. When Tony Blair was elected leader of the Labour party, the public satisfaction and dissatisfaction which under John Smith had been practically level at around 35 per cent began to widen out, with the dissatisfaction figure falling away to below 10 per cent. In September 1994, MORI reported that while Blair had yet to prove himself, he had already opened up extensive leads over Major on a range of leadership measures (e.g. handling the economy, understanding Britain's problems, being concerned for the country, effectiveness, competence, decisiveness and trust).[12] John Major, on the other hand, continued to languish in chronically low levels of public esteem. According to MORI, the proportion regarding him as a capable leader had dropped from 40 per cent in 1991 to just 10 per cent in September 1994. During the same period, those who saw him as being good in a crisis had fallen from 30 per cent to 7 per cent. By the end of 1994, Gallup had announced more records. Labour had reached an unprecedented 62 per cent in voting intentions. The Conservatives had never previously fallen below 20 per cent in opinion polls but were now registering 18.5 per cent, which constituted a lead of 43.5 per cent for Labour. Prior to this poll, neither major party had ever led the other by more than forty points in Gallup's history of opinion sampling. Other all-time records were also broken: 'In December only 9.7 per cent of voters said they approved of the Government's record to date. No Government before had ever fallen below 10 per cent. Also last month only 18.1 per cent of voters professed themselves satisfied with Mr Major as Prime Minister – a lower figure than even he had previously achieved.'[13] This persistent lack of public outreach fuelled a profusion of analyses, scenarios and manoeuvres, as observers and participants alike speculated on the reasons for the slump, the possibility of recovery and the political opportunities afforded to those who aspired to the leadership.[14]

It has to be acknowledged that Major's position was a complex and difficult one. He was the only senior Tory capable of brokering a form of peaceful co-existence between the different wings of the party and yet his authority was continually undermined by precisely this role. He was dogged not only by the model and the continual presence of his predecessor, but also by a proliferation of surreptitious contenders for the leadership. All of them were only too well aware of Major's own precedent in 1990, when his displacement of Margaret Thatcher had dramatically revived the party's public standing. The economic recession and the Conservatives' prolonged period in office made new departures in policy difficult. The government needed to consolidate the radical economic legislation of the 1980s, while maintaining a Thatcherite edge in specific areas of British industry. At the same time, it was attempting to devise innovative policies in the field of social problems (e.g. crime, inner cities, family breakdown and the 'underclass').

The previously uncharted depths of the Conservative deficit, in combination with disastrous results in the 1994 European elections, the 1995 local government elections and in key by-elections, seriously undermined the professional reputation and political standing of the administration. In many respects, the succession of failures delegitimised the Major administration as a functioning institutional force of governance. Critics such as the sacked Chancellor, Norman Lamont, fulminated publicly against a government that had all the appearances of being dysfunctional:

> There is something wrong with the way in which we make our decisions. The

> Government listens too much to the pollsters and party managers ... The trouble is that ... they are entering too much into policy decisions. As a result, there is too much short-termism, too much reacting to events, not enough shaping of events. We give the impression of being in office but not in power. Far too many important decisions are made for 36 hours' publicity.[15]

The sense of disarray fuelled a resurgence of critical analysis into the foundations of British government. To a growing extent the Labour party now openly embraced constitutional reform as a means of challenging the authority of the government.

Getting Major across

Ironically, what was seen to be one of the chief problems for the Conservatives was also regarded as representing the party's best chance of overcoming its difficulties and achieving re-election. John Major may have become a liability as party leader in parliament, but in the 1992 general election he had proved himself to be a formidable campaigner. He had been particularly adept at forging a relationship of trust and integrity with the public. The party now needed to unify around a leader in order to reconnect with its own constituency of core supporters. For most of the time, Major seemed the only figure likely to provide the focus of allegiance that would allow the party to re-engage effectively with the public. Opinion polls showed that a change of leader would have made little or no difference to the party's public image or its position in voting intentions. The Conservatives were, therefore, stuck with a leader who had the virtue of being less divisive than any of his senior colleagues.

The challenge for Major and the party lay in reviving the spirit of '92. This was tantamount to an admission that the disciplines and drives of the election campaign had become marginalised once the Conservatives had commenced a fourth term of office. As they could no longer depend upon the main opposition party to self-destruct, the Conservatives had to attend urgently to the question of its public face, which more than ever meant addressing the question of Major's public persona. John Major had always had a problem with presenting himself to a large audience. He was recognised, even by his opponents, as a very personable, charming and engaging individual in private. In public settings, however, he came across as defensive, colourless and uninspiring – a manager rather than an activist, a healer more than a warrior, a seeker of consensus instead of an evangelist.

For some the difficulty lay in releasing the private man into the public dimension. In the view of Bruce Anderson, for example, Major had 'the assets to take a formidable and enduring hold on public opinion'.[16] In the challenge to widen the Thatcherite cause and to construct a broader-based Conservative coalition, Major needed to remember that there was very little tradition of Tory politicians offering 'visions':

> His very ordinariness is an asset. Traditionally, the British feel comfortable with extraordinary ordinary men and distrust flashy politicians ... He is trying to persuade everyone in Britain that there are no barriers to their achieving what they wish to achieve. Mrs Thatcher had a similar message, but Mr Major can deliver his effectively for, unlike her, he understands the mentality of those at the bottom of the heap. He can offer encouragement where she had only exhortation.[17]

To Anderson, it was necessary, therefore, to let the full prosaic qualities of Major shine through, in order to allow the leader to personify his message of hope and reassurance.

David McKie, on the other hand, believed that the media saturation of politics, and especially the intense and unremitting attention given to the prime minister, required far from ordinary gifts, even in conveying a sense of ordinariness. While much of Major's appeal may have been based upon the appearance of being familiar, accessible and commonplace, McKie pointed to a voice and delivery that was out of synch with the visual impression. 'No leader since Wilson had come over better than Major in the difficult 1992 election campaign as a man of the people. Yet where Wilson sounded like a man of the people, Major's stilted, formal style of speaking jarred with the visual image. Informal language seemed to elude him.'[18] But it was not simply a linguistic problem. It has been shown that 'lack of variety in intonation, stress, phrasing, gesture and so on is likely to convey to an audience a lack of real passion, emotion and commitment for the cause you are advocating'.[19] Major suffered from precisely these deficiencies, prompting McKie to ask: '[C]an you hope to enthuse a depressed and demoralised Conservative Party, let alone the broader electorate, when the party is led by a man who apparently lacks the talent (which Heseltine has in abundance) for picking up resonant themes and making them sing?'[20]

Such points have a resonance with the themes of the 'rhetorical presidency' referred to in chapter 5. In this context, it was no longer possible for John Major to conduct his premiership, or expect to have it appraised, according to the categories of a pre-electronic media age. It was no longer sufficient to rely upon the intermediary assistance of the press or the party in painting a leader as a man or woman of the people. A leader like Major had actively to project himself into the public's consciousness and to inject a personal rhetoric into the public domain that would relate the media to a mass audience and to mobilise a popular interest into a set of branded themes conjoined to the leader's identity. The attempt to formulate a position that could be defined as 'Majorism' was abandoned at an early stage in his premiership.[21] Major's preferred posture of sensible consolidation and brokered moderation, however, was no substitute for an identifying theme. As a result, he had very little upon which to base an effective strategy of public engagement. The lack of an effective public dialogue also meant that he had few resources with which to counteract his critics and the leadership aspirants within his own party.

For others the difficulty lay less with Major himself and more with the state of media relations. The Major administration was synonymous with 'inept media management'.[22] This reputation was acquired not just as a result of having to deal with so many crises within the party and the government, but because of the administration's apparent inability to grasp the essential requirements of running an effective media strategy. In a study of the 'Major effect' in relation to the mass media, Colin Seymour-Ure mused upon whether the real issue at stake was the 'effect *on* John Major, not one caused *by* him. He was the victim, as time went on, of a slither of publicity disasters – about policies, colleagues and his own leadership.'[23] To Seymour-Ure, 'Downing Street news operations' under Major were 'woefully ineffective'.[24] Consequently, it was difficult to believe that 'the connection between the government's unpopularity and its many presentational mishaps was wholly fortuitous, rather than one of cause and effect'.[25] Among the many high profile episodes of media mismanagement during Major's second administration were the disastrous U-turn over ERM in September 1992; the poorly conceived plan to announce a *fait accompli* of a coal mine closure programme without prior consultation in October 1992; the succession of public disputes over the Maastricht Treaty during 1993; and the prime minister's rage over the BBC's coverage of his trip to Japan (September 1993), which resulted in his visit being further eclipsed by Major's domestic difficulties with the media and with critics inside his own party. But the event which encapsulated the Major administration's problems with media management came with a speech given by the prime minister himself. Major had every opportunity to control its meaning, its reporting and its effects but in every respect he conspicuously failed to maintain the initiative.

Back to basics

In his leader's address to the Conservative party conference in October 1993, Major set out to try and stamp his authority upon the party by defining an agenda of unifying themes that would provide the party with a renewed sense of identity. After a period of intense speculation over Major's leadership and at a time when the imminent publication of Margaret Thatcher's memoirs generated a host of unfavourable comparisons with her successor, Major needed to rally the party. He had to demonstrate that it still had a mission and that he was the figure that could define it. In a speech which was widely seen to mark a shift to the right, Major gave special emphasis to the erosion of social values and to the need to return to the core principles of civility, neighbourliness, decency and courtesy. It was, in Major's view, a 'time to get back to basics'.[26] In an explicitly populist attack upon the educational elite, pornography, tower blocks and soft regimes for criminal offenders, Major offered comfort to those who were disturbed by what seemed to be a world that was 'changing too fast for comfort [with] old certainties crumbling [and] traditional values falling away'.[27]

The prime minister poured scorn on 'fashionable opinion'[28] and urged a revival in traditional Conservative impulses: 'It is time to return to core values ... to self-discipline and respect for the law, to consideration for others, to accepting responsibility for yourself and your family.'[29] He reiterated the need to return to basic principles and promised that a Conservative party reawakened to its role would 'lead the country back to those basics right across the board'.[30] The speech was a classic example of Major employing the vision of his own past as the guiding frame of reference for his party's position. As *The Times* noted, Major's depiction of conservative values was brought to life by his own life and experience that provided a 'vision steeped in nostalgia for his tranquil London boyhood: a country in which people were polite to each other, the law was respected and common sense prevailed. The golden age of the Thatcherites may be the 1980s, but for John Major it is the 1950s.'[31] Margaret Thatcher gave her approval to the speech and thought that the Thatcherite inheritance was more secure than it had been before the Blackpool conference. It was thought that Major might after all be able to unify the party by redirecting populist impulses away from the divisive European issue and towards more unifying targets in the social policy field.

While the speech itself was seen to be effective in the context of a party conference, it subsequently generated a succession of new problems for the beleaguered prime minister. In retrospect, as Anthony Seldon notes, the seeds of the problem were sown in the 'hectic nature of Major government decision-making'.[32] The consequences of Major's chosen theme had not been given sufficient consideration:

> The plan was to go into the conference fighting on three issues of the Conservatives' own choosing, the economy, law and order, and education. But Number 10 produced the words 'back to basics' in John Major's keynote speech, a phrase

> intended to pull together the broad drift of the strategy. Insufficient thought had been given to the words, which were subsequently invested with interpretations that the hurried process of speech-writing and policy-making had overlooked.[33]

Apart from the fact that the government found it difficult to provide any follow-up to the back to basics exhortation, other than negative responses such as tougher sentences and more police resources, the breadth of the theme meant that it was susceptible to differing interpretations. Major was later to insist that he had been referring to social morality and respect for the law rather than to individual behaviour, sexual standards or family values. Nevertheless, the latter categories could fairly be construed as being a necessary part of Major's message, especially as he had specifically placed his back to basics call in a context of family respect. Whether the media were looking for a lead from the Major administration and Conservative party in respect to the theme, or whether they were united upon looking for hypocrisy, it rapidly became clear that the 'individual moral stands of senior party figures could not withstand the extra scrutiny which the speech unintentionally invited'.[34]

A succession of scandals followed the launch of the 'back to basics' campaign. Four ministers, two Parliamentary Private Secretaries and a government whip were forced to resign as a result of adverse publicity concerning their private lives. Most damaging of all were the disclosures that two Conservative MPs had been discovered accepting £1,000 each to table questions in the House of Commons on areas related to commercially valuable government information. By October 1994, the 'cash for questions' scandal had forced John Major to set up the Nolan Committee on Standards in Public Life to investigate the contemporary ethics of political conduct. The subsequent inquiry highlighted the problem of 'sleaze' at the heart of the political process and drew attention to what the Committee referred to as a 'culture of moral vagueness'.[35] Major's attempt to introduce a renewed sense of traditional community into the political landscape ended ignominiously. It succeeded only in heightening the public's awareness of the dangers presented by a party in office for a prolonged period. As a consequence, the 'back to basics' campaign was 'widely regarded as an own goal by the Major government'.[36]

Crisis in the premier's linkage to the public

One of the key problems faced in the area of media relations was that of personnel. In contrast to his predecessor who had the support of the robustly assertive Bernard Ingham as her press secretary, John Major preferred the more measured competence of civil servants such as Gus O'Donnell and Chris Meyer. They attempted to give the prime minister greater visibility through the introduction of mini-press conferences outside Number 10 and the open attribution of 'Downing Street sources' in lobby briefings. But they lacked Bernard Ingham's weight both as an ex-journalist and as a publicly recognised confidante of the prime minister. As Colin Seymour-Ure notes, for 'a prime minister with Major's leadership problems, a press secretary with strong political instinct and an experienced news sense would have had a better chance of success'.[37] It is true that Chris Meyer was forceful in projecting Number 10's daily priorities on to the news-gathering agenda. Nicholas Jones recognised that Meyer's tight focus helped Downing Street to influence the development of emerging news stories. Meyer would often open 'his briefings with what [was] clearly a carefully crafted response to the main news story ... He intend[ed] it to be used by TV and radio journalists as the sound-bite of the day. Lobby correspondents, just like other journalists, are always searching for a top line to their story. With Meyer there [was] no mistake about Downing Street's stance.'[38] But in spite of Meyer's efforts in this respect, his success in developing a deeper relationship with the media remained limited. This was due to a lack of resonance with the visceral community of senior reporters, editors and proprietors, and also to the absence of any senior cabinet figure committed to cultivating the media elites. But most significantly of all, the problem was a reflection of the deep antagonism of the press towards the Major government.

The antipathy towards Major was not limited to the left-of-centre press. It extended to many of the traditional vehicles of Tory promotion that had been central to the pursuit of the Thatcherite agenda of the 1980s. Major became a victim of a self-perpetuating dynamic. A critical press would stimulate disarray, division and ambition within Conservative ranks, which would lead in turn to a greater deterioration in the government's public standing and to an intensification of media complaint and condemnation. The organsational, doctrinal and electoral threat to the Conservative party posed by the Major administration generated a disjunction in the Tory press between an instinctive 'long-term onslaught on socialism' and a 'short-run but vehement, disenchantment with the post-Thatcher Tory party'.[39] For Major, there appeared to be very little slack in a system of media coverage that normally favoured the Conservative party. By 1994, newspapers like *The Times*, *The Sun*, the *Daily Telegraph* and the *Sunday Times*, which were traditionally conservative in temperament, had become Major's sternest critics and were responsible for underwriting much of the speculation over Major's continued leadership of the party.

The occasion on which this disillusionment was given its most forcible expression was the leadership election of 1995. In an effort to end the plots against his leadership and to renew his authority in the party, Major dramatically resigned the leadership and dared his opponents to declare themselves in an open contest. His call to 'put up or shut up' was designed to rally the party around his leadership and to mobilise the support base of the Conservative organisation in preparation for the general election. It quickly became evident that the Tory press would not answer the call for unity. Many newspapers that had traditionally provided the links between the Conservative party and its sympathisers in the constituencies saw their role as one of developing the indictment against the prime minister. Even though the leadership contest propelled the party into a position of aroused public interest, much of the Tory press saw its role as one of making the case for a genuine challenge to the leadership.

In the *Daily Telegraph*, for example, Simon Heffer declared that it would be in the party's interest to transform Major's voluntary retirement into a coercive and permanent one. Heffer did not prevaricate:

> The evidence of Mr Major's weaknesses is plentiful; the concatenation of crises and scandals ever since the summer of 1992, when the pound came under pressure in the ERM, have shown him to be a poor prime minister ... It would be best for his party, in my view, if it replaced him now, for there is nothing to suggest that he will govern more effectively in the future.[40]

In *The Times*, William Rees-Mogg continued his long-established indictment of Major's leadership. Although Major's resignation was acknowledged to be a bold stroke, it did not resolve any of the underlying issues that had afflicted the premiership. It did not 'even resolve the question of John Major's temperamental weakness as a leader' or 'his underlying weakness ... in the direction of national policy'.[41] Under Major's leadership, 'British policy ha[d] been adrift during his five years in Downing Street'.[42] For Major to stand on his record and to decide 'not to make any new policy statement to justify his re-election' meant in effect that he was 'a candidate without a manifesto'[43] and therefore a leader offering no strategic direction for the country. The *Sunday Telegraph* thought that for Major to stand on his record was in itself a sign of incompetence because it was precisely 'his record which [had] caused the trouble'.[44] As there were 'real doubts about his competence, his electability and his European policy', the paper believed that 'Mr Major deserve[d] to be challenged'.[45] Andrew Neil, in the *Sunday Times*, was even more direct over the shortcomings of Major's period of office and over the corrective action required:

> His has been a government ... that has lurched from folly to gaffe to crisis, buffeted by events beyond its control under a limp leadership that has allowed squabbling nonentities to fill the vacuum left by an absence of firm government ... The Tory party is in dire need of a prime minister who offers a fresh start, new inspiration and strong, determined leadership ... [T]here is nothing in Mr Major's make-up or track record to suggest he has the ability to re-invent himself or his government.[46]

Even though no senior cabinet figure emerged to contest the leadership, *The Times*, the *Sunday Times*, the *News of the World*, the *Daily Telegraph*, the *Sunday Telegraph*, the *Daily Mail* and the *Sun* all adopted a position against Major in the leadership election. Only the *Mail on Sunday*, the *Evening Standard*, and the *Express* newspapers remained loyal to the leadership. In the event, John Major secured victory over John Redwood in the election but this did not resolve the underlying problems in the party and the government as a whole. While it did provide the prime minister with a temporary boost in his approval ratings and prompted another reassessment of Number 10's media strategy, the election succeeded only in demonstrating the chronic condition of the Major administration. Notwithstanding an improvement in the economy, Major found it increasingly difficult to penetrate the defences of a deeply resistant public or to shift the media away from its preoccupation with sleaze, division and decay.

Labour and the rise of Millbank

Major's problems in public projection were made all the more acute by the high levels of news management that had been achieved by the Labour party. Media relations constituted an integral part of the New Labour project, in terms of both guiding philosophy and operational priorities. As a consequence, enormous resources were applied to the monitoring of news coverage and to the mobilisation and co-ordination of party output to the news-gathering processes. Labour's communications headquarters at Millbank became a byword for high resolution news organisation. With a staff of approximately 200 and with access to a profusion of research materials, policy documents, databases, press releases, polling intelligence and high-tech analytical and communication equipment, Millbank represented the logistical, managerial and presentational instrument of the Blairite project. The Millbank headquarters was designed to provide the most sophisticated sensory device for tackling news stories and comment, and for giving the party the maximum opportunity of reacting to them in order to counter misinformation and to advance its own news priorities.

Millbank allowed the party to develop a continual engagement with the mass media in what was rapidly becoming a permanent political campaign conducted incessantly through increasing media outlets that were creating a continuous news cycle. Modelled upon Bill Clinton's 'war room' from the 1992 presidential election, Millbank drew together the previously atomised units of the party's media and electoral agencies and melded them together for maximum effect. Again like Clinton's war room, Millbank was given an open-plan design that was intended to promote integration, focus, single-mindedness and a sense of community dedicated to the overriding objective of securing a Labour victory in the next general election. The emphasis given to Millbank and the missionary zeal with which it was invested reflected Blair's conviction that media relations were essential to the party's prospects. As leader, he saw 'handling the media as an essential part of doing the job, explaining to the public and party what he [was] doing and why'.[47] Millbank facilitated this role but it also allowed the leadership to mobilise the party in support of its electoral strategy through the authority and reach of its communications network.

Millbank, therefore, was not just an instrument for monitoring and interacting with the mass media. It was an action agency in keeping the party at large 'on message'. Through phones, faxes, modems and pagers, shadow spokespersons and candidates were continually informed of the party's line in the public arena. Millbank pioneered the intensive and centralised usage of telephone canvassing in marginal seats. In effect, 'Labour's old retail network of local branches [was] superseded by ... direct marketing in key constituencies ... combined with mass marketing to the rest of the population through television and radio'.[48] The emancipation from the party's branch network afforded the 'leadership far greater control over the message ... and a unified command that [could] respond swiftly to events'.[49] 'Conservative media specialists watched in admiration as Labour politicians repeated their soundbites on the main evening news programmes.'[50] While John Major's government was openly riven with splits, divisions, rebellions and talk of leadership crises, Tony Blair was able to present New Labour as a government-in-waiting, with all the discipline normally associated with the Conservative party. To his detractors, Blair was expending valuable resources and energies by placing the party on a war footing. Given that the election could be over two years away, such a heightened level of preparedness was seen as unnecessary, wasteful and artificial. The party was in effect behaving as if it were fighting an election campaign when no election was in prospect. But to the leadership, this was precisely the strategy that Millbank had been created to pursue.

In Philip Gould's view, New Labour's emphasis upon media management and communications was a necessary response to a changed context of political exchange. To Gould, '[c]ampaigns now go on not just for weeks, but for years. Perpetual, continuous campaigning has become the norm.'[51] As it can take years to build up a basis of public trust, so an opposition party can never relax its vigilance in the quest for public approval in a media-saturated environment. Gould continues:

> In a campaign, you must always seek and keep the momentum ... Gaining momentum means dominating the news agenda, entering the news cycle at the earliest possible time, and repeatedly re-entering it, with stories and initiatives that ensure that subsequent news coverage is set on your terms. It means anticipating and pre-empting your opponents' likely manoeuvres, giving them no room to breathe, keeping them on the defensive.[52]

These sentiments were no doubt influenced by Gould's experiences in the Clinton campaigns. Nevertheless, they were to prove apposite in the New Labour campaign, which proceeded on the premise that the election constituted an extension to, rather than a disjunction from, normal politics.

Millbank rapidly became synonymous with professionalism and sophistication. Whether it was market research, private polling, telephone targeting or focus group technologies, Labour's communications headquarters acquired a reputation for being incapable of relaxing its grip on the propagation of the party's message and on the prosecution of its electoral strategy. Millbank was the centre of the party's action plan to target ninety marginal seats at the expense of drastically reducing the resources assigned to other areas. Pippa Norris explains the chosen technique:

> For two years before polling day, a Labour task force was designed to switch 5,000 votes in each of the ninety target marginal seats. Those identified as potential Labour converts in these seats were contacted by teams of volunteers on the doorstep and by a canvassing operation run from twenty telephone banks around the country, coordinated from Millbank. In January 1997 'get out to the vote' letters were sent to each type of target voter, and young people received a video of Tony Blair.[53]

But perhaps the most impressive element in Millbank's armoury was 'Excalibur' or EFS (i.e. Electronic Filing System). This was a database of speeches, comments, policy statements, figures and reports that allowed Labour strategists to check facts and issue 'instant rebuttals' to any Conservative claims which the party deemed to be fallacious. The New Labour leadership was aware that the Conservatives' research department and its traditional press support had in the past often given the party the edge over Labour in the battle over public information. It was now determined to prevent Labour's opponents from engaging in the kinds of negative campaigning that proved so successful in the 1992 general election.

Labour took its cue from Bill Clinton's 1992 presidential campaign, which in its turn had been intent upon avoiding the mistakes of Michael Dukakis's campaign in 1988. In that election, the Democratic leader had allowed inflammatory attacks upon him to go unanswered in the mistaken belief that they would have no effect upon voter choice. By 1992, this was seen to have been a strategic error. It led Clinton to give a high priority to the need for 'instant rebuttal' where the objective was to prevent the opposition from controlling a single day's news cycle. By responding quickly enough to an opponent's allegation, it was possible to ensure that the counter would be integrated into the succeeding news broadcasts, thereby preventing the original claim from dominating a news cycle unchallenged. Philip Gould had observed the effect of Clinton's model usage of instant rebuttal at first hand and was so impressed by its utility that it became the source of his ten fixed principles of campaigning. According to Gould, any 'political assertion, however false, can spread through [the] media jungle with the speed of a panther'.[54] False claims could quickly become plausible if they remained unanswered:

> An unrebutted lie becomes accepted as the truth. You must always rebut a political attack if leaving it unanswered will harm you. And you must do it instantly, within minutes at best, within hours at worst, and with a defence supported by facts. That is what the computer Excalibur and the Rapid Rebuttal Unit at Millbank were about. The first big Tory tax attack in November 1996 was smashed back within three hours with a convincing rebuttal document, and that effectively was the beginning of the end of the Tories' tax campaign.[55]

The rapid retrieval of material and the organisation of counterclaims through Excalibur's daily updated database helped Labour to retain the initiative against the Major administration and to enhance its image of an organisation outperforming the government in the conspicuous field of information management.

Conservative responses to Millbank

On the day that a special Labour party conference gave its approval to the replacement of Clause Four in the party constitution, John Major condemned Blair as a shallow front man for a still dangerous organisation that had expropriated Conservative ideas and policies while retaining its old agendas. He denounced Blair as a leader wedded to 'soundbite politics'.[56] Major complained: 'Blair doesn't ask me questions about anything that is of serious interest. It's whatever is the soundbite issue of the day.'[57] To Major, New Labour amounted to a cynical piece of marketing with 'everything pre-packaged as though you were selling a soap powder'.[58]

In spite of these condemnations, Major could not fail to have seen that Blair's capture and transformation of the Labour party amounted to a quantum leap in the development of leadership politics in the British system. It also represented a challenge to him as prime minister to make a political response in the terms that his opponent had helped to establish. In some respects, the decision by Major to give himself and his leadership greater public prominence was influenced by a personal conviction that he had been pivotal in snatching victory from the jaws of defeat in the 1992 general election. He believed it was possible to repeat the exercise. Given the faction-ridden state of the Conservative party, it could also be said that Major had no alternative other than to distract attention from the chronic condition of his own party. But it was Blair's precedent in effectively distancing himself from the Labour party and its negative connotations that provided the impetus to Major's choice to adopt a presidential campaign strategy.

Resigning the leadership in 1995 in an effort to reclaim it with revived authority had not resolved Major's problems. The party remained divided and preoccupied with different doctrinal and sectarian agendas. The prime minister continued to be publicly condemned as an 'incompetent, shifty, amoral, self-centred leader of few principles'[59] by conservative commentators. Furthermore, he remained the object of incessantly unfavourable contrasts with Tony Blair, who was seen to have 'treated the Labour Party with a ruthlessness that Wilson never showed'.[60] Prior to the leadership contest, Major demonstrated an awareness of the need to re-establish links with the party's grassroots and with the public at large. 'I think it is true that we have not communicated',[61] Major declared in May 1995. 'I suppose we spent too much time on the politics of policy and too little time explaining to people why we are doing what we are doing.'[62] For the leader of a party that in its recent history had given specific emphasis to ideological prescription, Major appealed to the country to help him construct a 'people's policy'.[63] He announced that in order to 'bridge the gap between the doorsteps of Britain and the corridors of power',[64] he and his cabinet would engage in a grand tour of the country to consult party activists and the public about the next Conservative programme.

As part of a general refit at Number 10, designed to convey an impression of public responsiveness and policy initiative, Major appointed Norman Blackwell as head of the prime minister's Policy Unit. It was hoped that Blackwell would provide the Policy Unit with a focal point of policy advice, analysis and direction. Blackwell's predecessor, Sarah Hogg, had become bogged down in short-term crisis management, which only added to Major's appearance of being controlled by events. Blackwell was assisted by the flamboyant Howell James, who had replaced Jonathan Hill as the prime minister's Political Secretary in November 1994. Howell James's career in advertising, commercial radio and the BBC had at one point led him to become press spokesman for the ill-fated TV-am Company. During this period, James had been instrumental in turning the company around from a position of almost total collapse. Thereafter, he described himself as having been press officer to Roland Rat. A Tory admirer referred to his appointment in the following terms: 'You could say the man who rescued TV-am from disaster has arrived to do the same for this government.'[65]

It was individuals such as Norman Blackwell, Howell James, and Major's press secretary Chris Meyer and his successor Jonathan Haslam who supported and encouraged the prime minister in his strategy of reviving Conservative fortunes through a long campaign. It was envisaged that this would focus attention upon Major himself as an antidote to the public's fatigue with the party and the government. Major's team at Number 10 regarded the prime minister as the party's only remaining asset and believed that by marketing him in an explicit and concerted manner, it would be possible to create an entirely different public conception of the party. As a consequence, Major began an explicit campaign to cultivate the media and to project himself as the calming and accessible centre of stability in an otherwise agitated, and even paranoid, state of public debate.

In June 1994, the prime minister had experimented with an on-the-record press conference for reporters in the Downing Street garden. In some respects, it was designed to be an act of defiance in which the prime minister would face down criticism following the catastrophic European elections in which the Conservatives secured only 27.8 per cent of the popular vote. In a more positive light, it provided a stage for the prime minister to look and sound authoritative. He fielded questions from reporters in a presidential format, in which he projected an individual presence expressing on camera his reactions to the issues and themes in an unstructured context. The way the event set the prime minister visually apart from the government, accentuated the authority of the office and attracted immense media attention established it as a key precedent in Major's presidential strategy for the general election campaign. The exercise was repeated in January 1995. On this occasion, the venue was the state dining room in Downing Street but the open-ended on-the-record format of the garden press conference remained the same. Major used the event in an attempt to regain the political initiative by engaging in a direct appeal for the public's trust, both in his government's long-term policies and in his personal commitments to social improvement and to constitutional continuity. In June 1995, the prime minister was back in the Downing Street garden, but this time the press and media had been assembled to cover at first hand the prime minister's statement in which he resigned the leadership of the party and challenged his critics to challenge him. No regular pattern of press conferences was established by these events, but they did provide insights into the potential for prime ministerial outreach which helped to determine a direction that, by the end of 1996, had become clearly evident.

Opting for a presidential election

On 5 January 1997, Major announced that he would adopt a more presidential approach to the run-up to the next general election. Specifically, he would hold a series of White House-style on-the-record press conferences. His intention was to establish a personal rapport with the public: 'I hope that I can get directly through to the public without having my views enshrined in someone else's words. So in future if people read "friends of John Major say" they can discount it. The media will have the opportunity of asking me directly and I will tell them directly.'[66] The press conferences would be held every three to four weeks until the election was called, at which point they would be scheduled on a daily basis. Major wanted to create as much of a monopoly as possible on the party's media relations. Government strategists believed that the press conference format would not only secure valuable media coverage but also give Mr Major an additional source of authority as the premier in a presidential context providing an individual embodiment of the party and government. Major's determination to take a personal case to the people even led him to state that he would keep an open mind on the idea of a televised debate with Tony Blair.

Political commentators were quick to seize the significance of such an announcement. Major was staking the future of his party upon an election campaign that would be geared to the prime minister's capacity to shape the agenda and to select those issues most favourable to his record and style of leadership. In effect, Major wanted to make himself the key issue. To Donald Macintyre of *The Independent*, Major was seeking to imitate Tony Blair: 'For it is he, rather than his party, whom the voters are explicitly being asked to endorse. For all the Tory claims that their opponents are a one-man band, it is they who now offer up a single figure as their champion, their prize electoral asset. On Tuesday, Mr Major stood alone against a backdrop on which the word Conservative was nowhere to be seen.'[67] But in Macintyre's view, the strategy to emulate Blair was flawed because Major's decision was born out of weakness and party disintegration rather than on the basis of a supportive party propelling its leader into sweeping prerogative and unembarrassed public exposure. Blair's achievement was that he had 'at last turned Labour into the party most capable of leading'.[68]

While Major had long criticised New Labour's emphasis upon Tony Blair as a way of concealing the recidivist tendencies of Old Labour, the prime minister now appeared to be endorsing such a form of concealment himself. Major's presidential strategy was a proposed device for drawing attention away from the ungovernable state of the Conservative party. The plan was a sign not merely of the prime minister's isolation but of the strategic imperative of his remaining in isolation. To Hugo Young, the Conservatives could not win the election as a party. They were 'an entity incapable of performing the task'[69] for which they were putting themselves forward as a governing party. Major's avowed presidentialism, therefore, was less of a choice and more a 'reflection of his predicament ... of being so terribly alone'.[70] As such, the presidential strategy was the only conceivable alternative: 'He is driven to extremes and contradictory lengths. The only chance he has of re-election is by creating the illusion that the parliamentary system, of which party is the basic building block, has been replaced by something else.'[71]

Major looked forward to the 1997 general election because it afforded him the opportunity to revisit his triumph in the 1992 general election and to relaunch himself as a natural and formidable campaigner. Now at last he could leave the divisions and misbehaviour of his party to one side and concentrate upon his virtues as 'honest John'. The populist gesture in 1992 of publicly abandoning the accoutrements of political marketing and image building in favour of a trusted soapbox was repeated in 1997. This time, Major began his campaign with the soapbox and proceeded upon the premise that the longer and greater his contact with the public, the more likely it was that the Conservatives could close the gap on Labour. Accordingly, the prime minister opted for the longest possible campaigning period. The time would be used to publicise the good news on the economic recovery, to arouse voter fears over the taxation threat of a Labour government and to pressurise the Labour party into making mistakes, revealing self-doubt and disclosing previously concealed divisions and hidden agendas. This may have been a viable strategy if Major had had only one source of opposition. But the prime minister faced competitors on several fronts. In addition to Labour, he had to contend with those who were alienated within his own party and who were already reconciled to electoral defeat, to parliamentary opposition and to a new Conservative leadership. Major also had to confront the threat of the Liberal Democrats, who were set to squeeze Conservative majorities in the South and West of England. Finally, the prime minister was faced with the corrosive force of Sir James Goldsmith's Referendum party, whose virulently Eurosceptic posture threatened to split the Conservative vote.

The British Perot

The Referendum party was potentially dangerous because its effect was unpredictable. Fuelled by James Goldsmith's fortune, the party's £20 million media blitz attacked politicians in general for taking Britain 'into a federal European superstate by deceit'[72] and for continuing to surrender sovereign rights and powers through concealment and an avoidance of open debate. In Goldsmith's view, politicians were the 'most despicable human subspecies' he had ever experienced in his life.[73] He condemned them with a populist elan worthy of Ross Perot:

> They go from university into the research departments of parliamentary parties, are offered a losing seat at 27 and a winning seat at 33; become a PPS [Parliamentary Private Secretary]. Most have never visited the real world for a second. To me they are trash compared with a small businessman who faces reality every day. They are trimmers, careerists and opportunists.[74]

Although he thought Blair was 'dumb',[75] he reserved particular disdain for recent Conservative leaders who had been instrumental in involving Britain in the misadventure of European integration. His anti-politics populism led him to disavow any intention of becoming permanently involved in politics: 'we are not politicians and do not want to be politicians'.[76] His controlling premise was, 'the people as a whole have a wisdom which the elite lacks'.[77] A referendum on Britain's future would release that native prudence into the political arena and subject the policies of accumulated Conservative administrations to direct popular review.

The evident resonance of the Referendum party with the Eurosceptic wing of his own party prompted Major into another highly conspicuous public exercise of personal defiance. It was reminiscent of the occasion in the 1992 general election when he abandoned set-piece electioneering and resorted to the direct approach by immersing himself in crowds and speaking with a loud-hailer on top of a soapbox. On 16 April 1997, Major at short notice ditched the theme of unemployment in his morning press conference. He abandoned the prepared text for release and decided he would tackle head on the European question on his own, without the use of notes and teleprompts. Elements in his own party had often gone public in opposition to Major's policy of 'wait and see' in relation to the European single currency. Now he would go public in his appeal to them not to restrict his freedom of manoeuvre as a leader to 'wring the best deal out of our partners'. He implored his Eurosceptic colleagues to back off: 'Like me or loathe me, do not bind my hands when I'm negotiating on behalf of the British nation.'[78] That evening's party election broadcast was also suddenly abandoned in favour of John Major talking to camera on the same theme with the same message. Its improvised quality conveyed directness and urgency. The prime minister produced an impassioned appeal to the country at large to support his 'negotiate and decide' position on the single currency. In effect this was a request for his personal judgement and political skills to be endorsed in preparation for a political context that would be dominated by mutual pressure and leverage. The simplicity of the appeal and the starkness of the setting provoked widespread comment. One analyst of the media discerned a clear objective in the selected format:

> Apart from invoking the television of national emergencies, the broadcast also intriguingly had another more recent forbear. The only other modern politician to have devoted an election broadcast to himself at his desk was Sir James Goldsmith in his Referendum Party broadcast ... Few critics at the time expected this bleak and tedious style to be copied by other parties but now it has been. This is surely not a coincidence, for it is at the Goldsmith-sympathisers in Major's party that his ad was aimed.[79]

In some respects, it could be claimed that this was the 'first British party election broadcast addressed entirely to members of a party rather than the electorate at large'.[80] But in another sense, it could be seen as a public reprimand by a leader seeking to shame and to disgrace his party into disciplined compliance that would allow him palpably to distance himself from its influence. Others believed that the broadcast demonstrated both facets of Major's predicament – namely the weakness of his political position and the extraordinary level of self-belief in his own leadership and his own rapport with the general public. To Paul Goodman, here was a prime minister assured in the knowledge that he had a back channel at his disposal which was not available to the critics and dissenters:

> In his fury and fatigue – and that strange, eerie calm that succeeds fatigue – he has fallen back on the primal, stubborn drive that bore him from the streets of Brixton to 10 Downing Street ... The Prime Minister is not, surely, a superstitious man. But he holds ... to a belief almost primitive in its force: that he maintains a mysterious, personal power of communication with the British people ... What we saw yesterday was ... John Major *contra mundum*. The repeated use of the personal pronoun, and the reference to the 'scars' inflicted by the ERM debacle, struck an even more personal note than before. Mr Major

> more than any other party leader in recent history, has now placed the fate of an election squarely in one man's hands.[81]

John Major not only felt besieged on all sides, he used television to underline his sense of isolation and his credentials for a higher calling than that of merely party leader or prime minister.

Leadership campaigning

Major pursued several set themes in the election campaign. He alluded to the improving economy and for the need for political experience in European negotiations. The prime minister sought to marginalise the Referendum party by ignoring it and the threat it posed to the Conservatives. Major attempted to dent the customarily flamboyant and leadership-centred campaign of the Liberal Democrats by claiming that a vote for Ashdown would in effect be a vote for Tony Blair. This strategy could cut both ways because it reminded voters in safe Tory seats of the potential power of voting for the Lib Dems. In many constituencies a vote for the Liberal Democrats was the only way of registering a vote against the Conservatives or of taking action that would contribute towards the formation of a Labour government. New Labour, however, remained Major's central concern. He referred to Labour's historical inability either to control public spending or to resist tax increases. He also made an issue of the dangers posed by Labour's endorsement of constitutional reform.

But the most persistent and penetrating theme pressed both consciously and incidentally by Major was that of the benefits and utility of his leadership. He declared himself to be emancipated by the campaign as it allowed him to break away from the physical centre of power in London. 'It is a very artificial life, the centre of politics', he said. 'It is not real, and you are subjected to all sorts of artificial influences.'[82] Being away from it was synonymous with being where he belonged and where from his origins he remained – namely in touch with the ordinary citizenry where he could play to his strengths as a natural communicator. It was only in the campaign that he could revive his communion with the people and allow it to determine his agendas, schedules and priorities. In doing so, his own position could once again be enhanced by what he sensed would be the direct injection of popular consciousness. In effect, he felt that he was finally in charge of his own destiny:

> He's the orchestrator of his own campaign: composer, conductor and most of the wind section, if not the brass. For the final two weeks, the terrible party has at last been silenced whilst its leader takes centre stage. He calls the shots,

> decides what Saatchis will not spend, pushes himself as the only Tory asset the voters might want to vote for. He goes on television, face to face, looking down the lens, warning the nation more in sorrow than in anger against what it is about to do.[83]

While Major's campaign could be characterised by improvisation and unpredictability, Blair's campaign was the epitome of smooth professionalism, with themes, news events and venues all calibrated to produce the desired effects in support of the leadership's central strategy and objectives. New Labour had been so geared to the general election and had become so accustomed to the disciplines of a permanent election over the preceding two years that there was barely a discernible difference for the leadership between the two conditions of opposition politics and actual campaigning. The continuity was evident from the repeated invocation of issues that had already become familiar to the public during Blair's leadership. In respect to the Conservatives, the message remained that it was time for a change and that enough was enough. The pressure points of sleaze, betrayal, drift, stagnation, privilege, weak leadership and the priority of privilege over people continued to be exploited as they had been over the previous two years. In respect to Labour, the insistent claims were those of modernisation, renewal and the future of Britain. Particular emphasis was given to the leader's contractual pledges on investment, training, education, health and constitutional change. The key priority, however, was that of strong leadership and a personal project based upon the need to build public reassurance. Accordingly, Labour strategy concentrated upon the youth, strength and dynamism of Blair as the party's top strength. By the same token, it regarded the alleged failures and incompetence of John Major as a key Conservative weakness that required continual re-emphasis as a campaign priority.[84]

Blair's task all along had been to demonstrate that Labour was now responsible and worthy of public trust. As Blair made clear at the beginning of the campaign, the achievements of Labour modernisation were to be deployed as collateral in the campaign to secure public confidence:

> Labour needs to show that it has changed. The choice which the British people will face will not be between old Left and the new Right. New Labour is a transformed political force which offers a new political programme. We have changed our constitution so that it accurately reflects the needs of a modern country. We have revolutionised our relations with the trade unions, to make clear that we offer fairness, not favours, in government. Our early manifesto, New Labour to its core, was approved by 95 per cent of our members. That programme does not rely on out-of-date ideology, but offers practical solutions to Britain's problems.[85]

It was Blair's role to provide public reassurance that the leadership would ensure that there would be no retreat to Old Labour, no implosion into traditional identities and no derailments into the tax-and-spend excesses of the past. The conspicuous projection of Blair's leadership was depicted as neither a screen nor a diversion. It was portrayed as a genuine and decisive sign of a radical metamorphosis. The change would not only allow Labour to withstand public scrutiny, but was in its own right an expression of the party's new responsiveness to a general and more undifferentiated constituency of public concerns.

The leadership was portrayed as the party's talisman of trust. It gave physical form to New Labour's subliminal inference that it was *de facto* a different party to the one it had been in the past. Blair did not just personify the refit. He was its active and originating agent; he was its defining symbol, its pivotal underwriter and the chief means of substantiating its claims of being free of vested interests. Blair was depicted as being the public point of access to, and the individual guarantor of, the New Labour project. Public awareness of these images and claims associated with the Blair leadership had been cultivated over the previous two and half years. Labour's election campaign was now dedicated to preserving the integrity of these associations and to extending them to the point of making them impregnable to any negative campaign tactics employed by the party's opponents.

The presidential debate issue

Negotiations over the staging of a live television debate between the contenders for the premiership had begun as early as April 1996. Rival broadcasting organisations were engaged in their own campaigns to capture the prize of the first presidential-style confrontation between a sitting prime minister and a challenger. The proposal for a live debate was not new. The ritual of the challenge and its rebuff had almost become part of the architecture of general elections. While opposition leaders such as Harold Wilson (1964), Edward Heath (1966), Michael Foot (1983) and Neil Kinnock (1987, 1992) had regularly challenged prime ministers to a televised duel, premiers had invariably refused the invitations. In 1983, when Margaret Thatcher commanded a solid lead in the polls, she reacted to Michael Foot's challenge with a stern reproof: 'We are not electing a president.'[86] There was some irony to this statement as it was precisely the prospect of an opposition leader appearing with the prime minister that carried the threat of compromising the premier's authority and assigning prime ministerial potential to the challenger. On occasion, the normal stimulus–response pattern has been reversed. In 1979, when the prime minister, James Callaghan, suggested a confrontation with Margaret Thatcher, her advisors pressed her to decline. John Major was faced with similar problems in 1997. The Conservatives were willing to chance anything to cut into Labour's twenty point lead and, therefore, were not averse in principle to conceding a prime minister debate. For his part, Blair had been in favour of such an encounter since April 1996. The Major team believed that the prime minister could extend the primacy he had regularly achieved over Blair at Prime Minister's Questions to the format of a televised confrontation. Moreover, the prime minister was the Conservatives' chief asset in terms of their public appeal and, therefore, to give John Major even greater visibility might be an advantage to an otherwise discredited party. Private polls conducted for the Labour party showed that the more the public saw of Tony Blair, the more they liked him. Labour strategists saw a televised debate as an opportunity to enhance Blair's appeal still further by projecting a clear contrast between the opposition leader and a dithering prime minister presiding over a disintegrating government.

The debate project, which was agreed to in principle by both the main parties, ultimately failed to materialise owing to a profusion of problems that could not be resolved quickly enough to allow for a debate within the election timetable. Disputes arose over the number and length of the debates, over whether an audience should be included and how it should be selected, and over whether it would interact with the principal contenders. The proposal also generated questions over the form and organisation of the moderating function, the staging arrangements, and the level and type of questioning. But the most problematic issue related to the broadcaster's legal requirement to maintain balance and impartiality, which led to severe problems over the status of the Liberal Democratic leader in such a setting. Various devices were advanced to resolve this difficulty but it remained a political and constitutional barrier. Major did not wish to be outnumbered by two opposition leaders, especially in front of a studio audience that would be weighted against an established government. On the other hand, 'Labour was content to issue challenges, secure in the knowledge that the Conservatives would appear scared if they declined, but vulnerable to a two-pronged assault if they accepted'.[87] It is probable that both main parties were nervous over the prospect of Ashdown repeating what Ross Perot had achieved in the 1992 presidential election, when the stock and credibility of the third-party candidate increased following his appearance in the presidential debates.

Ultimately, the debate proposal foundered, but in doing so it revealed first the extent to which public outreach by the leaders had become an established and increasing part of the election itinerary, and second the way in which leader–public linkages now dominated election strategies. The issue of a prime ministerial debate was fuelled by the broadcasting organisations' growing confidence and authority in their role as a component of the democratic process. Many of the arguments in favour of a televised debate were based upon the idea that a leader-to-leader spectacle would be the natural outcome to the televising of parliament and to television news becoming the main source of political information. If the leaders sought media coverage so assiduously, then it seemed appropriate to draw them together within a media-enriched context. There was a need for a format that would 'allow the best campaign between the two contenders'.[88] The media would be providing a public service: 'Voters do not only need to see candidates on television and judge their performance on the medium, they are entitled to it.'[89] A leader in *The Independent* pursued the implication that television would be performing a civic duty by arranging a debate:

> Here we are not (yet) electing a president. But television already plays a huge – if little understood – role in political choice ... Use of television (which may often turn into use by television) is nowadays part of the governing process. What minister can hope to put over a controversial policy to the House of Commons alone, without attempting to persuade and inform in the television studios? Even their own backbenchers judge them as much by their performance on TV as on their performance in the debating chamber. Now that the proceedings of Parliament itself are televised, and now that politicians are so comfortable with the grammar of the medium and its opportunities for attack and defence, it is only logical to do what the Americans do and bring the party leaders into a formal televised election debate.[90]

The Times recognised that Britain did not have a presidential system. But it was 'nonsense to claim that it is exclusively parliamentary either. The quality of political leadership is fundamental to policy outcome.'[91] As a consequence, a debate would provide a searching examination of the leaders on the very grounds of imagery and media management that they themselves had adopted. This element of calling the leaders' own bluff on election strategy was clearly evident in many of the responses to the debate proposal. In a review of the failed negotiations, Stephen Coleman concluded that the party leaders 'should be expected to rehearse their positions ... because this form of democratic dialogue is what voters want, and because it enhances informed democratic citizenship'[92] and with it greater transparency and accountability.

The debate issue also revealed how extraordinarily sensitive the parties were to anything that might endanger their chief electoral investments. Their leaders were offered the prospect of a political spectacle that was likely to attract an audience of approximately half the adult population. In spite of this inducement, the party strategists advised against the venture. They did so for a variety of stated reasons, but behind the diverse objections to the format or its timing lay the factor of fear. The campaigns of the two main contenders represented the culmination of an intense process of planning designed to preserve, protect and defend each individual's claim to be the national and political leader with the qualifications to be premier. A debate threatened not only the respective autonomies of each campaign strategy, but also the individuality of each leader's appeal. Those carefully cultivated public images would be jeopardised through the unscripted and unpredictable nature of a direct exchange, either with one another or with an unknown audience. A debate would force the 'candidates to tackle a multitude of issues, without any assistance, in the full glare of the television camera'.[93] A debate would be 'by far the most searching experience any contender encounters'.[94] But it was precisely these properties that deterred both the candidates and their organisations.

As opposition leader, Tony Blair had every incentive to run a risk-averse campaign. In Millbank, New Labour had created an alternative media organisation to maximise the party's opportunities of generating a favourable impression in an environment that was traditionally hostile to Labour. The dynamics of a presidential-style debate threatened the intricacies of such an operation, especially as no guiding precedent had been established in previous elections. While Blair and the other leaders agreed to individual question-and-answer sessions in a range of formats,[95] they maintained their distance from one another in both time and space. The contrast in attitudes between a prime ministerial debate and other types of head-to-head confrontation was very noticeable. Constitutional objections, strategic reservations and political caution were conspicuously swept aside to allow for a series of other encounters. The contenders for the position of Chancellor of the Exchequer (i.e. Kenneth Clarke, Gordon Brown, Malcolm Bruce) engaged in two encounters that featured a three-way head-to-head debate (BBC2, *The Money Programme*; BBC1, *On the Record*). The same individuals were also involved in a three-way format that centred upon questions from a 300-strong audience. Similar debates featured the contenders for the positions of Deputy Prime Minister (i.e. Michael Heseltine, John Prescott, Alan Beith) and Home Secretary (i.e. Michael Howard, Jack Straw, Alex Carlile). Logically, in a system of cabinet government and collective responsibility, there should be no substantive difference between a prime ministerial debate and a debate between the deputy leaders, or between the Chancellor and his shadows. That this was not the case was conspicuously evident and served further to underline the distinctiveness between leaders and the rest.

Tony Blair and the professionalisation of public outreach

Notwithstanding the breakdown over the presidential debate, the party leaders pressed on with their strategic imperatives of reaching out to the public. In dispensing with a head-to-head leadership confrontation, Blair managed to turn the collapse in negotiations into an opportunity to reaffirm his commitment to engage directly with the voters and to connect his leadership with a sense of public immediacy and accessibility. 'This campaign is not going to be some presidential exchange', Blair said. 'It's got to be about the real questions that concern people ... We will be out very much with the people, talking about the things that matter to them, as we've been doing for the last nine months. I've done question and answer sessions all round the country, and I will carry on doing so.'[96] Major and Ashdown followed suit, joining Blair with their individual claims to superiority in the field of citizen empathy. It was Blair however, who, with the formidable planning, monitoring and co-ordination resources of Millbank at his disposal, was particularly adept at tuning his appearances to gain the maximum publicity at the optimum times in the right locations.

The trend towards media-centred campaigning established in previous elections was continued in 1997 with extensive efforts to exhibit the leaders without risking their leadership credentials in too many unstructured contexts. It is important for leaders to be seen and located in the midst of public gatherings and for them to be physically relating to popular concerns in visceral settings outside television and radio studios. By the same token, it is equally important for parties to minimise the chances of negative constructions being drawn from the unpredictable nature of such encounters. Press conferences, briefings, party election broadcasts, rallies and other set-piece arenas provide the best opportunities for generating precise imagery and statements. Nevertheless, this can lead to the disembodiment of candidates if they are seen to exist only in an artificially conflict-free habitat at a time of intense political competition. Journalists covering the 1992 general election complained that the daily press conferences were becoming a substitute for the cut and thrust of the hustings. The same complaints were made with even greater severity in 1997, when the election campaigns were more scripted and professionally staged for media consumption than ever. Even when the main party leaders appeared in unscripted and unstructured territory, every effort was made in their campaign organisations to reduce the attendant uncertainties. The following description of the Blair campaign out on the road conveys the priority given to the projection, but also to the protection, of the party's major investment:

> Journalists stand in fenced pens during walkabouts, are often excluded from

> parts of visits and are kept well away from the Labour leader. So tight is the rein on which reporters are kept that on Wednesday the Press Association correspondent was asked to take off her brown coat during a photo opportunity because it was deemed to be a depressing colour on a sunny day … The organisation – first class briefings, facilities for sending words and pictures, even refreshments to keep the mood upbeat – all help the Blair message in our papers and on our screens.[97]

Arguably, Blair had most to risk from the election campaign. John Major was prime minister and an established media figure whose 1992 track record, combined with the Conservatives' proven capacity as election campaign specialists, made the party a threat even with an opinion poll deficit of twenty-five points. Because of this, the Labour leadership required the most sophisticated and refined campaigning and news management organisation.

The Labour leadership's success both in cultivating the support of the press, and especially the tabloids, and in maximising the potential of the media in promoting its election campaign stung other party leaders into a response. Fearful that New Labour would win a landslide victory, thereby diminishing his leverage as kingmaker and prospective coalition partner, Paddy Ashdown turned his fire on Labour's lack of radicalism. He complained of the 'puniness of the commitments'[98] from a Labour party that gave priority to electoral calculation over principled conviction. In a section of a keynote address that was released to the press but which was cut just prior to the speech, Ashdown portrayed Blair as a cold politician who lacked the passion of Neil Kinnock. John Major decided to play the populist card and to attack what he saw to be the elitism of New Labour's conjunction with the media: 'There are two elections being fought: the one I read about and I see occasionally when I watch the media or listen to it; and the election that is being fought on the doorstep. I'm interested about the election that is being fought on the doorstep; I think that's a hard-fought election and one which I think we are going to win.'[99] Whether it was in reality a sign of retreat or a symptom of organisational disarray, or a genuine act of defiance, Major began to publicise his own revolt against the slickness and stage management of contemporary electioneering that was epitomised in his view by the Blair campaign. For example, at an election rally in Aberdeen on 23 April he conspicuously departed from the speech he was scheduled to give that evening. He wished to make a point.

> This meant tearing up his planned script, to the bemusement of the media, who had been given the intended text at 3 p.m. that afternoon, and some of whom had already filed their reports based on it … Major was pleased by his extempore speech. His entourage was not. Neither were the media, alienated

by the script change, nor the organisers, by his abandoning the podium and speaking from the front of the stage.[100]

By the end of the campaign, Major was prepared to give up key slots in the television schedules and to be the only main party leader not to participate in the *ITV 500* panel programme in order to take his simple and unsophisticated message direct to the voters. Paddy Ashdown, on the other hand, relished the publicity and the impression of comparability afforded by the general election campaign, where the third party could usually make gains in popularity. As the second choice of most voters, Ashdown was almost always assured of positive crowd reactions. As such, he made a point of engaging in extensive travel and numerous 'meet the people' sessions as part of a deliberate attempt to act as a contrast with the more measured approach of the main party leaders.

Among the three leaders, Blair was the junior partner and represented a party that had until very recently been notorious for losing elections. His lead in the polls was considered to be fragile and he feared the effect of Conservative propaganda upon Labour's ability to control the agenda and to maintain party cohesion. Nevertheless, as the campaign progressed it became clear that Labour's election machine was not faltering, its discipline was holding up and its poll lead was proving impregnable. The manifest importance of public outreach as a condition of effective political and party leadership laid great emphasis as well as responsibility upon the individual party leader. In contemporary British politics, a leader is expected to be the emblematic and substantive personification of party principles and priorities. The leader has to be effective as the point of both access and sale for the general public. He or she has to be the centre of individual reassurance, providing an authoritative presence and a discernible ability to satisfy the functional requirements of national leadership and government management. A party leader has to act as an effective hinge between the public and the party. As this study has repeatedly shown, the publicisation of leaders has gone hand in hand with the personalisation of leadership. The techniques, channels and dynamics of leadership projection have led inextricably to an increasing emphasis upon the exploitation of leadership politics. In this respect, as in so many others, the 1997 general election was to witness a further turn on the ratchet towards a material presidentialisation of political engagement in this country.

During the long pre-election period, the public had become increasingly accustomed to the figure of Tony Blair embodying New Labour and its project. Whether it was the appeals and advertisements surrounding the party's membership drive, or Labour's glossy pledge cards, or the party's magazines and promotional material, or the projection of the Blair persona in the stagecraft and props of party conferences, New Labour had been branded and marketed through the individual form of its leader. The election campaign was the culmination of New Labour's interior campaign to inject a decisive change of identity into the party. Blair's face, his background and his vision were continually publicised with a complete absence of self-consciousness or embarrassment. Labour's manifesto was the textual expression of Blair's personal vision. Moreover, in order to remove any doubt as to its origins and authorship, the manifesto cover featured a single photograph of the leader. Blair's face fills the picture. He is half hidden in shadow and is presented as the man apart, prepared for destiny with a determined and wholly focused attitude. The theme is repeated inside, with no fewer than ten pictures of Blair providing visual reassurance to the text of the manifesto. For Blair and New Labour, the defining theme is that 'this election is about trust'.[101] There would be no hidden agendas or 'magic wands or instant solutions'.[102] This could be counted on because of the watchful eye of Tony Blair. Labour could be trusted as the people's party because Blair could be trusted as its leader. This trustworthiness was in its turn derived from the public's cultivation of Blair as a person who could be known and understood as an individual rather than as a figurehead. Blair himself had never made a secret of his scepticism of professional politics. In the election, he sought to identify with people's ambivalence over the whole exercise:

> If you said to me at eighteen or nineteen, 'you're going to be a politician', I would have said 'forget it'. Anything else, anything but being a politician because I thought that politicians were complete pains in the backside. There is a part of me that constantly wonders whether it is worth staying in politics because of all the rubbish you have to do. You just have to do it. You have just got to keep a grip of yourself and hope your humanity sees you through and in the end understand why you want to be in it.[103]

Although he had achieved an extraordinary position, Blair portrayed himself as an ordinary person: 'I think most people who know me know that I'm a pretty normal guy.'[104] Just as he hoped that people could identify with him, so he made a point of trying to identify with them. For example, at the beginning of an election campaign which would represent the culmination of the entire New Labour project, Blair remained conscious of the ordinary person's low tolerance threshold for party politics: 'Now the great campaign has begun. We can carry on with this for another six weeks which will drive us all absolutely crazy.'[105] An integral element of Blair's message was that the country needed strong leadership and that it could only be provided by an individual giving a sense of direction, but also an identifiable centre of responsibility and accountability, to individual citizens. 'There are many differences between us and the Tories', Blair remarked. 'Here is another one – the buck stops with me.'[106]

If public access to the modernised Labour party came primarily through its leadership, then access to the leadership was a matter of understanding Tony Blair. The strategic need to provide reassuring insights into the life and mind of the New Labour leader was first given prominence in the 1996 Labour party conference. During the leader's address, Blair gave an emotional and apparently unscripted description of how his father's sudden illness had traumatised him when he was eleven years old:

> [W]hen you look back on your past you try to think of the things that shaped you ... My father was a very ambitious man; he was successful; he was a go-getter. One morning I woke to be told he had had a stroke and might not live through the day, and my whole world fell apart ... I don't pretend to you that I had a deprived childhood: I didn't, but I learnt a sense of values in my childhood.[107]

Blair explained that the experience had strongly influenced the development of his character and outlook. Moreover, it had been a factor in his decision to join the Labour party. The impulse to share his childhood, his father's illness, his personal reflections and his domestic life in a public arena was repeated in the party election broadcast of 24 April 1997. That night the viewing public could observe the Labour leader at home in a documentary that fused Blair's private life with his public face. Blair was shown casually dressed in his kitchen chivvying his son over his homework and chatting to the camera with a mug of tea in his hand. It was as if the viewer were a neighbour who had just dropped in.

The format of the specially commissioned film was not entirely new. It was reminiscent of 'Kinnock The Movie' (1987) and of 'Major The Journey' (1992), the prime minister's celebrated tour of his childhood haunts in Brixton. Yet there were important differences. Kinnock's adventure into a visual stream of consciousness was an episode in a general strategy to divert attention away from the insider culture of an unreformed party. As a film director, Hugh Hudson had elevated and dramatised his subject and sought to accentuate the man of destiny through panoramic scenes, 'crane shots' and emotive music. The references to Kinnock the man were used to exemplify Kinnock the leader. His background and origins were used to reveal the leader's roots and the conditions from which he had emerged to take up his metropolitan mantle. Notwithstanding Kinnock's denial that he was in any way out of the ordinary, the juxtaposition of his impoverished background with the position he had achieved did imply an exceptionalism that was consistent with the triumphant character of the film. The pattern for Kinnock was that his Old Labour background in South Wales did not provide general reassurance or a sense of familiarity. On the contrary, it conveyed to many voters a closed, and even alien, world of ingrown sentimentality and inverted snobbery. 'Kinnock The Movie' may have helped underline Kinnock's personal qualities but it could not disguise the lack of distance between him and his unreconstructed party.

In 1992 John Major was an already well-established leader when he decided to journey into his past. But in travelling around Brixton, the predominant visual message was that of a voyeur toying dispassionately with his geographical origins from the security of his chauffeur-driven government car. Although it was intended to link government policy and prime ministerial commitments to Major's life story, the personal element was primarily backward looking. Like 'Kinnock The Movie', it was geared to a past that had been left behind. To this extent, the exercise seemed contrived and out of character. Blair's biopic, by contrast, had a different quality. It was made by the distinguished documentary filmmaker, Molly Dineen, who specialised in intimate 'fly on the wall' productions. Blair was already publicly accepted as a leadership figure with an emphatic authority over his party. The film's purpose was not to show leadership or to suggest it but to reveal the leader as he really was – i.e. to give substance to his apparent integrity. As Blair himself exhorted: 'What I keep saying to people is get behind the image. It is quite difficult to bring people to actually see the kind of person you are.'[108] By revealing himself, Blair could reassure the voters of Middle England that he was identifiably middle class and not born and bred Labour. He could convey that he genuinely understood common concerns, had a practically minded social conscience, and could be relied upon to make voting the Conservatives out of office a safe option.

Blair was shown to be disarming and tough but, more importantly, devoid of artifice and duplicity. He provided material proof that Labour must have been transformed to have him as its leader. Blair's film, therefore, was thoroughly congruent with both the campaign and the entire New Labour ethos. It merged seamlessly into the central themes of the campaign. It recognised the need to demonstrate the core drives, motives and ideas of the leadership. It sought to instil trust and reassurance by examining the leader at source. It reflected the contemporary trends and formats of televised intimacy, personal self-expression, political transparency, social informality and emotional release. In effect, the film amounted to a public vetting of Blair the person for the purposes of providing an insight into the integrity and safety of the New Labour project as a whole. By coming to know him as a person, the public could come to know the reasons for his mission, to appreciate the authenticity of his shared empathy, and to associate with a common impulse to make things better in practical and unthreatening ways. The climax of the broadcast came with Blair's final observation in his kitchen. It related to the idea that an ordinary person placed in an extraordinary position could make a substantial difference. Given the opportunity, he impressed upon his audience that he could be relied upon to discharge the responsibilities of office on behalf of all of us: 'You see I couldn't imagine myself sitting in Downing Street doing the job, having those things going on out there and not be just like some sort of galvanising force driving through the change to make things better. I couldn't imagine doing it.'[109]

Fighting personality with personality

As a member of a party that had been in power for eighteen years and as a prime minister during an unprecedented decline in the respect given to the behavioural and ethical standards of professional politicians, John Major found it difficult to engage in personal exercises of populist dissociation. Nevertheless, he did seek to maximise the distance between himself and his party. In November 1996, for example, he published a defence of his government's record and an outline of its future plans without ever once mentioning the Conservative party.[110] By 1997, references made by Major to his personal ability to secure victory in the forthcoming election had become commonplace. For example, when his aides complained that he had been 'off message' in a House of Commons confrontation with Blair, Major's response was sharp and to the point: 'I am the message', he retorted.[111] In taking command of the party, or at least in being permitted to take command by a party whose only hope lay with Major, the prime minister shamelessly accentuated the positive through the use of the first person. In his view, the only way of talking up the party was by talking up the qualities and principles of John Major.

The prime minister agreed with the leader of the opposition that the election was about trust, and in particular about who could be trusted with the country's future. In Major's view, Blair was not worthy of trust because he had abandoned previously held positions for the sake of electoral viability, and he was conspicuously vague on a range of policy commitments. The Conservatives had floated the slogan of 'New Labour, New Danger' in 1996 and portrayed the warning in the form of a pair of Devil eyes looking out menacingly from a variety of dark surroundings. There was no question that these were meant to depict Blair's eyes and his temperament at the prospect of government. As the Conservatives failed to make inroads into Labour's lead, this negative device was reintroduced in order to weaken Blair's prodigious lead in the leadership approval ratings. The Conservatives did their best to launch a decapitation strike upon their Labour opponents. While Major attacked Blair for being opportunistic and for his 'shameless hypocrisy',[112] Stephen Dorrell accused Blair of 'dishonesty' and of panicking in the face of questions on the economy – 'the more he panics, the more he lies, telling bare-faced, despicable lies'.[113] Blair increasingly became the subject of direct personal attacks on the grounds of character, trustworthiness and experience. Conservative strategists were prompted into refuting Labour's insistent message of Major as a weak and ineffectual leader, by referring to the individual failings of Tony Blair. No comparison was more personal than that made by Michael Heseltine on 9 April 1997:

> Tony Blair started this campaign on the slogan 'Trust me' ... He asked to personalise it; he wanted to be trusted. And therefore it is legitimate and right that we should make the point that there is nothing in his record that gives any indication that he can be relied upon. The great thing about this prime minister is that he tells you the truth. Tony Blair will say almost anything to get a headline or a soundbite. This prime minister has been proved in the job, while Tony Blair to the best of my knowledge has never been in charge of anything. This prime minister can take the pressure. Tony Blair is cracking under the strain.[114]

For his part, Major concentrated upon personalising what the Conservatives had to offer. Like Labour, the front cover of the party's manifesto featured a full-page picture of the prime minister's face. Unlike Labour, there were only two photographs of the leader in the Conservative manifesto, but these amounted to the total number of pictures dedicated to politicians in the publication. Major increasingly claimed the manifesto as his own. During the campaign, he went to considerable lengths to reassure voters that the manifesto carried the leader's imprimatur. For example, at a meeting of party activists in Scotland, Major sought to raise morale by reaffirming that the party manifesto was essentially his prospectus. 'It has my imprint upon it', he said. 'It is my manifesto, not just to my constituents but to the whole of the country.'[115] As Major increasingly distanced himself from his party, he even issued a separate statement of his government's record and reasons for re-election. It was published in *The Times* under Major's chosen title: 'My personal manifesto'.[116]

By the end of the campaign, Major was even implying that voters should forget about the Conservative party in the calculation of their electoral choice: 'I appeal to you. Don't let whatever doubts you may have had about the Conservative Party in the past weigh with you, when the future of the

United Kingdom is at stake. Think about it. Think seriously. Think again. Look into my eyes and know this. I will always deal fair and true by this great nation.'[117] Major himself was the sales pitch. Major was the guarantor of the manifesto. To Major, this was the essence of his political appeal. His personality and his life experiences were the collateral for his party's message. At the 1994 Conservative party conference, for example, he revealed that it was his personal experience of having had his left leg shattered in a car crash which provided the guarantee to his commitment to the NHS. These types of personal account had been deployed throughout his premiership. Now they were intensified to an unprecedented level, in order to convey an extraordinary understanding of ordinary needs and an individualised source of familiar reassurance. Nowhere was this presidential level of personalisation more apparent than in Major's last throw, which came in the form of the party's final tranche of full-page press advertisements. On 29 April, below a picture of Major accompanied by school children and the caption 'True to Britain', appeared a list of no fewer than fifteen personal pledges from a prime minister appealing directly to the voter. They included the following:

> For me, Britain is the best country in the world in which to live.
>
> You can be sure I will keep our great United Kingdom as one country.
>
> You can be sure I will not let Britain go into a federal Europe.
>
> You can be sure I would give Britain a referendum on a single currency.
>
> You can be sure I will give every four-year-old a voucher for nursery education.
>
> You can be sure I will demand higher standards from every school and give every parent more choice.
>
> You can be sure I will give every school-leaver the further education or training they need.
>
> You can be sure I will think first of the victims of crime and take repeat offenders off the streets.
>
> You can be sure I will provide the money for more police to keep us safer on the streets.
>
> You can be sure I will improve our National Health Service, freely available to all, with more money year by year.
>
> You can be sure I will always protect the state retirement pension and offer dignity and security to the elderly.[118]

The personal assurances culminated with:

> You can be sure I will govern for everyone.
>
> On Thursday, be sure you mark your cross where you know you can place your trust.
>
> You can be sure I will be true to Britain.[119]

This extraordinary address finished with Major's signature and conspicuously no mention whatsoever of the Conservative party.

John Major's efforts were to no avail. It had been an election in which '[e]ach party relied heavily on its leader to carry the message, or rather each party leader assumed such a role for himself'.[120] In such an encounter, it was Blair who emerged as the ascendant figure. The post-election celebrations, the triumphant entry into Downing Street, the explanations of the victory and the interpretations of the mandate were all refracted through the lens of Tony Blair's leadership. If New Labour had been a marketing exercise, it had now been vindicated and revealed as a superbly conceived and implemented strategy whose primary symbol and animating force had now secured the central prize in the British political system. The landslide character of the result produced a 179-seat majority for Blair's party, a dramatic increase in the contingent of Paddy Ashdown's Liberal Democrats to 46 seats, and the collapse of John Major's party from 321 to 165 seats. The radical transformation from one era to another seemed complete when John Major finally relinquished the leadership position that had generated almost continuous speculation and in-fighting over the preceding four years, stretching even into the election campaign period itself.

Governing as New Labour

And yet, in spite of so many indications of a political sea-change, the disjunction was not quite as great as might have been supposed. This was because New Labour had been in a position of a viable government-in-waiting for so long a period that the leadership had grown concerned over the deleterious effects of 'reverse incumbency'. This referred to a condition where the opposition party was deemed to have acquired a vulnerability normally reserved for governments. The Labour leadership had feared that the prominence and familiarity of the New Labour message and programme would lead to public complacency and even fatigue. This risked placing the opposition in a position of having to defend its performance against a government seeking to place the burden of argument upon the party out of power. Labour's accession to power also seemed less convulsive than it might otherwise have been because it fitted into a pattern of successive changes that had all featured high levels of public participation. After the leadership election in 1994, the Clause Four campaign in 1995 and the Road to the Manifesto consultation exercise in 1996, the general election represented a difference of degree, but of not of kind, to what had become an increasingly open-textured and campaign-oriented Labour party. The leadership's view was that the party had functioned best and served the needs of leadership politics most effectively when it had been in a heightened state of electoral preparedness and when its engagement with the general public remained at its most intense.

The 1997 general election campaign was seen by the leadership to be an element in a continuum of public and electoral consciousness that had made the party into such a cohesive and disciplined organisation. The election of a Labour government was certainly a key objective but it was not seen as the point of culmination. It was not interpreted as a process in which abnormal means had been used to achieve conventional ends that would herald the resumption of peacetime conditions. Blair announced that New Labour would govern as New Labour. This declaration did not just refer to the programme of policy pledges. It would apply to the behaviour of the party and to the style of its administration. The method of New Labour's rise would be the means of retaining office. The guard would not be lowered. The party would not turn in on itself. The leader would not become preoccupied with party management. The crusade of earning public trust as a responsible and competent governing party would not be relaxed. The cautionary tale of the Conservative party's complacency and loss of public touch would remain a guiding force. It was not in spite of the large majority and a docile press that Blair insisted upon vigilance. On the contrary, it was because of the seductive appearances of security that the party needed a constant reminder that the campaign could never, and should never, cease operations and that the 'war room' mind-set was the best protection against the rapid erosion of New Labour's public esteem.

Blair believed he faced formidable problems. New Labour would now be operating in a more critical environment, not just because it now constituted the government but because it had campaigned on a set of specific promises and a challenge to the electorate to hold the leadership accountable for delivering them. In addition, Labour's majority had been inflated by voters more disenchanted with the Major government than by an enthusiasm for the Labour alternative. The prime minister therefore had the problem of only having secured 42 per cent of the popular vote, while at the same time having to deal with over 400 Labour MPs that threatened to pose considerable managerial difficulties for the party leadership in the future.

The inflated ranks of Labour's parliamentary representation provided a permanent reminder to Blair of the volatility of electoral attachments. To make matters worse, New Labour had to contend with high levels of public cynicism over the nature and conduct of politics, and with a press that had a historical antipathy to incoming Labour administrations. Blair felt there could be no rest from disproving Labour's traditional negatives or from protecting New Labour's hard-won positives. As a consequence, Blair quickly established that for New Labour to succeed in its project to produce a New Britain a second term of office would be an absolute necessity. Accordingly, re-election became an overriding objective and controlling obligation of the New Labour government.

At the outset of the incoming Labour government, great emphasis was laid upon the presentation and co-ordination of policy, on the continued cultivation of the press and in particular the tabloids, and on the need to maintain party discipline and ministerial coherence in the continued campaign of public outreach. The introduction of Millbank's methods, personnel and ethos into Whitehall had many implications, not least for the integrity of cabinet decision making and for the clarity of government policy (see pp. 310–23). The problems associated with spin doctors, unauthorised briefings and strategic leaks were in many respects attributable to the priority given media relations at the centre. The Blair team operated openly on the premise that the leadership's active engagement and symbolic identification with the public needed to be sustained and developed for the benefit of the government and the party.

Nothing epitomised the attachment to the need for effective public projection or signified the impulse attached to centralising the government's message from Number 10 than the position of Blair's press secretary, Alastair Campbell. His task was to provide the key reference point for a media operation that sought to emulate Millbank's prodigious achievement during the rise of New Labour. Campbell not only constituted a central clearance facility for news and information, but also actively promoted the timing and propagation of government news to produce the optimum effect. He gave professional guidance and political advice. Campbell was able to draw upon his extensive experience of working in the newspaper industry. From his professional origins at *The Mirror* group, he moved to be news editor of *Today* in 1986. He returned to *The Mirror* to become political editor, and it was there that he was headhunted by Tony Blair in 1994. Campbell rapidly became a key strategist of the New Labour project, but more significantly Blair's closest aide and most trusted advisor. Blair and Campbell became inseparable partners in the campaign to maximise Labour's news coverage and to promote the modernisation project to both Labour and non-Labour constituencies. The smooth transition of New Labour from opposition to government was in many respects a reflection of the effectiveness and continuity of the relationship between Blair and Campbell. The dynamic was one of mutual dependence. According to Clare Short, the two played out a 'good cop, bad cop'[121] double act, with Blair providing the emollient smile while Campbell engaged in the dirty work of press relations. As Blair fed off Campbell's tabloid instincts, his press secretary acquired a reputation for a ruthless devotion to an individual rather than to the government.

With the decimation and demoralisation of a Conservative party wholly unaccustomed to opposition, Campbell saw the likeliest centre of critical assault upon the new Labour government as coming from the media, whose congenital mode of operation had become one of 'split and gaffe'.[122] He believed that '[b]ecause John Major's government was in near-permanent crisis and the last election campaign effectively ran for two years, newspapers came to expect daily political drama'.[123] Government was more complex than opposition and the problem of controlling information was proportionally more severe. Nevertheless, Campbell believed that through extraordinary efforts and zealous application it would be possible to produce a central counterweight to a media that was becoming not only more centrifugal in character but also more conditioned to the adversarial approach to covering government.[124] Campbell rapidly acquired the reputation of being the prime minister's 'enforcer'. His status as 'the most powerful unelected politician at the very heart of the British Government'[125] was a reflection of the importance of news management in the Blair administration. Campbell's position was an expression of both his skills and the value attached to them by New Labour, which was an organisation whose origins had lain in public projection and presentation. After a year in government, Campbell's position was so secure that its potential for controversy had been neutralised. As Kevin Toolis noted, his power base was literally that of Tony Blair:

> Blair never moves from Downing Street without Campbell. He never appears on a platform without Campbell nearby. Never makes a speech that Campbell has not read or rewritten. Never walks into an important room without Campbell close behind. Never takes a decision that Campbell has not been consulted on. Never holds a significant meeting that Campbell does not attend or at least know about. Other Cabinet ministers slavishly repeat Campbell's line on the latest twist of Government policy in their broadcast interviews. Not vice versa.[126]

Such a power base was sufficient to quell any political or constitutional objections to the position of Alastair Campbell in the administration. As a result, he quickly became a far more formidable figure than Bernard Ingham had been in Margaret Thatcher's governments. Unlike Ingham, Campbell sat in cabinet meetings, attended party conferences, and was visibly engaged in campaign strategy and electioneering.

For a party that had become leadership centred in its rise to power, Campbell's emancipation from the restraints of previous press secretaries was exemplified by the priority given by the government to keeping as much of the media as possible 'on side'. It also reflected the importance of retaining the government's close identity with the figure and personality of Tony Blair. It was Campbell's role to maintain the status of the leader's brand name upon the government and, by extension, the reputation of the government in the public domain. He was instrumental in ensuring that selected elements of government activity would be seen to be derivative of Blair's leadership. By the same token, Campbell would give advice on the choice and timing of prime ministerial interviews in high profile areas. Campbell was also a key figure behind Blair's publicity coups where the premier's image and words became central to the presentation of singular news events (e.g. the death of Diana Princess of Wales, the NATO action in Kosovo). Even though the Blair administration received the most favourable news coverage of any incoming Labour government, Campbell remained alarmed that the machinery of government information remained far below the standards of professionalism achieved by Millbank prior to and during the election period. Mr Blair and his cabinet colleagues felt persistently 'frustrated at being unable to replicate what they had done in Opposition with everyone sticking to one message'.[127] So much so in fact that upon entering office many ministers continued to rely upon the daily bulletins prepared by Millbank's media monitoring unit.

The disciplines and priorities of news management

Tony Blair is a prime minister who has an equal regard for both the content of policy and its effective presentation. In fact, where policy is concerned these two elements are 'pushed parallel in his evaluation of it'.[128] The importance of selling policy effectively became a priority at the very outset of the administration. The government's need to sustain political momentum, to push policies through and to retain its public stature in order to secure a second term led quickly to a series of initiatives designed to improve Whitehall's media relationships. In a directive to all government press officers in September 1997, Alastair Campbell spelt out the need for them to change their outlook from the simple conveyancing of given information to a more proactive role. They were now expected to use their positions to attend to the media implications of policy, while it was in the process of being formed. He stated that the issue of handling the media in relation to policy should be built into the decision-making process at the earliest possible stage: 'As a policy is devised, how it will be explained and communicated should be an integral part of the process.' It was essential for the government to 'lay down big messages around every event'[129] and always to 'know how big stories [would] be playing in the next day's papers'.[130] The Government Information Service in effect needed to 'raise its game and be right at the heart of government'.[131]

Notwithstanding any improvement in the media consciousness of Whitehall departments, the problem of co-ordination remained an issue with the government. This had been recognised as early as July 1997, when Downing Street announced that ministers would need prior permission to engage in media appearances and interviews. Under the Major administration, 'most ministers used to do their own thing, making up their own mind whether or not they should appear',[132] recalled one senior BBC interviewer. An ITN rival agreed: 'It was a constant game, with no downside for us ... They knew that if a minister wouldn't come on the programme John Redwood would. You could threaten them with it, you had them over a barrel.'[133] Blair put an immediate stop to this practice. Intent upon preventing any recurrence of such mayhem, Number 10 amended the official code of conduct for ministers to reflect the imperative of centrally co-ordinating the presentation of government policy. Just as the 'policy content of all major speeches, press releases and new policy initiatives should be cleared in good time with the No 10 Private Office', so the 'timing and form of announcements should be cleared with the No 10 Press Office'.[134]

Blair's determination to maintain the initiative even extended on occasions to the point of refusing to provide any government spokespersons for programmes. During the 1997 European summit in Amsterdam, for example, Blair declined to make himself available for any formal interviews. Michael White recalled that this was the 'first time old media lags could remember such a slight'.[135] To make matters worse, Blair signalled his intention to bypass the pressroom altogether in order to ensure that his message would not suffer from distortions and misinterpretations. To White, this typified an approach that sought to minimise the risk of misplaced briefings and fractured messages through a coherent centre of prime ministerial communication: 'Radio and TV are used to addressing the voters directly and, in effect, to briefing the wider media which interprets the mere words ... [T]he dominant tone is set by Campbell and his allies: centralised, picture-driven and presentational, rather than concerned to dot the i's of policy details. Its instincts are tabloid in tone.'[136] While such exercises in prime ministerial projection could be very effective instruments of news co-ordination, they did not constitute an overall solution. The problem of news emanating from the disparate and largely autonomous departments in Whitehall remained a challenge.

In order to improve the quality of media coverage, co-ordination and responsiveness, Downing Street established the Strategic Communications Unit in November 1997. This was to provide a media monitoring and rapid reaction facility modelled upon the service provided by Millbank during the election period. The objective was to provide an internal pool of information and ideas for government departments. It would record, analyse and, where necessary, rebut items of news relating to government policy. The Unit would keep ministers informed of how their statements or actions were being treated by the media. It would also provide an in-house critique of any alleged mistakes or misinterpretations made by journalists that would allow ministers or their representatives to issue corrective statements as early as possible in the news cycle. This initiative was combined with a cross-fertilisation on the one hand of Millbank employees into government and the media, and on the other hand of experienced journalists taking up government positions.[137] Taken together, these developments provided the Blair administration with a highly advanced and sensitive news management organisation. It was explicitly geared to maximising favourable coverage by being attentive not merely to the news value of policy announcements, but to the importance of prior preparation and planning and to the need for effective and sustained 'follow-through'.

'Blair direct'

As an example of this continued concern for leadership outreach, Blair announced soon after his election triumph that he would establish a series of regular unscripted 'question and answer' sessions around the country. In what would be an experiment in direct democracy, members of the public would be given an opportunity to put their views to the prime minister. By the same token, Blair would be able to trail policy ideas, to explain government policy and to defend his administration's performance in a televised format that would show members of the public directly engaging with the premier. The format of the prime minister's personalised linkage with the public followed the example set by President Clinton's 'town meetings' and was designed with the same objective in mind – i.e. 'to allow ordinary people to hold ordinary people to account'.[138] These tangible 'Talk to Tony' shows would demonstrate that Blair was serious about his electoral commitment to keep in close touch with his public constituency. They would provide clear evidence that Labour was intent upon justifying its own appellation as the 'people's party'. The populist rationale was often matched by the populist content of the sessions. In the first session, the prime minister travelled to Worcester to face a 130-strong audience of law and order professionals and community group representatives. Blair addressed the problem of 'alcopops' among teenagers, the issue of vandals having to repair damage to property and the protection of vulnerable witnesses in criminal trials, as well as answering questions on drug abuse, domestic violence and aggressive begging. Other sessions included trips to Dudley to address the issue of welfare reform, to South Wales where the theme was devolution, and to London to discuss the 1998 Budget.

The 'town meetings' have been an integral part of a general strategy intended to maintain prime ministerial prominence at the same level as a general election campaign. 'More than any recent prime minister, Blair is aware of the importance of presentation to promote policy and himself. Like Presidents Reagan and Clinton, he is prepared to "go public" ... to carry his case directly to the voters.'[139] Blair has used his own media status to highlight selected issue areas and to promote the general party agenda of modernisation. In addition to public speeches, press conferences and media interviews, Blair has adopted other elements of the presidential strategy of circumvention. 'In a conscious attempt to go direct to the public and avoid hostile editorialising', Kavanagh and Seldon point out that Blair has 'made much use of the national and regional press to provide signed articles on the issues of the day'.[140] They estimate that in his first two years as prime minister, over 150 articles appeared under his name.

Critics have objected to Blair's cultivation of the media as an affront to parliamentary democracy and a way of further subverting the intermediary role of the party in providing a linkage between the citizenry and government. Number 10 waved away such complaints and stressed the overriding need to keep in touch with the currents of public opinion. One participant in a prime ministerial question session said that 'you at least get him directly'.[141] By giving an example of getting out and about, Blair hoped to induce his ministers to follow his lead. This would keep them from becoming enmeshed in Whitehall bureaucracy. In the final analysis, such outings were seen to be part of New Labour's continuing contract and personal covenant with the British people. Blair made clear at the very outset that this rationale lay at the very heart of these prime ministerial safaris: 'We have been elected as New Labour with a set of specific promises to fulfil. It's our contract with the British people. Like any contract, it's dependent on the satisfaction of both sides. That's why I want the British people to have the chance regularly to intervene to make sure we are living up to our promises.'[142]

Alastair Campbell's initiatives were not confined to the general theme of the government's media competence. He was influential in the development of innovating methods to cultivate the populist elements of Blair's personalised connections with New Labour's avowed client base of public opinion. Other initiatives were devised to perpetuate the visceral properties of the leadership's election-style connection with the public. They included the introduction of an annual 'state of the nation' report given by the premier on the government's progress with fulfilling its election commitments. The first report was given in the Downing Street Rose Garden to an audience of government ministers and senior civil servants. The staging and the style of the event immediately provoked comparisons with presidential statements from the White House. Blair's report amounted to a personal statement to the public. It occurred outside any party or parliamentary setting and it amounted to a report on the premier's own record in fulfilling his ten point 'contract with the people' that had characterised his election campaign. Developments were also made in the area of the Internet.

The Downing Street web site was first established by John Major in December 1996. In contrast to the Labour party and the White House sites, Major resisted the trend towards interactivity. Apart from the invitation by Humphrey the Downing Street cat for callers to sign the visitor's book, the first web site at Number 10 did not embrace two-way links with the public. That policy changed under Blair, who drew upon the highly advanced information technology that Labour had developed during the election period. Apart from its extensive usage of email to keep in close contact with its candidates in the field on a twice-daily basis, Labour boasted that it had the 'most developed website of any party anywhere in the world'.[143] In addition to disseminating information on policy statements, media rebuttals and campaign news, it offered an interactive facility for individuals to register and exchange views. Using this background as well as the experience of independent organisations[144] in establishing computer-generated discussion forums, the Labour leadership moved swiftly to develop the potential of such linkages to enhance its contacts with the public. The Number 10 web site was thoroughly overhauled to give access to government news on proposals, policies and performance, including specific prime ministerial issues, briefings, speeches and interview transcripts. The web site was also developed to give it the capacity to relay both live and recorded broadcasts of prime ministerial events.[145] More significantly, the web site offered a variety of interactive facilities that encouraged individuals to participate in discussion forums relating to such issue areas as health, education, welfare, the economy, foreign policy and the modernisation of government. Such a web site generates an in-house source of information on public opinion. It also provides a prodigious quantity of premier-centric information that allows an ordinary citizen not only to receive prime ministerial statements direct from Number 10, but also to access a database of the premier's responses to questions posed on news outlets outside the United Kingdom (e.g. *Larry King Live*, *Jim Lehrer NewsHour*). In February 2000, a revamped Downing Street web site was launched by the prime minister. Apart from acting as a central gateway to information on the government machine, Blair announced that the site would also offer a range of extra features, including an electronic Downing Street magazine and a weekly 'desktop chat' by the prime minister from his own PC. These direct personal messages would be accessible in audio, video or text form to the on-line sector of the public.

But perhaps the most significant innovation in the projection of the premiership came in the usage of alternative outlets on established channels. In a development strongly suggestive of President Clinton's cultivation of shows such as *Larry King Live* and *Good Morning America*, Tony Blair sought to diversify his media appearances in a way that would break the monopoly of the premier news programmes and give him more discretion to make appearances on programmes that would allow him the time and space to make his points free of excessive interruption, persistent confrontation and critical analysis. Political parties in general have come to recognise the benefit of targeting audience-based shows or chat shows, which attract higher viewing figures than the straight interview programmes. The proliferation of channels and outlets allows the media advisors of senior politicians increasingly to select programmes that will optimise the fit between the format, the message and the target audience. This has been particularly the case with Blair, who has made pioneering prime ministerial appearances on the daytime television programme *This Morning* with Richard Madeley and Judy Finnigan, and on both *The Frank Skinner Show* and *Des O'Connor Tonight*.

John Major described the development as a 'dumbing down of politics'.[146] Alastair Campbell's reaction to the charges of trivialising the premiership has been to claim that 'there is a metropolitan media snobbery about these programmes' which are seen by 'an awful lot of people who don't watch Prime Minister's Questions or read the papers'.[147] Furthermore, he asserted that the more traditionally inquisitorial outlets were failing or failed formats. BBC2's *Newsnight*, for example, was described as having 'a dwindling audience'and BBC Radio 4's *The World At One* was dismissed as a programme 'which very few take seriously'.[148] The appeal of soft format shows over hardball programmes was quite evident to media professionals: 'Although they can be high-risk, with politicians fielding unexpected questions, the spin doctors see huge potential in "humanising" their subjects. And dangerous and detailed questioning on policy is avoided.'[149] There was an additional advantage:

> [W]hile the spin doctors may be reviled, they are no fools whatever the former Tory Prime Minister might think. They know that Mr O'Connor's invitation to a soft shoe shuffle, like that of the other 'sofa shows', reaches the C and D social groups, people more likely than the more upmarket *Today* listeners to change their vote – the very folk who deserted Labour for Margaret Thatcher and came home to Tony Blair at last year's May election.[150]

Audience size and type, however, are not the only factors. Timing is another. This is why *Breakfast With Frost* on Sunday morning is so influential. Although its audience is small (i.e. 900,000) and it is interview based, the material generated by the programme is regularly taken up by news and political editors and fed into succeeding news bulletins, thereby shaping the agenda of the news cycle for the beginning of the week. The priority of such programmes over outlets such as *Panorama* and *Newsnight* means that the prime minister is able to avoid extensive and intensive television interviews. In many respects, he can determine the rules of engagement by circumventing established media hierarchies for more unmediated access points to selected television audiences.

The selection is now far greater than it used to be and Blair has sought to widen the range of opportunity still further. It was significant that Blair's appearance on the *This Morning* was preceded by a press briefing by Alastair Campbell that the exercise had been part of 'an all-out assault on the national press'.[151] Campbell noted with satisfaction that Blair's appearance on *This Morning* 'appear[ed] to have got beneath the skin of the press'.[152] This unprecedented assault upon the national press represented a strike against the press's traditional linkages with the electorate. It was also a sign of Downing Street's confidence that the British public was following its American counterpart in becoming more sceptical of the national media's authority in the interpretation, evaluation and construction of news agendas. Alastair Campbell urged the BBC to disconnect itself from the agenda of the national press and to create its own set of priorities. He claimed that important policy announcements and developments were being repeatedly 'dumbed down' by a national press that was more concerned with giving prominence to stories about governmental travel expenses and ministerial flights. To Campbell, it was important for the BBC and others to detach themselves from the downmarket orientation of the national press.[153]

Downing Street's strategy was in part motivated by the need to start laying down markers for the future propaganda battle over Britain's membership of the single European currency. This was an issue that threatened to revive the traditional antipathy of the tabloid press against Labour and to lead to a loss in prime ministerial authority in what could degenerate into a crudely nationalistic crusade against the EU. But the media strategy was also prompted by New Labour's drive to diversify structures and points of access into a more pluralist matrix that would be less amenable to dominant intermediaries such as the national press. In the 1996 presidential election, Bill Clinton sought to counteract the critical metropolitan agendas of the Washington elites by pouring resources into regional and local media markets where presidential appearances could be injected directly into segmented publics. Blair followed suit in the 1997 general election with a concerted strategy to cultivate local radio stations and regional news outlets. In Number 10, the Blair leadership continued the thrust of diversification. By 1999, Campbell had made it clear that he intended to 'work more closely with provincial newspapers, women's magazines and ethnic publications'.[154] For example, when the government had become irritated over what it took to be the disinterest of the national press in the government's New Deal programme on unemployment, Downing Street invited reporters from the regional newspapers for a briefing on the New Deal. This resulted in a profusion of front-page splashes on the success of the programme. It was followed up a week later with a variation on the strategy. Overseas journalists were given similar treatment in order to achieve positive coverage abroad that would subsequently be reported back to this country by foreign correspondents. The employment of alternative media outlets, therefore, is integrally related to the usage of soft format shows. They both represent a general policy on the part of the Blair premiership to encourage and to exploit the fragmentation of media linkages to the public.

The strains of displacement

In giving such extensive attention to the media and to their linkage between a reinvented party and a volatile electorate, New Labour accelerated the development in British politics towards a condition of permanent election. In doing so, it has helped to establish competence in media relations as an integral element of governing competence. Even with a majority of over 170, the Blair administration has acted with a habitual sense of insecurity in respect to a media that is in many ways its most important life-line to an increasingly volatile electorate. Party management remains a vital role to the leadership, but under the Labour government media management has been seen as a function of comparable significance – especially so when the fourth estate is perceived to be a more likely source of political opposition than any of the institutional centres of power. The explicit cultivation of the tabloids has been symptomatic of the government's thrust towards pre-empting the development of any competing agency of populist expression.

The battle cry keeping order in the inflated ranks of Labour MPs and allowing such a priority to be given to media relations is precisely the same message that enhanced the party's organisational integrity and increased the leadership's status in opposition – i.e. electoral viability. The immediate entrenchment of a second term of office as a key objective of the Blair administration ensured that New Labour would indeed intend to govern as New Labour. In many respects, it would be tantamount to continuing in opposition by different means.

Just as the party's investment in leadership politics became a driving imperative for extended political success, so the leadership's initial role as a means of achieving office became a *raison d'être* for the party in government to remain in power. This dynamic not only increased the scale and value of the leader's media penetration but developed in its wake a genre of political critique that bore a close resemblance to the form and content of opposition politics in the American presidential system. For example, during his administration Blair has often been accused of increasing the visibility of his office while at the same time reducing the public's accessibility to it. In enhancing the prominence of the premiership and opening it up to greater public inspection, Blair has also been accused of reducing the status of the office and encouraging a more passive, voyeuristic and non-participatory citizenry. Moreover, by seeking to empower himself through personalised appeals and public contracts, he is seen as substituting durable political bases for temporary coalitions that will provide fewer defences in difficult times and make for less rather than more stability for the government. But perhaps the most persistent and penetrating complaint is the one that is a standard criticism of contemporary presidents – namely that of mistaking media strategy for government action. Even though the 'shift towards the permanent campaign in Britain has still not gone as far as in the United States … the techniques are becoming merged with the techniques of governing'.[155] Blair is routinely questioned not merely for subordinating government schedules and decisions to media criteria, but for allowing the campaigning ethos to become a style of government and even arguably a substitute for effective governance. The threat of the media becoming an active source of opposition, together with the proportional response by New Labour towards channelling resources to news management, has led to a host of complaints over the status and activities of the government's spin doctors.

Dissidents within the party have found spin doctors to be a useful device for criticising the leadership without directly attacking the leader. Ken Livingstone, for example, has complained that the spinners are less concerned with acting as a link between the government and the public than with 'rubbishing members of their own party'.[156] A figure like Peter Mandelson 'always saw his role as promoting the Leader of the Labour Party rather than the party itself'.[157] Livingstone claims that while spin doctors are 'very good at spinning about their own omnipotence',[158] they are firstly incompetent in their professional abilities, and secondly provocative in the way they provoke populist responses to their avowed elitism as technical specialists. Accordingly, he took mischievous pleasure in puncturing their pretensions: 'One of the reasons I love politics in general and the Labour Party in particular is that, given the chance, people have the unerring ability to produce results that confound the spin doctors.'[159]

Joy Johnson, who had been Labour's head of communications until January 1996, took an altogether graver view of the party's dependence upon media consultants and advisors. She had found the party's spin doctors to be a serious cause for concern even prior to the general election. In May 1996, she objected to them for 'obscuring the language of politics ... for trivialising its content' and for 'slowly dripping poison into the body politic'.[160] She complained that their activities relied on 'a view that politics is and should be run secretively from the centre'.[161] By October 1997, Johnson was warning that New Labour, which had always seen news management as part of its professionalism, was running the risk of allowing process to supplant policy: 'What they practised so ruthlessly and successfully in opposition they have taken into government. But what is happening now is mismanagement. Instead of pushing stories through the media, the spin-doctors are the story.'[162] By May 1999, Johnson had become convinced that 'New Labour's distinctive fusion of policy with spin'[163] had become a dangerous obsession:

> After two years, the outstanding feature of this government is that its overwhelming desire to appease Middle England has led it to conceive policies not so much to solve a problem as to conjure an appearance ... As image-making becomes progressively blurred with policy development, politicians are moving from objective reality to a virtual world of their own creation. It's no wonder that their policy advisers are employed mainly as doctors of spin.[164]

Spin doctors also offered a means of political critique for the media themselves. Commentators such as Michael White, for example, warned that Labour had 'thrived for so long on brilliant presentation that it [was] in danger of forgetting that there is no substitute for substance'.[165] Matthew Parris was far less tolerant. He saw the activities of 'image-smiths'[166] as being responsible for generating 'a big, fuzzy generalised unease about something shallow, something hollow, something narcissistic, unrooted and opportunistic about the whole Blair thing; a sense of outward varnish and exterior panic. Damage *limitation*? This is the damage. It's the varnish which is rotting the woodwork.'[167] Political opponents were swift to exploit the opportunities for attack. For example, John Redwood claimed that Britain was now 'governed by spin doctors rather than by ministers'.[168] Alan Beith for the Liberal Democrats expressed a general anxiety that ministers preferred to make statements on radio and television or through leaks rather than speaking in the House of Commons. As a result, there was a 'real danger' that the government would 'feel immune to censure if it oversteps the mark'.[169] Significantly, Labour's spin doctors were even criticised by the Speaker of the House of Commons. In an interview in 1998, Betty Boothroyd publicly objected to their practice of leaking political decisions to the media prior to their official announcement in parliament: 'There are far too many of what I term apparatchiks who are working in government departments and who have been accustomed, when a party was in opposition, to want to get the maximum publicity. That's understandable. Now in government they have to be harnessed a little more.'[170] Betty Boothroyd went on to state that, under Labour, the practice of leaking information had become 'rather blatant'[171] and she regularly had to urge ministers to restrain their spin doctors.

In setting such store in achieving electoral and governmental success through effective media relations, New Labour had helped to generate its own source of vulnerability. It was instrumental in creating a reactive set of positions and arguments against the actual or perceived forms of influence at the disposal of the government's media advisors. Paradoxically, the emphasis placed upon news management to defuse opposition had opened up a point of access where opponents could develop leverage against the government and especially the leadership. The public projection and private protectiveness of a leader-centred party and government carried concomitant risks of decapitation strikes through the development of a critical dimension related to the alleged abuses and excesses of media manipulation. New Labour's strategy of news management had been epitomised by, and geared towards, the enhancement of Blair's leadership position. By the same token, the leadership's consequent centrality ensured that the value and effort it placed upon media relations would radiate through the controlling principles and operating methods of the party and government. To attack spin doctors, therefore, was in effect an assault upon the public outreach and political *modus operandi* of the leader and his party.

New Labour had equated political effectiveness with the successful shaping of news agendas. It was for this reason that the most serious crisis to confront the Labour government in its first three years came in December 1998, when the party's news management devices experienced a dramatic failure. The crisis, which was set in a context of competing sources of news briefing within government, centred upon the financial irregularities of the Paymaster General, Sir Geoffrey Robinson, and the Secretary of State for Trade and Industry, Peter Mandelson. Both ministers were forced to resign from office. As a consequence of the crisis, Gordon Brown's press secretary, Charlie Whelan, also left the government shortly afterwards. These events constituted a particularly damaging episode in Tony Blair's government. The prime minister had lost his closest confidante and fellow architect of the New Labour project. More seriously, the crisis was occasioned by a chronic breakdown in the very discipline that Mandelson had always advocated for the effective management of government news.

Notes

1 See Michael Foley, *The Rise of the British Presidency* (Manchester, Manchester University Press, 1993), chs 4, 7, 8; Margaret Scammell, *Designer Politics: How Elections are Won* (Basingstoke, Macmillan, 1995); Dennis Kavanagh, *Election Campaigning: The New Marketing of Politics* (Oxford, Blackwell, 1995); Martin Rosenbaum, *From Soapbox to Soundbite: Political Campaigning in Britain since 1945* (Basingstoke, Macmillan, 1997); Bob Franklin, *Packaging Politics: Political Communications in Britain's Media Democracy* (London, Edward Arnold, 1994), ch. 7.

2 Michael White, 'The Major years: nothing more than a lottery?', *The Guardian*, 3 May 1997.

3 Allan Massie, 'Worst year of his life', *Weekly Telegraph*, 4–10 August 1993.

4 Massie, 'Worst year of his life'.

5 John Major, *John Major: The Autobiography* (London, HarperCollins, 1999), p. 384.

6 Michael Jones, 'Keep on smiling through', *Sunday Times*, 23 March 1997.

7 Anthony King, 'Major fails the voters' 14-plus exam', *Daily Telegraph*, 7 May 1993.

8 Anthony King, 'Major's team tops unpopularity stakes', *Daily Telegraph*, 4 June 1993.

9 King, 'Major's team tops unpopularity stakes'.

10 King, 'Major's team tops unpopularity stakes'.

11 Anthony King, 'Outlook bleak for Tories as they plumb new depths', *Daily Telegraph*, 4 October 1999.

12 See Peter Riddell, 'Tory defectors redefine state of the parties', *The Times*, 19 September 1994.

13 Anthony King, 'Tories who dare not speak their name', *Daily Telegraph*, 13 January 1995.

14 See Hywel Williams, *Guilty Men: Conservative Decline and Fall, 1992–1997* (London, Aurum, 1998).

15 HC *Parliamentary Debates* (Hansard), Sixth Series, vol. 226, 7 June 1993–18 June 1993, House of Commons, Session 1992–93, cols 284–5.

16 Bruce Anderson, 'The extraordinarily ordinary Mr Major', *The Independent*, 11 January 1993.

17 Anderson, 'The extraordinarily ordinary Mr Major'.

18 David McKie, 'Why John Major's not on speaking terms with Joe Public', *The Guardian*, 18 April 1994.

19 Max Atkinson referred to in McKie, 'Why John Major's not on speaking terms with Joe Public'.
20 McKie, 'Why John Major's not on speaking terms with Joe Public'.
21 See Dennis Kavanagh, *The Reordering of British Politics: Politics After Thatcher* (Oxford, Oxford University Press, 1997), pp. 200–9.
22 Colin Seymour-Ure, 'Mass Media', in Dennis Kavanagh and Anthony Seldon (eds), *The Major Effect* (London, Macmillan, 1994), p. 412.
23 Seymour-Ure, 'Mass Media', p. 399.
24 Seymour-Ure, 'Mass Media', p. 400.
25 Seymour-Ure, 'Mass Media', p. 412.
26 John Major's address to the Conservative party conference, 1993, *The Guardian*, 9 October 1993.
27 John Major's address to the Conservative party conference 1993.
28 John Major's address to the Conservative party conference 1993.
29 John Major's address to the Conservative party conference 1993.
30 John Major's address to the Conservative party conference 1993.
31 'Years of gold', *The Times*, 9 October 1993.
32 Anthony Seldon, 'The Conservative Party', in Seldon and Kavanagh (eds), *The Major Effect*, p. 36.
33 Seldon in *The Major Effect*, p. 36.
34 Mark Garnett, *Principles and Politics in Contemporary Britain* (London, Longman, 1996), p. 152.
35 *First Report of the Committee on Standards in Public Life, Volume 1: Report*, Cm 2850–1 (London, HMSO, 1995), p. 16.
36 Garnett, *Principles and Politics in Contemporary Britain*, p. 152.
37 Seymour-Ure, 'Mass Media', p. 413.
38 Nicholas Jones, 'Press-ganged', *The Guardian*, 24 October 1994.
39 David McKie, 'Finding the right tone', *The Guardian*, 8 May 1995.
40 Simon Heffer, 'John Major is right to fight but he ought to go', *Daily Telegraph*, 23 July 1995.
41 William Rees-Mogg, 'Ahead but still adrift', *The Times*, 23 June 1995.
42 Rees-Mogg, 'Ahead but still adrift'.
43 Rees-Mogg, 'Ahead but still adrift'.
44 'Who governs Britain?', *Sunday Telegraph*, 25 June 1995.
45 'Who governs Britain?'.
46 Andrew Neil, 'Don't flunk it – Major is a loser and must go', *Sunday Times*, 25 June 1995.
47 Peter Mandelson and Roger Liddle, *The Blair Revolution: Can New Labour Deliver?* (London, Faber and Faber, 1996), p. 53.
48 Charles Leadbeater, 'Re-engineered at Labour HQ', *Financial Times*, 30 April 1997.
49 Leadbeater, 'Re-engineered at Labour HQ'.
50 David Butler and Dennis Kavanagh, *The British General Election of 1997* (Basingstoke, Macmillan, 1997), p. 58.
51 Philip Gould, *The Unfinished Revolution: How the Modernisers Saved the Labour Party* (London, Little Brown, 1998), p. 295.
52 Gould, *The Unfinished Revolution*, p. 294.
53 Pippa Norris, 'The Battle for the Campaign Agenda', in Anthony King *et al.* (eds), *New Labour Triumphs: Britain at the Polls* (Chatham, Chatham House, 1998), p. 127.
54 Gould, *The Unfinished Revolution*, p. 295.

55 Gould, *The Unfinished Revolution*, p. 295.
56 Quoted in Michael Jones, 'It's no more Mr Nice Guys', *Sunday Times*, 30 April 1995.
57 Quoted in Jones, 'It's no more Mr Nice Guys'.
58 Quoted in Jones, 'It's no more Mr Nice Guys'.
59 Simon Heffer, 'Die hard', *The Observer*, 26 November 1995.
60 William Rees-Mogg, 'Tactics aren't enough to run the country', *The Times*, 8 January 1996.
61 Quoted in Nicholas Wood, 'Portillo calls for plain speaking to win voters', *The Times*, 8 May 1995.
62 Quoted in Wood, 'Portillo calls for plain speaking to win voters'.
63 Quoted in Nicholas Wood, 'Major sets out on quest for a people's policy', *The Times*, 13 May 1995.
64 Quoted in Wood, 'Major sets out on quest for a people's policy'.
65 Quoted in Andrew Grice and Michael Prescott, 'Dancing to the spin doctors', *Sunday Times*, 22 January 1995.
66 Quoted in Fran Adams, 'Major takes a lesson from US President in hunt for image', *The Independent*, 6 January 1997.
67 Donald Macintyre, 'The man who would be president, until he's elected', *The Independent*, 9 January 1997.
68 Macintyre, 'The man who would be president, until he's elected'.
69 Hugo Young, 'President Major sails on in a sinking ship', *The Guardian*, 9 January 1997.
70 Young, 'President Major sails on in a sinking ship'.
71 Young, 'President Major sails on in a sinking ship'.
72 Quoted in a Referendum Party advertisement, *The Guardian*, 10 January 1997.
73 Quoted in 'Politicians are the most despicable human subspecies I have come across', Sir James Goldsmith interviewed by Judi Bevan, *Sunday Telegraph*, 13 October 1996.
74 Quoted in 'Politicians are the most despicable human subspecies I have come across', Sir James Goldsmith interviewed by Judi Bevan.
75 Quoted in a Referendum Party advertisement, *Independent on Sunday*, 17 November 1996.
76 Quoted in a Referendum Party advertisement, *Sunday Times*, 13 October 1996.
77 Quoted in 'Politicians are the most despicable human subspecies I have come across', Sir James Goldsmith interviewed by Judi Bevan.
78 Quoted in Kamal Ahmed, Rebecca Smithers and Christopher Elliot, 'Major seizes lifeline as tide turns', *The Guardian*, 17 April 1997.
79 Mark Lawson, '"Wartime address" adds to sense of crisis for Tories', *The Guardian*, 17 April 1997.
80 Lawson, '"Wartime address" adds to sense of crisis for Tories'.
81 Paul Goodman, 'John Major makes his last stand', *Daily Telegraph*, 17 August 1997.
82 Quoted in Hugo Young, 'No vision thing', *The Guardian*, 28 April 1997.
83 Young, 'No vision thing'.
84 See the leaked plans of Labour's campaign strategy, 'War book: version 3', *The Guardian*, 24 April 1997.
85 Tony Blair, 'It's safe for you to back Labour', *Daily Telegraph*, 18 March 1997.
86 Quoted in Stephen Coleman, 'The Televised Leaders' Debate in Britain: From Talking Heads to Headless Chickens', *Parliamentary Affairs*, 51, no. 2 (April 1998), p. 183.
87 Coleman, 'The Televised Leaders' Debate in Britain', p. 188.
88 'Talk about talks', *The Times*, 25 March 1997.
89 'It's time for our leaders to face trial by TV', *The Independent*, 8 October 1996.

90 'It's time for our leaders to face trial by TV'.
91 'Speak your mind', *The Times*, 3 March 1997.
92 Coleman, 'The Televised Leaders' Debate in Britain', p. 195.
93 'Speak your mind'.
94 'Speak your mind'.
95 For example, *Panorama*, *Breakfast with Frost*, *On the Record*, *The World This Weekend*, *The Jimmy Young Programme*, *Roscoe on 5*, and *The Enormous Election*.
96 Quoted in Anthony Bevins, 'The Tory underdog should be put out of its misery', *The Independent*, 17 March 1997.
97 'Pastries, punks and peptalks … on the road with Tony, John and Paddy', *The Independent*, 12 April 1997.
98 Quoted in Rebecca Smithers, 'Lib Dems lash "puny" Labour', *The Guardian*, 9 April 1997.
99 Quoted in Andrew Grice, Sebastian Hamilton, Sarah Higgins, Michael Jones, Michael Prescott, David Smith and Rajeev Syal, 'In the gutter', *Sunday Times*, 27 April 1997.
100 Anthony Seldon, *Major: A Political Life* (London, Phoenix, 1997), p. 728.
101 Quoted in Michael White, 'I'm the one to trust – Blair', *The Guardian*, 4 April 1997.
102 Quoted in White, 'I'm the one to trust – Blair'.
103 Party election broadcast, 24 April 1997.
104 Quoted in 'Quotes of the campaign', *Daily Telegraph*, 2 May 1997.
105 Quoted in Joy Copley and Robert Shrimsley, 'Long campaign will drive us absolutely crazy, says Blair', *Daily Telegraph*, 18 March 1997.
106 Quoted in Toby Moore and Roland Watson, 'Facing up to victory day', *The Express*, 30 April 1997.
107 Quoted in Arthur Leathley, 'Father's stroke changed son's politics', *The Times*, 2 October 1996.
108 Quoted in party election broadcast for the Labour party, 24 April 1997.
109 Quoted in party election broadcast for the Labour party, 24 April 1997.
110 See John Major, 'What's right with Britain', *Daily Telegraph*, 11 November 1996.
111 Quoted in David Butler and Dennis Kavanagh, *The British General Election of 1997* (Basingstoke, Macmillan, 1997), p. 40.
112 Quoted in Michael White, '"Hypocrisy" outburst by Major', *The Guardian*, 15 April 1997.
113 Quoted in Michael White, 'Major and Blair go for the kill', *The Guardian*, 25 April 1997.
114 Quoted in Michael White, 'Tories to make it personal', *The Guardian*, 10 April 1997.
115 Quoted in Arthur Leathley, 'Cast your doubts aside and trust me, pleads Major', *The Times*, 24 April 1997.
116 John Major, 'My personal manifesto', *The Times*, 9 April 1997.
117 Quoted in Leathley, 'Cast your doubts aside and trust me, pleads Major'.
118 *Daily Telegraph*, 29 April 1997.
119 *Daily Telegraph*, 29 April 1997.
120 Butler and Kavanagh, *The British General Election of 1997*, p. 226.
121 Quoted in Roy Hattersley, 'Let's hear it for Tony', *The Observer*, 22 February 1998.
122 Alastair Campbell quoted in John Mulholland, 'Labour's Mr Media', *The Guardian*, 12 February 1997.
123 Stephen Castle, 'Labour's spin doctors hit back at bad press', *Independent on Sunday*, 1 February 1998.
124 See Peter Oborne, *Alastair Campbell: New Labour and the Art of Media Management* (London, Aurum, 1999).

125 Kevin Toolis, 'The Enforcer', *The Guardian*, 4 April 1998.
126 Toolis, 'The Enforcer'.
127 Ewan MacAskill, 'No 10 to control Whitehall "spin"', *The Guardian*, 27 November 1997.
128 Sir Geoffrey Robinson, quoted in Channel Four, *Blair's Way*, 1 May 1999.
129 Quoted in Valerie Elliot and Nicholas Wood, 'Whitehall press officers get lessons in spin', *The Times*, 2 October 1997.
130 Quoted in Michael Streeter, 'Whitehall's press machine "sidelined"', *The Independent*, 3 October 1997.
131 Quoted in Elliot and Wood, 'Whitehall press officers get lessons in spin'.
132 Quoted in Michael White, 'In the frame', *The Guardian*, 7 July 1997.
133 Quoted in White, 'In the frame'.
134 http://www.cabinet-office.gov.uk/central/1997/mcode/index.htm.
135 White, 'In the frame'.
136 White, 'In the frame'.
137 For example, Martin Sixsmith, the BBC's Moscow correspondent, left the Corporation to become chief press officer at the Department of Social Security. The BBC's political correspondent, Lance Price, left to join the Number 10 communications team.
138 'A senior government source' quoted in James Landale, 'Blair takes question time to the heart of Middle England', *The Times*, 14 June 1997.
139 Dennis Kavanagh and Anthony Seldon, *The Powers Behind the Prime Minister: The Hidden Influence of Number Ten* (London, HarperCollins, 1999), p. 278.
140 Kavanagh and Seldon, *The Powers Behind the Prime Minister*, p. 278.
141 Quoted in Landale, 'Blair takes question time to the heart of Middle England'.
142 Quoted in Patrick Wintour, 'PM stages public Question Time', *The Observer*, 8 June 1997.
143 Tony Blair, quoted in Butler and Kavanagh, *The British General Election of 1997*, p. 213.
144 For example, the BBC, ITN, Microsoft Network, *The Guardian*, and the *Daily Telegraph*.
145 For example, the first prime ministerial interview exclusive to the Internet was conducted by Sir David Frost and broadcast on 29 April 1998.
146 Quoted in Matthew Parris, 'Why the press is turning', *The Times*, 10 July 1998.
147 Quoted in Stephen Castle, 'We only speak if we feel like it', *Independent on Sunday*, 5 July 1998.
148 Quoted in Robert Shrimsley, 'Big beasts of the political jungle go for the jugular', *Daily Telegraph*, 3 July 1998.
149 Castle, 'We only speak if we feel like it'.
150 Chris Buckland, 'Who sets the news agenda?', *The Times*, 10 July 1998.
151 Alice Miles, 'The impotence of the press', *The Spectator*, 27 February 1999.
152 Quoted in Miles, 'The impotence of the press'.
153 See Nicholas Jones, *Sultans of Spin: The Media and the New Labour Government* (London, Victor Gollanz, 1999), p. 291.
154 Jones, *Sultans of Spin*, p. 291.
155 Norris, 'The Battle for the Campaign Agenda', p. 129.
156 Ken Livingstone, 'The truth about our spin doctors – they're really not much good', *The Independent*, 24 June 1998.
157 Ken Livingstone, 'These spin doctors thrive in our backstabbing culture', *The Independent*, 6 January 1999.
158 Livingstone, 'The truth about our spin doctors.
159 Ken Livingstone 'The joy of politics – a chance to upset the spin doctors', *The Independent*, 12 August 1998.

160 Joy Johnson, 'Doctor, doctor, my head is in a whirl', *New Statesman and Society*, 24 May 1996.
161 Johnson, 'Doctor, doctor, my head is in a whirl'.
162 Joy Johnson, 'Simply mesmerised by the sultans of spin', *Sunday Times*, 19 October 1997.
163 Joy Johnson, 'Spinner takes all', *Red Pepper*, May 1999.
164 Johnson, 'Spinner takes all'.
165 Michael White, 'Spinning out of control', *The Guardian*, 21 October 1997.
166 Matthew Parris, 'Why the press is turning', *The Times*, 10 July 1998.
167 Parris, 'Why the press is turning'.
168 John Redwood, 'Blair's soundbite strategy keeps us on the sidelines', *The Times*, 5 January 1998.
169 Quoted in Daisy Sampson, 'Labour prefers the press to parliament', *The Independent*, 22 July 1998.
170 Quoted in Jill Sherman, 'Labour spinning out of control, says Boothroyd', *The Times*, 9 April 1998.
171 Quoted in Sherman, 'Labour spinning out of control, says Boothroyd'.

CHAPTER 7

Leadership stretch in Britain

The propulsion of leaders into public arenas and the drive to commit party agendas and programmes to a process of public outreach through the agency of leadership projection has led party leaders to become increasingly differentiated from their colleagues. Leaders are no longer merely party spokespeople, but the ostentatious flagships of their respective fleets. They have no choice. They are simply part of a self-generating and self-intensifying process that compels party leaders to achieve high levels of public attention and recognition by moulding themselves successfully to the channels of political communication that can best provide it. Leaders struggle with one another on a continued basis to be the most effective expression of popular convictions and anxieties. What were once media opportunities to reach a wider audience have now been turned into overriding media obligations to publicise political positions through the effective projection of party leaders as national figures.

In modern British politics, the possession of a public identity is a political resource in its own right. Party leaders have to be able to command public attention in order to maintain the confidence of their parties. Leaders who are known to the public have access to the public domain. They can float ideas, discredit opponents, allay doubts, share concerns, sell policies and change the agenda of public debate. How well leaders perform these public functions, how effectively they use the public facilities of leadership to convey messages, and how proficient they are in commanding public confidence are themselves matters of public scrutiny and popular appraisal. The extent of the public's access to, and interest in, the words, images and behaviour of leaders – together with the scale of the media's leader-centred presentation of the news – produces an effect that can be called 'leadership stretch'. The term refers to the way that party leaders have increasingly stretched away from their senior colleagues in terms of media attention and popular awareness.

The profound significance that is attached to a leader's capacity to acquire and use public attention is driven by fears of competitive disadvantage in the battle over the next general election. This event is the pole star that guides parties in their drive for public access and that allows leaders to navigate their way to increasingly advanced states of personal prominence. The conspicuous nature of contemporary political leadership is reflected in the disparity of press coverage between the party leaders and their senior political colleagues. But it is the electronic media, and particularly television, which lie at the centre of a synergy between the media, the party leaderships and electoral motivations. For example, much of the recent exposure and public attention given to leaders has come as a result of an underlying dynamic between the mass media and party politics. In short, television's inclination to personalise the treatment and presentation of politics has been matched by the willingness of parties to provide their leaders with the prominence and licence to fit the party product to its optimal form of communication. Just as 'the dominance of television helps to presidentialize the message of the parties',[1] so the messengers themselves have become increasingly presidentialised. In turn, in doing so, leaders acquire further public prominence which enhances their television news value to an even greater extent than before. As a result of this process, a leader can improve the security of his or her position in the party, and thereupon claim further executive discretion to exploit the visibility of that position for the party's interests and objectives.

An important qualification in leadership selection is now an individual's proven ability to attract publicity and media attention. For example, '[i]t was natural that the successor to Michael Foot as Labour leader in 1983 should be chosen with considerable care for TV skills.'[2] In fact, Neil Kinnock was said to have 'owed almost everything to television'.[3] He used it to compensate for his lack of political and governmental experience. As he himself said, 'I got to be Leader of the Labour Party by being good on television'.[4] David Owen was chosen as the SDP leader for much the same reason. Roy Jenkins, the party's first leader, had performed poorly on television in the 1983 general election. He felt obliged to make way for a leader who could better exploit the modern opportunities for personal and party publicisation. Shirley Williams explained the main reasons why Jenkins's successor had to be David Owen: 'David Owen had a remarkable capacity ... for being able to seize the attention of the media, capture it and turn it into headline after headline after headline.'[5] This relationship between party leaders, the mass media and public opinion is strengthened still further by the emphasis given to elections, and especially to general elections, by the broadcasting organisations. Television and radio news services devote enormous resources to covering a general election. It is regarded by them as the centrepiece of their political reporting efforts and as their main claim to being a public service. Coverage of an election, right through to the authoritative predictions before the official announcements, is the forte of the electronic news-gathering organisations. Elections are now not only conducted through the mass media, but to a large extent by them as well.

Given this symbiotic relationship between the mass media and elections, it is only to be expected that television and radio news programmes should reflect their interest in the electoral dimension of political events and disputes. This takes various forms but the most conspicuous effect is the way that political news is often presented and analysed in reference to its significance for a forthcoming election – even if that election is some years away. As a result, the handling of domestic news is riddled with allusions to electoral timing and voting projections, and to American-style calculations as to who is ahead, who is falling behind and who might not reach the starting line. By-elections, for example, are now seen and treated as being prototypical of general elections. Accordingly, they are subjected to a blaze of publicity in which the party heavyweights spar with one another in preparation for the big contest. Such elections provide not only a testing ground for the parties' campaigning techniques, but also a proving ground for the media's own capacity to impose general election categories of analysis and evaluation upon a local voting exercise.

When general elections finally arrive, dynamics of leadership stretch are already well established and the media report the election according to their pre-set priorities. This is reflected in the proportion of attention given to the party leaders in relation to the other members of the cabinet and shadow cabinet teams. In the 1992 general election, Holli Semetko, Margaret Scammell and Tom Nossiter concluded that the 'party leaders were the single most visible actors in the press'.[6] Nearly a third of all the politicians featured on the front pages came from the tiny minority of party leaders. A similar pattern of press coverage was repeated in the 1997 general election (see table 7.1).

The figures reveal that 'over a third of all the press stories concerned party leadership and candidates'.[7] Both John Major and Tony Blair received over four times the press coverage of their nearest party colleagues. The coverage devoted to Paddy Ashdown 'was even more pronounced, with almost no stories about any of his colleagues'.[8] This reflected a common strategy on the part of third parties to concentrate attention upon the leadership. The assiduous cultivation of the medium of leadership projection creates an impression of comparability with the main parties. Although Ashdown was unable to match either Blair or Major in terms of absolute coverage, he was able to maximise the impression of comparable leadership status by attracting almost all the coverage apportioned to the Liberal Democrats.

Table 7.1. *Press coverage of major political figures in the 1997 general election (in percentages of the total coverage given to individual politicians)*

Conservatives	
John Major	17.7
Neil Hamilton	3.9
Margaret Thatcher	3.9
Kenneth Clarke	3.7
Michael Heseltine	3.4
Michael Howard	1.7
Brian Mawhinney	1.7
Michael Portillo	1.4
John Redwood	1.4
Peter Lilley	1.1
Tim Smith	1.1
Others	4.0
Labour	
Tony Blair	19.7
Gordon Brown	4.6
John Prescott	2.3
Peter Mandelson	1.7
Robin Cook	1.5
Cherie Booth	1.1
Neil Kinnock	1.0
Others	1.6
Liberal Democrat	
Paddy Ashdown	4.3
Lord Holme	0.3
David Steel	0.2
Simon Hughes	0.2
Others	0.3
Other candidates	13.5
'Celebrities'	2.8

Source: Content analysis of 6,072 articles published in the national press over the period 17 March to 1 May 1997. The analysis was produced by CARMA and published in Pippa Norris, 'The Battle for the Campaign Agenda', in Anthony King *et al.*, *New Labour Triumphs: Britain at the Polls* (Chatham, Chatham House, 1998), p.137.

Table 7.2. *Number of times politicians quoted in selected radio and television news, 1997 general election*

	BBC 1	*ITV*	*C4*	*R4*	*Total*
Conservative					
Major	116	109	37	86	348
Heseltine	31	25	11	19	86
Clarke	17	17	4	11	49
Howard	12	6	4	13	35
Dorrell	10	9	6	8	33
The Hamiltons	8	6	4	8	28
Forsyth	9	5	3	7	24
Mawhinney	9	3	2	7	21
Portillo	6	5	2	7	20
Thatcher	6	5	1	1	13
Shephard	5	4	1	3	13
Currie	1	6	1	4	12
Lang	5	1	1	5	12
Lilley	7	1	1	3	12
Browning	3	3	1	4	11
53 'others'	50	26	19	45	130
Labour					
Blair	117	94	38	79	328
Brown	34	30	7	23	94
Cook	10	4	7	13	34
Straw	11	8	4	11	34
Robertson	6	8	4	8	27
Prescott	7	9	7	—	23
Blunkett	5	6	2	2	15
Mandelson	6	5	1	2	14
A. Smith	5	—	1	3	9
Beckett	1	1	3	3	8
38 'others'	41	14	23	12	90
Liberal Democrats					
Ashdown	117	99	28	84	328
Beith	10	5	1	10	26
Holme	14	3	1	7	25
Wallace	9	8	1	5	23
Hughes	6	7	3	6	22
Bruce	5	5	2	6	17
Foster	4	5	2	5	16
Carlile	4	2	3	4	13
Taylor	3	4	—	6	12
Kennedy	5	2	2	3	12
27 'others'	28	30	11	16	85

Source: Martin Harrison, 'Politics on the Air', in David Butler and Dennis Kavanagh, *The British General Election of 1997* (Basingstoke, Macmillan, 1997), p. 144.

Campaign exposure

Figures produced by Martin Harrison in the Nuffield studies of British general elections reveal the magnitude of leadership stretch where the broadcasting media are concerned. Working on the basis of the number of times that politicians had been quoted in radio and television news programmes during the election campaigns, Professor Harrison shows in graphic form the dominance of the party leaders over other senior political figures in respect to media coverage. The results of the 1997 election are given in table 7.2.

These figures demonstrate the advantage accrued to a third-party leader such as Ashdown from the broadcasting media's statutory obligations to provide balanced reporting. In this set of measurements, Ashdown records the same number of appearances (i.e. 328) as Blair. But it is the disparity between party leaders and senior colleagues which is the most significant feature of this table. John Major accounts for 41.1 per cent of the total number of appearances made by Conservative politicians. The equivalent proportions for Tony Blair within the Labour ranks is 48.5 per cent and for Paddy Ashdown within the complement of Liberal Democrat spokespersons 56.7 per cent. These levels of domination are considerably greater than even the disparities recorded in the distribution of press coverage. They show an emphatic disjunction between the party leaders and even those figures in their respective parties who occupied key positions in the electoral campaigns. At this level of news appearances, John Major outscores the Conservative party chairman, Brian Mawhinney, by a factor of 16.6 to 1. Tony Blair eclipses the Deputy Leader of the Labour party, John Prescott,

Table 7.3. *Differential in television and radio news appearances between Conservative prime ministers and their party chairmen, and between Labour leaders and their deputy leaders (1983, 1987 and 1992 general elections)*

	1983	*1987*	*1992*
Conservative leader	Thatcher	Thatcher	Major
Conservative chairman	Parkinson	Tebbit	Patten
Leader/chairman news ratio	5.6	3.0	4.9
Labour leader	Foot	Kinnock	Kinnock
Deputy leader	Healey	Hattersley	Hattersley
Leader/deputy news ratio	1.8	5.1	12.6

Source: David Butler and Dennis Kavanagh, *The British General Election of 1983* (London, Macmillan, 1983); David Butler and Dennis Kavanagh, *The British General Election of 1987* (Basingstoke, Macmillan, 1988); David Butler and Dennis Kavanagh, *The British General Election of 1992* (Basingstoke, Macmillan, 1992).

by a ratio of 14.3 to 1. These disjunctions represent significant increases over the three previous elections (see table 7.3).

In order to give a clearer picture of the disparities in broadcasting penetration between the party leaders and the other prominent performers in their respective parties over the election period, the top five below the leadership level in all three main parties are taken as aggregate groups. By calculating the average number of their appearances, it is possible to arrive at a more accurate measurement of general disparity that is based upon the differences between the leaders and the norm of 'heavy hitters' within each of the parties (see table 7.4). Table 7.4 clearly shows the overall level of disjunction between the appearance rates of the leaders and those of the senior figures inside their cabinets or shadow cabinets. The ratios of leadership preponderance are revealed as 7.53 and 7.74 for the leaderships of Major and Blair over their respective parties. Predictably, the ratio for the Liberal Democrats is higher (14.51), and this helps to inflate the overall rate of leadership preponderance to 9.93.

Table 7.4. *Differential in television and radio news appearances between the party leaders and the top five spokespersons below the leadership level within their respective parties (1997 general election)*

Party	*Number of times leader quoted*	*Average of the top five below leader level*	*Difference between leader and top five average*	*Leader's news count as a proportion of top five average*
Conservative	348	46.2	301.8	7.53
Labour	328	42.4	285.6	7.74
Liberal Democrat	328	22.6	305.4	14.51
OVERALL	333.7	37.1	207.6	9.93

Source: David Butler and Dennis Kavanagh, *The British General Election of 1997* (Basingstoke, Macmillan, 1997).

The figures on media appearances produced by the Nuffield studies of British elections reveal that over the last twenty years, the number of occasions that leaders have been quoted in accordance with this measure has grown from 390 in 1979 to 1,004 in 1997. While this shows a general, if not always consistent, trend-line,[9] the measure is not a precise expression of leadership attention by the broadcasting media. For example, in the 1983 election the number of outlets included in the measure increased to accommodate the news programmes on Channel 4. In addition, news organisations have sought to introduce some element of diversification to their election coverage. This has included an attempt to provide a greater range of party spokespersons who would perhaps be less likely to echo the predictable message of the leaders' ever more tightly controlled campaign teams. In the view of Martin Harrison, the 'need for variety probably creates a natural limit'[10] to the exposure of the party leaders. The counter-weight to the 'forms of "presidentialisation" has come with the greater role of other party spokespersons across a range of current affairs sequences from *GMTV* right through to *The World Tonight*'.[11]

Notwithstanding these caveats, the important element of the measure is not so much one of the aggregate increase in the leaders' overall quotation levels, but the difference between the leaders and the rest. Here the trend-line has been a consistent movement towards an increasingly marked gulf between the two classes of politician (see table 7.5). From a relatively high level of 69.8 in 1983, the average of the 'top five' category has dropped in successive elections to 37.1 in 1997. The global figures for party leaders have fluctuated in accordance with factors such as editorial policy towards election coverage (e.g. responding to the balance of the parties and the likelihood of a close finish) and the deliberate attempt by Labour in 1992 to make its campaign more team based. Nevertheless, the proportionality of the leaders' contributions has shown a marked increase upon the 1983 figures. Over the past three general elections, leaders have attracted approximately ten times the television and radio news coverage of the leading figures in the cabinet and shadow cabinets. These results underline Martin Harrison's conclusion that a fusion of forces is present in this sector of news generation. 'The commitment of such large resources to the leaders confirm[s] the tendency of the broadcast media over a succession of elections to presidentialise their presentation.'[12]

It can be claimed that by concentrating upon mainline news programmes, the Nuffield figures under-represent the political notables who appear on other news and current affairs outlets. This may be true but, by the same token, the measure also underestimates the scale of the leaders' domination of the news during an election period. The Nuffield statistics are based upon the incidence of quotations. By their very nature, they include neither the length of quotations nor any reference to visual sequences, even where there is a direct connection to a policy or personal statement. As Martin Harrison himself points out, because the measures are based upon reported utterances, they overlook other forms of leadership projection. For example, leaders are 'seen extensively in non-speaking situations like photo-opportunities' and they are also 'interviewed at length on many programmes outside the news'.[13] In this respect, the Nuffield figures clearly understate the scale of attention given to the party leaders during election periods.

Table 7.5. *Differential in television and radio news appearances between the party leaders and the top five spokespersons below the leadership level within their respective parties (1983, 1987 and 1992 general elections)*

Party	*Number of times leader quoted*	*Average of the top five below leader level*	*Difference between leader and top five average*	*Leader's news count as a proportion of top five average*
1983 general election				
Conservative	330	50.8	279.2	6.50
Labour	307	82.0	225.0	3.74
Liberal Democrat	230.5 [a]	76.5 [b]	154.0	3.01
OVERALL	289.2	69.8	219.4	4.42
1987 general election				
Conservative	421	63.0	358.0	6.68
Labour	481	51.6	429.4	9.32
Liberal Democrat	335.5 [a]	23.4	312.1	14.34
OVERALL	412.5	46.0	366.5	10.11
1992 general election				
Conservative	469	60.8	408.2	6.71
Labour	452	54.2	397.8	7.34
Liberal Democrat	419	26.2	392.8	14.99
OVERALL	446.7	47.1	399.6	9.68

Source: David Butler and Dennis Kavanagh, *The British General Election of 1983* (London, Macmillan, 1983); David Butler and Dennis Kavanagh, *The British General Election of 1987* (Basingstoke, Macmillan, 1988); David Butler and Dennis Kavanagh, *The British General Election of 1992* (Basingstoke, Macmillan, 1992).

[a] In the 1983 and 1987 elections, the individual totals for the two Alliance leaders were aggregated and given an average to produce a composite figure for the Alliance leadership.

[b] Due to a lack of data, the only two non-leadership Alliance politicians to be given appearance ratings (Owen and Williams) were aggregated and given an average that was used as an 'average of the top five below leader level'.

Analysis of the 1997 general election produced by the Communications Research Centre at Loughborough University helps to overcome some of the limitations alluded to by Harrison. To begin with, the CRC has generated an aggregate measurement of the campaign's leading figures that combines appearance levels in the press with those recorded in the broadcast media. Figure 7.1 reveals the scale of the leaders' exposure in graphic form. The

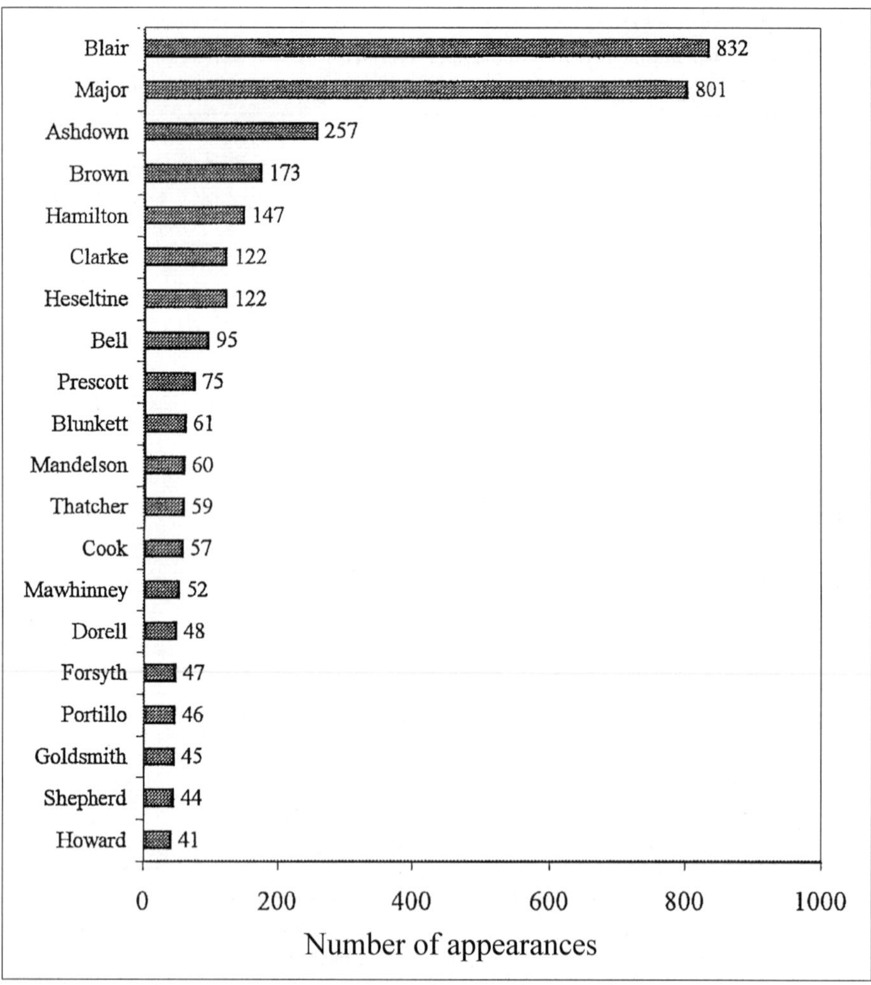

Figure 7.1 News appearances league table for the period 1 April–31 April 1997. The top twenty politicians are drawn from an aggregate measure of appearances in all media.* An appearance is allocated when an individual is a featured player in a news story.

* Media analysed: *Television*: BBC1, *Nine O'Clock News*; ITN, *News At Ten*; BBC2, *Newsnight*; Channel Four, *Channel 4 News*; Channel 5, *5 News*. *Radio*: BBC4, *Today* (8.00–9.00). *Newspapers*: *The Mirror*, *The Sun*, *Daily Star*, *Daily Mail*, *The Express*, *The Times*, *Financial Times*, *Daily Telegraph*, *The Guardian*, *The Independent*.

Source: Communications Research Centre, Loughborough University, by permission.

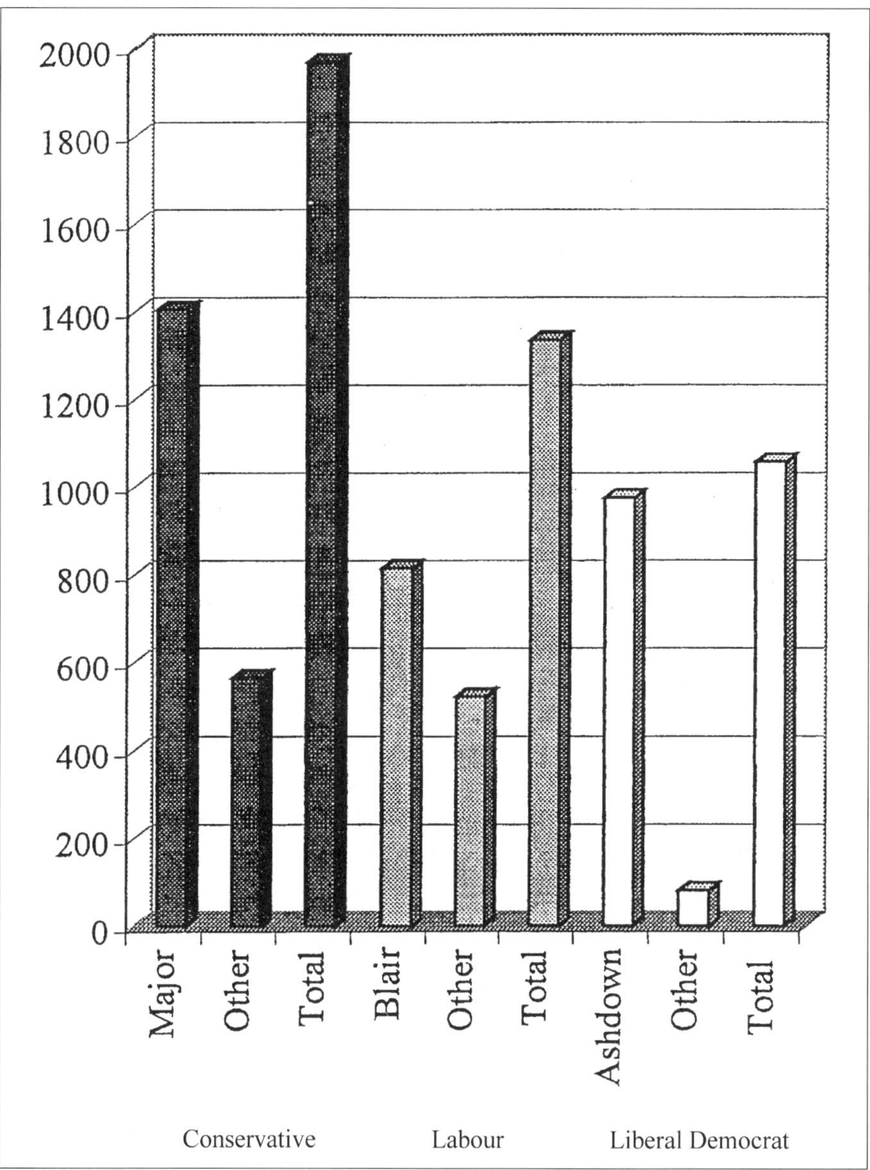

Figure 7.2 The time taken up by the party leaders on television news* as a proportion of the total time occupied by individuals from their respective parties during the period 31 March–18 April 1997.

* BBC1, *Nine O'Clock News*; ITN, *News At Ten*.

Source: Communications Research Centre, Loughborough University, by permission.

top twenty in the league account for 57 per cent of all the appearances made by politicians. The top ten account for 48 per cent. But the appearance measurements of just three individuals – namely Major, Blair and Ashdown – constitute over a third (34 per cent) of the total of 5,542 recorded appearances. More revealing are the figures relating to the length of time that the leaders appeared on television news. During a three week period, the CRC measured the time that was occupied by politicians on BBC1's *Nine O'Clock News* and ITN's *News at Ten*. Figure 7.2 demonstrates the scale of the leaders' actual predominance over all their party colleagues in talking to the viewers and in filling their field of vision. Instead of registering merely the incidence of appearances, this more sophisticated measure conveys something of the substantive level of leadership stretch that lies within the simple itemisation of individual appearances.

Keep on running

Even though it can be shown that the party leaders achieve exceptional levels of media domination over other senior party figures, this may be an effect confined to campaign periods. It is possible that a general election may represent an extreme set of circumstances that produce an atypical concentration of news reports centring upon the party leaders. In order to gauge whether the priorities of election coverage are representative or unrepresentative of normal periods of political news reporting, it is necessary to have some set of time-series data relating to the news coverage of political figures. Comparable data that cover different periods to a degree of consistency sufficient to produce an integrity of scale and a continuity of categories are largely unavailable. Nevertheless, in order to acquire a general grasp of the distribution of news attention among senior political figures, recourse has been made to a simple yet effective device that was first employed by Richard Rose.

In a pioneer study of prime ministerial prominence published in 1980, Rose showed that prime ministers regularly received more press coverage than the Foreign Secretary, the Chancellor of the Exchequer and Leader of the House of Commons put together[14] (see table 7.6). It was also revealed that the coverage given to the leader of the opposition had grown in parallel with the increased publicity given to the prime minister. In 1956, for example, Anthony Eden and Hugh Gaitskell together accounted for approximately the same number of references as the Chancellor, Foreign Secretary and Leader of the House of Commons combined.[15] By 1977, Callaghan and Thatcher were not far from having doubled the number of references given to the holders of the same three senior offices of state.[16]

Table 7.6. *Volume of references to senior politicians in* The Times Index[a], *selected years*

Year	*Prime minister* (1)	*Leader of opposition* (2)	*(1) as % of (2)*	*Chancellor of Exchequer* (3)	*Foreign Secretary* (4)	*Leader of House of Commons* (5)	*(1) as % of total of (3–5)*
1949	Attlee 94	Churchill 62	152	Cripps 110	Bevin 96	Morrison 56	36
1952	Churchill 302	Attlee 64	472	Butler 136	Eden 197	Crookshank 38	81
1956	Eden 193	Gaitskell 70	276	Macmillan 93	Lloyd 111	Butler 50	76
1960	Macmillan 303	Gaitskell 88	344	Amory 44	Lloyd 76	Butler 109	132
1964	Douglas-Hume 278	Wilson 169	164	Maudling 47	Butler 106	Lloyd 23	158
1968	Wilson 147	Heath 50	294	Jenkins 46	Brown 45	Crossman 14	140
1972	Heath 141	Wilson 82	172	Barber 18	Douglas-Hume 74	Whitelaw 24	122
1977	Callaghan 170	Thatcher 78	218	Healey 37	Crosland/ Owen[b] 39	Foot 59	126

[a] Publications indexed relate to *The Times*, *The Sunday Times*, *Times Educational Supplement*, *Times Scottish Educational Supplement*, *Times Higher Education Supplement* and *Times Literary Supplement*

[b] Stories on the death of Anthony Crosland and the appointment of David Owen are omitted.

Source: Richard Rose, 'British Government: The Job at the Top', in Richard Rose and Ezra N. Suleiman (eds), *Presidents and Prime Ministers* (Washington, DC, American Enterprise Institute, 1980), p. 20.

New calculations covering selected years during the premierships of Margaret Thatcher, John Major and Tony Blair are produced in table 7.7. This reveals a pattern of sustained prime ministerial preponderance. In 1980, Margaret Thatcher utterly eclipsed the leader of the opposition, Michael Foot. It is true that she was unable to emulate this level of pre-eminence when Foot was replaced by the high profile leadership of Neil Kinnock. Nevertheless, the prime minister remained the dominant news figure throughout the 1980s. The 1990 figures demonstrate the effect of a leadership election and the transfer of power from one prime minister to another. The leader

Table 7.7. *Volume*[a] *of references to senior politicians in* The Times Index[b], *selected years*

Year	*Prime minister* (1)	*Leader of opposition* (2)	*(1) as % of (2)*	*Chancellor of Exchequer* (3)	*Foreign Secretary* (4)	*Leader of House of Commons* (5)	*(1) as % of total of (3–5)*
1980	Thatcher	Foot		Howe	Carrington	St John Stevas	
	302.8	77.3	392	90.5	101.5	47.9	126
1984	Thatcher	Kinnock		Lawson	Howe	Biffen	
	342.5	185.1	185	73.8	109.3	17.9	171
1988	Thatcher	Kinnock		Lawson	Howe	Wakeham	
	383.8	145.6	264	59.0	59.1	21.1	275
1990	Thatcher/ Major	Kinnock		Major/ Lamont	Hurd	Howe/ MacGregor	
	346.7	80.2	432	56.6	104.5	46.4	167
1992	Major	Smith		Lamont	Hurd	MacGregor/ Newton	
	519.9	97.0	536	215.2	88.2	11.7	165
1994	Major	Smith/ Blair[a]		Clarke	Hurd	Newton	
	344.3	147.6	233	105.8	125.2	4.6	146
1996	Major	Blair		Clarke	Rifkind	Newton	
	389.0	340.3	114	230.0	87.3	3.8	121
1998	Blair	Hague		Brown	Cook	Taylor/ Beckett	
	424.9	122.7	346	184.4	158.6	10.7	120

[a] The volume is measured by the length (in centimetres) of the columns of entries relating to each politician cited in *The Times Index* for each of the years shown in the table.

[b] Publications indexed relate to *The Times*, *The Sunday Times*, *Times Educational Supplement*, *Times Scottish Educational Supplement*, *Times Higher Education Supplement* and *Times Literary Supplement*.

[c] The figures do not include the period between John Smith's death (12 May 1994) and the selection of Tony Blair as Labour leader (21 July 1994).

of the opposition slumps to only a quarter of the news stories generated by Margaret Thatcher and John Major. In 1992, the drama surrounding 'Black Wednesday' and the government's withdrawal from the ERM helps to boost the Chancellor's level of news coverage to over twice the level recorded by any Chancellor in the 1980s. Notwithstanding this surge, the prime minister remains dominant, with over twice the coverage of that recorded for Norman Lamont. During what became a crisis point for the Major administration, it is noticeable that the quiet leadership of John Smith was even quieter than usual, with a news volume measure under a fifth of that registered by the prime minister.

The figures return to a more settled pattern in 1994. The only exception relates to the coverage of the leader of the opposition. This reaches a level of nearly half that of the prime minister. Once again this reveals the influence of a change of leadership. This time it is the transition from John Smith to Tony Blair. Even though the figures do not include the period between John Smith's death (12 May 1994) and the selection of Blair as Labour party leader (21 July 1994), the effect of the new leadership upon news coverage is immediate. Whereas Smith had achieved a volume measure of 38.6 in the first five months of 1994, Blair was registered at 109.0 for the final five months of the year. The full impact of Blair's leadership is discernible in 1996, when he nearly succeeds in reaching parity with the prime minister. The ratio between the prime minister and the opposition leader falls to a level of 1.1 to 1 – i.e. the lowest recorded in this set of measures. The weakened authority of the prime minister is also reflected in a slump in Major's preponderance over his Chancellor, Kenneth Clarke. Prior to 1996, the average level of prime ministerial superiority over the Chancellor of the Exchequer was 342 per cent. In the case of John Major and Kenneth Clarke, it had declined to 169 per cent in 1996.

In 1998, the picture shifts back to one of clear dominance on the part of the prime minister. Despite the myriad references to a dual leadership, the volume differential between premier and Chancellor widens and returns to a more familiar pattern. The figures also underline the problems of a new opposition leader in attracting public attention. Even in a newspaper such as *The Times*, which traditionally supports the Conservative party, Hague is overwhelmed by Blair by a factor of 3.5 to 1. Moreover, the opposition leader is outscored by two of the other offices (i.e. the Chancellor and the Foreign Secretary). In terms of these *Times Index* tables, such a situation had not occurred since 1952. Although the 1998 figures also show a marked increase in the news coverage of the Foreign Secretary's post, some of this was due to Robin Cook's marital problems rather than to any substantive factor. Another office to show a significant gain in news coverage is that of the Leader of the House of Commons, but despite the increase it remains far removed from the levels achieved in table 7.6 that covered a period when the House of Commons had a higher news value.

The reliability of this rudimentary measure of news coverage is supported by the more advanced data searches that are occasionally conducted to give comprehensive snapshots of the media penetration achieved by public figures. For example, in one such exercise the databases of all the national newspapers were surveyed to reveal the number of stories referring to each individual politician that appeared between 1 January and 23 December 1998. The results, which are said to give an 'indication of the Prime Minister's presidential style',[17] are given in table 7.8. They confirm the emphatic predominance of the prime minister, with no senior politician able to achieve even half Blair's number of references. Alastair Campbell's recorded appearances exceed those of nine cabinet ministers and nearly the whole of the shadow cabinet. William Hague struggles not only to reach a fifth of the prime minister's measure but even to exceed the number of appearances by Margaret Thatcher (i.e. 5,859).[18]

Tables 7.7 and 7.8 show that the various pressures which orientate election coverage to an identifiable cadre of leaders are not peculiar to an election period. They may be particularly intense during a campaign, but they are symptomatic of a more general trend towards a permanent election, in which the effective leadership of a political party and the effective marketing of political issues are closely tied up with one another.

Leaders, polls and lists

The distinctive properties of 'leadership stretch', and the ramifying nature of its consequences upon leadership politics, are probably shown to their fullest effect in the content and treatment of public opinion polls. The polls are a product of the public's fascination with party leaders. They are also a stimulus to even greater public interest in the leaders' qualifications for leadership and in their performance as public figures. Opinion polls used to be primarily concerned with the level of public support for the various parties. But over recent years they have become progressively more oriented towards categories of leadership assessment. Polls commissioned by, and published in, the national press regularly feature questions not only on how well the party leaders are doing in leading their parties, but also on how well the prime minister is doing in his or her job, together with how effective the other party leaders might be as premier.

These polls, along with their accompanying commentaries, follow an internal logic of their own that gives a self-perpetuating quality to the interest they show in leadership. To begin with, polls are expensive and the newspapers that commission them want to ensure that they will derive the maximum publicity from their investment. Large shifts of support between the parties will provide headlines, but as there are now so many polls it is unlikely that one poll will catch an attention-grabbing swing to one or other

Table 7.8. *Database of ranking of senior politicians and political notables based upon the incidence of individuals referred to in news stories covering the period 1 January to 23 December 1998*

The leaders	
Tony Blair	28,653
Alastair Campbell	2,241
Cherie Blair	991
William Hague	5,991
Ffion Hague	79
Paddy Ashdown	1,484
Jane Ashdown	1

Cabinet		*Shadow cabinet*	
Gordon Brown	11,753	Michael Howard	1,358
Robin Cook	6,861	John Redwood	1,004
John Prescott	6,402	Francis Maude	818
Jack Straw	6,385	Ann Widdecombe	783
David Blunkett	3,358	Sir Norman Fowler	330
Donald Dewar	3,221	Andrew Mackay	307
Chris Smith	3,198	Liam Fox	237
Lord Irvine of Lairg	3,067	Gillian Shepherd	232
Mo Mowlam	3,009	John Maples	194
Frank Dobson	2,383	Sir George Young	184
Margaret Beckett	2,134	Peter Ainsworth	174
George Robertson	1,558	Lord Strathclyde	155
Jack Cunningham	1,217	Tim Yeo	138
Stephen Byers	1,119	Gary Streeter	88
Clare Short	1,010	David Willetts	78
Nick Brown	765	Iain Duncan Smith	57
Baroness Jay of Paddington	543	Sir Nicholas Lyell	33
Alun Michael	534	James Arbuthnot	29
Alan Milburn	501	Lord Kingsland	14
Ann Taylor	427		
Other Labour			
Peter Mandelson	6,323		
Ron Davies	1,329		

Note: Database covers all national newspapers published within the period.
Source: *The Times*, 30 December 1998.

of the main parties. Levels of party support are no longer enough to command public attention. Questions on the leaders and on the requirements of leadership not only provide a colourful background to the party figures, but tap a different dimension of political interest and allegiance. It is a personal dimension that has an immediate popular appeal. It provides a subject area in which questions and opinions can freely proliferate by drawing upon different facets of the public's perception and judgement of the party leaders. Furthermore, the greater the number of questions, the higher will be the probability of newsworthy fluctuations in the categories of response. Indeed, it is this high volume of information generated by leadership polls which provides the raw materials, and to some extent the licence, for all manner of speculative inferences concerning the political significance of the leaders' personalities and behaviour.

These polls, and the myriad conclusions drawn from them, often give rise to eye catching and highly suggestive headlines about leaders and the effect of leadership:

> Major's rating up as Labour lead is halved
> *The Independent*, 19 July 1991
>
> 'Blair effect' undermines Major and lifts Labour to record high
> *The Times*, 26 August 1994
>
> Blair raises Labour to new heights of popularity
> *The Times*, 28 October 1994
>
> Major left reeling as Blair wipes out Tory gains
> *Daily Telegraph*, 3 November 1995
>
> Blair's oratory sways undecided
> *Daily Telegraph*, 5 October 1996
>
> Honest John losing out to Trustworthy Tony
> *Daily Telegraph*, 10 April 1997
>
> Ashdown's ratings up as attacks damage Blair's standing
> *The Guardian*, 16 April 1997
>
> Tories believe Labour has the best party leader
> *The Times*, 2 October 1997
>
> Hague must make most of chance to impress the electorate
> *Daily Telegraph*, 6 October 1997

The net effect of such polls, and of the reviews and headlines generated by them, serves both to reaffirm and to enhance still further the news value of leaders. This in turn promotes even greater coverage of leaders, and increases their centrality in political interpretation and explanation. The commentaries and speculations prompted by such leadership polls feed back into the public domain by way of the newspapers themselves and through television and radio – thereby generating controversy and arousing further public interest in the significance of political leadership. This increases the momentum for more polls, more questions, more analyses, and for the nature and location of leadership to become a rolling public issue. If it is true that opinion polls have become an integral part of the British system's emergence into a condition of permanent election, then it is equally true that leadership has become a defining characteristic of that condition.

It is clear from any examination of the way polls are presented in the national press that extensive coverage is given to the categories relating to the leadership of the political parties. Great emphasis is attached to the theme both as a component of public choice and as an indication of prevailing public trends. The significance of leadership is registered in terms of both the priority given to leadership categories in the presentation of poll findings and the relative space reserved for the subject in proportion to other polling categories. For example, opinion poll commentaries now have a conventional set of priorities in the presentation of findings. The customary format is to start with the levels of party support. This is very often followed by the responses to questions concerning the personal leadership record of the prime minister, either singly or in comparison with the leader of the opposition, or alternatively with the leaders of both main opposition parties. It is only after addressing the leaders that the polls generally move on to presenting the public's responses to current political issues.

The prominence given to the leaders and to the dimension of leadership becomes even more marked in the volume of column inches reserved for discussing the significance of the findings. The attention given to leadership analysis not only underlines the importance assigned to the leaders' rankings in the overall poll, but often has the effect of reversing the original priority given to parties over leaders. On occasions, concern over the leadership categories can completely displace all references to, and evaluations of, other analytical themes. This is particularly the case during periods of intense leadership speculation, when the position of a government or a party is seen to be critically attached to a decline in the public's estimation of a leader's political skills or personal characteristics. For example, much of the second Major administration was marked by a near continuous leadership crisis within the governing party. This ensured that the public evaluation of leadership categories and of alternative leaders remained a high priority, both in the polling organisations' selection of salient questions and in the media's subsequent coverage of the poll results. Pressure was repeatedly placed upon the prime minister by the incessant publication of polls that documented the linkage between poor leadership and his party's standing in the country. They flagged his low approval ratings, the government's lack of leadership, the prime minister's comparative deficiencies in relation to other party leaders, and the market testing of other potential Conservative leaders.

The *de facto* elevation of leadership into a high profile consideration is exemplified, and further exaggerated, by the disposition of editors to use arresting graphics, diagrams and pictures in their page design to give maximum visual prominence to the leadership poll results. A representative sample is given in figures 7.3 to 7.7. These sorts of design draw particular attention to the information presented and, in so doing, give their contents a much greater impact and sense of significance than they might otherwise have received had they been left in plain print or kept to the main body of the commentary. The inclination to give leadership material a high priority through the use of visually appealing boxes and insets is often completed by the positioning of such features at the head of the articles involved.

The weight given to leadership in opinion poll findings and analyses in terms of space, design and positioning is considerable, but the emphasis on leaders and the significance afforded to them in the polls are not confined solely to such presentational techniques. More substantive constructions of leadership salience arise from the juxtaposition of questions and responses in the polls. The progression of findings, from party support to leader assessment and subsequently to issue identification and measurement,

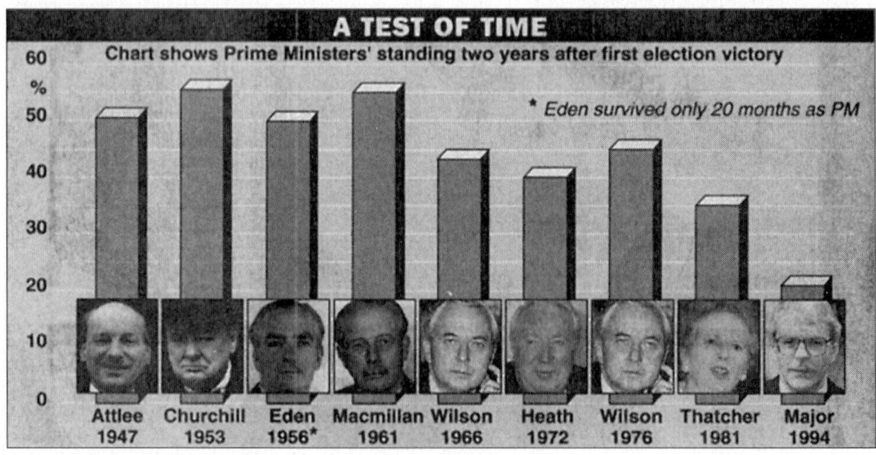

Figure 7.3 A test of time.

Source: *Daily Telegraph*, 8 April 1994.

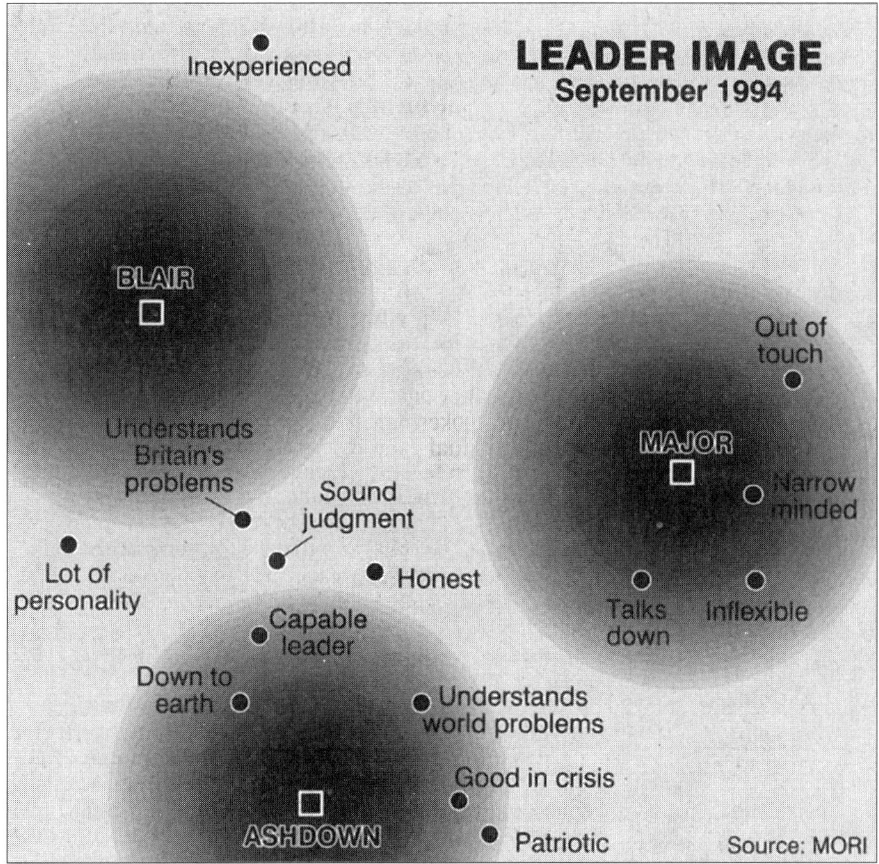

Figure 7.4 Leader image.
Source: *The Times*, 3 October 1994.

generates a system of autosuggestion within the polls themselves. The succession of findings on party, leadership and issues leads the analysis and commentary of each category to run into one another. If the result is not exactly a seamless web, the impulse to make connections, either implicitly or explicitly, seems quite irresistible. The presumption becomes one of interaction and interdependency as analysis follows the inertial properties of the polls' own progression from party to leadership and on to policy connotations. The varied assessments of party leaders become bound up with the current level of support for their parties and with the nature of contemporary issues in uninhibited, and often quite arbitrary, forms of conjecture. It is true that this frenetic confection of causal assumptions and attributed effects is greater in the more popular and openly partisan newspapers.

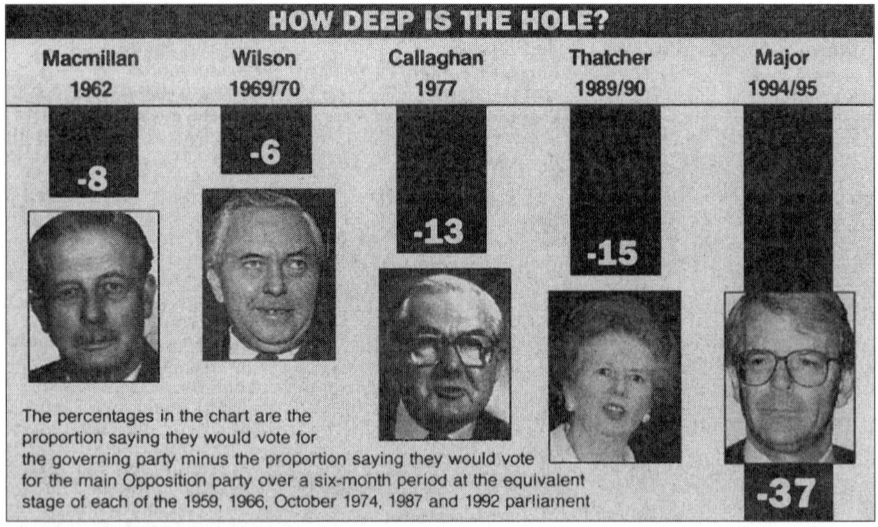

Figure 7.5 How deep is the hole?

Source: *Daily Telegraph*, 18 March 1995.

Nevertheless, senior political correspondents, experienced editors and respected political scientists, who are most aware of the problematic nature of drawing conclusions in this area, are not immune from the autosuggestive properties of the opinion polls.

The provision of the data, and the need to report upon the figures and relate them to recent developments in the news, prompt an exceptional interest in the party leaders. Leaders are not only seen as being instrumental in the generation of news, but are regarded as encapsulations of it, especially in respect to the effects that recent developments have had upon their standing and reputations. The impulse to draw conclusions of political changes by reference to the state of respective party leaderships is fired by the need to comment upon and explain why one poll is different to its predecessor. An opinion poll is largely meaningless on its own. Its usefulness is drawn from what it can show in comparison to either one or a series of previous polls. This means that analysts are often put in a position of trying to explain changes in the configuration of opinion by reference to events and developments that have occurred in the previous two or three weeks. The public prominence of leaders, the volatility in their support levels, and the way that issues are so often portrayed on news programmes as having a leadership dimension, draw commentators to leaders as one of the most conspicuous agents and objects of opinion variation. Such concentrated attention upon the party leaders carries the implication that they are not

Figure 7.6 Best ratings over the years.
Source: *Daily Telegraph*, 6 June 1995.

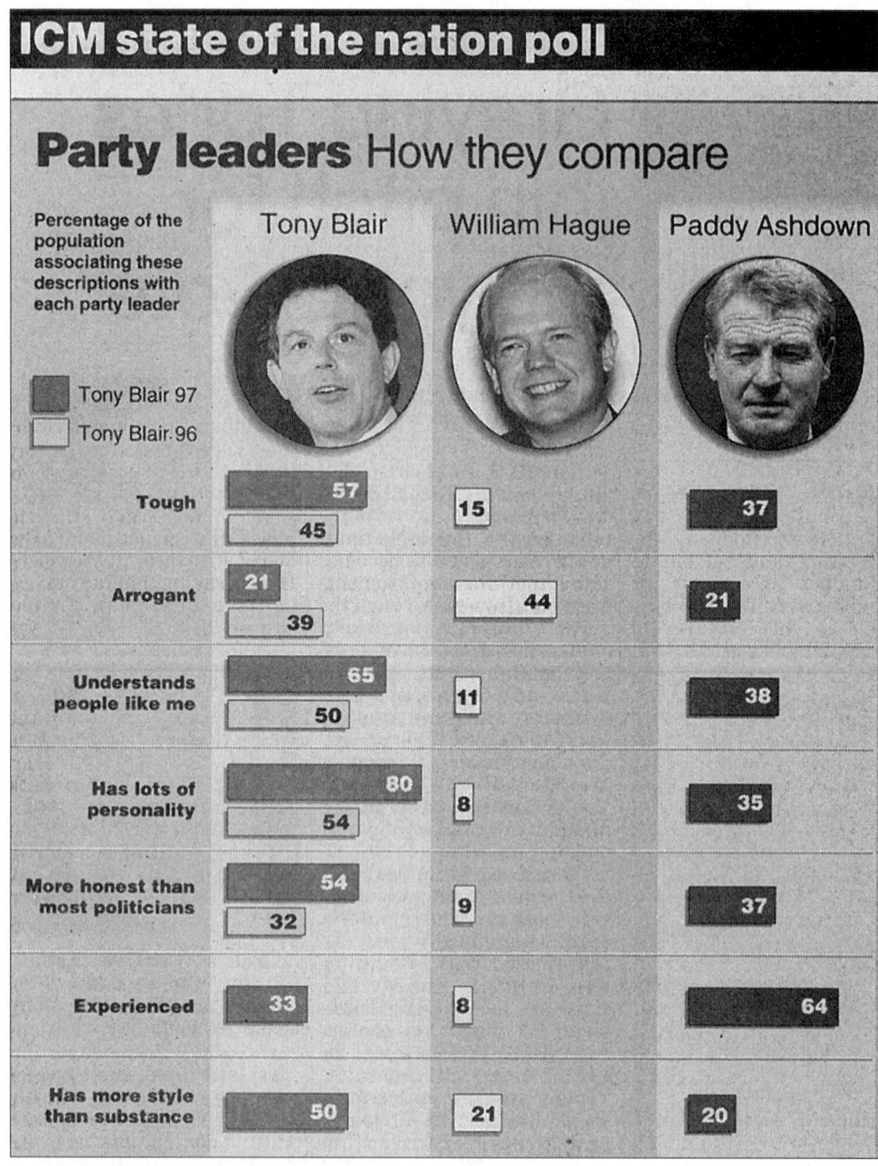

Figure 7.7 ICM 'state of the nation' poll.
Source: *The Guardian*, 8 October 1997.

merely sensitive registers of news developments and opinion movements; they are also active agents of explanation in the varied fortunes of the government and opposition parties, and in their prospects for retaining or acquiring power.

In many cases, the nature of this implication operates at the level of inference. By juxtaposing references to leadership with allusions to party support or government approval, the aggregate effect can often be one of imputed causality. For example, in June 1993 the *Independent on Sunday* splashed the front page with a poll analysis showing that the Conservatives had slumped to their lowest level of voter support for twelve years. The accompanying article, however, consisted almost entirely of an analysis of John Major's leadership which supported the implication that his premiership was responsible for the party support figures. The inference was drawn in the opening sentence: 'John Major's approval rating has plumbed new depths in an opinion poll which puts the Conservatives at their lowest ebb since 1981.'[19] Another example is provided by *The Times* in 1997. On 10 April, it reported upon a MORI poll that suggested the Conservatives had started to make inroads into Labour's lead. 'The MORI poll ... puts the Tories on 34 per cent, up six points since last week, while Labour is down by a similar amount to 49 per cent.' The report then simply added: 'Tony Blair's rating as the most capable prime minister has also dropped sharply over the past week.'[20] In a report on an ICM poll in *The Guardian* during the same month, another imputed linkage was conveyed by way of juxtaposed items. After a 'week of sustained personal attacks on the Labour leader by the Conservatives',[21] Blair's approval figures had fallen by five points. But the beneficiary was not the Tory leadership. It was Paddy Ashdown's ratings that had risen by five points. Following this disclosure, the report concluded with the party's standings, which were Labour down a point, the Conservatives down three points, but the Liberal Democrats up from 15 per cent to 19 per cent.[22]

The explanatory appeal of the leaders and the stimulus they provide to political conjecture are not limited, however, to such implicit assertions or intuitive associations. Serious analyses of the polls are replete with remarkably explicit claims regarding the wider significance of the leaders' performances. A representative selection of examples is given below:

> The importance of Mr Major in sustaining the Government's standing in voters' eyes would be hard to overstate. He is liked personally and seems to symbolise competence and decency. His presence almost certainly pervades voters' answers to other questions, not just questions relating to him as Prime Minister. For the time being at least, many voters give him the benefit of any doubts and therefore give the Government as a whole the benefit of the same doubts.
> *Daily Telegraph*, 5 July 1991[23]

> The Blair effect has boosted Labour to its highest poll ratings ... The latest MORI poll ... shows that the election of Tony Blair as Labour leader has

resulted in a big shift of middle-class voters, women and southern voters behind the party.
The Times, 26 August 1994 [24]

The Blair bubble has burst and Labour's opinion poll lead over the Tories has tumbled.
The Guardian, 15 September 1994 [25]

Labour has risen to its highest ever opinion poll rating as the Blair effect has squeezed support for the Liberal Democrats.
The Times, 28 October 1994 [26]

Mr Major's confrontation with his Conservative critics appears to have enhanced both his own standing and that of the Tory Party.
Daily Telegraph, 7 July 1995 [27]

Support for Labour and Tony Blair has dipped during August after rumblings of discontent within the party over his leadership.
The Times, 31 August 1995 [28]

The Conservatives have less chance of winning the next election if they dump John Major than if they keep him, a Sunday Express poll showed last night.
Sunday Express, 5 May 1996 [29]

No modern prime minister has entered 10 Downing Street with more goodwill behind him than Tony Blair ... [H]e had been responsible, more than anyone, for ridding the country of a tired Tory party.
Sunday Times, 21 December 1997 [30]

Support for Labour and approval of the Government's overall record are declining gradually but there are still no sounds of breaking crockery ... The explanation probably lies in the fund of personal goodwill Tony Blair has built up since becoming Labour leader.
Daily Telegraph, 6 February 1998 [31]

Tony Blair's stranglehold over British public opinion was reinforced by the latest poll last night ... A MORI survey ... showed that Conservative support has fallen even further this month and that Mr Blair and Labour have strengthened their position.
The Times, 30 September 1999 [32]

These statements reflect the extent to which leadership has become a medium of political discourse and explanation. For their part, the polls, together with the increasing proliferation and elaboration of questions on leadership, help to enhance the profile of leadership as an issue and to provoke assertions, arguments and debates about the individual party leaders. It is the sheer volume of opinion taking on leadership and the tenor of the accompanying commentaries that actively promote a political vocabulary and a medium of political appraisal that are conspicuously leadership centred in nature.

When the polls, with their hinterland of inference and associations, are combined with the media's preoccupation with the electoral credentials of the party's respective leaders, the result is a continual public orientation towards the issue of leadership. The projection of leaders into arenas and contexts where they stretch away from party and organisation anchorages is a reflection of the extent to which a new and highly advanced form of leadership politics has developed in British public life. This dimension of politics is qualitatively different from the traditional or basic leadership politics that revolves around a loose mixture of political issues and party leaders. The presupposition of this new form of political competition hinges upon leadership itself. It is geared to the components, conditions and usages of leadership. In effect, it casts leadership as a political issue in its own right – one which is employed as an evaluative category of political judgement and one to which substantive political effects are repeatedly attributed. This type of politics centres upon what the properties and credentials of leadership are, who has the personal attributes to fulfil these requirements, and how such considerations relate back to party politics, policy programmes and government performances. While the more general form of leadership politics tends to concentrate on the projection of political issues through publicly prominent leaders, this more developed form of leadership politics takes leadership itself as a primary political consideration and as a basis for political analysis. It would be more accurate to call this not leadership politics but the 'politics of leadership'. This is because leadership itself is the subject of political controversy and the vehicle for a continuous form of political appraisal. The presence of this distinction is a subtle but highly significant one and denotes a radical change in the character of British politics.

The dynamics of opinion polls and their high profile analyses both reflect and fuel the rising public consciousness of leadership as a separate entity of political motivation and choice. Whether or not the assertions made about individual leaders and their effect, for example, on the current support or electoral prospects of their parties are always accurate, they do have an effect on how politics is perceived and argued in the media and by politicians themselves. Even if the various propositions which are floated in the polls are not verifiable, they do possess self-authenticating properties that alter the context within which the main battle between parties and over issues is fought. These authenticating characteristics are born out of what politicians, party workers, commentators and especially political leaders believe to be true, or likely to be true.

The same point can be applied to polls and to the politics of leadership that they evoke so strikingly. Poll findings and the responses they generate among politicians prompt leaders to monitor their relationships with the public ever more closely. They become aware that they are being subjected to a form of continuous personal appraisal. They become intent upon improving their poll ratings or, at least, preventing any deterioration in their level of public approval. They will arrange public appearances and participate in media events solely in order to achieve an effect on their public estimation as a leader. This may well intensify the drive for public exposure, but in contemporary politics there is little alternative other than to conform to such popular and professional expectations. No modern party leader can afford to ignore what the public image of leadership might provide to those individuals who are seen to have it.

Leadership has become central to a political culture and to a society that have become progressively influenced by the dogmas of neo-liberalism. Leaders no longer operate as the figureheads of different forms of collective enterprise. They have to be seen and heard and experienced primarily as individuals competing for recognition within a social matrix increasingly disposed to measure and value achievement on an individual basis. For party leaders to be successful, they have to stake a claim to the prevailing social value of leadership. In current circumstances, that value is one of personal differentiation and individual merit. Just as contemporary leaders contribute to the personalisation of collective entities, so leaders are also expected to be the defining symbols and expressions of a competitively individualised society.

During the 1990s, the assumptions and expectations of leadership within a social context of personal achievement and comparative appraisal have been well captured by the development of highly publicised charts seeking to list the most accomplished individuals in British society. *The Sunday Times* 'Power List', for example, rank orders those individuals who, in the view of a monitoring committee, have been most effective in wielding power in Britain during a given year. The assessment takes into account 'whether the impact of an act of power was high, either on the number of people affected or in enhancing value or opportunity'.[33] In the 'Power List 1999', ratings from 31 separate sub-fields helped to construct an overall chart of the 500 most powerful individuals in Britain. The climactic culmination – arguably the defining objective – of such an exercise is the identification of the most powerful person. In 1999, the number one slot was filled by Tony Blair. The citation referred to Blair being 'presidential in his authority'.[34] This was less a derivative of his position, and more a product of his individual skills and personal temperament. 'As was abundantly clear when John Major was in government, the prime minister is not always the most powerful person in the country. But Blair is … Blair really does govern the country.'[35] Only one other member of the cabinet (i.e. Gordon Brown at number 5) was included in the top ten ratings. Those closest to the prime minister (e.g. Alastair Campbell at number 9, Peter Mandelson at number 26, Jonathan Powell at number 40, Philip Gould at number 41) featured strongly, and in many cases were listed above members of the cabinet (e.g. Robin Cook at number 61 and Stephen Byers at number 85).

A similar rating exercise is produced by Channel 4 and *The Observer*. The 'Power 300' list for 1999 shows Blair in the top position above figures such as Rupert Murdoch, Bill Gates, Alan Greenspan and Bill Clinton. These rankings also suggest an increasing emphasis upon the power resources of 10 Downing Street. Apart from Gordon Brown and John Prescott, every Secretary of State, along with 'their permanent secretaries who run their departments'[36] had been demoted from their 1998 positions. The accompanying commentary was not equivocal in its conclusion: 'What the panel is signalling is its collective judgement that power has become more concentrated in the centre. Blair runs a presidential system of government.'[37] Charts like these are self-evidently subjective in nature, but they do convey a scale of values. They epitomise both a social perception of power as individualistic in nature and a cultural fascination for those persons who appear to possess it. They also underline the contemporary status of the premiership as the ultimate prize in a context of attributed personal merit, social mobility and leadership skill.

Leadership 'effect' and leadership affect

Multiple references to the levels of public projection achieved by leaders and to the proliferation of opinion polls relating to leader qualities raise important questions over the political significance that can be attached to the prominence of leaders in the conduct of political engagement in Britain. What is often depicted as being the most significant issue comes in the form of an objection to the assertion that leadership prominence carries with it implications for the traditionally collective and corporate nature of British government. The controlling rationale of the British system is a reductionist scheme that links structures and processes back to the central event of a general election as the originating agency of popular consent, parliamentary sovereignty and party government. By the same token, if party leaders cannot be shown to have a material effect upon electoral outcomes then their prominence and public standing can be construed as being largely irrelevant both to the electoral calculations of parties and to the subsequent status of the winning party in government. In essence, if the party leaders cannot be reduced to a palpable and proportional influence upon voting behaviour then their prominence is ephemeral and lacking in substance.

This issue of leadership effect in an electoral context has duly become a subject of controversy in survey projects and electoral analysis. The general norm of British elections is one in which the parties provide the main structure of public choice. 'So important are the parties in giving meaning to contests in the individual parliamentary constituencies in Britain that for many voters candidates have no identity other than their partisan one.'[38] This outlook is closely tied to the defining purpose of a general election, which is to choose a party to form a government, rather than to select a leader to fill the premiership. An extensive literature supports the conventional position that party leaders have only a marginal effect upon electoral choice. It is conceded that party leaders have developed a higher visibility since the inception of television and that they have become clearly differentiated figures through the increased scale of public presentation. Moreover, it is also possible to conclude that 'personalities and images of party leaders have become more important factors in elections as a consequence of dealignment'.[39] Nevertheless, in many quarters these factors are not thought to lead to any substantive impact upon voting preferences or upon the formation and maintenance of governments. The only caveat that is customarily attached to this outlook is the same as that originally acknowledged by Butler and Stokes over thirty years ago – namely that leaders could have an effect on the party balance if the reputation of one or other of them was 'preponderantly positive or negative'.[40] In other words, party leaders can exert an electoral influence but 'only when there is a large difference in how they are regarded by the voters. Even then their impact is muted.'[41]

In spite of the purported impact of the 'Blair effect' and the presentational skills of New Labour, therefore, the result of the 1997 general election can and has been accounted for as a party-based verdict upon the performance of the Conservative government. For example, in *Explaining Labour's Landslide*,[42] Robert Worcester and Roger Mortimer claim that the attribution of Labour's decisive victory is a myth and that John Smith and even Neil Kinnock would have won after the Tories had effectively self-destructed following the debacle of 'Black Wednesday' in 1992. Havng a popular and attractive leader, therefore, is widely seen to be an epi-phenomenon of the Labour party's organisational competence and policy programme. Another study draws attention to the fact that over a period of intense leader exposure, 'the impact of the campaign on changes in leadership ratings were', with the exception of Paddy Ashdown, 'all either neutral or slightly negative'.[43] John Bartle, Ivor Crewe and Anthony King have no doubts that the leadership effect is a red herring in the pursuit of electoral explanation:

> [B]y and large, and with relatively few exceptions, the personal appeal to the voters that some democratic politicians are said to possess does not in fact lead to the success of themselves or their party; the success of themselves or their party leads to their appearing to have personal appeal to the voters.

Far from being decisive, the attribution to a leadership effect is claimed to be 'not merely wrong but 180° wrong. The causal arrow actually points in the opposite direction'.[44] The conventional perspective, therefore, is that leadership effects are mostly reducible to other attitudinal factors. Moreover, even when these effects are significant, they are not large in scale and are hardly ever decisive, except in finely balanced contests where there is a very marked disparity in the public estimation of the two main leaders.

On the other side of the argument is a set of propositions that build upon the evident personalisation of electoral competition and the exponential use of television in political communications[45] to create a case for leaders possessing an electoral impact independent of their party identity and their party base.[46] Research conducted by Brian Graetz and Ian McAllister, for example, suggests that leader popularity is one of the two main causes of voters defecting from their normal party commitments.[47] In other research findings, Clive Bean and Anthony Mughan look at the relative appeal of different leadership qualities on party voting in the parliamentary systems of Britain and Australia. They identify a uniformity of response to different leadership characteristics, and especially the way that perceptions of leadership effectiveness dominate how voters respond to leaders. This uniformity prompts Bean and Mughan to conclude that 'prime ministerial candidates are judged against some kind of well-defined schema in the public mind and that they will have an electoral impact to the extent they conform to this mental image of what a leader should be like'.[48] As there is increasing evidence that American voters also evaluate their presidential candidates in relation to a similar structure of preferred characteristics,[49] Bean and Mughan find it is

> interesting to speculate that presidential and parliamentary elections may be converging not only with respect to the lesser role for party ideologies and the personalisation of television-dominated election campaigns, but also with respect to the way party leaders affect the vote. The 'presidentialisation' of British politics may have progressed further than many commentators and analysts suspect.[50]

In a recent study, Anthony Mughan develops this theme and finds that parliamentary party leaders are acquiring a level of visibility, political influence and independence from party that is normally associated with American presidents. Mughan suggests that the commonly asserted disjunction between the presentation and impact is far less of a distinction in the developing dynamics of contemporary elections. Contrary to the conventional minimisation of leader effects, Mughan concludes that party leaders are not only more electorally significant than they used to be, but are increasing in salience to the point where they can be more pivotal than issues to an election outcome.[51]

This is a highly complex and contested debate that centres upon deeply problematic issues relating to voter perceptions and motivations, and to the difficulties of differentiating leader effects from party identity, party policies and party performance. It is not within the remit of this study to seek to resolve the debate or even to take sides. What is significant is the debate itself. In a parliamentary system, it is a debate where no debate ought to exist. The dispute over the magnitude of the leaders' public presence has leached into the area that is widely accepted to lie at the core of parliamentary democracy – namely the system of electoral competition and the point of origin of party government. The controversy, therefore, is a reflection of the unprecedented public projection and general salience of contemporary party leaders and, in particular, the prime minister. It is symptomatic of what has become a continuing public discourse that centres the meaning, language, location and utility of leadership.

Ivor Crewe and Anthony King are fully aware of this cultural fascination disjunction with the presumptive significance of party leaders:

> The belief is almost universal in Britain that the leaders of the major political parties are figures of great electoral significance. Politicians in the run-up to general elections talk endlessly about whether their party would do better or worse under some alternative leader. Journalists and opinion pollsters are equally pre-occupied with various political leaders' electoral appeal or lack of it. Casual political conversation is likewise remarkably leader-centred ... There are few commentators on British elections, and probably few British citizens, who do not incline to this view ... Leaders are thought to matter.[52]

Crewe and King, however, also realise that they, along with other specialists on voting behaviour, are themselves part of the discourse. They point out that when those political scientists who investigate electoral behaviour talk among themselves they ignore party leaders: 'It is not shown ... that the leaders do not matter. They are simply, for practical purposes, written out of the script'[53] as a matter of course. And yet when these self-same specialists converse outside their professional circles, they intuitively adopt the view and the language that leaders do matter: 'Most political scientists ... incline to this view. Or, more precisely they incline to it when they are talking as ordinary citizens. To eavesdrop on most political scientists' conversation about electoral politics is to hear them using a language not so very different from that of politicians and journalists ... The leaders loom large.'[54] The general preoccupation with leaders afflicts even those who are most resistant to it.

It is precisely this unremitting and compulsive public exchange upon the attributes of leaders and the characteristics and imperatives of leadership that provides the core of the presidential dimension with which this study is concerned. The social fixation with leadership is intense and eclipses the extent to which leadership influence can be pivotal on election day. The precise nature of the leaders' effects upon voter choice is less critical than the generative properties and ramifying effects of an individualised leadership culture that has now assumed a central and permanent position in British politics. As we will see in chapter 8, it is through this medium that British premiers have extended the presidential dimension by developing roles and positions more normally associated with presidential politics.

Notes

1 David Butler and Dennis Kavanagh, *The British General Election of 1987* (Basingstoke, Macmillan, 1988), p. 249.

2 Colin Seymour-Ure, 'Political Television: Four Stages of Growth', *Contemporary Record*, 4, no. 2 (November 1990), p. 22.

3 Michael Cockerell, *Live from Number 10: The Inside Story of Prime Ministers and Television* (London, Faber, 1988), p. 287.

4 Quoted in Cockerell, *Live from Number 10*, p. 287.

5 Quoted in BBC Radio 3, *The Gang That Fell Apart*, Part 2, broadcast 18 September 1991.

6 Holli Semetko, Margaret Scammell and Tom Nossiter, 'The Media's Coverage of the Campaign', in Anthony Heath, Roger Jowell and John Curtice (eds), *Labour's Last Chance?* (Aldershot, Dartmouth, 1994), p. 28.

7 Pippa Norris, 'The Battle for the Campaign Agenda', in Anthony King *et al.*, *New Labour Triumphs: Britain at the Polls* (Chatham, Chatham House, 1998), p. 136.

8 Norris, 'The Battle for the Campaign Agenda', p. 136.

9 The current high-water mark of 1,573 was recorded in 1987. This inflated total has been attributed not only to the double-counting properties of the Alliance's dual leadership, but also to the heavily presidential nature of Labour's campaign and the predicted closeness of the election.

10 Martin Harrison, 'Politics on the Air', in David Butler and Dennis Kavanagh, *The British General Election of 1997* (Basingstoke, Macmillan, 1997), p. 145.

11 Harrison, 'Politics on the Air', p. 146.

12 Martin Harrison, 'Politics on the Air', in David Butler and Dennis Kavanagh, *The British General Election of 1992* (Basingstoke, Macmillan, 1992), p. 168.

13 Harrison, 'Politics on the Air', 1997, p. 146.
14 Richard Rose, 'British Government: The Job at the Top', in Richard Rose and Ezra N. Suleiman (eds), *Presidents and Prime Ministers* (Washington, DC, American Enterprise Institute, 1980), p. 20.
15 Columns 1 and 2 of table 7.6 (1956) as a percentage of columns 3, 4 and 5 give a figure of 104 per cent.
16 Columns 1 and 2 of table 7.6 (1977) as a percentage of columns 3, 4 and 5 give a figure of 184 per cent.
17 James Landale, Hannah Betts and Elizabeth Judge, 'Tony Blair – has he got news for us', *The Times*, 30 December 1998.
18 See Landale, Betts and Judge, 'Tony Blair – has he got news for us'.
19 Stephen Castle, 'Tories lurch to 12-year low', *Independent on Sunday*, 13 June 1993.
20 Peter Riddell, 'Labour poll slashed by the Tories', *The Times*, 10 April 1997.
21 Martin Kettle, 'Ashdown's ratings up as attacks damage Blair's standing', *The Guardian*, 16 April 1997.
22 Kettle, 'Ashdown's ratings up as attacks damage Blair's standing'.
23 Anthony King, 'Major's popularity with voters is key to Tory fortunes', *Daily Telegraph*, 5 July 1991.
24 Peter Riddell, '"Blair effect" undermines Major and lifts Labour to record high', *The Times*, 26 August 1994.
25 Martin Linton, 'Blair's bubble bursts', *The Guardian*, 15 September 1994.
26 Peter Riddell, 'Blair raises Labour to new heights of popularity', *The Times*, 28 October 1994.
27 Anthony King, 'Premier and party gain from fight', *Daily Telegraph*, 7 July 1995.
28 Peter Riddell, 'Internal rumbling shakes Labour lead', *The Times*, 31 August 1995.
29 Simon Walters, 'At last Major is ahead in the polls', *Sunday Express*, 5 May 1996.
30 David Smith, 'How tarnished is Teflon Tony?', *Sunday Times*, 21 December 1997.
31 Anthony King, 'Blair enjoys happy marriage with voters', *Daily Telegraph*, 6 February 1998.
32 Peter Riddell and Philip Webster, 'Times poll deepens Tory gloom', *The Times*, 30 September 1999.
33 Stewart Clegg, 'Rules of engagement', *Sunday Times*, 26 September 1999.
34 'The Power List 1999: the 500 most powerful people in Britain', *Sunday Times*, 26 September 1999.
35 'The Power List 1999'.
36 'Power 300: The most powerful in Britain', *The Observer*, 24 October 1999.
37 'Power 300'.
38 David Butler and Donald Stokes, *Political Change in Britain: Forces Shaping Electoral Choice* (London, Macmillan, 1969), p. 8.
39 David Denver, *Elections and Voting Behaviour in Britain*, 2nd edn (Hemel Hempstead, Harvester Wheatsheaf, 1994), p. 112.
40 Butler and Stokes, *Political Change in Britain*, p. 357.
41 David Denver, *Elections and Voting Behaviour in Britain* (Hemel Hempstead, Philip Allan, 1989), p. 93. See also Ivor Crewe and Anthony King, 'Are British Elections Becoming More "Presidential"', in M. Kent Jennings and Thomas E. Mann (eds), *Elections at Home and Abroad: Essays in Honor of Warren E. Miller* (Ann Arbor, University of Michigan Press, 1993), pp. 181–206.
42 Robert Worcester and Roger Mortimore, *Explaining Labour's Landslide* (London, Politicos, 1999).

43 Pippa Norris, John Curtice, David Sanders, Margaret Scammell and Holli A. Semetko, *On Message: Communicating the Campaign* (London, Sage, 1999), p. 179.

44 John Bartle, Ivor Crewe and Anthony King, *Was It Blair Who Won It?: Leadership Effects and the 1997 British General Election* (Colchester, Department of Government, University of Essex, 1998), p. 32.

45 See Shaun Bowler and David M. Farrell (eds), *Electoral Strategies and Political Marketing* (Basingstoke, Macmillan, 1992); Lynda Lee Kaid and Christina Holz-Bacha (eds), *Political Advertising in Western Democracies: Parties and Candidates on Television* (London, Sage, 1995); David L. Swanson and Paolo Mancini (eds), *Politics, Media and Modern Democracy: An International Study of Innovations in Electoral Campaigning and Their Consequences* (Westport, Praeger, 1996).

46 See Anthony Mughan, 'Electoral Change in Britain: The Campaign Reassessed', *British Journal of Political Science*, 8, no. 2 (April 1978), pp. 245–53; Brian Graetz and Ian McAllister, 'Party Leaders and Election Outcomes in Britain, 1974–1983', *Comparative Political Studies*, 19 (1987), pp. 484–507; Clive Bean and Anthony Mughan, 'Leadership Effects in Parliamentary Elections in Australia and Britain', *American Political Science Review*, 83, no. 4 (December 1989), pp. 1165–79; Marianne C. Stewart and Harold D. Clark, 'The (Un)importance of Party Leaders: Leaders Images and Party Choice in the 1987 British Election', *Journal of Politics*, 54, no. 2 (May 1992), pp. 447–70; Anthony Mughan, 'Party Leaders and Presidentialism in the 1992 Election: A Post-War Perspective', in David Denver, Pippa Norris, David Broughton and Colin Rallings (eds), *British Elections and Parties Yearbook 1993* (London, Harvester Wheatsheaf, 1993), pp. 193–204; Philip Jones and John Hudson, 'The Quality of Political Leadership: A Case Study of John Major', *British Journal of Political Science*, 26, no. 2 (April 1996), pp. 229–44.

47 Graetz and McAllister, 'Party Leaders and Election Outcomes in Britain, 1974–1983'.

48 Clive Bean and Anthony Mughan, 'Party Leaders and the Vote', *Contemporary Record*, 4, no. 2 (November 1990), p. 25.

49 Donald R. Kinder, Mark D. Peters, Robert P. Abelson and Susan T. Fiske, 'Presidential Prototypes', *Political Behaviour*, 2 (1980), pp. 315–37; Arthur Miller, Martin P. Wattenberg and Oksana Malanchuk, 'Schematic Assessments of Presidential Candidates', *American Political Science Review*, 80, no. 2 (June 1986), pp. 521–40.

50 Bean and Mughan, 'Party Leaders and the Vote', p. 25.

51 Anthony Mughan, *Media and the Presidentialization of Parliamentary Elections* (Basingstoke, Macmillan, 2000).

52 Ivor Crewe and Anthony King, 'Did Major Win? Did Kinnock Lose?', in Anthony Heath, Roger Jowell and John Curtice (eds), *Labour's Last Chance?* (Aldershot, Dartmouth, 1994), pp. 125, 126.

53 Crewe and King, 'Did Major Win? Did Kinnock Lose?', p. 126.

54 Crewe and King, 'Did Major Win? Did Kinnock Lose?', p. 126.

CHAPTER 8

The presidency and the premiership: power, constitution and nation

The politics of leadership do not end with a general election and with the onset of a fresh, or refreshed, administration. It is true that the ultimate purpose behind the various individualising facets of contemporary political competition is the acquisition of the premiership. In order to capture Number 10, individual leaders are expected not merely to withstand, but also to exploit, the rigours of media attention, opinion polling, personal campaigning and public engagement. But once there, a prime minister quickly finds that holding the premiership is not an antidote to leadership politics so much as a further stimulant to its varied dynamics. In the rise to power, a modern prime minister comes to embody the many factors that contribute to the development of competitive public engagement and leadership stretch. The prime minister's comparability with the American presidency in these particular respects has been acknowledged and appraised in previous chapters. Nevertheless, the analogies with the presidency do not stop there.

Having acquired a position of enhanced political status within the governing party and within the government as a whole, a prime minister has to convert that status into a form of workable authority. Like an American president, a British premier will often find that his or her position is more provisional and his or her power more contested than formal status would at first suggest. The already contingent nature of such leadership is made worse by a system increasingly permeated with the strictures and strategies of leadership politics. In seeking to use their leadership position to acquire an approximate condition of leadership, modern prime ministers have to make considerable efforts to diversify their political resources and to augment their influence within government. It is these problems of life at the centre, and the solution pursued by prime ministers to correct them, together with the reactions they generate, which reveal a clear resonance between the present state of the premiership and the president's position inside Washington. Three areas of direct comparability are particularly significant in this respect. They are important because they demonstrate the extent to which American parallels can illuminate the nature and ramifications of current British developments.

The three areas in question are: (1) the properties of executive power in an increasingly pluralist society; (2) the conditioning effects of constitutional considerations and constraints upon the exercise of political leadership; and (3) the relationship of national interests and nationalist attachments to the role of chief executive. These subjects will be considered individually in the following three sections.

Power

AMERICAN CONCEPTIONS OF PRESIDENTIAL POWER

If there is one thing that is quite clear about the American presidency, it is the fundamental ambiguity of its powers. In one respect, presidents benefit from a set of formal executive powers, which are constitutionally guaranteed by virtue of the office's established status in a separation of powers system. In another respect, presidents have to operate in a scheme of government that is fragmented into multiple centres of power, whose divisiveness is supported and promoted by the constitution's checks and balances. A president cannot rely solely upon his formal executive powers to fulfil even his basic responsibilities – let alone the prodigious social, economic and military obligations that presidents have acquired since the Depression in the 1930s and World War II and its aftermath in the 1940s and 1950s. The unbridled force of American political competition among parties and groups, and the American enthusiasm for legal dispute over the powers and demarcation of the separate branches of government, render presidential power a highly provisional form of influence. These conditioning agents, together with the general American disposition to challenge political authority wherever it is most evident, means the president does not even have assured access to his basic executive powers.

Richard Neustadt is the figure that has done most to point out that the chief executive's powers are not always available, and that even when they are, they are not always workable. Neustadt suggests that, contrary to appearances, the presidency is continually confronted by a system which imposes severe limits on the exercise of executive command. In fact, 'the mere assertion of a formal power is rarely enough'[1] to ensure its actual presence. In a study that relies upon aphorisms for its effect, Neustadt is at his most succinct in driving home this point about the provisional nature of presidential authority. 'Formal powers have no bearing upon influence' because, in his view, '"powers" are no guarantee of power'.[2] Neustadt emphasises that presidents do not inherit their power, but appropriate it through their own proficiency in persuasion and bargaining. A president needs to have a professional politician's sixth sense in locating and exploiting the possibilities of power. In a system where so many participants have political resources at their disposal and where executive authority is far from being intact, let alone complete, a president is required to maximise his position by working with and through the reciprocal nature of power relationships.

Neustadt's revision of presidential power, from a fixed corpus of executive authority to a highly mutable and unpredictable state of influence, has spawned a large literature on the ways and means of the presidency. Much of it is centred upon the central thrust of the chief executive's position being contingent upon a range of factors such as the state of the economy, the incidence of international crises, the level of presidential popularity, and the political skills and personal temperament of the president himself. The last has led to the creation of an entire genre of analysis based upon the working premise that because the nature of the presidency is one of personally acquired power, then the office can best be explained by reference to the person who holds the office. This entails studying not merely the individual president, but what lies beneath the person and determines his character, his behaviour and, ultimately, his decisions. According to James Barber, who represents the vanguard of this form of study, a president's character is the critical factor in understanding the office; 'the connection between his character and his presidential actions emerges as paramount'.[3] The basic objective of this type of analysis is to trace a line of causation from childhood to adulthood, from personality to action, and from the subconscious to political decision. It has been claimed that such analysis can even provide a predictive capacity and that this could be, and moreover should be, used to assess the suitability of prospective presidential candidates. Whether this type of analysis is or is not as fruitful as its defenders assert, it is a reflection in its own right of the abiding interest in presidents not merely as individuals, and not even as different individuals, but as significantly different individuals.

Even though both Neustadt and Barber's schemes of analysis have been criticised on a number of grounds,[4] their basic conclusions remain central to an understanding of the modern presidency. Despite all the formal appearances of a solid executive hierarchy, the presidency is now comprehended far more as a contingent entity. It is an office dependent upon the active agency of a president in the construction and maintenance of his own *de facto* hierarchy in an openly pluralistic system. A president may have certain bargaining advantages because of his position. Nevertheless, his strength has to be negotiated in relation to other centres of power. These have to be consulted and accommodated in order for the president to exercise that authority which, to many outside observers, he seems to exert without effort. The story of the American presidency, therefore, is one of mutability and continual evolution. The institution has developed in a system which is designed to inhibit the establishment of a strong centre, while at the same time being dependent upon an organising force to achieve a modicum of government direction and policy coherence. The presidency in effect is *in* the American system but is not expected to be *of* it. It is seen to be the only possible device in a framework of reciprocal checks and countervailing powers, which will allow some respite from the self-nullifying properties of political and institutional interaction. Modern presidents are expected to confront structural constraints and to challenge systemic forces. They are required to provide leadership by possessing a vision or programme in support of the public interest. They need to have the political skills both to maximise the available sources of power and to deploy influence as effectively as possible in support of their selected objectives. In a system renowned for its mechanistic character, presidents are exceptional for their singularity and individuality. Their assigned role is one of transcending the normal dynamics of pluralist democracy to provide a compensatory dimension of active and conscious political will. As a result, the personal contributions to leadership and the personal qualities of leadership are central to political activity, commentary and analysis in the United States. As Bert Rockman notes, Americans are 'enchanted by the rhetoric of leadership, but the American system mostly operates to deny its possibilities'.[5]

It is the fascination with the narrow opportunities for leadership that generates interest in the exceptionalism of those individuals who can operate within its boundaries. '[C]oherent leadership is a topic of concern in the American system because it defies that which the system was structured to prevent. Not surprisingly, therefore, much attention is paid to the prospects for generating effective political leadership – indeed, it is often a passionate obsession.'[6] This interest extends to presidential analysis where there is a marked emphasis upon personality in the shaping and playing of presidential roles, in the formulation of decisions and policy, and in the methods of persuasion and mobilisation. It gives rise to a marked interest in the role of individual morality and personal ethics in the effective political leadership.[7] To Erwin Hargrove, 'the issue is not, Do individuals make a difference? But under what conditions do they make a difference?'[8] This analytical agenda has generated a host of studies into the relationship between individual personality and the political environment. The main thrust of this genre can be reduced to three types of analysis. They are: (1) inquiries into the influence of an individual's needs, beliefs, values and experiences upon political motives and choices; (2) the effect of a president's cognitive and emotional inheritance upon attitudes to conflict, advice and the management of political decision making; and (3) the nature of the dynamics between patterns of individual temperament and political action.[9] James Barber's pioneering studies on presidential character can be criticised for giving insufficient weight to the structural properties of the presidency and to 'tremendous historical forces lodged in the laws, traditions and commitments of institutions'.[10] Nevertheless, his work has come to typify an analytical approach that has gained enormous social currency in the United States. Barber continues not only to provide the most prominent expression of a burgeoning genre of psychobiography and political psychoanalysis, but to reflect a disposition in American political culture that relates the presidency to the incumbent's personality – so much so in fact that President Reagan felt compelled to challenge the depiction of him as a 'passive-positive' president in Barber's typology of presidential character.[11]

PRIME MINISTERIAL POWER AS A CONSTITUTIONAL 'UNCONVENTION'

The British prime minister has traditionally been thought of as a given unit of authority, functioning within a system of disciplined parties and collective government. 'The very high degree of institutionalisation in British government' is widely regarded as the 'most powerful determinant of what a prime minister can and cannot do.'[12] A prime minister is thought to assume the office, and the functions and power attached to it. The centralisation of authority in the British system produces a chief executive figure, whose formal position is well established and who is generally secure from any open and direct competition for the influence at his or her disposal in Number 10. According to this traditional view of the premiership, the personal characteristics of a prime minister are not really relevant to an understanding of either the position or an individual's conduct within it. Richard Rose explains:

> Personal style influences how a Prime Minister carries out the demands of Office, but it does not determine what is done. The first priority of a Prime Minister is to do what is expected of him or her. How a Prime Minister meets these role expectations reflects not only his or her basic personality, whatever that may be, but even more what the incumbent has learned in a quarter century of socialisation in Westminster and Whitehall.[13]

As a result of this view of the office and of the orderly system that allegedly surrounds it, the role of personal leadership has often been disregarded as something of an aberration in British political life. Except for the most extreme conditions of wartime, leadership has been seen as unnecessary, unseemly and largely non-existent. Accordingly, 'British political science has little or no literature on political leadership. In Britain we refer to the office of prime minister and his or her performance rather than national leadership or individual leaders.'[14]

The clear significance of leadership in British politics is combined with a cultural inhibition in considering its properties. John Gaffney expresses this mixture in a penetrating observation:

> Political personalism is a complex and influential phenomenon in British political life which affects both the electorate and party organisation but which – possibly because of the near taboo placed on the discussion of leadership because of the European experience of Fascism in the twentieth century – has been little considered outside analyses of totalitarianism on the one hand or 'personality politics' on the other, which associates the projection of political leadership with the selling of soap powder.[15]

The traditional distaste for taking leadership very seriously in peacetime politics can lead to a contemptuous attitude in which the role of personality in politics is ridiculed and thereupon dismissed. Edward Pearce's demolition of Michael Heseltine is instructive in its content and tone:

> He is everywhere praised for charisma. I always thought of charisma as a South American dance rhythm. But one observes that the most desirable rulers – Cavour, Guizot, Peel, Truman, Attlee, Monet and Kohl – have been without it. Michael Heseltine admires J. F. Kennedy, a crashing error of taste which suggests that from a Heseltine government we shall have charisma the way we otherwise have chips.[16]

Pearce continues the theme:

> For elections we require personalities who, in turn, need charisma. The result will be a festival of eager self-promotion, the parade of dwarves on tiptoe ... Charisma is an odd word. I always think of it as a three-beats-to-the-bar Latin American dance rhythm vaguely associated with Edmundo Ros. 'Down Sao Paulo way, this is how we do the charisma'. It suggests a shake of maracas and spangles in the hair, and nowhere is this more the case than when Michael Heseltine does the charisma.[17]

This type of scornful scepticism helps to sustain and promote an instinctive assumption that the theme of personality and politics is a superficial and risible distraction. Such attitudes have traditionally contributed to the view that the characteristic stability of British politics has a systemic property in which leadership is reduced to a predominantly aggregate feature that diminishes the role and significance of any one personality. The dearth of systematic studies on the individual characteristics of prime ministers and on the personal components of leadership has remained a highly conspicuous lapse in an otherwise burgeoning field of British political analysis. The deficiency also betrays a basic cultural aversion to taking the role of personality in politics very seriously. This customary disposition is well captured in the following passage written by Anthony King in 1977:

> Psychobiography as an art form if that is not too strong a term has never really arrived in Britain. Anthony Storr once wrote a perceptive essay on the origins and consequences of Churchill's 'black dog' moods, but otherwise we have not been treated to accounts of how the repressions inflicted upon Lord Home by his nanny caused him to develop a phallic fixation on matchsticks, or of how the rigours of Harold Wilson's toilet training wrought such havoc on his cognitive structures that he came to imagine that a week was a long time.[18]

In part this is a gentle satire on the excesses of the personality theorists that have colonised the study of the American presidency and in part an acceptance that 'American journalists and political scientists ... enjoy a greater intimacy with prominent politicians and are better able to deal with such questions of political personality'.[19] More significantly, it is recognition that a disjunction exists between the individual prominence given to British prime ministers and the level of substantive significance attached to such concerted attention.

The nature of political leadership and the relation of power to personal attributes have in Britain almost invariably fallen between two stools. On the one hand, political science has normally been wary of studying individuals. Research design and hypothesis formulation in political science are normally geared to eliciting regularities and generalisations by working across discrete entities and looking for common features. Individual political leaders are so limited in number and so idiosyncratic in nature that their very atomisation deters systematic analysis. Analytical effort is related to explanatory potential. In Britain the controlling cultural premises have inhibited such effort on the grounds that political leadership and, therefore, personality are of secondary importance in the political system. Political biography, on the other hand, is a very popular idiom in this country but the genre itself imposes limits on the study of political leadership. This is because political biography, by the very nature of the exercise, perpetuates a longitudinal approach to the subject in which prominent politicians remain discrete units locked within their own contexts. There are normally very few grounds for latitudinal comparison or generalisation. The *raison d'être* of a biography is to explain the individual. Biographies, like individuals, are inherently *sui generis*. Furthermore, very few biographies are motivated by the desire to provide an explicit analysis of the properties and attributes of political leadership. Even fewer are concerned with relating the idiosyncrasies of a particular leader with any systematic study of the general theme of leadership.

MARGARET THATCHER AND THE PERSONALISATION OF POWER

In reality, this phlegmatic indifference towards the personal properties of prime ministerial leadership has always been slightly misplaced. Prime ministers in the past have all needed to have an awareness of the sources of power and an ability to cultivate and protect their own access to those sources, in order to remain prime ministers. A premier and the properties of his or her position could never be satisfactorily reduced to the exterior status of a servant to the crown. The true position was always more akin to the analysis of organisational power and the conditions of its usage, which Richard Neustadt pioneered in his study of the presidency. If it had been the case in the past that the British premiership had developed close parallels with the American presidency on the basis of their common experience of the contingent and provisional nature of power relationships, then this comparison became far more direct and immediate during Margaret Thatcher's premiership.

Mrs Thatcher had entered office in 1979 after the governments of her two Labour predecessors had been wracked by the effects of economic stagflation, industrial unrest, social dissent, civil strife, electoral volatility and nationalist revivals. After the events of the 1970s, the old collective certainties of cabinet government and the two-party system had begun to evaporate in the face of claims that Britain and its corporate state were becoming ungovernable and that the Northern Ireland problem was a sign of a deeper malaise spreading throughout the United Kingdom. The claims made upon government were alleged to be too many, too strident and too contradictory to be satisfactorily accommodated. As a result, government was often seen to be helpless in the face of intransigent demands from such powerful participants as trade unions and producer groups.[20] The disarray culminated in the humiliation of the Callaghan government in the 'winter of discontent', when a number of union organisations had openly defied the Labour administration's negotiated pay norms.

In some respects, Margaret Thatcher represented a reaction against this form of governance. In many other respects, however, she inherited its infrastructure and its characteristics. Despite her advocacy of conviction politics and her reputation for intransigence, Margaret Thatcher had to conduct her premiership in the now customary glare of the public arena, where political forces were far more uninhibited and insistent in their demands than they had been in the recent past. It was a system where the veto powers of its component parts were conspicuously evident. The Labour party, for example, was in opposition, but it was quite clear that it held an effective veto power over any serious attempt to dismantle the welfare state. Mrs Thatcher, in effect, had to optimise her chances of governing in a system that was now recognised to be one of internal conflict and dissent. She also had to operate in a context of increasing demands for public information and a growing insistence on the right to know. These conditions compounded the already prodigious problems facing the government (e.g. recession, growth of public expenditure, inner city disorder). Contrary to her public reputation for strident inflexibility, her private conduct was much more measured – much more akin to Neustadt's description of presidential power. In the words of Anthony King,

> Thatcher is in fact a remarkably cautious politician. Not only is she cautious, but she respects power and has an unusually well-developed capacity for weighing it, for seeing who has it and who has not, for calculating who can damage her and who cannot. She is often described as an emotional person; in her ability to weigh power, she is more like a precision instrument.[21]

Margaret Thatcher realised the limitations of her position but she also had an ability to work within those constraints to maximise the potential for power that was available in the office. Her professional reputation in Whitehall and Westminster as a leader who could and would exploit all the bargaining advantages of the office increased her leverage. It also enhanced her public prestige as a leader, which, as Neustadt recognised in the presidency, was essential to preserving her status as a leader inside the government machinery.

Mrs Thatcher's attempts to maintain her effectiveness by seeking to maximise her leverage in the competitive interplay with other power centres provoked charges of imperiousness. Her private distaste of weakness was thought to have led to a compulsive form of overcompensation against the countervailing forces within the system. While it was widely believed that Margaret Thatcher was perpetually in danger of exceeding her power beyond the lines of legitimate usage, her pre-eminence had the effect of demolishing the case in support of Britain's ungovernability. In doing so, public and critical attention became centred upon an individual who engaged the political process so effectively that she acquired a level of personal influence and authority that would have been unimaginable to her peacetime successors. In summing up Thatcher's premiership, Dennis Kavanagh pointed out that the profound changes wrought in local government, Whitehall bureaucracy, trade union law, nationalised industries and the post-war consensus meant that the 'signposts in the textbooks [would] have to be rewritten'.[22] She may have been 'uninteresting', 'commonplace', 'rude' and 'fortunate'.[23] 'Many of her ideas and policies [were] not original.'[24] Nevertheless, to Kavanagh, the pivotal factor was that she had been the driving force and central catalyst: 'What is crucial is the political *push*, will, determination and energy which she has provided.'[25]

JOHN MAJOR AND THE PERSONALISATION OF FAILURE

Margaret Thatcher had provided graphic evidence that one person could make a dramatic difference and that a gifted politician with drive, skill and conviction could be pivotal in changing the policy and position of government in society. Thatcher not only exposed the developing politics of leadership but explored its possibilities and enlarged its potential. As the prime minister increasingly stamped her authority on government, strong leadership was increasingly attributed to her personal qualities. It spawned a host of premises, associations and equations concerning the relationship between governing competence, political leadership and individual character. Until the time of Margaret Thatcher's fall, any discussion of power was almost exclusively centred upon the individual qualities she brought to the role of premier. It was precisely this nexus of power and personality that stimulated such a habitual interest in the properties of Mrs Thatcher's character. Initially, public fascination with the person inside Number 10 did not extend to the premiership of John Major. Once Mrs Thatcher had been replaced as prime minister, critical concern over the issue of the premier's personality underwent a marked decline.

In part, this diminished interest was due to the explicit intention on the part of John Major to eliminate the stridency that had marked his predecessor's premiership and to replace it with a more consultative and consensual style of government. Major had 'found Mrs Thatcher's style of "macho leadership" personally distasteful'[26] and prided himself on a collegiate approach to decision making that built up agreement through mutual consent. He saw himself as a practical politician that eschewed ideology in preference for the pragmatic traditions of Disraeli, Baldwin and Macmillan. He described his style as going to a 'great deal of trouble to take the views of colleagues, to take colleagues through all the options and reach a considered view that all colleagues [would] rally behind'.[27] The emphasis upon the term 'colleague' exemplified Major's preferred method of problem resolution. In a veiled reference to his predecessor, Major stated the functional value of his collegiate ethos: 'It is a matter of instinct that if you carry people with you rather than ride through people you will get a better outcome than otherwise.'[28]

The initial decline in interest in the personal dimensions of political leadership reflected the shift in outlook and working philosophy of the new prime minister. It also mirrored what increasingly came to be seen as the predominantly grey and allegedly anodyne nature of the prime minister. The Wagnerian scale of Margaret Thatcher's dramas was supplanted by the managerial utility of a compromise candidate whose conciliatory and technocratic style carried with it an implicit suggestion of the dispensability of high profile leadership. This influence was taken up by political commentators seeking to analyse and to rationalise the less fevered and more equable features of the immediate post-Thatcher premiership. Peter Riddell, for example, stressed the importance of historical perspective in locating the significance of Thatcher's leadership and in conveying the sheer normality of Major's premiership:

> The real lesson to be drawn is that weak government is not unusual in post-war Britain. It has been the norm and strong government the exception ... Her eleven and a half years in power stand out as a highly unusual long period of strong government, aided by a divided Opposition. Judged by the post-war record, they were, however, an aberration.[29]

Major was less interesting as a person, therefore, because he was less powerful as a prime minister. By the same token, because he was a less formidable premier his power seemed less significant and the personal contributions to his role and position less salient as explanatory factors.

Just as Thatcher's power in retrospect could be safely accepted as abnormally personal, so Major's premiership was presented as normal and, therefore, heavily based upon institutional processes and dynamics. Nevertheless, it was the very prominence of his predecessor that was instrumental in subverting the conceptions of normality associated with his successor. It became evident that Mrs Thatcher had helped to redefine the evaluative and performance-related categories of British political leadership. It was not simply a matter of nostalgia over a lost leader. Major's leadership suffered by and because of comparison with Margaret Thatcher. She had acted as a conditioning agent to the Major premiership. It would have been difficult for any leader to follow one who had been in office for over eleven years, but the position was made even more problematic by Major's stated intention to depart from Mrs Thatcher's style of government. The situation was further exacerbated by the active presence of his predecessor in the febrile atmosphere of a party and government riven by the polarities that had initially been induced by Thatcher herself.

At first, Major gained a reprieve from the manner of his elevation and the fault-lines in his own party through the successes of the Gulf War (1991) and the 1992 general election. But as the second Major administration began to suffer from a series of setbacks, failures, crises and revolts, questions began to be raised over Major's decisions and judgements. Speculation over culpability moved remorselessly from Major being *a* factor to him being *the* factor. With ever increasing rapidity, critical discussion moved from the political choices of the prime minister to the personal element of his character. By 1993, criticism of the government had become instinctively personalised. Questions were continually raised concerning Major's personal fitness for office and even the state of his mind. The extent to which the prime minister had become a public commodity was typified by an edition of BBC2's *Newsnight*[30] which investigated whether John Major was cracking up. The item featured an interview with the editor of the *British Journal of Psychiatry*, who was asked whether the prime minister might be going mad and what advice might be offered to a premier in such palpably stressful circumstances.

It was not simply that Major had become identified as an abstracted centre of accountability for an unpopular government. It was that he was being continually subjected to the proposition that there was something about him and his personal make-up that was undermining the government. As a consequence, he did not merely characterise decline, he was made to embody it through personal flaws and deficiencies. In many respects this was wholly unfair, both in terms of the conventional rubric of collective responsibility and the structural and circumstantial nature of the government's problems. Major was confronted with a series of formidable challenges. He had to contend with a severe economic recession, a declining party membership, a small majority in the House of Commons, and the presence of over seventy brooding ex-ministers on the back-benches. He was badly affected by the quickening pace of European integration, the dissident activities of a set of irreconcilable Eurosceptics in the parliamentary party, and a lack of available heavyweights for collective support. He was expected to assert himself in the face of a contracting base of new ideas and agendas, a series of allegations relating to sleaze and complacency, and a revived opposition in the form of New Labour with its central themes of modernity and strong leadership.

Problems on such a scale would have debilitated any prime minister. Nevertheless, the instinctive response from most quarters was that the government was weak because the prime minister was weak. The conditioned reflexes that had been formed during the Thatcher years remained undiminished. In fact, they had been strengthened by the publicity given to her political memoirs, to her personal reflections on her rise to power, to the multiple insider accounts by her ex-ministers, and to her interventions into highly charged policy debates. As a result, while Major sought to present a pragmatic and assimilative style of government in the traditional grain of the Conservative party and the British constitution, he found himself increasingly entangled in a critical web of asserted requirements of strong leadership, radical vision and personal power. He was continually admonished for not having cultivated a Thatcher-like authority and for not exerting whatever leverage he possessed on his unruly party. Margaret Thatcher may have exceeded, and even abused, her position but at least she had had the power to do so. John Major's lack of power was equally seen to be derivative of character. 'Major could not lead a cinema queue, let alone a country'[31] screamed *The Sun* in 1995. This was not an untypical political comment during the Major years when the ingredients, usages and solutions of leadership, together with the language of leadership critiques, crises and challenges, became an entire political discourse. Even when the prime minister provoked a leadership contest in June 1995 in order to reassert his authority over the party, it was seen as a sign of personal weakness. In his autobiography, Major juxtaposes the decision to resign the leadership with a personal revelation of a previously concealed weakness. But to him, it was not simply psychological or social in origin: 'There were moments when I became profoundly depressed ... I had been working the usual seventeen-hour day ... and suffering throughout the period from very severe pain in my back and shoulder and in the base of my neck – a problem that had been recurring for years and was now getting worse.'[32]

During the second Major administration, there were many subtleties and variations to the insistent inquiries over the prime minister's leadership. John Major tried to draw upon conservative ideas and traditions to distance himself from the presumptions of a personal vision: 'I was never very attracted to the term Thatcherism or Majorism or anything else. Politics is largely about tolerance. I don't think it is necessarily about imposing what you happen to think is right upon other people.'[33] The *Daily Telegraph* agreed that visions could 'too often turn out to be so much hot air'.[34] Nevertheless, it also pointed out that 'while a government may survive without a political vision, it cannot prosper unless it possesses at least a visible sense of direction behind which its supporters can unite'.[35] William Rees-Mogg also believed that Major was 'not a good leader because it [was] the job of a leader to decide'.[36] Rees-Mogg explained the unpopularity of the Conservative government as a popular reaction against the leadership of the prime minister: 'He seems to be the most over-promoted of the seven [post-war Conservative prime ministers]. He is not a natural leader; he cannot speak; he has a weak cabinet which he has chosen; he lacks self-confidence; he has no sense of strategy or direction ... His ideal level of political competence would be deputy chief whip, or something of that standing.'[37] As cartoons mercilessly depicted Major as a well-intentioned but hapless and incompetent buffoon, it was difficult to sustain his moral authority as party leader and prime minister.

The prime minister was continually given public advice on how he needed to get a grip and to raise his performance as a leader. The highly experienced Conservative MP, George Walden, found it impossible to take John Major seriously: 'I could never convince myself that he was Prime Minister or, come to that, a real person.'[38] A senior Conservative strategist denounced the prime minister in public as 'a wimp'.[39] Paul Johnson complained that the problem with Major's premiership lay in his personality. There was 'virtually nothing there', concluded Johnson.[40] Friends and allies of John Major tried to convey something of the personality, style and resolve of the prime minister which was evident in intimate gatherings but conspicuously absent on public occasions. In 1992, Bill Clinton had been one of a pack of Democratic hopefuls until his advisors decided to differentiate him from the other runners by giving emphasis to the person rather than to the politician – his background and his journey from impoverished home to reformist governor.[41] Penny Junor,[42] Nesta Wyn Ellis[43] and Bruce Anderson[44] attempted to emulate this device with accounts of Major's own childhood and his early difficulties, together with their formative influence upon his leadership.

It was largely to no avail. In the eyes of many of his contemporaries, it was precisely these domestic travails which were responsible for Major's social vulnerabilities and for the limitations of his leadership. His biographer, Anthony Seldon, conceded that Major's 'vulnerability and lack of inner confidence, which dated back fifty years or more'[45] had had a material influence upon his leadership. Some of the criticism of the prime minister was driven by views of his actual performance, but other critiques were prompted more by intellectual and class snobbery, especially within his own party. While Seldon believed that many of the attacks on Major were unbalanced and paid insufficient attention to the political context within which the prime minister had to operate, he recognised that many of Major's problems were due to him not being a 'first-order leader'.[46] In Seldon's view, the 'worst that can be said of his unassertive style of leadership was that it may have encouraged divisions to grow, whereas a strong line earlier might have resolved some issues sooner'.[47] Major was, however, constrained not least by those 'weaknesses [that] date back ... to his childhood insecurities'.[48]

TONY BLAIR AND THE CULT OF PERSONAL POWER

In the 1997 general election, John Major tried to make the political limitations of his personality into a public virtue. He was overwhelmed by the armour-plated appeal of Tony Blair, whose cultivated image appeared flawless and whose two year campaign for the premiership had been based upon the need for an effective antidote to John Major's leadership. Blair's iron grip upon his party, combined with his strategic awareness, clear convictions and organised discipline, generated the kind of respect and fear among colleagues and adversaries that Margaret Thatcher had once achieved. In opposition and in government, Blair has had no inhibitions over fostering a cult of personality (see pp. 102–12, 190–5). The 1997 general election represented the culmination of a three year process to mould the Labour party around the figure and promise of a single individual. 'I listen carefully to colleagues', Blair said, 'but in the end it's like running a business. You can't do it by committee ... and I'm aware of this. If you have made this extraordinary claim that you can lead the country ... if you have put yourself very much up front, as I have, you take the downside. The buck stops with me and that's that.'[49] Blair had long since acknowledged the loneliness of his leadership position, but he had always accepted that it was an integral component of a personal campaign. It was, in essence, 'part of the deal'.[50]

The stylistic accessibility of Blair at work and play, the invocation of childhood experiences and formative influences in the prime minister's decision-making processes, and the public expression of his religious and moral convictions have made the figure of Blair into the distinctive trademark of his party and government. As a result, the definition of the New Labour project, the continued identity of the administration, the meaning of the 'third way', and the drive and energy of the government have all been palpably dependent upon the intensive presentation of Blair's persona. Just as the processes of leadership stretch and personalised power have been both actively and unwittingly advanced by the Blair leadership, so the actions of the Labour government have increasingly been refracted through the lens of the prime minister.

The tone was set at the very outset when, seven days into the administration, the first major television examination of the Blair administration concentrated exclusively upon the personality of the prime minister. The *Dispatches* programme,[51] produced by the company responsible for *Psychology News*, aimed explicitly to reach into Blair's mind by relating his background and formative influences to the New Labour project. The same theme and the same agenda have been persistently followed ever since. Political disjunctions within government, therefore, have not merely been reduced to some alleged deficiency in leadership. They have increasingly been seen as symptoms of the Labour prime minister's inner impulses and psychic turmoil. Blair has been depicted as being at one and the same time both Labour's conscience and the party's crushing disciplinarian.[52] David Marquand, for example, is alert to Blair's contradictions because, in his estimation, they matter to the conduct of British politics and policy making. 'Plainly he is a radical. As plainly, he is also a conservative. He is a child of the 1960s, who is also a child of the 1980s; a participative democrat who has imposed a Prussian discipline on his own party; the darling of the Sedgefield Labour Party who has managed to charm the Murdoch press.'[53] According to Marquand, New Labour and the Labour government cannot help but be influenced by the 'tensions within the psyche of the Prime Minister'.[54] Others believed the tensions to be so severe that they constituted a form of schizophrenia.[55] The compulsion to attribute political and explanatory significance to the state of the prime minister's mind and to his religious affiliations is the reverse side of a process of personalisation to which contemporary premiers are increasingly drawn.

This personalising process on the part of Tony Blair has been a key component in the promotion of issues and policies by Number 10. This prime ministerial imprimatur in the presentation of news is typified by the following sample of representative headlines:

Blair apologises to Ireland for potato famine
Daily Telegraph, 2 June 1997

Blair vows to tackle tearaways
Daily Telegraph, 14 June 1997

Blair pledge to low paid
The Guardian, 15 November 1997

Blair acts on 'cronyism culture'
The Guardian, 13 July 1998

Blair to hire 20,000 for millennium bug army
The Independent, 30 August 1998

Blair invents secular vicars to save family
Sunday Times, 27 September 1998

Blair offers advice to parents
The Guardian, 20 November 1998

Blair sharpens his axe to end 'feudal domination' of Lords
The Independent, 25 November 1998

Blair reasserts his will to build Lib Dem links
Financial Times, 11 January 1999

Blair bid to break Ulster peace deadlock
The Observer, 7 February 1999

Blair promises to end child poverty within 20 years
The Times, 19 March 1999

Blair pledge to refugees
The Guardian, 4 May 1999

Blair tells Serbians to overthrow Milosevic's 'corrupt dictatorship'
The Independent, 5 May 1999

Blair battles to cast Britain in role of world's conscience
Financial Times, 28 May 1999

Blair puts hunt ban beyond doubt
The Times, 9 July 1999

Blair tells TUC: I am in charge
The Times, 15 September 1999

Blair promises to speed 'top to bottom' modernisation of Britain
The Independent, 28 September 1999

Blair acts after unit's plans are ignored by Whitehall
The Times, 15 October 1999

Teacher 'excuse culture' attacked by Blair
The Times, 21 October 1999

Blair backs 30,000 strong Euro army
Sunday Times, 14 November 1999

Blair's war on drivers
The Express, 18 November 1999

Blair halts plans for 1.1m homes in the South
Daily Mail, 30 November 1999

The personal convictions and experiences of the premier have often been flagged in the launch of policy initiatives and reviews. It has been a feature of the Blair premiership that so many of these initiatives have borne the imprint of the prime minister's personal interest in a new scheme or course of action. Sometimes this has taken the form of the prime minister actively using his position to publicise an issue as a matter of personal concern (e.g. Northern Ireland, education, welfare reform, the NHS and the future of the European Union). On other occasions, Blair has explicitly associated an issue with a deep personal experience. For example, in highlighting the need to address the issue of rising cancer rates, Blair not only made it a Downing Street priority with a publicised meeting of cancer experts, but personalised the force behind this commitment. Writing in the *Daily Mail* on the day that he launched a 'war on cancer' with the objective of cutting the death rate from the disease by 20 per cent, the prime minister drew upon his family's experience with the illness:

> It has certainly left its deep mark on our family. My mother died at 52 from throat cancer. Her early death, just weeks after I left university, had a profound impact on me. And Cherie has written in *The Mail* about the death of her Aunt Audrey, who was a great support to both of us when our children were young. It's why Cherie is now such a campaigner on breast cancer.[56]

Real political substance therefore inheres in the prime minister's experiences, impulses and interests.

The interest in the prime minister's thought processes is reflected in Alastair Campbell's briefings to lobby correspondents, where Tony Blair's mind is quoted as a constant and authoritative insight into the government's plans and reactions. 'Every nuance means something'[57] to the assembled company. Blair's feelings are now part of the political currency. They have also in their turn contributed to a political environment which generates demands for personal revelation and which elevates the private as the key to understanding public actions. The biosphere that Blair has come to inhabit is one which is geared both to display and to intrusion. It is characterised by a medium of permanent political campaigning, a continuous news cycle, an obsessive search for inside-track stories and new perspectives, and a magazine culture that gravitates to the prime minister as a super-celebrity and reads significance into every feature of his life and the lives of his family (e.g. Tony Blair's Stratocruiser guitar; his Ford Galaxy; his views on smacking children; Cherie Blair's 'makeovers'; her time management as working mother and career woman; her pendant providing protection from 'bioelectric rays'; the Blairs' choice of schools; their holiday locations in Tuscany; the pressures on their family life; Cherie's unexpected pregnancy, and the timing and location of the conception).[58] The popular fascination with Blair and his family has contributed to the prime minister becoming a recognised figure of cultural, and even religious, authority. In a poll conducted by the *Sunday Times* on who we look up to in Britain, Tony Blair came top.[59] The prime minister's well-known religious convictions and moral views placed him in a position of spiritual leadership above the Archbishop of Canterbury, Cardinal Hume, the Chief Rabbi and the Queen. In another listing of spiritual leaders, being Blair's spiritual advisor was sufficient to raise Peter Thompson to a position above that of Desmond Tutu, the Archbishop of York and the Chief Rabbi.[60]

The various dynamics involved in the progressive personalisation of power can be of great benefit to a prime minister when he or she is in a dominant position. At a time when the prime minister appears to constitute the command and control centre of an effective government, has a demonstrable grasp of the levers of power and possesses the political skill to cultivate new sources of influence, then the personalised depiction of government can provide extensive political advantages. However, the very prominence given to premiers through the extensive publicisation of their personas can backfire in more difficult times. The various agencies and processes involved in personalising the perceptions and analysis of the government, the party and the 'project' have the potential for being deployed for critical effect. For the first two years of his premiership, Blair was untroubled by such a reversal into personalised critique and condemnation but the threat of personal responsibility for personal power remained a threat. John Major once complained that one of the things he most disliked about being prime minister was 'the way everything you said was analysed and analysed ... I read this amazing analysis of me by strangers and I don't know why they say it.' He went on to offer advice: 'I think these people should be psychoanalysed.'[61] The predilection to psychoanalyse the prime minister has intensified even further with Tony Blair because of his centrality to what the government does and, more significantly, why it selects and pursues certain objectives.

Even though British dispositions towards looking systematically at leaders have yet to reach the levels of preoccupation that characterise the American approach to the presidency, there is a growing inclination for perceiving and analysing politics and government through the most prominent single feature within the system. The position of the premier, the political skills needed to be a prime minister and the extent to which the government's outlook reflects the leader's own temperament have become subjects of public interest and debate. Being a prime minister is no longer seen as simply being an occupant of a position. The office itself is now interpreted as being far less institutionalised than it used to be and far more dependent upon the individual incumbent for its meaning and effect. This being so, there has arisen a much greater British interest in the psychological analysis of leadership, and in the wider explanatory significance of personality and its formative influences upon the development and behaviour of leaders.

Whether it is Margaret Thatcher's relationship with her mother and especially her father, or the pivotal effect upon Tony Blair of his mother's death and his father's subsequent illness, or the influence of his father's unemployment upon John Major, there is now a much greater willingness to regard such information as materially significant.[62] All three leaders consciously played upon childhood themes for political effect. Margaret Thatcher, for example, used her earlier experiences in her father's corner shop to substantiate her claims of having an intuitive understanding of capitalism: 'There is no better course for understanding free-market economics than life in a corner shop. What I learned in Grantham ensured that abstract criticisms I would hear of capitalism came up against the reality of my own experience.'[63] Similar purchase was given to the backgrounds of Major and Blair in their efforts to give integrity and insight to their leadership claims (see pp. 177–83). Many observers returned the favour by moving from the sphere of the conscious and deliberate to that of the unconscious and unintentional. While Major's priorities and insecurities were traced back to childhood experiences, the psychological origins of Blair's moralism and religiosity generated protracted speculation.[64] Given that the key to New Labour was Tony Blair, then the formative influences of the leader were now considered to be highly significant to an analysis of the Labour government. Political journalists have been continually prompted to comment on the psychic contradiction between Blair's emphasis upon compassion, consideration and community on the one hand, and the prime minister's ruthlessness and 'obsession with not looking weak'[65] on the other. Such examples are indicative of a general trend towards ascribing a higher level of political meaning and of current significance to the personal constitutions and histories of leaders, and especially prime ministers. Memoirs and biographies may previously have touched on such themes after the event. Today, they have a public currency and a political force that is relevant to premiers while they are premiers.

Just as political significance increasingly devolves upon leadership figures, so analytical attention becomes focused upon the individual variants of power. The concentration of attention upon the prime minister for insights and meanings into current and future government action bears witness to the salience of the premier within the machinery of state. When this point of explanatory access is combined with the growing significance of inquiries into the core components of leadership, the contribution of individual leadership to political solutions and the congruence of personality types to the political roles of a mutable office, it is clear that the discussion of executive power within British governance has been increasingly conditioned to the proposition that there exists a presidential dimension in the system.

Constitution

CONSTITUTIONAL CONSCIOUSNESS IN THE UNITED STATES

The second area in which a justifiable case can now be made for comparing the prime minister with the presidency is that of constitutionalism. The United States possesses not only a written and entrenched constitution, but also a highly developed constitutional culture that accepts the constitution as the ultimate source of sovereignty and, therefore, as the ultimate reference point of society. The constitution is seen as exemplifying the form and ideal of a government under law. Political institutions are defined, their powers enumerated and their relationships specified, and the rights and liberties of the citizenry are specified. The underlying objective is one of ensuring that the exercise of power is conducted according to legal criteria with the object of preventing the occurrence of arbitrary and unlimited government. The central principle of American constitutionalism, therefore, has been one of determinable powers, ascertainable rights and government restricted under the higher law doctrine of constitutional sanction.

Alongside this characteristic feature of constitutionalism lies the concomitant constitutional objective of sustaining a political community and providing it with a structure of government commensurate with the needs of that community. This was always as important a purpose to the Founders as the objective of self-restraint. The two features were aggregated together, rather than fused into an organic conception of community interest and individual rights being served by a government integral to both. The danger of the state was identified quantitatively as being the physical bulk of government entrusted with the power of coercive force. This was confined to a separate department demarcated as the executive and designated as a co-equal branch of government.

As the republic grew in size and power it became increasingly evident that the executive could not be reduced to a defined condition. The executive was increasingly expected to use the instruments of state to provide central direction, forceful energy and initiating drive on behalf of society's welfare and the nation's interest. While the executive's authority had constantly to be legitimised by recourse to constitutional validation, it also became evident that the executive possessed inherent prerogative powers that were not based upon the procedures of consent or upon any general understanding of the rule of law. Executive prerogative sat very uneasily in such an explicitly constitutional system. As Harvey Mansfield has pointed out, '[f]or a constitutional people, nothing is more difficult, nor more necessary, than to define what executive power is'.[66] But in having said that, Mansfield recognises that executive power is 'the power that most resists definition'.[67] During the era of the modern presidency, the problematic position of the executive's discretionary power was thought to have been resolved by steady recognition and assimilation of the need for a strong and active president. Implicit in the modern presidency was the idea that it was both the agent and the outward evidence of the political system's necessary evolution into a form and function necessary for modern conditions. The modern presidency was presented as a rising and irreversible curve of accumulated power, delegated authority and assimilated prerogative.

The 'imperial presidency' episode of the late 1960s and early 1970s, however, dramatically revealed the extent to which the nature and scale of presidential power had not been settled by convention and precedent. What had seemed an irreversible fact of modern governing conditions was suddenly challenged by a popular front of constitutional fundamentalism. Critics of the Nixon administration reasserted another key feature of the American constitution – namely the ethos of checks and balances. The use of executive power, especially in foreign policy and national security, had in many respects superseded the formal arrangement of separated power held in competitive tension by the interplay of reciprocal checks. In this field, the adversarial claims and counterclaims to contested constitutional authority that normally permeate American political debate were largely suspended. They were replaced by a general acquiescence in the overriding need for executive power in a world dangerously polarised into competing ideologies, military alliances and nuclear arsenals. It was when presidents began to project their international prerogatives into domestic affairs that the public renewed its interest in the old principles of constitutional dispute, legal challenge and institutional friction.

The Watergate scandal represented the climax of this revival in the constitution's checks and balances. Watergate's 'importance was in the way it brought to the surface, symbolised and made politically accessible the great question posed by the Nixon administration ... the question of the unwarranted and unprecedented expansion of presidential power'.[68] The executive power of the chief executive had been politically accommodated and selectively sanctioned by the courts, but the issue had never been fully resolved. This was because the executive's access to, and its cultivation of, the coercive powers of the state ran against the constitutional grain of dispersed powers and delimited government. The Watergate crisis opened up the fundamental question of executive power to intensive analysis and critical evaluation. It subjected the executive to a form of scrutiny which it was unaccustomed to receiving and unable to withstand. The insurgents demanded precision in the definition and demarcation of executive force. Such a demand was quite alien to the conventional negligence by which the presidency was normally accommodated within the constitution's sphere of legitimacy. The end result was a presidency broken on the wheels and cogs of a refurbished constitutional machine that drew its strength from a heightened public interest in the potential abuse of power and in the value of checks and balances to prevent it. Progressive evolution was no longer interpreted as a form of advance but as the sign of constitutional subversion and degeneration. The legitimacy of executive power was suddenly brought into question. The problematic nature of the executive's constitutional position was exposed. Critics and reformers became constitutional zealots, insisting that executive power was reversible and that the presidential office should be reduced to a definable position.

The same zeal for textual analysis and for debate over final authority was shown during the 'Iran-contra scandal'. This incident also led to calls for balanced government and, in particular, to a restoration of 'the constitutional roles of both Congress and the courts as active players in a system of balanced institutional participation'.[69] Over the period 1998–99, another presidency was effectively subverted by a scandal pursued to its fullest extent as an instrument of political opposition. President Clinton's multiple evasions over his sexual misconduct with Monica Lewinsky led to an accumulation of charges relating to perjury and obstruction of justice. As a result, his Republican opponents 'put the nation through months of hearings, debate, and trial, weakening the presidency, preoccupying Congress, and monopolizing public attention'.[70] The controversy culminated in President Clinton's impeachment by the House of Representatives. He escaped conviction in the subsequent Senate trial but the authority of his presidency had been undermined by an issue that had derailed the normal conduct of politics. Like the Watergate and the Iran-contra episodes, the scandal had generated an intense debate over the misuse and abuse of power in a system noted for its constitutional self-consciousness.[71] In all three scandals, presidents had provided the stimulus for full-scale constitutional dispute. They did so by their actions but, more importantly, by their status as chief executives, which not only attracted critical concern over the demarcation and rightful use of executive power, but made discussion of the whole system that much more accessible because of the presidency's central role within it. It is the presidency's very conspicuousness as the 'state personified'[72] which can accentuate any public dismay over government into charges of an executive blight upon the whole of America's constitutional democracy.

SOCIAL CONVENTION AND CONSTITUTIONAL MANAGEMENT IN BRITAIN

Until recently, Britain did not have the sort of constitutional awareness to foster concerns such as the distribution of political power and the legitimacy of government action. The British had no modern tradition of challenging, on constitutional grounds, the performance and authority of any part of the political system. As for contesting the rights and prerogatives of the state's executive heartland, with its heavy responsibilities for national security and its high status as the epitome of parliamentary development, such effrontery was unthinkable. Apart from being inconceivable, it was also regarded as unnecessary. The British constitution was distinguished by its spontaneous flair for absorbing stress and assimilating change without disturbing the continuity of British society. It had been able to adapt to the demands for popular participation while retaining the heritage of established structures of traditional authority.

The British constitution's reputation for stability and equilibrium was based upon three main factors. First was the widespread conviction that British political development was evolutionary in form and, as a consequence, progressive and benevolent in outcome. Second was the way in which parliamentary sovereignty provided a controlling principle that could explain the organisation of the state. The principle foreclosed damaging discussion about the location of final authority and invested the entire system with a prevailing legitimacy rooted, ultimately, in parliament's democratic credentials. And third was the central importance given to the spirit of custom and tradition, both in the constitution's essentials and in its usage.

As a result of these factors, the British constitution has generally been noted for its dependence upon conventions and unwritten understandings in the task of managing government, and for the necessary dependability of government's participants to abide by such informal arrangements. The constitution's silences were thought to be not only the sign of its viability, but also its chief means of maintaining life. Social outlook, political manners and self-restraint became the substitute for any consciously conceived constitutional doctrine. What was in effect an improvised bundle of laws, customs and institutions defying collective definition nevertheless assumed an 'irrefutable authority as an embodiment of historical progression and social obligation'.[73] Habits and sentiments were the 'works managers'[74] of the constitution. They obscured its anomalies and contradictions and made its arrangements workable to the general satisfaction of those whose mutual trust sustained its integrity. Liberties were protected by public authorities being confined to their statutory powers by the courts. Democratic accountability was assured by parliamentary checks and the ministerial system. The British constitution, therefore, had a tradition of stability based upon the intuitive capabilities of its participants to conform to the spirit of its understandings. The constitution operated on the basis of a public trust that its anomalies and areas of unsettlement would not be exploited for political gain. The constitution, therefore, was dependent upon a strong sense of political and public propriety. Reciprocity and manners at the top were complemented by a common core of liberal beliefs concerning the importance of individual rights and the permanent need to limit the sphere of the state's coercive powers.

When this collegiate style of government began to corrode is not clear, but what is certain is that by the 1970s its internal points of conflict and the political attitudes supporting the structure and style of its operation were coming under severe pressure. The economic and social turmoil of the period was translated into a form of constitutional irreverence that led to a series of public critiques and a range of proposed reforms. The stark realism of the 1970s stripped away the comfortable securities of the 1950s and laid bare the problematic nature of many of the British constitution's governing arrangements. The British were placed in the unaccustomed position of having seriously to question their constitution.

MARGARET THATCHER AND THE POLITICS OF CONSTITUTIONAL CRITIQUE

In many respects, Margaret Thatcher's accession to power curtailed the crisis of the constitution. Her administration was committed to reducing the powers of the state and, in particular, to scaling back the heavy accoutrements of corporate government. The effort to return responsibilities and liberties to the individual, however, led to the widely recognised 'Thatcher paradox'. In order to release personal energies and to emancipate the productive potential of the market, the Thatcher governments had to draw increasingly upon their central powers. They found that their libertarian crusade had to be a government-directed campaign for less government. Instead of defusing the controversies over centralism and 'elective dictatorship' which had afflicted the 1970s, the Thatcher governments had the opposite effect. The earlier constitutional disarray of 'ungovernability' and the colonised state was replaced by a new constitutional affliction of 'overgovernability' and the spectre of coercive statism. It was said that Thatcher 'showed little regard for the spirit of any constitution'.[75] In spite of her professed radicalism, she was thought in many quarters to show a worryingly conventional attitude towards the prize of British parliamentary democracy. 'Deep in Thatcher's psyche was a characteristic shared with traditional British socialism: a faith not in parliament but in government. Her instincts were "democratic centralist", rooted in the legitimacy of a single, all-powerful executive subject only to periodic election.'[76] This outlook on the part of Thatcher prompted an enriched form of new constitutional debate that was able to focus on the natural object of constitution – namely, the nature and scale of executive power.

The critical reflection of governmental power, and of Mrs Thatcher's relationship to it, was rooted in the public's impression of her conduct in, and usage of, the cabinet. The Thatcher years were replete with stories of the prime minister's personal domination of the cabinet. A number of insider accounts disputed this view,[77] but they were never able to dislodge the overriding impression that Mrs Thatcher openly defied the ethos of cabinet government. What made matters worse for Thatcher was that her public persona gave the stories of her cabinet behaviour an immediate credibility. Moreover, the palpable evidence of her cabinet style in the form of sackings and resignations all seemed to point in one direction.

The record shows that Thatcher did intervene in her ministers' departmental affairs, she did remove ministers who were in her view not 'one of us', and she did engage in the tactical use of cabinet committees and informal groups to achieve objectives. Writing in 1986, Peter Hennessy concluded that the

> Cabinet does meet less frequently, it discusses fewer formal papers, it is presented with more virtual *faits accomplis* at the last moment, and she does prefer to work in ad hoc groups – many of the most important ones remaining outside the Cabinet-committee structure. She has certainly flouted the spirit of traditional cabinet governments.[78]

It is likely that Mrs Thatcher believed herself to be confronted by a multiplicity of constraints and that, in the political style celebrated in Richard Neustadt's study of the presidency, she was necessarily exploiting her limited political resources to the fullest effect. In the public domain, however, Mrs Thatcher's attempts to maximise her executive influence created doubts that provided the basis for a deeper scepticism about the state of the British constitution. Her detractors used the outward impression of her style of cabinet management to popularise the view that she was the source of the 'predatory, authoritarian and dishonest trends in government'.[79] When Michael Heseltine resigned from the cabinet during the Westland crisis, he made explicit allusions to the constitutional irregularities in Mrs Thatcher's management of cabinet government.[80] This was not just a case of a senior minister justifying his withdrawal from government on spurious grounds. He deliberately invoked constitutional impropriety because it had become such a potent term of political dissent. In doing so and in withdrawing so dramatically from the cabinet room, he strengthened the public's impression that there were constitutional issues at stake; that they were worth resigning for; and that the ethos of cabinet government was not a private value system restricted to the interior of government, but was a subject of genuine concern.

The Labour opposition came to appreciate the potential of the issue for generating government discomfort and for providing a focused theme that could be exploited for political effect. In the 1987 general election, Neil Kinnock spoke of 'Thatcher totalitarianism'.[81] He charged the prime minister with having inaugurated a 'long process of removing all opposition in the great institutions of Britain'.[82] The working assumption, which gained popular credence, was that Mrs Thatcher's departure from the post-war consensus was synonymous with a deviation in constitutional practice. Mrs Thatcher and the British constitution had in effect become mutually deranged. This type of criticism was not confined to the opposition parties, or to the realms of simple partisanship. Concern over the constitution and over what was widely seen as Mrs Thatcher's cavalier disregard of constitutional proprieties was expressed by legal scholars, political analysts and senior political figures. The tone and subject of their criticisms varied, but they shared a sense of disquiet over the aggressive way that power was being exercised and over the increasingly casual manner in which legal and customary controls on the use of government power were being set aside. David Marquand pointed out that it had always been a supposition of Britain's traditional 'club government' that 'no one would push his formal constitutional rights to the limit: that governments would use the huge battery of powers available to them'.[83] After the Thatcher era, Marquand noted, 'no such assumption could be made today'.[84]

The absence of self-restraint and consequent lack of collective restraint had led to the suspension of rights, to the restriction of freedoms and to a further increase in central power. As part of the same pattern, Margaret Thatcher was seen to challenge the influence of other centres of political authority that had traditionally constituted a form of corporate countervailing power in the British system. The trade unions, the civil service, the universities, professions and the church all received critical attention from the government. In particular, the Thatcher governments were accused of attempting 'to whittle down, reduce or eliminate the role of local electoral institutions; local participation in the administration of services affecting local areas; and local opposition, lawfully expressed, to central government policies'.[85] In sum, the strident style of Thatcher's conviction politics raised the issue of the government's own legitimacy. Its 'arrogance in the use of power', its 'general pattern of contempt for ... the constraints on power' and 'its belief that the rightness of the policies to be executed, excused or justified the methods whereby they were executed'[86] all added weight to the charge that the government was acting improperly. To many, even raising the question of the government's legitimacy was demonstrable proof of its damnable properties. The question suggested its own answer. It betrayed the existence of a 'concentration of power in the hands of the executive – and the prime minister in particular – and the absence of any effective checks and balances'.[87] The necessary consequence was that 'civil liberties in Britain were in a state of crisis'.[88]

The thrust of these critiques was strongly suggestive of the sort of challenges that American presidents have often been subjected to in the past. First, there was a strong sense that Mrs Thatcher's success in rearranging the priorities of the political agenda was achieved by her willingness and her ability to 'use the vagueness and flexibility of the constitution to her own ends'.[89] Second, her reputation for dominance and intervention increased the susceptibility of the public to see the hand of Thatcher in practically every area of government action. Third, the tendency to see British government transmuted into prime ministerial government increased the tendency to view the state of the nation, as a whole, in the light of Margaret Thatcher and her programme. The term 'Thatcherism' was especially important in this respect for, like the programmes of American presidents in the past, Thatcherism among other things gave Margaret Thatcher herself the appearance of a universal presence in society. Her prominence gave her considerable influence at the centre of government, but it also rendered her personally accountable for nearly every point of stress and maladjustment in society. It increased, rather than decreased, the tendency to hold government culpable for the state of civil society. It might even be said that because Thatcherism was widely characterised as the consequence of one person's idiosyncrasies, it was interpreted as an aberration at the centre of government that in its turn multiplied social complaints and laid them directly at the door of Number 10.

This led to a fourth development in the form of an aroused constitutional consciousness generating an American-style fusion of policy criticism and constitutional dispute. The linkage made between Mrs Thatcher's programme and her success in pushing it through, together with its social and economic consequences, and the scale – real or imagined – of her power as prime minister, fostered an increase in the use of constitutional principles to analyse and evaluate her government. While Thatcher's position and her behaviour were often taken as a barometer of the state of the constitution, the idea of a constitution was increasingly employed as an evaluative point of reference and as an instrument of dissent.

The fifth and final factor in this development was the search for a solution to what had been defined in many quarters as a constitutional problem. In this way, Mrs Thatcher and the 'extent of her unchallenged success signalled the need for new forms and structures'.[90] The most notable example of such constitutional concern was the Charter 88 organisation, which called for a new constitutional settlement. According to Charter 88, political rights were being curtailed while the powers of the executive were increasing in scale. This 'identification of authoritarian rule had only recently begun' through the government's exploitation of the 'dark side of a constitutional settlement which was deficient in democracy'.[91] Because freedoms were not encoded and powers were not defined, the old constitutional order had 'enabled the government to discipline British society to its ends'.[92] What was now required to reverse this process was a comprehensive restructuring of British government in a written constitution embracing such measures as a bill of rights, a freedom of information act, proportional representation, and the subjection of executive powers, prerogatives and agencies to the rule of law and to the control of a democratically renewed parliament.

It would be no exaggeration to say that Margaret Thatcher's premiership provided the catalyst to this revival in constitutional fundamentalism. Whether prime ministerial power is seen as having been the general spur to a number of specific constitutional proposals, or a specific spur to a search for a new constitutional settlement, there is no doubt that Mrs Thatcher's conduct in office directed attention to constitutional constraint. Her premiership dramatised the problem of centralised power inside British government and fostered a much greater interest in looking at government not from the traditional outlook of *ad hoc* improvisations and discrete issues, but from the point of view of general principles of political authority and citizenship.

JOHN MAJOR AND THE CONSTITUTIONAL ISSUE OF CENTRAL EXECUTIVE POWER

In one way, the removal of Margaret Thatcher provided an initial solution to the issue of the constitutional contentiousness of her premiership. In the best tradition of Britain's political constitution, in which constitutional forms and processes should rightfully be seen as derivatives of political exchange, John Major's personal preference for consultation and conciliation, together with his revival of collective decision making, embodied a type of corrective to the inflammatory figure of his predecessor. In the light of such a perspective, the installation of John Major in Downing Street could be construed as a systemic response on the part of the constitution to an identified problem of disequilibrium. However, in another way Major was not so much a solution as a restatement of the original problem. The style and tone of the government may have changed and the provocation of the 'poll tax' may have been defused, but in general the shape and direction of the Thatcherite agenda remained intact. The policies that had had immense constitutional repercussions were not only continued but extended in scope.

In his study of the period, Simon Jenkins states that Major 'brought no new insight into policy' and 'announced no change of approach'.[93] On the contrary, Major's response to the public sector was 'if anything more rather than less Thatcherite than Thatcher's'.[94] The governing culture in Whitehall had now become fixed upon privatisation and centralisation. Accordingly, the Major governments pressed onward into areas such as the railways, the coal industry and the post office[95] that had been seen by Thatcher to be beyond the outer limits of denationalisation. In those sectors that remained in the public domain, the Major response was one of furthering the level of centralised control and auditing (e.g. the NHS, police authorities, housing, schools, universities and local government finance). In Jenkins's view, it was 'hard to put daylight between the actual deeds of John Major's Cabinet and those of Lady Thatcher had she been in office'. Indeed, she may have opposed some of Major's policies, 'but only on the grounds that they went too far and too fast'.[96] The net effect of the Major administration on the constitutional audit was, therefore, neutral. Mrs Thatcher's cavalier disregard for constitutional protocols was replaced by John Major's open-textured pragmatism that provided a similar myopia towards the constitutional implications of policy that characterised the Thatcher era. To Major, the creation of more natural monopolies and the increased centralisation of control over the public sector were not only well motivated by the desire to deliver improved public services but were the product of a more open process of political accommodation. To the government's opponents, the constitutional dimension remained an instrument of critique and a frame of reference that could provide a source of positional constancy and critical anchorage in a rapidly developing policy regime that no longer had the conditioning factor of an ideological alternative.

It is true that Major sought to respond to the demands for constitutional reform through a series of guarded initiatives (e.g. The Code of Practice on Access to Government Information to be supervised by the parliamentary ombudsman; the concession to allow ministers to appear at meetings of the Scottish Grand Committee held north of the border). It is also true that the legality, rationality and fairness of the actions undertaken by public authorities were increasingly subjected to judicial review as part of a 'remarkable march of administrative law calling governments to account in court'.[97] But these elements did not satisfy what had become a well organised and highly sophisticated movement in support of constitutional reform. The maturing of its proposals and arguments into a coherent agenda, together with its capacity to propagate a language of constitutional critique, to enlist political support and to influence political parties, amounted to a significant point of challenge to the government. In 1996, the establishment of a Joint Consultative Committee on Constitutional Reform gave formal expression to the political potential of collaboration between Labour and the Liberal Democrats over the issue of constitutional reform. The Joint Committee had been conceived at a time when Paddy Ashdown was publicly speculating on a ten year partnership with Labour based upon its acceptance of the Lib Dems' *full* programme of constitutional reform. During the same period, Tony Blair shifted his stance against electoral reform to one of giving it serious consideration and even pledging a referendum on the issue during the lifetime of the first parliament under a future Labour government. The New Labour leadership was conscious of the need to demonstrate its radical credentials and to gain the support of this influential source of opposition impulse. It recognised the prudence of reaching an accommodation with the Lib Dems, which had traditionally been the party most closely aligned to constitutional reform and which could provide Labour with electoral and coalitional backing. Accordingly, Blair allowed his party to absorb much of the reform agenda.

In March 1997, the Joint Committee announced an agreement between Labour and the Liberal Democrats to collaborate in a full agenda of constitutional change. Although the agreement reflected the priorities of the senior partner, it amounted to a working partnership of historic importance not least because it committed the main opposition party to full-scale reform and provided the support of a third party to secure it. In the election, Major believed that by dwelling on the dangers of constitutional reform he could repeat his victory of 1992 when in his own mind the popular fear over the future of the United Kingdom had been pivotal to the re-election of a Conservative government. Although constitutional reform divided the two main parties more than any other issue, it was not a theme of high salience to the voting public. Notwithstanding the ever deepening tone of Major's fearful prognoses – 'we have 72 hours to make sure that the system of government that has prevailed in this country for a very long time is … not broken up',[98] – Blair secured a landslide victory. In the process, he acquired a governing position of prodigious strength with a mandate to dismantle both the means by which it achieved power and the methods used to maintain that power.

RIDING THE TIGER

Even though he did not have to contend with a hung parliament and, therefore, had no immediate need for the Lib Dems as coalition partners, Blair was nevertheless committed to constitutional reform and quickly put into effect measures towards achieving devolution for Scotland and Wales. As part of New Labour's project to modernise the British system of government, the new government also introduced legislation to incorporate the European Convention of Human Rights into British law and to establish an elected authority and mayor for London. Moreover, it voluntarily relinquished the control of interest rates to the Bank of England. It rapidly became apparent that the issue of the constitution would dominate at least the first half of the Blair government and would lead to the greatest change in the country's constitutional arrangements since World War I. Despite the gains made in the constitutional reform agenda, questions were promptly raised over whether the early momentum for reform could be maintained and whether New Labour's acclimatisation to the drives and complexities of government would lead to the postponement, and even the abandonment, of the remaining reform items. The Blair government had satisfied the proponents of Scottish and Welsh devolution and responded adequately, if belatedly, to the issue of proportional representation for elections to the European parliament. The government was never going to appease the proponents of a full democratic settlement and written constitution. Nevertheless, its delays and prevarication generated doubts over New Labour's commitment to a revised constitutional culture, and its disjointed and compartmentalised approach to constitutional reform raised concern over the coherence of any finished product.

To an articulate and suspicious reform lobby, the Blair government was attending only to the outer fringes of what was a multifaceted issue. It was possible to regard such criticisms as being premature and overdrawn, coming as they did from a purist perspective that gave little weight or credence to the factors of government time, political resources, legal problems, party positioning and prudent caution in the pace of a reform programme. On the other hand, a strong case could be made in support of the proposition that the Blair government, for all its reforming activity, had shown great circumspection over any change that challenged the linkages between the principles of parliamentary sovereignty and crown prerogative, and the authority of the central government. Blair was a believer in strong leadership and radical government. During the first two years of his government, he showed few signs of actively seeking to extend the ethos of modernisation and constitutional restraint to the government's powerhouse of the core executive. Furthermore, Blair was criticised not only for the strong-arm methods that the party leadership employed to drive reforms through parliament but for having a strategic wariness over anything that could exert a countervailing force upon executive government. The government was nervous over the ramifications of constitutional reform for the maintenance of its discretionary executive powers. This disquiet was reflected in its evident anxiety over the shape and authority of a reformed second chamber, its concern over the extension of proportional representation to the House of Commons and its insistence that the legislation incorporating the European Convention of Human Rights into British law should not challenge parliamentary sovereignty. Labour worries were also reflected in the successive postponements of freedom of information legislation, culminating in the publication of a Freedom of Information Bill (May 1999) that was conspicuously weaker in effect than even the much delayed Freedom of Information White Paper (December 1997). After two years of a Blair administration,

The Observer concluded that a constitutional revolution was still far from being achieved:

> The party is formally committed to the democratisation of Britain, yet its devolution proposals devolve little formal political control with purse-strings held tightly in Whitehall. In Wales Mr Blair shamelessly resorted to the union block vote to ensure his favoured candidate, Alun Michael, won [the] leadership of the Welsh Labour party ... The voting rights of hereditary peers are to be abolished, but Mr Blair wants the second chamber to be appointed. Increasingly constitutional reform looks compromised, ill-thought through and above all not animated by a desire to democratise the country.[99]

This attitude was claimed to be not just consistent with, but a direct consequence, of a 'fundamental illiberalism that [ran] through the government'.[100] To Simon Jenkins, his critique of the Thatcher–Major years was similarly applicable to the Blair government. Although the language may have changed from the statism of Old Labour, Blair's administration had demonstrated that it was 'dirigiste at home and interventionist abroad'.[101] Blair had established what Jenkins termed 'Blatcherism'[102] as Britain's national ideology. Upon taking office, the prime minister had inherited and assimilated the previous regime's 'privatise-or-centralise authoritarianism'[103] and given it merely a different exterior form: 'It is marinated in clichés about One Nation, Third Way, social inclusion and aspirational society. But its appeal is as clear as a focus group memo, to offer a rigidly controlled state sector to the tax-conscious floating voters of Middle England.'[104] Stuart Hall had similar misgivings. In spite of the clamour over participation, decentralisation and constitutional reform, Hall experienced 'the queasy feeling that New Labour increasingly finds the rituals of democratic practice tiresome, and in practice if not formally, would be happy to move in the direction of a more "direct", plebiscitary referendum style of governance'.[105] This may not have been exactly the same kind of populism associated with Mrs Thatcher but it was a 'variant species of "authoritarian populism" none the less – corporate and managerialist in its "downward" leadership style and its moralising attitude to those to whom good is being done. It's also deeply manipulative in the way that it represents the authority it imposes as somehow "empowering us".'[106] Needless to say, both authoritarianism and populism sit uneasily with the ethos of constitutionalism with its filters, processes, checks, entrenchments and legal mechanics.

In spite of Blair's emphatic conversion to constitutional reform prior to the general election, Labour's manifesto pledges and the Labour government's huge majority in the House of Commons, the resistance to advanced constitutional modernisation has been extensive. What has been an optimum period of constitutional reconstruction and what should have been the culmination of a prolonged process towards fundamental constitutional change has demonstrated instead the durability and tenacity of the central executive's resistance to incursion. Blair's revision to the constitution would not be extended to Blair's backyard.[107] The role of a United States president is to uphold the constitution, while at the same time protecting the office's authority, which is implicitly based upon the irreducibility of executive prerogative to constitutional categories. In a similar manner, Blair has come to inhabit an environment that is increasingly oriented to constitutional consciousness and constitutional inclusion, but which remains predisposed to the claims of executive exclusion. Away from the core executive, much of the system has become geared to the positivist properties of constitutionalism and to its central purpose of governmental limitation. By contrast, the prime minister has become situated in a dual existence well understood by American presidents. One side of the duality relates to the need by the prime minister to embody the executive force of government and, therefore, the main rationale for a constitutional order based upon the rule of law. On the other side, the prime minister exemplifies an extra-constitutional dimension geared to providing a centre of decision and discretion without recourse to law on the grounds of protecting the public and national interest and maintaining the constitutional order itself. Presidents are accustomed to dramatising this paradox in a democratic polity. Blair is new to such a position but he has quickly had to acclimatise himself to the twin role by which he symbolises the movement towards a more defined and modernised constitutional system, while at the same time personifying the elusive and mercurial features of executive power.

Nation

AMERICA'S PAST AS A POLITICAL RESOURCE

The third selected area of comparability between the modern presidency and the contemporary premiership in Britain concerns the theme of nationalism. The presidency has always had a close association with the American nation: 'The presidency has grown and expanded as the nation has grown and expanded.'[108] This dual growth has not been coincidental. Great presidents of the past contributed not only to the development of their own office but, in doing so, they were instrumental in the rise of the American nation. The office and the nation grew up together and progressed very much in terms of one another. The integration and progress of the nation are habitually portrayed through the lives of American presidents, as if personal leadership was the main causal agency of a nation being born and advancing in development. Likewise, the nation's ideals are commonly embodied in the form of national archetypes that have achieved the ideal of becoming president.

In the modern era, the presidency and the nation have achieved an even closer identity. The 'redeemer nation' is regularly expressed through the power, centrality and singularity of its redeemer presidents who in national emergencies can, for all practical purposes, reformulate government to respond to national needs. At the same time that America's nationhood finds expression in the presidency's foreign policy and national security powers, the presidency itself can stimulate, focus and enhance the level of national consciousness. It is not merely that 'the power of the nation is identified with the power of the president',[109] it is that, to all intents and purposes, 'the president can symbolise the nation and [its] government'[110] to the American people. Studies show that a president enduring low levels of public approval and suffering from the myriad restrictions of a pluralist society and of a constitutional framework of checks and balances can suddenly be given a prodigious freedom of action and a high level of popular support whenever America finds itself implicated in an international crisis.[111] This 'rally round the flag' effect is even evident when the president himself is seen as being responsible for the crisis. Events such as military interventions, major diplomatic initiatives and actions leading to international tension confront the nation as a whole through the person of the president. As such, they generate an intense national loyalty that devolves upon the presidential office as the only entity capable of giving symbolic and material substance to the idea of the nation. Nationalism has proved to be such a palpable and potent political resource that it is not uncommon for presidents to try and establish international affairs as the centrepiece of their administrations. Foreign policy can provide a refuge from domestic factionalism and a way of rising above politics by exploiting the disjunction in the American constitution that limits a president at home, while providing him with generous emergency powers and executive prerogatives in the hazardous area of international relations.

The nationalist card, however, has by no means been confined to the field of foreign policy. The compulsive forces attached to American nationalism are strongly rooted in American ideals and principles. Indeed, it is often observed that America's unanimity on the precepts of liberty, democracy, equality, human rights and the rule of law provides the fundamental cohesion to a highly heterogeneous culture that would otherwise be incapable of generating a national community:

> The United States indeed, virtually alone among nations, found and to some extent still finds its identity not so much in ethnic community or shared historical

> experience as in dedication to a value system; and the reiteration of these values, the repeated proclamation of and dedication to the liberal creed has always been a fundamental element in the cohesion of American society.[112]

While this dedication can be seen as 'an absolute national morality',[113] it does contain within it an extraordinary scope for conflicting interpretations and varying applications. Presidents are normally adept at characterising American foreign policy decisions in terms of America's obligations to its own principles and to its destiny in propagating these principles to the outside world. But presidents have also attempted to exploit the mobilising properties of national ideals to arouse public support for their domestic policies and programmes.

The colouring of domestic issues in nationalist tones can take the form of an association of a domestic policy either with military terminology (e.g. 'war on poverty', 'war on drugs') or with an ultimate pay-off for national security. Occasionally, presidents have used their national and public prominence to instil a direct linkage between national instinct and social policy. No recent president was more proficient at channelling the nationalist potential for political mobilisation into internal affairs than Ronald Reagan. Reagan sought to fuse together what was a conventional technique of using national security anxieties to expand America's military capability, with a radical strategy of using these same nationalist drives to reduce the level of central government inside the United States. Reagan attempted to generate a national revival, in which America's armed forces would be built up by central government at the same time that Reagan would be leading a crusade against the government's domestic presence. Reagan used his position at the centre of the state to evoke a traditionally American and libertarian response to the state. He encouraged his countrymen to give maximum expression to their ancient anti-statist impulses. Reagan hoped that America could recover its lost sense of national confidence by returning to that laissez-faire posture which had coincided with America's rise as a world power.[114]

Reagan's attempt to fuse his own programme of tax and expenditure cuts with a nationalist fervour, that might best express itself through an insurgency against the abstraction of government, was remarkably successful during the early part of his presidency. It was also a strategy that was thoroughly consistent with the maintenance of media attention upon the president and with Reagan's own brand of spatial leadership. In fact, it was often difficult to discern whether national sentiment was used in the service of a campaign against the state, or whether Reagan's antipathy towards 'government' was a device to fuel his national revival. It could even be contended that both were used as the best available means by which to sustain a position of 'spatial leadership' in the modern system of American government. Whatever the true position, the mass media gave him the opportunity and the tools to engage in a dual appeal to mass temperament. In the past, modern presidents had generally sought to depress the raw anti-statist prejudices of American nationalism in favour of a national democracy and a positive state. Ronald Reagan set out to use his considerable skills in popular communication to unleash America's primal drives against the state in a sustained display of patriotic emotion and national self-assertion. Reagan was able to combine the portrayal of himself as a national archetype with the unique national symbolism of his office and, thereupon, to equate the display of his own convictions with that of an authentic national spirit. He urged his audience to recognise that it was his ideals that had made America into a nation. Americans are not averse to their presidents taking upon themselves the task of revealing the inner light of their national idealism. Reagan was not averse to using this licence to define America's moral self-image along the lines of a public philosophy of national liberation – even from its own government.

Even after Reagan had reached the limits of public consent on the issue of the positive state's diminishment, he was still able to marshal popular support for his presidency by virtue of his appeal to national sentiment. His successor, George Bush, continued with the same tactic. He came under attack for the drift in domestic policy and for his opposition to the growth in government expenditure. And yet at the same time he also successfully appealed to America's sense of patriotism, first over the Panamanian invasion and then over the Gulf War. The spectacular victory against Iraq was not just a vindication of Bush's leadership. As Bush himself was swift to point out, it represented nothing less than a national revival that would finally allow America to recover from the trauma it had suffered in South-east Asia during the late 1960s and early 1970s. 'By God, we've kicked the Vietnam syndrome once and for all',[115] declared a jubilant President Bush after the liberation of Kuwait. As the president's public approval rating soared to unprecedented levels,[116] Bush was made acutely conscious of the political force of American nationalism when it is uninhibited and fixed upon a particular success. As president, he had sound political reasons to ruminate publicly about national pride. In the afterglow of Operation Desert Storm against Iraq, Bush said, 'I sense there is something noble and majestic about patriotism in this country now.'[117] Given this groundswell of American national fervour and the president's capacity to express and symbolise the nation's spirit, Bush emerged from the war with his position so enhanced that even his Democratic opponents conceded that his re-election in two years' time was practically assured.

Despite these advantages, President Bush did not succeed in securing a second term of office. His successor, Bill Clinton, had outflanked the president on the domestic agenda by implying that the Republicans' foreign policy successes were achieved at the direct expense of presidential attention to economic and social problems. Like many incoming American presidents, Clinton was primarily a domestic politician reared on indigenous concerns and animated by the immediate needs of a public that is always open to the suspicion of being overlooked by the cosmopolitan preoccupations of Washington. And yet, Clinton was no different to any of his predecessors. In spite of the Bush precedent, Clinton became progressively susceptible to the lure of the national leadership in an international context. He became more aware of the opportunities afforded by foreign policy issues to escape from the frustrations of domestic issues, which invariably become enmeshed in a constitutional system geared to checks and balances. It might be said that he gravitated to the international stage in order to withdraw from the gridlock of Washington, or to distract attention from the political effects of his personal misbehaviour. It is probably fairer to say that, like most presidents, Clinton found that the role of foreign policy leader most closely approximated to the resources and opportunities at his disposal in the office. This dimension permits a president to substantiate his claims of being a centre of national unity. It is during times of international crisis that a president's position as an expression of national ideals can be decisively enhanced.

Clinton's predicament as the first post-cold war president placed him in the uncharted ambiguity of being the leader of the only remaining superpower, but without the urgency of a global threat to act as a stimulus or rationale for action, or even for a sense of identity. In one sense, the United States was the triumphant model of the 'end of history'. It was the progenitor and inspiration of a set of Western values that were now seen as universal. In another sense, the United States had not resolved the 'Vietnam syndrome' and remained more cautious than ever over the licence it had acquired for the projection of military power. Clinton was able to summon up national pride over the expanding reach of the American economy and over the Americanised process of democratisation in Eastern Europe and the former Soviet Union. Nevertheless, he found it difficult to translate economic and cultural hegemony into public support for American involvement in regional crises. Just as Clinton increasingly found himself engaged in foreign policy issues, so he experienced an ever greater need to appeal to American notions of moral obligations and national mission in order to target public attention and support to the succession of discrete crises that had come to characterise the post-cold war arena. As early as 1995, Clinton's indictment of Bush as a foreign policy president and his promise to concentrate exclusively upon

American problems at home had become a distant memory. At the end of 1995, with his domestic agenda and his Democratic party in ruins, Clinton travelled to Europe to embark 'on a victory tour of diplomatic achievements',[118] the climax of which would be the formal signing of the Bosnian peace agreement. Martin Walker observed that Clinton 'look[ed] strangely like the man George Bush had wanted to be: a president visibly confident of reelection, facing a parade of unconvincing campaign rivals, presiding over the world's healthiest economy and above all, the very embodiment of global leadership'.[119] Walker concluded: 'If the concept of a superpower meant anything, it defined a state with the ability to choose to intervene for the sake of its preferences. And by this test, in Haiti and Bosnia, in Ukraine and in the Baltic, in the Middle East and in Ulster, Clinton had usually, if belatedly, justified his office.'[120]

Four years later, when the president was confronted with the need to institute a campaign for public support over the Kosovo crisis, Clinton once again drew upon the president's prerogative obligations: 'I have a responsibility as President to deal with problems such as this before they do permanent harm to our national interests.'[121] In announcing a bombing campaign against Serbian forces in Kosovo and Serbia itself, the president reassured his national audience that by taking action the United States was fulfilling a historic role. Clinton quoted from Franklin Roosevelt's final address: 'We as Americans do not choose to deny our responsibilities.'[122] He continued: 'By acting now we are upholding our values ... and advancing the cause of peace.'[123] Clinton's rallying cry was a fusion of the president's claims to interpret the national interest and also to give voice to the theme of American exceptionalism as a nation with a unique purpose: 'Ending this tragedy is a moral imperative.'[124]

THE THATCHERITE CLAIM OF THE BRITISH PAST

There is no sense in which British nationalism is comparable to the legendary patriotic fervour of the United States. This being so, a British prime minister does not have the same potential for eliciting nationalist drives or for embodying the spirit of the nation. By contrast, a 'president is such a constant presence in the nation's consciousness, that the nation is subject to mood swings as a result of the ups and downs of his performance'.[125] Apart from such extreme conditions as World War II, prime ministers cannot hope to emulate the symbolic and emotive properties of America's nationally elected office. In British politics, it has always been dangerously unconventional to risk the presumption of identifying political leadership and the allegiance to it directly with the nation's interest and purpose. According to the British political tradition, prime ministers are expected to be the main representatives of the national government, not to be the personification of the nation itself. Any effort by a party leader to unite the nation by claiming it for his or her own had always risked dividing the nation and undermining his or her own position of leadership. Margaret Thatcher's premiership represented a departure from this tradition. She attempted to use her position in a way very similar to President Reagan's usage of the presidency. She sought to project herself and her office as an embodiment of national principles and values. This extended a lot further than rousing appeals to British industry to improve its international performance or to a loose symbolic usage of the Union Jack. It was a concerted policy to identify the Thatcher programme with the essence of Britain itself. Thatcher consistently sought to identify her values of individual freedom, hard work and courage as native British qualities and to denote her opponents' values as alien, false and divisive.

In this guise, Margaret Thatcher tried to make her economic reforms into the equivalent of a national revival, in which Britain could be construed as returning to that authentic state which had once given rise to an empire. The prime minister promoted her radical programme on the radical ground that Thatcherism would integrate the people into a nation at one with its origins. To Mrs Thatcher, the Falklands War had evident connotations with the state of British society and the economic challenges of the 1980s. In her eyes, Britain's victory demonstrated the fact that modern Britain could still emulate the achievements of its forebears. The same determination and willpower could release the same inspiring national spirit of the original empire builders. The war characterised the possibilities and promise of national will, both in the South Atlantic and at home, where Mrs Thatcher was engaged in another war of liberation. The spirit of the South Atlantic was regularly invoked by the prime minister to lend inspiration and legitimacy to her economic vision through which Britain would reclaim itself:

> The battle of the South Atlantic was not won by ignoring the dangers or denying the risks. It was achieved by men and women who had no illusions about the difficulties. They faced them squarely and were determined to overcome them. That is increasingly the mood of Britain. And that's why the rail strike won't do. What has indeed happened is that now, once again, Britain is not prepared to be pushed around. We have ceased to be a nation in retreat. We have instead a new-found confidence – born in the economic battles at home and tested and found true 8,000 miles away. That confidence comes from the rediscovery of ourselves, and grows with the recovery of our self-respect.[126]

Margaret Thatcher's attempt to mobilise the public around the idea of the nation was particularly reflected in her habitual use of national history to validate her positions. Like Ronald Reagan's, Thatcher's deployment of history was erratic and eclectic, but it was used with the same purpose in mind – to convey a sense that Thatcherism offered a process of revitalisation upon which Britain depended for its continuity as a nation. The prime minister promoted her radical programme on the radical ground that Thatcherism would integrate the people into a nation at one again with its own rediscovered nature. In this context, socialism and collectivism were denounced not just for being wrong or misguided, but as national aberrations that had made Britain deviate from its true course. Margaret Thatcher's numerous and varied references to Britain's Saxon origins and Norman ancestry, to Magna Carta and the Glorious Revolution, and to common law, Protestant individualism and the empire of free-born Englishmen were all geared to the same end of proving that Britain has one all-embracing national tradition.[127]

According to Sarah Benton's study of Margaret Thatcher's speeches, the prime minister sought to appeal 'over the conflict to the "spirit of Britain"',[128] which she always presupposed to be unified in nature: 'Her resolution of all conflict was to deny that it existed. Her history of democracy in Britain admitted of no fights, no opposition ... History in fact abolished politics. There is only one truth, and we have access to it through our "hearts" and "instincts".'[129] The alleged unity of British history and national life afforded Margaret Thatcher the prospect of acquiring a status that is more commonly associated with the American presidency. In the United States, the president is not merely in a good position to present a public philosophy.[130] It is that the very centrality and enriched national symbolism of the office arouses a historical consciousness of American society and evokes a belief in the existence of a public philosophy.

It is of course harder for a prime minister to establish both the office and the policies of the chief executive at the centre of some mainstream national consciousness. While 'Americanness' has always been closely tied to the theme of national principles and ideals, Britain has not generally been regarded as a moral concept in its own right, or as a solid entity of timeless and unifying values. Indeed, 'the notion of a public purpose is alien to ... [Britain's] political class'.[131] The Whig tradition of historiography has certainly encouraged the British to value their political institutions of constitutional monarchy and parliamentary government as the culmination of a particular historical process. But the tradition has also encouraged the British to take their political institutions for granted. They are seen as being so self-evident and beyond reproach that they have become a silent substitute for the self-conscious doctrines associated with the rise of European nationalism. Political leaders have generally not sought to claim proprietorship of British nationalism for party gain. This is partly because of the traditional idea that Britain has no need of continental nationalist stimulants, bearing in mind that its unwritten constitution presupposes a fundamental unity. It is also partly because of the intuitive deterrent against using Britain and its history for explicitly political purposes for fear of opening up its course and development to damaging dispute. Notwithstanding these customary inhibitions, Mrs Thatcher immersed herself in national stories and symbols in an effort to project her programme and her office above party politics and doctrinaire divisions, into the transcendent realm of the national spirit. She tried to reawaken the national dimension to British liberty; she tried to root it explicitly in a national epic; and she tried to raise the public's consciousness over Britain's political institutions and traditions by engaging in an uninhibited celebration of them as the touchstone of British exceptionalism.

'NO, NO, NO': THE POLITICS OF EUROPEAN DEFIANCE

It is entirely consistent with this nationalistic style of leadership that Margaret Thatcher should have appreciated the advantages of resisting European integration. She had projected British nationalism as the spirit and content of her programme, and as the basis of her authority to move beyond party towards a national philosophy. As a consequence, Margaret Thatcher reacted to the prospect of enforced European integration as any professional politician would be expected to respond to such a challenge to her political resources. She was fortunate in that she was able to respond exactly in the manner that suited her leadership style. She was combative, solitary, righteous and outnumbered – a symbolic recollection of the nation's greatest modern myth of standing alone and at bay in 1940. In defending British sovereignty, she made it clear that 'you have to identify with something which has been part of your life, part of your experience, your memory, your ceremony, your culture'.[132] This defiant position not only matched her temperament, but was consistent with her crusade against socialism. This time the threat of state collectivism came from without. It was fuelled by Europeans who, in Margaret Thatcher's view, were seeking to reduce British sovereignty and compromise Britain's newly reclaimed national integrity by what she regarded as backdoor attempts to impose a European agenda of state-centred social and economic development. In the face of such provocation, she adopted her preferred role of outsider set, on this occasion, against foreign governments and Eurobureaucracy.

In her celebrated address to the College of Europe at Bruges on 20 September 1988, she openly distanced herself from the developing consensus on the subject of European integration. She warned that Europe must not become 'ossified by endless regulation'.[133] She went on: 'We have not successfully rolled back the frontiers of the state in Britain only to see them reimposed at a European level, with a European super-state exercising a new dominance from Brussels.'[134] For a leader with Margaret Thatcher's grasp of populist politics, she was well aware that what she might lose in party unity with such views, she would gain in personal stature as an expression of Britain's widespread anxiety over European integration. She knew how to tap the largely silent groundswell against the EEC in a country of largely reluctant Europeans. Although 'the nature and the ultimate sources of British national awareness remain obscure',[135] the British do know enough about themselves to be sensitive over the idea of Britain being progressively diminished by a distant and anonymous supranational entity.[136] Margaret Thatcher, who aspired to the presidential posture as the voice of the nation, was even prepared to jeopardise her entire administration to preserve her access to the public prejudices aroused by this issue. Her heightened sense of nation and her willingness and capacity to project it were central not just to her own self-image, and to the spirit of her political programme, but to her whole conception of the prime minister's role.

RUNNING DOWN THE THATCHER–REAGAN NARRATIVE

Ronald Reagan's appeal to Americans has often been attributed to his ability to tell stories. According to Ellen Reid Gold,

> What he developed over the years was a great cultural narrative incorporating fundamental American myths, orally transmitting the Horatio Alger vision of striving and succeeding, the Frederick Jackson Turner notion of the western frontier as the birthplace of individualism and democratic ideals, George Bancroft's version of American history, and 'epic of liberty', and Mark Twain's depiction of Americans as sturdy originals … Reagan's genius lay in his ability to establish a close relationship with his audiences and his ability to select vivid and compelling themes which spoke clearly to the deep-felt feelings of contemporary Americans … Like the old epics, Reagan's discourse is enriched with narratives, an easy-to-remember form which incorporates abstract ideals into a concrete form.[137]

Margaret Thatcher's style of leadership was very similar. She also 'made up stories … to tell the people their history', implying that she herself represented 'the essence of British values'[138] and was, therefore, uniquely positioned to tell the truth about Britain to the British. Both their successors were either unwilling or unable to conjure up the same sense of national identity in their own persons. Nevertheless, both George Bush and John Major were highly conscious of the extent to which the cultural identities of their respective countries are dependent upon the integrity of their nation's political principles and governing arrangements. Both of them were aware that the leadership appeal of their predecessors was rooted in a form of nationalist reaction against the onset of a world of increasing economic interdependence, international mass culture and diminishing national sovereignty.[139] The nationalism of Thatcher and Reagan was a form of cultural defiance. It acknowledged the progressive development of the international economy and the globalisation of political issues, but it also gave expression to the impulsive drives of national sentiment and communal resentment against the prospect of economic decline and limited national autonomy.

To a large extent, George Bush was able to replace Reagan's oral tradition of national celebration with an actual military victory in the Gulf War. John Major was also able to enjoy what was called at the time the British army's 'last adventure'. But in contrast to Bush, Major remained part of a political culture that is much more ambivalent over the political uses of nationalism. Even though the prime minister's personal reputation was enormously enhanced by the Gulf War, he had to give every impression of not exploiting the war for political gain. The political kudos and patriotic glow gained from the Gulf quickly evaporated in the prolonged and divisive controversy over the Maastricht Treaty and in the expensive chaos surrounding Britain's humiliating withdrawal from the ERM. The problems of exploiting national pride for political leadership were continually exacerbated both by Britain's need to remain in the European Union and by its traditional suspicions over the processes and politics of European integration. Major was persistently confronted by the dynamics of an issue that presented in stark form a dilemma between the populist drives of national identity and sovereignty, and the prudent attachment to the nation's economic interest in addressing the practicalities of international interdependency and progressive co-operation. Bill Clinton was able to accept the economic logic of the United States' membership of the North American Free Trade Agreement without having his national allegiance called into question. Major, on the other hand, was confronted with a process of regional integration that he felt unable to control and that threatened either to marginalise or to absorb Britain as a national entity. Like Reagan and Thatcher before him, Major tried to exert a nationalism of cultural defiance by evoking the spirit of the 1950s. By way of his leadership, he offered the security of his childhood England: 'long shadows on county grounds, warm beer, invincible green suburbs, dog lovers and old maids bicycling to holy communion through the morning mist'.[140] The problems for Major's vision of a future based upon a nostalgia for the past were that too many people believed the country was already stuck in the past and that Major's past did not have a sufficiently high recognition factor or cultural anchorage to be turned into a political movement. After eighteen years of Conservative radicalism and free market iconoclasm, Major found it difficult to operationalise a Tory affection for the past in ways that could avoid the simplistic xenophobia of Eurosceptics. His fragile substitute of a fundamentalist defence of the British constitution, combined with a wistful celebration of a suburban belle epoch, was crushed by Tony Blair's juggernaut of modernisation.

NEW LABOUR, NEW BRITAIN

At first sight, Blair's premiership could be construed as a departure from the use of national traditions and nationalist themes in the service of political leadership. Blair wished to distance himself from Thatcher's insular and negative conception of Britain as a necessarily non-European entity and from Major's nostalgic evocation of a Britain set in the 1950s. Blair was more unequivocally internationalist than either of his two Conservative predecessors. This found expression in the customary meetings of the leaders of the European socialist parties but much more significantly in Blair's advocacy of a deeper and more influential engagement in Europe. At the same time, the prime minister was committed to a policy of devolution that would not only provide a political outlet for Scottish and Welsh national identity, but would constitute a further threat to the status and authority of the British government.

And yet notwithstanding the apparent emphasis upon the sub-national and the supranational in these positions and outlooks, Blair was fervently attached to the instrumental and substantive dimensions of Britain's nationhood as a force in contemporary politics. He had repeatedly conjoined New Labour with the notion of a new Britain during the long campaign for office. He had insisted that his purpose was to respond to popular patriotism and to give it a new identity. He wanted Britain to be a 'young country again … [w]ith ideals we cherish and live up to. Not resting on past glories. Not fighting old battles. Not sitting back, hand on mouth, concealing a yawn of cynicism, but ready for the day's challenge. Ambitious. Idealistic. United.'[141] In his second speech as leader to the Labour party conference (1995), he employed a civic theme that was comparable to that used by President Kennedy in his inaugural address. Blair exhorted the nation to be an idealistic and cohesive entity where 'people succeed on the basis of what they give to their country, rather than what they take from their country. Saying not "This was a great country" but "Britain can and will be a great country again".'[142] Just as the objective of a New Britain helped to define and to market the New Labour project, so Blair's subsequent authority as prime minister was often supported by claims of a mandate to engage in a radical transformation of the country. As the British premier, Blair has increasingly used 'nation' and 'community' as interchangeable terms.

Community has 'changed from having a class to a one-nation meaning'.[143] As a consequence, 'when Blair talks of community ... he does not mean working class community, but the whole nation, all included, with a common purpose'.[144]

At one level, Blair's vision of a young country took the form of giving recognition to the contribution made to British society and to the national economy by individuals of creative talent who had achieved critical acclaim in a variety of sectors and markets (e.g. media, music, fashion, design, advertising, film, computer software, retailing). Blair sought to give new emphasis to new excellence. The rebranding exercise of 'Cool Britannia' took on a variety of expressions, from the plan to make the Anglo-French summit (November 1997) at Canary Wharf into a showcase for British interior design, to Number 10's open courting of figures from popular culture such as Noel Gallagher, Jeremy Irons, Kevin Keegan, Mick Hucknall, Ben Elton and Glenn Hoddle. Blair's objective was to publicise individual successes as exemplars of an emergent Britain in the process of formation. Creative talents and skills were already making Britain different to what it had been in the past. The Labour government set itself the task of maximising such national resources and of projecting those elements of the 'New Britain' that were already present and functioning effectively.

At another and more significant level Blair was committed actively to changing Britain. He was aware that the country and its economy had a negative image abroad, and that its own inhabitants had a weakening faith in British institutions and an eroded sense of what being British stood for.[145] Blair wanted to summon up Britain's national strengths and values in order to facilitate a transition to a national resurgence in which Britain's sense of itself would shift away from the closed categories of the past to be replaced with a modern, plural, inclusive and open-textured identity. Blair used the analogy of the Labour party itself. During the party's modernisation process, Labour values were said to have remained the same while the methods of their application had changed in the light of contemporary conditions. Modernisation allowed the party to return to its principles 'freed from the weight of outmoded ideology'.[146] Blair's objective of a 'New Britain' would follow the same format. An outmoded conception of British national identity would be challenged and displaced by another construction of Britain's role in the world. It would fuse the principles of the past with the contingencies and needs of the present. New Labour would not only be the inspiration and model, but also the active agency in securing and legitimising this new sense of nationality. In Blair's view, it is because people 'love this country that they look to Labour to change it'.[147]

Devolution, to Blair, was the opposite of nationalism because, in allowing a form of decentralisation, it would improve citizenship, increase political participation, strengthen the decision-making process, and make the UK into a stronger, more confident and less internally distracted country. In the past, Britain's identity had been based upon a dynamic rather than static relationship between its constituent elements. Devolution provided a renewed recognition of this process of mutual adjustment. To Blair, it was not something to be feared so much as a positive step to be accepted as part of Britain's historical continuity. New Labour's similarly positive approach to Europe was cast in the same light of making adjustments not merely to defend the national interest but to maintain Britain's national integrity by accepting evolutionary change and by recasting the nation's image and position in the EU. Since the future was seen to lie in Europe, then the modernisation of Britain's national identity would have to draw on the need for greater European engagement and integration.

Instead of seeing devolution and the Europe Union as the twin centrifugal forces condemning Britain and its political structure to dissolution, New Labour took them to be both the signs and the instruments of a necessary process of modernisation. During his rise to power, one of Blair's key principles had been that a 'government of national renewal require[d] a national renewal of government'.[148] Once in government, it was Blair's presence and leadership at the centre that gave reassurance to a society, noted for its constitutional caution and European scepticism, that change was not only plausible but beneficial. The implication of New Labour's extraordinary electoral success was that its own organisational modernisation gave it the technical and conceptual authority to administer the modernisation of Britain. The subtext was that exceptional leadership and vision would ensure the continuation of national confidence in British exceptionalism. Instead of mistrust and retreat, New Labour aimed to define a more forward-looking identity that was consciously open to outside experiences and alternative points of reference.

The reconfiguration of Britain has been an integral part of New Labour's political project to demonstrate that there is no necessary equation between 'Britishness', anti-Europeanism and constitutional changelessness. Change to the nation and to its self-image is conceived as being more of a virtue than a vice. The New Labour perspective is one in which Britain has the potential to create a 'unique pluralist democracy where diversity becomes a source of strength', allowing the nation to emerge as the 'first country in the world that can be a multicultural, multi-ethnic and multinational state'.[149] As constitutional reform has proceeded, the figure of Tony Blair has served as the centrepiece not only to signifying the altered state of the nation's institutions, but to personifying the shift in the nation's consciousness of its own changing character. This was exemplified in Blair's dramatic acknowledgement of the British government's role in the Irish potato famine of 1845–49. 'Those who governed in London at the time', Blair admitted, 'failed their people through standing by while a crop failure turned into a massive human tragedy.'[150] Even though Blair's intervention was not, strictly speaking, an apology, it nevertheless was an example of a prime minister who, in the cause of the Irish peace process, felt impelled to assume the nation's historic conscience and convey its moral debt.

BLAIR AND THE PREROGATIVES OF NATIONAL SYMBOLISM

Another dimension of national expression that was solicited by Blair is related to his presidential presumption to speak and act on behalf of the British nation. In many respects, Blair has been no different from his predecessors in invoking authority to define the national interest, to use executive discretion to make decisions, and to rally public opinion around themes of national unity and common concerns. But in other respects, it can be claimed that Blair has acted in a context of melting boundaries and disrupted hierarchies to provide a national point of reference that at times has appeared to be almost indistinguishable from that of a head of state. Instead of being merely a derivative of the crown in exercising executive prerogative, Blair's acute sense of public mood and his ability to articulate it has on occasion given him a status which, while differently grounded, has impinged upon the monarchy's social prominence and state function. This is not to say that Blair has consciously aspired to appropriate the monarchical role of the Royal Family. It is to point out that the expectations and energies of the Blair premiership have had sufficient political and social ramifications even for the monarchy's areas of traditional centrality to come under pressure.

Many factors have been at work in the monarchy's discomfiture. An ageing Queen, with no intention of abdicating in favour of her son and whose symbolic and historical associations were oriented to the British Empire and to the Commonwealth, essentially represented the past at a time when Britain's traditions were under assault from an allegedly belated process of modernisation. The Royal Family's predicament was made worse by its inability to project itself as a model of family life and Christian morality, owing to a succession of exposures, scandals and divorces. After the 1997 general election, the monarchy was suddenly confronted by the first Labour government in eighteen years. The contrast between the respective images of the monarchy and the new prime minister was made immediately apparent at the State Opening of Parliament two weeks after the general election. Tony and Cherie Blair decided to walk from Number 10 to the Palace of

Westminster, in order to portray a government intent upon breaking with tradition in the campaign to modernise Britain:

> On a day usually dominated by Parliamentary tradition and pomp, it is a powerful reminder that Blair is a new-broom Prime Minister determined to govern in a different way. [Alastair] Campbell knows that television news editors will have no choice but to juxtapose the image of an energetic and youthful Blair against the staid pageantry of Black Rod and the Serjeant at Arms. Blair on walkabout versus the Queen in her gilded coach.[151]

It was clear that the senior ranks of the Royal Family were confronted with a young dynamic prime minister, who was animated by a new future in Europe, by the need to give political recognition to the national identities of Scotland and Wales, and by an emphasis upon populist insurgency and cultural informality. He was the leader of a party whose programme included the reform of the House of Lords that entailed a direct assault upon the hereditary principle and with it palpable implications for the monarchy. It was known that Blair was close to Prince Charles and to Diana Princess of Wales, both of whom wished to modernise the monarchy – albeit in different ways. Moreover, Blair was an enduringly popular leader who had firm religious convictions, an evangelising political morality and an unequivocal attachment to the family as the primary element of social value.

In many ways, Blair appeared to constitute a counterpoint to the negative connotations of the House of Windsor. In addition to having 'the almost royal ability to represent any number of things at any one time and to inspire loyalty beyond the boundaries of party allegiance',[152] Blair attracted the attention of those who lamented the passing of one-nation Toryism and its connotations of patrician hierarchy. Instead of depending solely on a monarchy that seemed intent upon undermining its own continuity, the advocates of Establishment order and social cohesion looked favourably upon Blair's new magistracy. The prime minister's hauteur, and even arrogance, was a welcome sign to Peregrine Worsthorne of New Labour's intent 'to be its own ruling class and be itself deferred to'.[153] In Worsthorne's view, this represented the revival of a 'thoroughly British style of ruling'.[154] He concluded:

> Just as the old Tory patricians wanted to shape British society according to their own elevated values, rather than to leave them to be shaped exclusively by the free play of market forces, so now, with the same air of effortless superiority, do the New Labour paternalists; and just as the old Tory patricians saw how patriotism ... could mitigate and moderate the disintegrating effects of liberal individualism, so now with the same understanding of statecraft, do the New Labour paternalists.[155]

The High Tory–High Church frisson surrounding Blair's premiership had not gone unobserved at the Palace. After only a short period of the Blair administration, the Palace was reported to be anxious over the pace and direction of change. Specifically, concern was expressed over 'the "presidential style" of the new Prime Minister'.[156] Members of the Queen's inner circle broke their legendary silence to convey the Palace's alarm. They were concerned over the reputed informality of Blair's cabinet meetings, over the casual dress sense of the 'denim premier', over the number of political advisors brought into government, and over the media projection of Cherie Blair as the 'first lady' and the whole Blair family as a kind of 'first family'.[157] The problem was encapsulated by the Blairs' walkabout at the State Opening of Parliament in May 1997. Courtiers explained their concern to the *Express on Sunday*: 'It was supposed to be the State Opening of Parliament, not the State Opening of the Labour Government',[158] asserted one Palace source. Another source discerned a clear American influence: 'Mr Blair seems to be leading the Government more in the style of President Bill Clinton than the style we are accustomed to in this country. The change is obvious to the man in [*sic*] the Clapham omnibus and we have noticed it too.'[159] It was seen to be intrusive and contrary to protocol: 'Constitutionally, the Queen is at the head of society and the position is not open to question. The Prime Minister is head of the political part of society, and not the head of society. That is an important and intrinsic part of the monarchy.'[160]

Like New Labour, the monarchy was highly attuned to the power of symbolism and public ceremony and was, therefore, aware of the meaning of the Blairs' flouting of tradition and protocol. The changes introduced by Blair to the structure and style of government were important in their own right, but they were also significant for giving the impression of a disjunction between the past and present in what was formally Her Majesty's Government. The problematic nature of this disrupted relationship between prime minister and monarch was painfully revealed in the week following the fatal accident of Diana Princess of Wales in August 1997. '[I]t was Blair, not Queen Elizabeth II as head of state, who defined the country's grief and gave voice to the loss many in Britain were feeling.'[161] Blair was also instrumental in changing the Palace's public reaction to Diana's death and in fundamentally altering the organisation of the funeral to reflect the public outcry over the tragedy. It was Blair who redesignated Diana as the 'people's princess'[162] and worked behind the scenes to protect the Royal Family from its lack of public response and to exert pressure for a more publicly minded funeral. The occasion typified the co-existence of a prime minister with new and potent sources of authority with an experienced monarch who was no longer so assured of her own political judgement and constitutional anchorage in a swiftly changing context. Tony Blair's advocacy of large-scale constitutional reform and a 'new politics' could be seen as redefining the basis of the state and, therefore, the Queen's relationship to it. By the same token, his emphasis upon social consensus and the assimilative properties of New Labour's 'big tent' could be construed as a prime minister moving inexorably to a position of speaking not simply *for* society, but *as* society.

THE PRIME MINISTERIAL VISION OF BRITAIN'S NATIONAL MISSION

Finally, Blair has been placed in a situation where his stature at home has been translated into positions of conspicuous leadership abroad. Like all prime ministers, he has represented Britain in international negotiations and at collective meetings of heads of government. Nevertheless, Blair has experienced a proportionally higher profile in representing the nation and its interests in international contexts than many of his peacetime predecessors. This is not solely due to the rising incidence of European and G8 summitry that makes enormous contributions to the visibility of leaders. Some factors relate to circumstantial events, such as Britain's presidency of the EU soon after Blair's election victory. Other factors relate to circumstantial points in political cycles, such as the fortuitous combination of developments that led to Blair becoming the youngest and newest high profile Western leader at the very outset of his premiership. From merely representing his country, Blair quickly assumed the role of providing British leadership to overseas allies and to international organisations. Whether it was his advocacy of a 'third way' to European social democrats, or his forceful intervention to replace Jacques Santer with Romano Prodi as President of the European Commission following allegations of financial mismanagement, or the political support offered in Washington to a president mired in impeachment proceedings and a crisis over Iraq, Blair became an international figure whose leadership credentials commanded widespread respect.

In February 1998, Blair announced his long-term plan to place New Labour at the head of a worldwide movement of ideas that would aim to create a centre-left consensus for the twenty-first century.[163] He had no doubt that by becoming a model nation for the new century, Britain could be a 'beacon shining throughout the world'.[164] Blair was unequivocal that his vision of a 'post-Empire Britain' was to 'make this country pivotal, a leader in the world'.[165] Britain would rediscover its history. This would reveal that for 'four centuries or more, we have been a leading power in Europe'.[166] His task was to revive that tradition and to be instrumental in the construction of a 'people's Europe'.[167] In articulating his themes and in mobilising support for them, Blair conspicuously invoked British principles and values. He drew attention to their instructive utility and the contribution they could make in an international dimension. New Labour's guiding theme had been the modernisation of Britain. By the same token, Blair's impulse was to use his position so that Britain could modernise Europe and the foreign policy objectives of the West in the post-cold war world.

This adopted role was most noticeable during the Kosovo crisis, when Blair assumed such a formidable leadership role that many senior figures in Washington referred to him as the 'NATO leader'. At a time when the authority of President Clinton had been undermined by sex scandals and when NATO's credibility and even future existence were at stake, it was Blair who provided the alliance with direction and drive. He underlined the need to include the threat of ground forces in a strategy that was in danger of drifting into ineffectiveness. At the end of April 1999, in what was originally planned as a gala to celebrate NATO's fiftieth anniversary but which was hastily transformed into a NATO council of war, it was Blair's leadership that provided the injection of resolve both in public action and in private negotiation. The meeting occasioned what Ed Vulliamy and Patrick Wintour described as Blair's 'most remarkable 48 hours since becoming Prime Minister'.[168] Their reasons for reaching such an assessment were as follows:

> Blair single-handedly ensured the possibility of the West fighting a ground war against Milosevich's Serbia remained on the NATO agenda, in the face of Clinton's reservations and the outright opposition of other countries. Blair found himself not only pushing the Clinton Administration but working behind the scenes to win over the more sceptical leaders from France, Germany and others. And in by far the most uncompromising speech by any leader ... recalling the language of Churchill, Blair said that to stop ethnic cleansing in Kosovo would be 'the best memorial' to NATO's half-century.[169]

At the outset of this critical juncture in the Western alliance, Blair's personal address to the British people referred to the moral imperative of having to react to the ethnic cleansing being undertaken by Serb forces in Kosovo. 'Act or do nothing' was the stark choice. 'Do nothing and Milosevic will feel free to do as he likes with the civilian population. They will be ground under his heel at the very moment when these poor defenceless people are begging us to show strength and determination.'[170] To ignore the plight of 'our fellow human beings' would constitute 'unpardonable weakness and dereliction. That is not the tradition of Britain.'[171] It was a situation that required the assertion of simple truths conveyed by clear-sighted leadership: 'We are doing what is right for Britain, for Europe, for a world that must know that barbarity cannot be allowed to defeat justice. This is simply the right thing to do.'[172] During his visit to the Stankovich I refugee camp in Macedonia, Blair's attachment to British liberal traditions was reflected in his affirmation that the military action was motivated by a concerted regard for human rights: 'This is not a battle for Nato, this is not a battle for territory, this is a battle for humanity. It is a just cause.'[173]

In later statements, Blair elaborated upon the need for the specific circumstances of Kosovo to define a more general response to the balance between individual sovereignty and universal human rights. The 'Blair Doctrine' invited serious consideration to be given to a new framework in which the sovereignty of nations would no longer be accepted as a protective device to shield regions engaged in internal repression or ethnic cleansing. Globalisation to Blair meant that the strategic interests and national security of each state were now integrally connected to one another. If one state were to engage in the deportation of entire ethnic groups, it would have a serious effect on the security of the immediate region, the stability of the surrounding regions and, ultimately, on the equilibrium of the international community. As a consequence, Blair asserted that the international community had a stake in the conduct of other nations: 'Acts of genocide can never be a purely internal matter. When oppression produces massive flows of refugees which unsettle neighbouring countries then they can properly be described as "threats to international peace and security".'[174] In starting with ascribed British traditions, Blair had moved to an assertive derivative of British traditions in the form of a 'new internationalism'. British values would be central in defining the moral and military purposes of future humanitarian interventions by Western governments.

For a Labour prime minister, Blair's internationalism has no basis in the universal themes of socialism or in the traditions of trade union struggle and working-class consciousness. He has often been accused of exploiting Conservative devices of national celebration for maintaining political support in the same way that New Labour expropriated the Union Jack in the 1997 general election. It has been said many times that Blair makes better conservative speeches than the leader of the Conservative party. On a superficial level, this can be seen as a case of a Labour leader protecting his flanks and his radical programme from the debilitating effects of charges of national betrayal. On a more substantive level, it reflects the incentives and drives of contemporary leadership in locating and maximising currents of support that will not only sustain but advance the leader and his vision.

All effective United States presidents have known that mobilising American society for the future is best achieved by successfully alluding to the past, usually through the use of high rhetoric commemorating national values and social solidarity. Like Thatcher before him, Blair was aware of the radical properties of national appeal. 'I believe in Britain. I believe in the British people',[175] declared Blair in his first address to the party as Labour prime minister. 'One cross on the ballot paper, one nation was reborn.'[176] His task of building a model nation would mean 'drawing deep into the richness of the British character'.[177] Just as New Labour had drawn on Labour values to create a new entity, so a new Britain would be formed from British materials: 'Old British values but a new British confidence'.[178] Blair was not simply trying to co-opt nationalist objections to his project. He was engaged in a concerted attempt to draw British history and identity away from the proprietary presumptions of the Conservative party. He wanted to make Britain a contested category that would be susceptible to a left-of-centre construction in the service of radical purposes.

A number of anomalies were clearly implicit in working with such a theme. Devolution in response to ancient Celtic drives on the periphery sat uneasily with the idea of national renewal as an open-ended process of European integration. Notwithstanding the problematic nature of these distinctions, Blair was wholly unable to resist the theme of British nationhood as a leadership resource in a political system that was becoming demonstrably more fragmented both in terms of party dealignment and constitutional structure. Indeed, far from resisting it, Blair was impelled towards the medium of Britain's national distinction within a democratic polity. He used it to advance his leadership as an expression of national community, as a stabilising centre amid rapid change and as a method of acquiring alternative sources of leverage and authority in an otherwise compressed and inhibitory context. In sum, he used the nation as a presidential instrument.

Notes

1 Richard E. Neustadt, *Presidential Power: The Politics of Leadership* (New York, Wiley, 1960), p. 10.

2 Neustadt, *Presidential Power* p. 10.

3 James D. Barber, *The Presidential Character: Predicting Performance in the White House* (Englewood Cliffs, Prentice-Hall, 1972), p. 445. See also Michael Nelson, 'The Psychological Presidency', in Michael Nelson (ed.), *The Presidency and the Political System*, 2nd edn (Washington, DC, Congressional Quarterly, 1988), pp. 185–206.

4 See Peter W. Sperlich, 'Bargaining and Overload: An Essay on Presidential Power', in Aaron Wildavsky (ed.), *Perspectives of the Presidency* (Boston, Little Brown, 1975), pp. 406–30; John Hart, 'Presidential Power Revisited', *Political Studies*, 25, no. 1 (March 1977), pp. 48–61; Thomas Cronin, *The State of the Presidency*, 2nd edn (Boston, Little Brown, 1975), ch. 4; Arthur L. George, 'On Analysing Presidents', *World Politics*, 26, no. 2 (1974), pp. 234–89; J. H. Qualls, 'Barber's Typological Analysis of Political Leaders', *American Political Science Review*, 71, no. 1 (March 1977), pp. 182–211.

5 Bert Rockman, *The Leadership Question: The Presidency and the American System* (New York, Praeger, 1984), p. 15.
6 Rockman, *The Leadership Question*, p. 7.
7 For example, see Erwin C. Hargrove, *The President as Leader: Appealing to the Better Angels of our Nature* (Lawrence, University Press of Kansas, 1998).
8 E. C. Hargrove, 'Presidential Personality and Leadership Style', in George C. Edwards III, John H. Kessel and Bert A. Rockman (eds), *Researching the Presidency: Vital Questions* (Pittsburgh, University of Pittsburgh Press, 1993), p. 70.
9 See Hargrove, 'Presidential Personality and Leadership Style', pp. 69–110; Irving Janis, *Victims of Groupthink: A Psychological Study of Foreign Policy Decisions and Fiascoes*, 2nd edn (Boston, Little Brown, 1982); Bruce Mazlish, *In Search of Nixon: A Psychohistorical Inquiry* (New York, Basic, 1972); Doris Kearns, *Lyndon Johnson and the American Dream* (New York, Harper and Row, 1976); Fred I. Greenstein, *The Hidden Hand Presidency: Eisenhower as Leader* (New York, Basic, 1982); John P. Burke and Fred I. Greenstein, 'Presidential Personality and National Security Leadership: A Comparative Analysis of Vietnam Decision-Making', *International Political Science Review*, 10 no. 1 (January 1989), pp. 73–92; Stanley A. Renshon (ed.), *The Clinton Presidency: Campaigning, Governing, and the Psychology of Leadership* (Boulder, Westview, 1995).
10 Theodore Lowi quoted in Hargrove, 'Presidential Personality and Leadership Style', p. 72.
11 Robert Shogan, *The Riddle of Power: Presidential Leadership from Truman to Bush* (New York, Plume, 1992), p. 244.
12 Richard Rose, 'British Government: The Job at the Top', in Richard Rose and Ezra N. Suleiman (eds), *Presidents and Prime Ministers* (Washington, DC, American Enterprise Institute, 1980), p. 44.
13 Rose, 'British Government', p. 44.
14 Dennis Kavanagh, *Thatcherism and British Politics: The End of Consensus?*, 2nd edn (Oxford, Oxford University Press, 1990), p. 244.
15 John Gaffney, *The Language of Political Leadership in Contemporary Britain* (Basingstoke, Macmillan, 1991), p. 11.
16 Edward Pearce, 'Fighter with a golden tongue', *The Guardian*, 26 November 1990.
17 Edward Pearce, 'Cash 'n' carry charisma', *The Guardian*, 26 February 1992.
18 Anthony King, 'Psychic roots' (Review of Bruce Mazlish, *Kissinger: The European Mind in American Politics*), *New Society*, 13 October 1977.
19 Dennis Kavanagh, 'Making Sense of Thatcher', in Dennis Kavanagh, *Politics and Personalities* (Basingstoke, Macmillan, 1990), p. 87.
20 Nelson W. Polsby, *British Government and its Discontents* (New York, Basic, 1981); Andrew Gamble, *Britain in Decline: Economic Policy, Political Strategy and the British State* (London, Macmillan, 1980); Anthony King (ed.), *Why is Britain Becoming Harder to Govern?* (London, British Broadcasting Corporation, 1976); Samuel H. Beer, *Britain Against Itself: The Political Contradictions of Collectivism* (London, Faber, 1982).
21 Anthony King, 'Margaret Thatcher: The Style of a Prime Minister', in Anthony King (ed.), *The British Prime Minister*, 2nd edn (Basingstoke, Macmillan, 1985), p. 118.
22 Kavanagh, 'Making Sense of Thatcher', p. 88.
23 Kavanagh, 'Making Sense of Thatcher', p. 88.
24 Kavanagh, 'Making Sense of Thatcher', p. 88.
25 Kavanagh, 'Making Sense of Thatcher', p. 88.
26 Anthony Seldon, *Major: A Political Life* (London, Phoenix, 1997), p. 738.

27 Quoted in 'My first five years – by John Major', interview with Anthony Seldon, *Daily Telegraph*, 27 November 1995.
28 Quoted in 'My first five years – by John Major'.
29 Peter Riddell, 'Old weaknesses regained', *The Times*, 15 February 1993.
30 BBC2, Newsnight, 3 June 1993.
31 'No more, Prime Minister', *The Sun*, 3 July 1995.
32 John Major, *John Major: The Autobiography* (London, HarperCollins, 1999), p. 616.
33 Quoted in 'My first five years – by John Major'.
34 'Just waiting will not do', *Daily Telegraph*, 4 November 1994.
35 'Just waiting will not do'.
36 William Rees-Mogg, 'Tactics aren't enough to run the country', *The Times*, 8 January 1996.
37 William Rees-Mogg, 'Major fails the leadership test', *The Times*, 10 May 1993.
38 George Walden, *Lucky George: The Memoirs of an Anti-Politician* (London, Allen Lane, 1999), p. 335.
39 The disparaging remark is attributed to Steve Hilton, the 'head of M&C Saatchi's Tory Party account and one of the three most senior strategists in Mr Major's re-election campaign'; see Patrick Wintour, 'Major is a wimp, says Tory strategist', *The Observer*, 9 February 1997.
40 Paul Johnson, quoted in Seldon, *Major: A Political Life*, p. 735.
41 Martin Walker, *Clinton: The President They Deserve*, rev. edn (London, Vintage, 1997), pp. 135–8.
42 Penny Junor, *The Major Enigma* (London, Michael Joseph, 1993).
43 Nesta Wyn Ellis, *John Major* (London, Macdonald, 1991).
44 Bruce Anderson, *John Major: The Making of the Prime Minister* (London, Fourth Estate, 1991).
45 Seldon, *Major: A Political Life*, p. 735.
46 Seldon, *Major: A Political Life*, p. 741.
47 Seldon, *Major: A Political Life*, pp. 738–9.
48 Seldon, *Major: A Political Life*, p. 743. See also Channel 5, *Two Little Boys*, broadcast 23 April 1997; Major, *John Major: The Autobiography* chs 1–4.
49 Quoted in Lesley White, 'New man old boy', *Sunday Times*, 20 April 1997.
50 Quoted in Andrew Marr, 'Two year's hard Labour', *The Independent*, 13 July 1996.
51 Channel 4, *Dispatches*, broadcast 8 May 1997.
52 Simon Jenkins, 'The case of two Blairs', *The Times*, 26 April 1997.
53 David Marquand, 'Blair's split personality', *The Guardian*, 17 July 1997.
54 Marquand, 'Blair's split personality'.
55 For example, see Jenkins, 'The case of two Blairs'.
56 Tony Blair, 'Britain's treatment of cancer just isn't good enough. And I should know ... my mother died from the disease', *Daily Mail*, 20 May 1999.
57 Kevin Toolis, 'The Enforcer', *The Guardian*, 4 April 1998.
58 Cherie Blair even agreed to act as guest editor for a magazine when Tony Blair was leader of the opposition. See *Prima*, October 1996. See also the front-page feature given to the news of Cherie Blair's pregnancy in *Hello*, 30 November 1999.
59 See Alexandra Williams and Cherry Norton, 'All the saints go marching after St Tony', *Sunday Times*, 7 February 1999.
60 See 'The Power List 1999: the 500 most powerful people in Britain', *Sunday Times*, 26 September 1999.

61 'The secret life of John Major', interview with Petronella Wyatt, *Daily Telegraph*, 15 July 1996.
62 For example, see Leo Abse, *Margaret, Daughter of Beatrice: A Politician's Psycho-biography of Margaret Thatcher* (London, Jonathan Cape, 1989).
63 Margaret Thatcher, *The Path to Power* (London, HarperCollins, 1995), p. 566.
64 For example, see Seldon, *Major: A Political Life*; Leo Abse, *The Man Behind the Smile: Tony Blair and the Politics of Perversion* (London, Robson Books, 1996).
65 Andrew Rawnsley, 'Tony Blair's obsession with size', *The Observer*, 14 December 1997.
66 Harvey C. Mansfield, *Taming the Prince: The Ambivalence of Modern Executive Power* (New York, Free Press, 1989), p. 291.
67 Mansfield, *Taming the Prince*, p. 291. See also Edward S. Corwin, *The President: Office and Powers, 1787–1984*, 5th edn (New York, New York University Press, 1984); Louis Henkin, *Foreign Affairs and the Constitution* (Mineola, Foundation, 1972); Michael Foley, *The Silence of Constitutions: Gaps 'Abeyances' and Political Temperament in the Maintenance of Government* (London, Routledge, 1989) chs 3, 5; Louis Fisher, *Constitutional Conflicts between Congress and the President* (Princeton, Princeton University Press, 1985); Christopher H. Pyle and Richard M. Pious (eds), *The President, Congress and the Constitution: Power and Legitimacy in American Politics* (New York, Free Press, 1984).
68 Arthur M. Schlesinger, Jr, *The Imperial Presidency* (London, Andre Deutsch, 1974), p. 275.
69 Harold H. Koh, *The National Security Constitution: Sharing Power After the Iran-Contra Affair* (New Haven, Yale University Press, 1990), p. 204.
70 Ronald Dworkin, 'The wounded constitution', *New York Review of Books*, 18 March 1999.
71 Richard A. Posner, *An Affair of State: The Investigation, Impeachment and Trial of President Clinton* (Cambridge, Harvard University Press, 1999). See also *Presidential Studies Quarterly*, special edition, 'The Clinton Presidency in Crisis', 28, no. 4 (Fall 1998), pp. 754–60, 773–9, 806–15, 816–20, 851–5, 861–86, 898–904.
72 Theodore J. Lowi, 'Presidential Power: Restoring the Balance', *Political Science Quarterly*, 100, no. 2 (Summer 1985), p. 189.
73 Foley, *The Silence of Constitutions*, p. 88.
74 Foley, *The Silence of Constitutions*, p. 89.
75 Simon Jenkins, *Accountable to None: The Tory Nationalization of Britain* (London, Penguin, 1996), p. 9.
76 Jenkins, *Accountable to None*, p. 21.
77 For example, see Nicholas Ridley, *My Style of Government: The Thatcher Years* (London, Hutchinson, 1991); William Whitelaw, *The Whitelaw Memoirs* (London, Aurum, 1989); Norman Fowler, *Ministers Decide: A Memoir of the Thatcher Years* (London, Chapmans, 1991); Bernard Ingham, *Kill The Messenger* (London, HarperCollins, 1991).
78 Peter Hennessy, *Cabinet* (Oxford, Basil Blackwell, 1986), p. 122.
79 Tam Dalyell, *Misrule: How Mrs Thatcher Misled Parliament from the Sinking of the Belgrano to the Wright Affair* (London, New English Library, 1988), p. 36.
80 See Michael Heseltine's resignation statement, *The Times*, 10 January 1986.
81 Quoted in Robert Harris, *The Making of Neil Kinnock* (London, Faber, 1984), p. 206.
82 Quoted in Harris, *The Making of Neil Kinnock*, p. 206.
83 David Marquand, *The Unprincipled Society: New Demands and Old Politics* (London, Fontana, 1988) p. 194.
84 Marquand, *The Unprincipled Society*, p. 194.
85 Patrick McAuslan and John E. McEldowney, 'Legitimacy and the Constitution: The

Dissonance between Theory and Practice', in Patrick McAuslan and John E. MeEldowney (eds), *Law, Legitimacy and the Constitution* (London, Sweet and Maxwell, 1985), p. 17.
86 McAuslan and McEldowney, 'Legitimacy and the Constitution', pp. 32, 13.
87 K. D. Ewing and C. A. Gearty, *Freedom Under Thatcher: Civil Liberties in Modern Britain* (Oxford, Oxford University Press, 1990) p. 255.
88 Ewing and Gearty, *Freedom Under Thatcher*, p. 255.
89 Ewing and Gearty, *Freedom Under Thatcher*, p. 7.
90 Ewing and Gearty, *Freedom Under Thatcher*, p. 7.
91 'Charter 88', *New Statesman and Society*, 2 December 1990.
92 'Charter 88'.
93 Jenkins, *Accountable to None*, p. 14.
94 Jenkins, *Accountable to None*, p. 15.
95 The plans for the partial privatisation of the Post Office were abandoned after the 1992 election.
96 Simon Jenkins, 'The posthumous years', *The Times*, 24 May 1995.
97 Simon Lee, 'Law and the Constitution', in Dennis Kavanagh and Anthony Seldon (eds), *The Major Effect* (London, Macmillan, 1994), p. 138.
98 Quoted in Philip Webster, Jane Landale and Arthur Leatley, '72 hours left to save UK, says Major', *The Independent*, 29 April 1997.
99 'New Labour must try harder', *The Observer*, 2 May 1999.
100 'New Labour must try harder'.
101 Simon Jenkins, 'If the Tories had won ...', *The Times*, 29 April 1998.
102 Jenkins, 'If the Tories had won ...'.
103 Simon Jenkins, 'Turn left for No 10', *The Times*, 27 January 1999.
104 Jenkins, 'Turn left for No 10'.
105 Stuart Hall, 'The great moving nowhere show', *Marxism Today*, November/December 1998.
106 Hall, 'The great moving nowhere show'.
107 See Anthony Barnett, 'Please stop patronising us', *New Statesman*, 28 June 1999.
108 Thomas Cronin, *The State of the Presidency*, 2nd edn (Boston, Little Brown, 1975), p. 2.
109 Barbara Hinckley, *The Symbolic Presidency: How Presidents Portray Themselves* (New York, Routledge, 1990), p. 12.
110 Hinckley, *The Symbolic Presidency*, p. 11.
111 John E. Mueller, *War, Presidents and Public Opinion* (New York, Wiley, 1973); Jong R. Lee, 'Rallying Around the Flag: Foreign Policy Events and Presidential popularity', *Presidential Studies Quarterly*, 7, no. 3 (Fall 1977), pp. 252–6.
112 Michael Howard, *War and the Liberal Conscience* (Oxford, Oxford University Press, 1981), p. 116.
113 Louis Hartz, *The Liberal Tradition in America: An Interpretation of American Political Thought since the Revolution* (New York, Harcourt Brace Jovanovich, 1955), p. 286.
114 Stephen Burman, *America in the Modern World: The Transcendence of United States Hegemony* (Hemel Hempstead, Harvester Wheatsheaf, 1991), ch. 8; Paul D. Erickson, *Reagan Speaks: The Making of an American Myth* (New York, New York University Press, 1985), ch. 6; David Mervin, *Ronald Reagan and the American Presidency* (London, Longman, 1990), ch. 7.
115 Quoted in Stanley W. Cloud, 'Exorcising an old demon', *Time*, 11 March 1991.
116 A '*USA Today*' poll (1 March 1991) returned an approval rating level at a record 91 per cent.
117 Quoted in John Cassidy, 'A bit of unfinished agenda', *Sunday Times*, 3 March 1999.

118 Walker, *Clinton: The President They Deserve*, p. 281.
119 Walker, *Clinton: The President They Deserve*, p. 282.
120 Walker, *Clinton: The President They Deserve*, p. 284.
121 'Statement by the President to the Nation', 24 March 1999 (http://www.pub.whitehouse.gov/uri-es/I2R?urn:pdi://oma.eop. gov.us/1999/3/25/1.text. 1).
122 'Remarks by the President to Hampton Roads Military Community', 1 April 1999 (http://www.pub.whitehouse.gov/uri-res/I2R?urn:pdi://oma.eop.gov.us/1999/4/2/6.text.1).
123 'Statement by the President to the Nation'.
124 'Statement by the President to the Nation'.
125 George F. Will, 'How Congress shaded in our picture of the President', *Daily Telegraph*, 4 August 1987.
126 'Margaret Thatcher, *The Revival of Britain: Speeches on Home and European Affairs, 1975–1988*, compiled by Alistair B. Cooke (London, Aurum, 1989), p. 164.
127 For a critical commentary on Margaret Thatcher's use of nineteenth-century British history, see Raphael Samuel, *Island Stories: Unravelling Britain, Volume Two, Theatres of Memory* (London, Verso, 1998).
128 Sarah Benton, 'Tales of Thatcher', *New Statesman and Society*, 28 April 1989.
129 Benton, 'Tales of Thatcher'.
130 Kenneth W. Thompson, *The President and the Public Philosophy* (Baton Rouge, Louisiana State University Press, 1981).
131 Marquand, *The Unprincipled Society*, p. 11.
132 Quoted in an interview with Kenneth Auchinloss and David Pedersen, *Newsweek*, 15 October 1990.
133 Thatcher, *The Revival of Britain*, p. 259.
134 Thatcher, *The Revival of Britain*, p. 260.
135 Kenneth O. Morgan, *The People's Peace: British History, 1945–1989* (Oxford, Oxford University Press, 1990), p. 515. See also Paul Rich, 'The Quest for Englishness', *History Today* (June 1987), pp. 24–30; Raphael Samuel (ed.), *Patriotism: The Making and Unmaking of British National Identity, Volume 1: History and Politics* (London, Routledge, 1989); Ghita Ionescu, *Leadership in an Interdependent World: The Statesmanship of Adenauer, De Gaulle, Thatcher, Reagan and Gorbachev* (Harlow, Longman, 1991), pp. 167–82.
136 While the British may be reconciled to greater European integration, survey evidence shows that they do not identify closely with Europe. For example, to the question 'Does the thought ever occur to you that you are not just British but also European', 69 per cent said 'never' (*New Statesman and Society*, 22 June 1990). In another poll conducted for *The European* (21–23 June 1991), 66 per cent of British respondents answered 'no' to the question 'Do you feel more a European citizen than you did five years ago?' This was by far the highest negative response in the six nations surveyed (Italy, France, Germany, Spain, Denmark and Britain). See also the ICM poll in *The Guardian*, 14 November 1991.
137 Ellen R. Gold, 'Politics by wordpower', *Times Higher Education Supplement*, 28 October 1988. See also Paul D. Erickson, *Reagan Speaks: The Making of an American Myth* (New York, New York University Press, 1985), ch. 6; William K. Muir, 'Ronald Reagan: The Primacy of Rhetoric', in Fred I. Greenstein (ed.), *Leadership in the Modern Presidency* (Cambridge, Harvard University Press, 1988), pp. 260–95.
138 Benton, 'Tales of Thatcher'.

139 Richard Rose, *The Postmodern President: The White House Meets the World* (Chatham, Chatham House, 1988); Ionescu, *Leadership in an Interdependent World*, chs 3, 4.
140 John Major, quoted in Robert Harris, 'And is there honey still for Tory tea?', *The Sunday Times*, 23 February 1997.
141 'The young country', leader's speech to the Labour party conference 1995, in Tony Blair, *New Britain: My Vision of a Young Country* (London, Fourth Estate, 1996), p. 65.
142 'The young country', p. 65.
143 Stephen Driver and Luke Martell, *New Labour: Politics After Thatcherism* (Cambridge, Polity, 1998), p. 163.
144 Driver and Martell, *New Labour*, p. 163.
145 Mark Leonard, *Britain: Renewing Our Identity* (London, Demos, 1997).
146 'The young country', p. 62.
147 'The young country', p. 71.
148 Peter Mandelson and Roger Liddle, *The Blair Revolution: Can New Labour Deliver?* (London, Faber, 1996), p. 191.
149 Gordon Brown interviewed by Steve Richards, *New Statesman*, 19 April 1999.
150 Quoted in Toby Harnden, 'Blair apologises to Ireland for Potato Famine', *Daily Telegraph*, 2 June 1997. See also Paul Bew, 'The truth about the famine', *Daily Telegraph*, 2 June 1997; Ruth Dudley Edwards, 'No need to apologise for the potato famine', *The Independent*, 3 June 1997.
151 Derek Draper, *Blair's Hundred Days* (London, Faber, 1997), p. 49.
152 Anne McElvoy, 'Britain's new First Family', *Daily Telegraph*, 21 July 1997.
153 Peregrine Worsthorne, 'The rise of the new ruling class', *Daily Telegraph*, 12 July 1997.
154 Worsthorne, 'The rise of the new ruling class'.
155 Worsthorne, 'The rise of the new ruling class'.
156 Quoted in Simon Walters, 'Radical Blair worries Palace', *Express on Sunday*, 18 May 1997.
157 Quoted in Walters, 'Radical Blair worries Palace'.
158 Quoted in Walters, 'Radical Blair worries Palace'.
159 Quoted in Walters, 'Radical Blair worries Palace'.
160 Quoted in Walters, 'Radical Blair worries Palace'.
161 Dan Balz, 'Britain's Prime Minister assumes presidential air', *Washington Post*, 2 October 1997.
162 The phrase was used by the prime minister at Trimdon on 31 August 1997.
163 See Martin Kettle, 'The next step: a blueprint for New Labour's world role', *The Guardian*, 7 February 1998.
164 Leaders' speech to the Labour party conference 1997, *The Guardian*, 1 October 1997.
165 Leader's speech to the Labour party conference 1997.
166 Leader's speech to the Labour party conference 1997.
167 Leader's speech to the Labour party conference 1997.
168 'It is simply the right thing to do', transcript of the prime minister's televised address to the nation, *The Guardian*, 27 March 1999.
169 Ed Vulliamy and Patrick Wintour, 'The Pentagon prepares to put its trust in Blair', *The Observer*, 15 April 1999.
170 'It is simply the right thing to do'.
171 'It is simply the right thing to do'.
172 'It is simply the right thing to do'.
173 Quoted in Chris Bird and Lucy Ward, 'Blair pledge to refugees', *The Guardian*, 4 May 1999.

174 'Doctrine of the international community', speech by the prime minister to the Economic Club, Hilton Hotel, Chicago, 22 April 1999, http://www.number–10.gov.uk/public/info/index. html.
175 Leader's speech to the 1997 Labour party conference.
176 Leader's speech to the 1997 Labour party conference.
177 Leader's speech to the 1997 Labour party conference.
178 Leader's speech to the 1997 Labour party conference.

CHAPTER 9

Tony Blair and the British presidential dimension

Tony Blair's premiership has disrupted the superstructure of British government. His radicalism has extended beyond the substance of policy to the methods of decision making and administration. In a period when constitutional change has come to represent the defining property of the New Labour government, the status and authority of the prime minister's own position has become the subject of intense speculation. The proposition that constitutional flux has reached a level where even the anchorage points of the core executive are now open to question has become a seriously considered contention. At the very least, the extraordinary dominance of Tony Blair in his party and in his government has given renewed vigour to the old debate concerning the power of the prime minister in relation to the cabinet. With Blair the scale of change and the level of supremacy has prompted a profusion of references to the existence of a *de facto* presidency at large within the structures and processes of the system. As we have seen at an earlier stage of this study, the allusions and analogies are not only motivated by a variety of impulses but carry different levels of meaning and seriousness. Nevertheless, they all denote an awareness of change and the need to make sense of it. They serve to draw attention to the implications and to create an evaluative response to them. The term 'presidential' conjures up a profusion of associations relating to executive centralisation and personal power. As such, the presidential analogy has an immediate resonance in circumstances of such rapid fluidity. In the case of the Blair premiership, the usage of the presidential frame of reference seems particularly appropriate in reaching an understanding of developments that can be construed as departures from the conventional dynamics and traditional relationships at the heart of British government.

Blair and Labour

Where the distribution of power between institutions and organisations is concerned, the British premiership has had a material effect that has often been used to support the contention of a growing presidential element to British government. At the level of the Labour party, Tony Blair has succeeded in imposing unprecedented cohesion and discipline upon the party's organisation. The traditions and structures of the Labour movement's internal democracy that used to preoccupy Labour leaders with the need for protracted negotiation and accommodation through multiple layers of consultation have to a large extent, been either marginalised or superseded by New Labour's modernisation. The urge to become electorally competitive led to sweeping reforms to reduce the established power bases in favour of a less hierarchical and more broad-based structure, allowing more freedom of manoeuvre to the leadership. Extending the logic of the 'one man one vote' reforms under John Smith, New Labour pressed onward with a series of changes designed to create a flatter organisational structure with greater participation at the grassroots and a rolling programme of policy reviews to minimise any recurrence of high visibility confrontations within the party. In 1994, the Blair leadership introduced a campaign to enlarge the grassroots of the party. Within three years, it had succeeded in increasing the membership to 405,000, which represented a 40 per cent increase on the 1994 level. Moreover, the New Labour members were 'markedly more conservative than Old Labour on many issues'.[1]

The Blair leadership transformed the identity of the party away from its old attachments to trade unionism, public ownership, high taxation and large-scale redistribution towards a centre-left organisation that was attentive to the demands and opportunities of the global market and to the needs of business innovation and investment.[2] Blair's project and Blair's vision came to define the Labour party's brand image in an electoral context that was increasingly interpreted as a marketing exercise in product promotion. Innumerable American parallels were drawn, not just between the policy content of New Labour and the New Democrats, but also between the techniques of presidential campaigning and Blair's drive for the premiership. The strategy of New Labour had been to create a Blair coalition capable of maintaining its core supporters but with the capacity to appeal to traditionally non-Labour voters, especially in 'middle England'. In an increasingly dealigned electorate, depending upon class-based voting, ideological polarities and the social solidarity of the Labour heartlands was no longer a feasible proposition. Through opinion polling, focus groups, think-tank investigations and market research, the Labour party had to transform its entire image in order to break the Conservative hegemony and to reach out for the independents, the switchers, the floaters and the new voters.[3] Blair was the agent of expression and the chief beneficiary of Labour's shift into an openly coalitional party. In place of ideological fervour was an emphasis upon pragmatism. Instead of partisan conflict, there was a cross-party appeal for consensus and inclusive pluralism. References to 'our people' by past Labour leaders were replaced by invocations of 'the people'. This carried the clear implication that representation entailed a collective trust to protect the public interest at the expense of sectional preferences.

Loosening the texture of the party brought with it a proportionate need to tighten the leadership. This entailed changing the agenda of party management. Under normal circumstances, Labour's effectiveness as a party was conditional upon the creation and maintenance of an internal equilibrium between power bases at the highest reaches of the organisation. Under New Labour, party management was centred upon the mobilisation of the party's membership into a common cause to raise public confidence in Labour's potential as a party of government. Blair was determined to use his leadership to draw attention away from the party and to establish his own criteria for the public's evaluation of Labour. Blair was criticised for his iconoclasm, his presumption and his 'permanent revolution' of the party. Within a year of his election as leader, Blair and his advisors were denounced as 'Stalinist'. The Labour back-bencher, Richard Burden, typified the concern felt by many over the party's obsession with eliminating negative images of itself in the rush to appeal to mainstream opinion:

> Labour is drifting towards a US-style party – a ruthlessly effective electoral machine as the vehicle for those who want to go into politics rather than a radical party with a definable ideological base ... Americanisation has seen New Labour actually increasing its demands for internal discipline. Mechanisms for the party to communicate directly with its members may be more extensive than they have ever been. But such communication is essentially 'top down'. Power is increasingly centralised around the leader's office, with immense pressure on everyone else to fall in line.[4]

This type of criticism remained constant throughout Blair's period as leader of the opposition and it has been a marked feature of his premiership. In both cases, it has been prompted by a reaction to an alleged excess of power. It has not been a question of calling upon the party leader to exert leadership or of demanding new leadership. The complaint has been one of too much emphasis upon leadership and too much power lodged in the leadership.

Those inside the party warned that '[l]oyalty should not be tested to destruction'[5] by the leadership. It was an imposition upon the tolerance of the Labour movement that it should have to withstand the 'strutting conceit' and 'crude condescension' of the 'peacock throne'.[6] Labour critics complained that policy commissions, which were dominated by the party machine, had replaced the traditional wealth of debate inside the party. 'Instead of the NEC being a vital area of policy debate', Ken Livingstone reflected after a year of the Blair government that it had 'largely been reduced to a cross between the role of police informer and a collection of narrow-minded magistrates.'[7] Although the minimisation of open dissent and the maximisation of discipline provoked anxiety within the party, little organised expression of it had troubled the leadership after two and a half years of tight governmental control. Instead, political commentators and opinion leaders were astonished at the leadership's 'Leninist approach to power'[8] and its transformation of the party into what Siôn Simon described as a 'humourless Orwellian superstructure whose only purpose is the ruthless imposition of the Blairite will'.[9] To the modernisers, it was necessary for party people to 'understand that most things they hold most dear have been erased'.[10] Hugo Young sympathised with Old Labour having to come to terms with the fact that the government's 'acts of so called courage have tended to be directed against its lifelong friends not its old class enemies'.[11] The techniques of central control were considered so advanced that those who had earlier castigated John Major for the weak leadership of his party began to have doubts as to whether Blair's leadership had gone too far. William Rees-Mogg, for example, thought that because of Britain's liberal instincts, the government's 'obsession with control [would] come to no good'.[12] Siôn Simon, in the *Daily Telegraph*, agreed that even a large majority organised by Millbank was no security against accumulated resentment and ultimately rebellion: '[I]f Labour does not pay more sincere attention into co-opting the PLP into the business of government, the consequences will begin to erode its standing in the country.'[13]

Notwithstanding such warnings, Blair has continued to keep his distance from the party, to exert tighter management of its activities and to remind it of its exalted duty to the British public. His high visibility and continued popularity have reaffirmed the rationale of his authority. Just as the public and democratic manner of his election to party leader in 1994 served to inject his leadership with leverage greater than any other Labour leader, so the associations of his modernisation programme and style of leadership with the election triumph of 1997 have further enhanced his authority. And yet Blair's anxiety over Labour's capacity to lapse back into fissile dissidence has compelled him to continue making changes to the structure of the party in order to retain the leadership's leverage over it.[14] The once formidable NEC has been stripped of many of its powers over the party. In August 1998, it was announced that the party conference would be reorganised to eliminate the recurrence of damaging disputes being aired on the conference floor. What had been conceived as the sovereign parliament of the Labour movement and the arena where the party would monitor and confront a Labour government was now re-engineered to provide a showcase for the Blair administration and a rallying point for the leadership. The prime minister was determined that the party conference should not have the status of an alternative government that had been achieved under previous Labour administrations. Unpredictable and hastily devised 'composite motions' produced by union leaders and constituency organisations were replaced by a system of policy forums and refined options. It was further proposed that motions on controversial issues (e.g. tobacco sponsorship, public sector pay awards, welfare reform, student loans, the legalisation of cannabis) that might disrupt the organisational coherence of the conference would be debated in private with no press and television coverage. Left-wing MPs complained that the Labour conference was being turned into an American party convention, whose main purposes were to provide a presidential-style platform for the leadership and to suppress the critics and criticisms of government policy. The leadership remained undeterred and announced a further innovation designed to undercut the intermediate sector of the party hierarchy. Each party member would be given a unique security code that would allow the introduction of telephone voting in party elections. This would encourage greater participation by the non-active element of the party membership, which would further dilute the influence of the party's traditional power centres.

Blair's robust attitude to the party has been unrelenting. In February 1999, it was disclosed that the Blair administration had spent £22 million on research into social attitudes and public responses to policy. The expenditure had been made in the face of party criticism that the Labour movement should have been used to monitor and convey public opinion. Blair has always insisted that his original intention to engage in tough choices would be kept even in areas of great sensitivity to Labour party traditions (e.g. the welfare state, privatisation, immigration control, asylum rights). In spite of a majority of 175 seats, the prime minister has not only offered positions on a cabinet committee to leading Liberal Democrats but has been quite explicit in advocating a convergence of the two parties to create the conditions for a controlling left-of-centre realignment. Even after Labour's poor showing in the 1999 elections for the European parliament, which raised serious concerns over the loss of core support in, the Labour heartlands, the prime minister rounded on those critics who speculated on the need to bring 'traditional values' back into the party:

> [W]hilst I am leader of my Party and Prime Minister of this country, I will never again have Britain forced to choose between a Labour Party that ignored

> the importance of business and ambition, and a right-wing Conservative Party which ignored the need for justice and compassion. That is the New Labour message and it will remain 100% proof. We govern for all the people ... I see the nonsense written in the media about the electorate, as though policies on jobs appeal to one section of the community, policies on the economy and enterprise to another. We were elected to serve the whole country, those who voted for us and those who didn't. That is what we will continue to do.[15]

Significantly, Blair's response to the collapse in Labour's vote was to announce a new drive to take his premiership to the people. A round-Britain tour in July 1999 was designed to deflect attention away from the party's performance and place the prime minister at the centre of public interest through a series of speeches, question-and-answer sessions and radio interviews. At the end of 1999, Blair became the first Labour prime minister to address the Confederation of British Industry (CBI). In his speech, he described the role of government intervention in industry as a policy that had 'passed its sell-by date'.[16] He confirmed that under New Labour, the role of contemporary government was to 'encourage innovation and entrepreneurship' and to 'equip people and business for the new economy'.[17] He concluded that as a 'New Labour prime minister', he was 'proud to be pro-business' and proud to have 'transformed our relations with business'.[18]

Blair and parliament

A second institutional indicator of a presidential form of centralisation at work in the British system is provided by parliament. A number of features can be cited to support the contention of a burgeoning executive power which, while endorsing a process of devolved power, has at the same time demonstrated an authority that has seldom been more immune to effective challenge. For example, New Labour has always had a clear emphasis upon the need for discipline. New Labour was conceived as a corrective to Old Labour's sectarian divisions. After years of opposition, the party's modernisers had had direct experience of the disruptive effects of their own guerrilla tactics against the Conservative governments. They were also acutely conscious of the negative images incurred by the Major administration's fractious relations with its own MPs. As a result, the New Labour government was not prepared to take chances with the parliamentary party, especially as its ranks had become inflated with many almost unknown candidates who had unexpectedly won parliamentary seats in the 1997 landslide. To the prime minister, 'governing as New Labour' meant continuing in government what the party had achieved in opposition – namely forming a cohesive support structure for the leadership team whose right to expect consent was based upon the outcomes of a party election and a general election. Andrew Rawnsley explained the logic: 'In the Blairite conception of parliamentary democracy, the role of New Labour MPs is to sustain the Government ... New Labour did not get elected by licensing dissent, and it is not going to be re-elected by encouraging the habit now. That is an article of faith with the Prime Minister.'[19] Such an outlook was not born simply out of a political need to keep the prodigious ranks of New Labour MPs closed around the figure of the prime minister. It entailed a more fundamental expectation based upon legitimacy and obligation. Those closest to the prime minister operated on the belief that 'most of the New Labour horde occupying the government benches were not elected on their own wonderful merits, but because they swept to Parliament on Mr Blair's coat-tails'.[20] Even if this could not be shown to be precisely the case, Blair had been primarily responsible for the modernisation, message, campaign and face of the party in the election. In the eyes of his lieutenants and the Labour whips, this was tantamount to Blair having secured power on behalf of his party. In accordance with this concept of parliamentary democracy, MPs were obligated to the leadership and to its judgements and decisions.

New Labour had been formed as a public service that had facilitated Labour's reconnection with the British people. As a result, the leadership saw the party's MPs as the guardians of public trust. Given that they operated in a high profile arena during a period of a great public sensitivity over standards of behaviour in politics, the leadership put in place a range of stringent measures to maximise not just party discipline but party coherence in the face of an increasingly intrusive media. On occasions, the objective of solidarity produced complaints of excess. Critics cited Millbank's fax and pager instructions to keep MPs 'on message', the high incidence of 'planted questions asked by robotic New Labour MPs',[21] the chief whip's threat to report dissident MPs to their local parties, and the revelation that many Labour MPs had used Millbank briefings to issue near identical statements on the 1998 Budget.[22] In many quarters, the management of the party was seen as being so severe as to threaten the independence of parliament. The Conservative party had become a demoralised rump of 165 MPs with little hope of becoming electorally competitive for at least ten years. The Liberal Democrats were tied to Labour's promises of constitutional reform. Consequently, Millbank was seen as representing a threat to British parliamentary democracy through it efforts in squeezing the opposition out of a party in a position of hegemony.

The threat was not merely one of intention. It was that Millbank appeared to be achieving its objectives. Left-wingers were marginalised. Mavericks became strangely quiet. Independent thinkers confined their activities to thought. In June 1999, Tony Benn, Labour's leading parliamentarian, announced that he would resign his seat at the next general election in order to spend more time on politics. The net effect was to leave commentators speculating upon where dissent would ever come from and upon the need for diversity to be seen as a constitutional virtue rather than a political vice. Anne McElvoy, for example, thought that it was essential for governing parties to have the capacity for self-renewal though critical synergy: 'Mr Blair needs to encourage young men and women capable of looking ahead of their time, of laying out brave ideas which can be tested in the heat of debate. Instead, he has a chorus of regular approval.'[23] Donald Macintye believed that internal party friction had a functional utility not just for Labour but more significantly for the system as a whole: 'If the safety valves of dissent are not built anew into the system, then the vital task of opposition will be left to other more volatile and less democratic theatres of conflict.'[24]

Complaints over New Labour's attitude to parliament were given material support by government decisions such as those to impose a guillotine on the two most important Bills in the first session of parliament (i.e. the Referendums (Scotland and Wales) Bill and the Finance Bill). Further weight to the allegations was provided by the Labour whips' concerted efforts to control the membership of the select committees, and by their robust methods in pacifying critics and closing down back-bench mutinies. To an extent, these examples of strong-arm tactics are simply part and parcel of normal parliamentary management which operates through pressure, negotiation, patronage and sanctions. And yet, taken together, the rapidity and volume of such examples have raised questions over Labour's attitude to parliament, especially in light of the party's pre-election advocacy of the need for British politics to become more inclusive and less adversarial. More serious, however, is the charge that these cases of robust behaviour are representative of a deeper challenge to the stature and authority of parliament. This outlook was reflected in Blair's determination to confront the hereditary principle of the House of Lords and accordingly to transform the chamber into a wholly different body. The peremptory reduction of Prime Minister's Questions from Tuesday and Thursday to a single session on a Wednesday, on the grounds of allowing the premier 'to be questioned in greater depth',[25] was also seen to be symptomatic of New Labour's impatience with the current forms of parliamentary accountability. The Labour modernisers' stated intent was one of changing the institution: 'Parliament ... needs to be dragged (probably kicking and screaming) into modern times.'[26] With this in mind, the government arranged for a special select committee to be established that would investigate how parliamentary procedures could be modernised to produce 'an effective House of Commons'.[27]

Blair's challenge to parliament, however, was not thought to be limited simply to direct attempts to reshape the institution. More significant, and arguably more corrosive in effect, has been the belief that parliament is becoming marginalised as a political institution in contemporary British government and that the Labour government is simply giving expression to this underlying trend. The infusion of record numbers of unelected political advisors into government; the volume and authority of their unofficial briefings to the media; the release of Budget details prior to the Chancellor's statement to the House of Commons; and the low levels of parliamentary attendance and voting by members of the cabinet have all contributed to an impression of parliament being of secondary importance. This trend is underlined by the infrequent occasions when 'Tony Blair ... that aspirant presidential figure condescends to appear in the Commons'.[28] It is claimed that the Blair administration has a 'disregard for parliamentary procedure' and an 'arrogant disdain for constitutional propriety'.[29] It is even alleged that a 'contempt for parliament has become a hallmark of this government'.[30] This may be so, but it is more likely that the government's attitude to parliament has been based less on arrogance and more on hard-headed realism.

Political, constitutional and international dynamics are disrupting parliament's centrality to the British system, both on formal and informal terms. The devolution of legislative powers and political accountability from Westminster to the Scottish parliament and the Welsh assembly, the incorporation of the European Convention on Human Rights into British law, the progressive derogation of national policy choices to the machinery of the EU, and the rising incidence of referendums to determine major constitutional decisions have all had major repercussions upon parliament's role in the British system. On a less formal level, the government's usage of focus groups, citizen juries, road shows, task forces, 'the people's panel', the Internet and prime ministerial annual reports have all contributed to a sense in which political forces and means of exchange are increasingly transcending parliament. 'For Blairites, Parliament is no longer central, it is merely one means of communication.'[31] The long-term consequence was already clear to one noted parliamentary observer within one year of the Blair government: 'Government is becoming divorced from Parliament ... [I]n practice, as opposed to constitutional theory, a separation of powers is developing. The executive may still emerge out of the legislature, but the two are now increasingly distinct.'[32]

Blair and the government machine

The position and status of the cabinet are invariably seen as the litmus test of an emerging presidential dimension in the British system. In the case of the Blair administration, the political innovation of the incoming government appeared to be matched by a shift away from the norms of cabinet government. The New Labour government occasioned a profusion of references to the derogation of the cabinet as a decision-making body and as a central point of political clearance. They carried the imputation of a deliberate attempt on the part of the Blair leadership to replace the cabinet with a scheme of central control more akin to a presidential format. Even before its accession to office, New Labour had a clear intention to revitalise the centre of government, in order to develop the political and bureaucratic leverage required to modernise the country at large.

The nearest approximation to an official prospectus of Labour's modernisation movement was *The Blair Revolution* by Peter Mandelson and Roger Liddle. In it, they give emphasis to the need for a future Blair administration to take charge of a Whitehall structure that had been conditioned to eighteen years of Conservative priorities. In such a struggle, the new prime minister would have to get 'personal control of the central-government machine and drive it hard, in the knowledge that if the government does not run the machine the machine will run the government'.[33] In their view, 'the prime minister's writ must run in order to get results'.[34] In general, the 'whole government machine is, rightly, very responsive to the prime minister's will'.[35] The objective of a Blair administration had to be one ensuring that the machine was wholly and reliably responsive to Downing Street. Taking his cue from Margaret Thatcher's ability to drive policy changes through the system, Blair's aim had to be to 'achieve a similar level of policy fulfilment without the accompanying costs and damage to relations inside and outside government'.[36] Blair would need to 'harness the strengths of his cabinet colleagues ... [but] he will not be interested in needless conflicts'.[37] To Mandelson and Liddle, the radical policy change promised by New Labour would necessarily include a sweeping review of the centre of government, in order to maximise prime ministerial influence while minimising departmental and ministerial friction. 'The answer lies in a more formalised strengthening of the centre of government, which should not only give much-needed personal support to the prime minister ... but provide the means of formulating and driving forward strategy for the government as a whole.'[38] Prior to taking office, it was envisaged that New Labour empowerment would be integrally connected to the idea of prime ministerial aggrandisement.

Once in office Tony Blair was determined to fulfil his promise made during the election campaign that New Labour would 'run the centre and govern from the centre'.[39] He established a committee of inquiry under Sir Richard Wilson, the Cabinet Secretary, and assigned it the task to produce plans for the modernisation of government. The intention was to devise a more responsive and dynamic agency at the centre, in line with the recommendations set out by Mandelson and Liddle in *The Blair Revolution*. As Sir Richard Wilson embarked upon his brief, allusions were made by, or on behalf of, Blair's inner circle that the new premiership would entail a shift to a more Napoleonic system. The need for a tighter linkage between Number 10 and the Cabinet Office was deemed to be a priority. Similarly, the idea of a prime minister's department was extensively trailed as a plausible response to the need for a support agency to give Blair the capacity for co-ordinated intervention from the centre.

The intention to fuse the identity and the leverage of the centre with Number 10 was made evident in other respects. The Ministerial Code was amended to provide Number 10 with a capacity to exert an unprecedented level of central control upon the content and timing of policy initiatives and public announcements from ministers and their departments. Upon entering office, the Blair administration also established a profusion of task forces designed to examine complex issues in the round in place of the segmented approach inherent in the cross-cutting departmental perspectives and jurisdictions. Task forces were intended to convey a spirit of urgency and commitment on the part of a new administration intent upon action and delivery. They were designed to be 'emblems of Labour's desire to be seen to be implementing manifesto pledges briskly and in a spirit of trust'.[40] Task forces were established to cover a range of different areas from 'welfare to work' and NHS efficiency, to youth justice, literacy and school standards. The rationale of the task force approach was to generate fresh insights on policy development away from the standard Whitehall hierarchies. They were free to recruit from any sector of society in order to widen the available knowledge base but also to provide forms of prior consent among constituencies involved in the formulation of policy. In one respect, the proliferation of task forces could be construed as a form of genuine pluralism that could not easily be controlled from the centre. In other respects, however, the task force template bore witness to New Labour's lack of confidence in the conventional arrangements of cabinet committees and interdepartmental structures in providing the creativity and coherence necessary for major overhauls in complex areas of policy.

The task force ethos was also significant for providing the basis of Number 10's flagship device for centrally conceived initiatives in policy. The

Social Exclusion Unit was formed not only to create a lateral and thematic organisation to co-ordinate policies in the field of poverty, but also to underline that the area was a high priority issue to the prime minister himself. The Social Exclusion Unit was conceived as a way of pooling resources across departments in a field of policy where 'solutions have been very hard to find'.[41] The Unit's objectives were to improve government's understanding of the problems, to 'promote co-operation between departments; and to make recommendations to tackle social exclusion more effectively'.[42] Half its membership was drawn from the civil service. The remainder was recruited from organisations with front-line experience of the problems of social exclusion (e.g. local government, business, the voluntary sector, the police and probation services). The Unit carried the authority and imprimatur of the prime minister. Its remit was determined by the prime minister and it reported directly to Number 10. In its first phase, Tony Blair requested that the Unit investigate both broad issues (e.g. the social deprivation of sixteen- to eighteen-year-olds not in education, training or employment; neighbourhood renewal) and specific areas of concern (e.g. teenage pregnancy, rough sleeping, truancy). Social exclusion was recognised as a generic problem requiring a collective and creative response in the form of an agency with the capability of breaking out of the structures and mind-sets endemic to Whitehall.

Peter Mandelson described the Social Exclusion Unit as the 'most important innovation'[43] that the Labour government had made in office. What lay behind the claim was based not merely upon a commitment to resolve an entrenched social problem through government action, but upon its relationship to an altogether separate agenda described by John Lloyd: 'It is explicitly meant to be a prototype for a reinvention of government. Those who are designing the unit believe that it will succeed in its first aim of inclusion only if it succeeds in its second aim of deconstructing, then reconstructing, Whitehall … [T]he aim of the unit is to slash bureaucracy – even to revolutionise government.'[44] The Social Exclusion Unit, therefore, was designed as an experiment in pioneering what was termed 'holistic government' or, as Blair termed it 'joined up government'. Being a top priority issue for the new Labour government and Tony Blair, social exclusion was intended to drive a movement for diminishing the turf wars between departments and for weakening the nexus between agencies and their clienteles. It was envisaged that Number 10 would provide the conceptual leadership for a concerted assault upon the problem and at the same time establish the Unit as a model in the pursuit of the general objective towards interdepartmental co-operation.

The need for prime ministerial clout in the machinery of government was a recognised feature of the Blair administration in the first year of government. In April 1998, Peter Mandelson was being widely tipped to be brought into the cabinet as the prime minister's 'enforcer'. It was thought that he would head an enhanced Cabinet Office which would move away from its formal role as a service agency and neutral broker for the collective interests of the cabinet to a new function designed to give greater political and administrative weight to the prime minister. Mandelson, however, was too divisive a figure to be considered for such a sensitive and controversial undertaking. Blair also drew back from trying to establish a prime minister's department. It would have been too politically and administratively disruptive. Nevertheless, he did endorse Sir Richard Wilson's report on the modernisation of central government. This called for the unification of policy formulation and delivery through the merging of the Cabinet Office and the Office of Public Service. It also recommended a new Policy and Innovation Unit (PIU), which would build on the experience of the Social Exclusion Unit by focusing on selected issues that cross departmental boundaries and by proposing policy innovations to improve the government's ability to achieve its stated objectives. Like the Social Exclusion Unit, the PIU would draw on the public and private sectors to assemble teams to carry out studies on interdepartmental co-operation and policy innovation. The PIU promised to give Number 10 much greater leverage in the field of policy analysis which, up to then, had traditionally been a preserve of the Treasury. Finally, Blair announced a set of initiatives designed to improve the corporate management of the civil service. These included a new Centre of Management and Policy Studies in the Cabinet Office. The Centre would be established to ensure that the civil service 'continues to be a learning organisation, open to new ideas ... and the best new thinking on current issues and new approaches to management'.[45] The prime minister's proposals also included a commitment to 'meet the corporate objectives of the Government as a whole, rather than just the objectives of the individual departments'.[46] Blair concluded that the extensive re-organisation of the Cabinet Office would give it a 'new focus as the corporate headquarters of the Civil Service'.[47]

Sir Richard Wilson's review had led to a considerable enhancement in the status of the Cabinet Office. It would accommodate a new crisis and command centre and what was effectively a government think-tank. Moreover, it was given a renewed authority and a fresh mission to maximise the collective character of the governmental machine. The Cabinet Office was to be enlarged and to be given priority in the allocation of office space to enable it to be as integrated as possible in a central location. Jack Cunningham was named Minister for the Cabinet Office and given the task of reducing the competitive friction between different departments and ministries. Given the nature of his brief, Cunningham was widely described as the prime minister's 'enforcer'. But Cunningham was the first to refute any such title and to deny that such a role even existed. In formal terms, he and Sir Richard Wilson were joint partners in the revamped Cabinet Office where their powers were drawn from the Cabinet Office's traditional remit of serving the collective interest of the cabinet as a whole. Despite the ambiguity in Cunningham's position, the strengthening of the Cabinet Office was interpreted at the time as a redistribution of power towards the centre, which was in turn equated with a further shift to a condition of prime ministerial administration. Just as the prime minister had instigated and driven the review, so Number 10 was seen to be the main beneficiary of an outcome which increased the potential for the centre's co-ordination of policy and personnel in Whitehall.

Factors in premier–cabinet relations: (1) New Labour culture

The effect of the Blair administration upon the cabinet has not been limited to changes in the formal machinery of government. The usage and status of the Blair cabinet have been influenced by at least three other major factors. First is what can be termed 'New Labour culture'. The transformation of Labour under the modernisation project of Tony Blair was based upon the need for organisational unity and political discipline. The emphasis was one of superseding Labour's traditions of entrenched divisions and fragmented structures. New Labour's colonisation of, and concentration upon, the centre ground was achieved and sustained by a leadership that set out to establish public trust based not merely upon policy grounds but upon a capacity to make Labour into a palpably leader-led party. Blair's management of the party, together with his cultivation of extra-party sources of public influence, made New Labour into a formidable campaigning organisation. As Kavanagh and Seldon make clear, once New Labour achieved power, it in many respects translated its opposition values, outlooks and techniques into government. 'These included a belief that political leadership is a stock of capital that can be replenished by personal integrity, good communications, and the achievement of visible objectives … that are effectively within the leader's and government's control; [and] a willingness to change established structures and patterns to enable him to work effectively and achieve his objectives'.[48] To the leadership, Old Whitehall was in many ways similar to Old Labour. Blair needed the support and resources of the departments of state, but he would not allow himself to be confined exclusively to their ambit. He wished to reserve a freedom of manoeuvre and a flexibility in approach that allowed him to pursue other sources of information, consultation and decision making.

In his premiership, Blair deliberately set out 'to create a new approach, setting the national mood and policy agenda via the media, rather than through the conventional channels of Westminster politics'.[49] By the same token, Blair's reaction to Whitehall and to the cabinet in particular was one of traditional dependence and radical departure. New Labour had featured public reaction in its strategy and calculations. In like manner, 'No 10, under Tony Blair the most presentation-conscious Downing Street ever, kept a tight grip on image (and ensured that image was a potent ingredient in policy-making from its very earliest stages)'.[50] Given the scale and intensity of the media's intrusion into national politics, the increasing speed of reporting and analysis, and the media's position as the primary point of political engagement, Blair apportioned prime ministerial resources accordingly. In many respects, handling the media simply transcended normal cabinet prerogatives. The responsibility ascribed to Number 10 in the field of protecting and cultivating Labour's public status, combined with the inherently technocratic character of media relations, served to enhance Blair's guardianship role and legitimise the position of his staff at the expense of the formal cabinet.

The special privileges assigned to the New Labour leader were complemented by New Labour's emphasis upon management. Just as New Labour's shadow cabinet was unified behind the Blairite project, so the Labour cabinet's unity has reflected the party consensus upon an established centrist agenda that envisages cabinet ministers primarily as managers of their departments. The strategic vision, and the 'big picture' issues, would be addressed by the prime minister. In the main, the remainder of the cabinet have been assigned to the role of achieving pre-set objectives and adhering to the government's spending targets. The New Labour project in government has been a 'managerial project in a way that attracts virtually no disagreement, left to right, old to new'.[51] This outlook has had a material effect upon the functional role of the cabinet: 'The business of modern ministers, as Blairism defines their role, is not argument but primarily management. They must ... address the problems, task the departments, [and] produce the results ... Never in the past 50 years has that been the presiding narrative of cabinet performance in the way it is today.'[52]

After a prolonged period during which the concept of 'governability' had once again become a cause for concern, Blair was determined that his administration would be a purposeful enterprise geared to service delivery. The election was seen as determining the major decisions. The business of government was a matter of attending to the contractual obligations occasioned by the manifesto but in particular by the leader's personal pledges to the British people. Nowhere has New Labour's emphasis upon the utility and value of management been more in evidence than the extent to which the cabinet itself has been managed into an expression of unity and resolve. In contrast to the sectarian divisions and protracted disputes that characterised the Wilson and Callaghan cabinets, the Blair cabinet has been marked by a New Labour intention to introduce commercial talent and best business practice into government and by a New Labour impulse to identify itself as the antidote to the organisational disarray of John Major's administrations.

Factors in premier–cabinet relations: (2) Blair's personal preferences

A second factor in Blair's relationship to the cabinet has been the prime minister's own personal inclinations towards decision making and policy formulation. By temperament, Blair is tolerant towards structures and practices if they can be shown to serve a purpose, but he is intolerant of tradition for its own sake. In opposition, his continuing theme was the need not merely to change the government but to change how government works. With this in mind, he has championed constitutional reform, transferred the control of monetary policy to the Bank of England, allowed Liberal Democrats to participate in cabinet committees, proposed the modernisation of government and public services, and introduced a range of new initiatives, agencies and task forces. The prime minister has set great store in the need to escape from past practices and to develop a creative and iconoclastic outlook to the challenge of governing in the twenty-first century. With this in mind, he has broken with Labour party traditions and made a virtue of recruiting top-level figures from business and commerce into the government in both advisory and government service roles. It was noteworthy that in Sir Richard Wilson's committee on government modernisation, the need for innovation and fresh thinking was given particular prominence. For example, the review underlined the importance of creating 'Learning Labs' that would 'encourage new ways of front-line working by suspending rules that stifle innovation'.[53]

In the same way that Blair marginalised the once mighty NEC in favour of a more ad hoc yet tighter group of fellow modernisers and personal confidantes, the prime minister has maintained a strong preference for small meetings instead of large and more diffuse gatherings of colleagues. He sees the former as being simply more efficient, coherent and effective. Small meetings are also more congruent with Blair's sense of spatial leadership that rests upon his detachment from the party and upon his lack of affinity with the clubby gregariousness of Westminster. In Blair's scale of values, adherence to institutional restrictions and social conventions has a far lower priority than the pursuit of a theme, or the need to adapt patterns of behaviour and thought to achieve objectives. Blair's endorsement of a 'third way' was based upon the need to escape from established outlooks and orthodox practices, in order to release a pragmatic inventiveness that would lead to more workable ways to address immediate problems. Given these values and motive forces, together with the prime minister's determination not to be sucked into the kind of leadership-sapping spectacles of government disintegration that marked the Major administration, Blair has viewed the cabinet and its system of cabinet committees with personal misgivings and not a little suspicion.

Factors in premier–cabinet relations: (3) origins of leadership

The circumstances surrounding Tony Blair's election as party leader and the conditions arising from that victory constitute the third factor that has had a material influence upon the Blair cabinet. It is often overlooked that Blair became leader by subjecting himself to the largest democratic exercise ever undertaken by a party in this country. This made Blair different to other Labour leaders and to other members of the shadow cabinet. This rite of passage not only invested his leadership with an enriched basis of democratic consent but generated a new set of social dynamics between the leader and his senior colleagues. The difference between them was no longer one merely of degree but of kind. Just as the leader could no longer be reduced to the same common denominator as the rest of the shadow cabinet, so the leader could no longer be regarded and treated as an emblematic first among equals. By broadening the franchise so extensively, it widened the difference between the leader and the rest into a gulf and changed the leader's position with his shadow cabinet accordingly. The relationship was still one of interdependence but the balance had shifted decisively in favour of the leader who, by virtue of the means and outcome of his election, no longer had to negotiate his leadership on a continual basis. Unlike Harold Wilson, for example, the process of Blair's elevation to leader dramatically undercut the political status of other senior figures in the party. Harold Wilson had to contend with the power and confrontational aspirations of individuals such as James Callaghan, Denis Healey, Anthony Crossland, Richard Crossman and Roy Jenkins, all of whom made no secret of the plausibility of their leadership ambitions. This was not a problem that troubled Blair either in opposition or in government.

Prior to the 1997 general election, Hugo Young observed that Blair's dominance as leader was not based, as it had been under Wilson, upon a 'capacity to balance and divert, to wheedle and deceive, to cross and double-cross in time-honoured style, the substantial giants around him'.[54] In contrast, Blair was simply supreme because the leadership election had allowed him to win all the arguments and to humble his rivals in the very act of becoming leader. The manner of his rise to office became the means of maintaining and extending his hegemony. Harold Wilson and James Callaghan were leaders on points. Blair's leadership was won by a knock-out.

> The biggest difference is that the power-bases of the rivals have tended to merge into the single power-base of the leader. Thirty years ago, the right to challenge him could be acquired by either interest or intellect. Faction was ritualised, with effects the leader could manipulate but not extinguish. Now, loyalty to the leader has been allotted first place in the canon of Labour virtues. Disagreement, once acknowledged as an eternal given of Labour politics, is no longer permitted to exist, let alone to penetrate the cabinet.[55]

Once in government, the same pattern not only held but was strengthened as a result of the leader's ability to reconstruct the election victory as both a vindication and an affirmation of his personal leadership. After six months of a Blair administration, Hugo Young drew conclusions that to him had been inescapable from the very inception of Blair's leadership:

> This is a government in thrall to its own disproportionate triumph on May 1 and to the leader who produced it. Its collective membership permits him to run it as a personal fiefdom, consulting here and there with selected colleagues, running the show through an inner cabinet, not all of whose members belong to the real thing or have any other base than as a Blair familiar. The cabinet itself has taken further giant strides into the desert of irrelevance towards which Mrs Thatcher propelled it. Nobody, these days even talks about the cabinet as a centre of power, or its meetings as occasions where difficult matters are thrashed out between people whose convictions matter to them.[56]

This is not to say that Blair has been free of potential rivals, or that the government has not been unaffected by political feuds. But the rivalry is muted and conditioned by the knowledge that a boardroom reshuffle is no longer an available option. Moreover, the feuds are almost invariably confined to disagreements between ministers. They are also limited in their effect because of the absence of any unified body of ideas that could be deployed as an alternative to Blair's project.

The only exception to the prevailing pattern has been Tony Blair's relationship with Gordon Brown. Blair has openly acknowledged Brown to be the most gifted politician of his generation and a likely successor as prime minister. Strains between Blair and his Chancellor of Exchequer have coloured much of the reporting on the upper reaches of the government. The cabinet reshuffle in July 1998, for example, was widely interpreted as a device by Blair to reduce the status of his Chancellor's allies in government and, by implication, the position of Gordon Brown himself. Nevertheless, the effectiveness of the New Labour government has been generally attributed to the success of the close partnership between Blair and Brown. While their respective entourages have generated friction between Number 10 and the Treasury, the working relationship between the two principals has appeared to be sound. Nevertheless, the potential for discord remains evident not simply because of the status afforded to their respective positions, but because it was Gordon Brown who, in 1994, absented himself from the race to succeed John Smith in order to allow his fellow moderniser a clear run for the party leadership.

A presidency in contention

The net effect of all these factors, in addition to the leadership's relationships with parliament and the Labour party, has resulted in a widespread questioning of the extent to which Blair's premiership has superseded traditional cabinet government to the point where it approximates more to a presidential form of governance. As the course of this analysis has demonstrated, the Blair administration has been associated with a prodigious number of discernible developments, priority shifts and operational changes. In the reputedly litmus test area of executive authority and organisation, these include the infrequency and truncated length of cabinet meetings; Blair's regular abandonment of cabinet agendas; and the prime minister's clear preference for informal *ad hoc* meetings with small numbers of selected ministers and staff around his sofa in the private office. After over a year of his office, *The Economist* concluded that power was moving increasingly into the prime minister's orbit: 'Part of the evidence is the sheer dull perfunctoriness of what now passes for cabinet meetings ... Agendas are vague, debate rare, dissent virtually unheard of. Typically, the prime minister simply recounts decisions already taken in more intimate gatherings.'[57]

Other developments also suggest a strengthening of the premier's position. Kavanagh and Seldon point out that 'Blair entered office determined to exercise a grip from Number Ten and made appointments and created and reformed institutions to suit that purpose'.[58] The doubling of the prime minister's staff during the first two years of the Blair premiership, the introduction of New Labour professionals from party positions to strategic posts relating to policy advice and media presentation in government departments, and the Cabinet Office reforms have all been referred to as evidence supporting a stronger association between Number 10 and the 'centre'. To Kavanagh and Seldon, the drive on the part of Blair to create a dynamic and professionalised centre has been exemplified by the influx of senior advisors with whom he had worked closely when he had been leader of the opposition: 'The scale of Blair's importation and his familiarity with them resembles the way in which a new US President brings in his own "team".'[59] These and the other initiatives demonstrate that the 'trend towards a collective premiership has continued steadily over the period 1997–2000'.[60] In Peter Hennessy's view the development of a collective premiership is closely correlated with the rapid accumulation of power in the office under Blair. '[T]he real hidden wiring' now lay in the 'agreements the Prime Minister concludes with every cabinet minister individually each year ahead of their aims and objectives ... ; and – this is even more amazing – with the permanent secretaries of all the main departments. We've never seen such a tangible instrument and extension of prime ministerial power, as this before.'[61]

One insider quoted by Peter Hennessy believed that the question of a prime minister's department was no longer a real issue in the system: 'Do we need a prime minister's department? It's largely an academic debate now, because we already have one ... Almost all the people in this structure hold office at the pleasure of the PM. It is *sui generis*, a case apart from the rest of the Whitehall machine'.[62] As an incoming administration, the Blair team had made its position on the cabinet very clear: '[T]he new Government did not want the old Cabinet system perhaps not even the Cabinet itself. The PM didn't see why you needed an elaborate and slow system of decision taking.'[63] While the forms of cabinet government were adopted, the essence remained in doubt. Cabinet committees no longer had the status and reach that they had possessed under previous administrations. Full sessions of the cabinet were preceded by more substantial planning and strategy meetings by the 'Big Four' (i.e. Tony Blair, John Prescott, Robin Cook, Gordon Brown) and selected prime ministerial aides (e.g. Jonathan Powell, Alastair Campbell). The overall effect was described by Philip Stephens as a system in which Blair 'preside[d] over a cabinet not so much of comrades but of strangers'.[64]

The use of the term 'strangers' was strongly suggestive of the United States cabinet, whose marginal and contingent significance had always been a reflection of the president's pre-eminent position as chief executive. In similar fashion, Tony Blair seemed able to place the cabinet on the periphery of decision making, or at least to be in a position to select when it should be central and when it should not. During the war in Kosovo in 1999, the cabinet was rarely involved in any substantive decision making or even in any consultation exercises. The prime minister mainly relied on bilateral meetings with Robin Cook, George Robertson and the Chief of the Defence Staff, Sir Charles Guthrie. At the conclusion of the war, a government insider believed that the experience had demonstrated the extraordinary supremacy of the prime minister: 'Because of the war, presidential government is more extreme than ever now.'[65]

It is not unusual for the decision-making apparatus of the British cabinet to contract in periods of emergency. The point about the Kosovo engagement and the Iraqi crisis in December 1998 was that they appeared not so much to deviate from the norm of the Blair administration, but to exemplify it. The prime minister has developed a capacity to intervene in a whole range of issues (e.g. Northern Ireland, welfare reform, health, education, Europe). These incursions have not been limited to the level of strategic oversight but have involved Number 10 engaging in the micro-management of issues. Commentators have recognised that the prime minister's 'ability to stand at some distance from his cabinet has been a source of strength'.[66] His detachment has enabled him to give focus to selected issues, to honour the pledges on constitutional reform against the reservations of the cabinet, and to engage successfully in highly sensitive areas 'requiring the skills of a quasi-presidential figure above the fray'.[67] Notwithstanding the possible benefits of prime ministerial micro-management, the scale of Blair's authority in the system has created anxiety not only within an increasingly restive party but in Whitehall itself. In Peter Hennessy's judgement, the Blair team has been engaged in a process to introduce a 'command and control premiership' in to the British system (see figure 9.1). This is reflected in Hennessy's adoption of a circular device in conveying the estimated distribution of power. To Hennessy, 'a model of concentric circles fitted the reality much more than a pyramidal, hierarchical arrangement of the kind usually produced when the traditionally collective Cabinet system is depicted'.[68]

As Burch and Holliday have shown in connection to the cabinet system, the precise configuration of network relationships at the centre will change in relation to different issue areas.[69] Nevertheless, this schematic device of concentric circles is intended to demonstrate the gravitational force of the prime ministerial centre. The pattern 'illustrates what has been called a "prime minister's department" in all but the formalised sense'.[70] It is true that the design reveals one cabinet minister to be exceptionally close to Blair. Gordon Brown's occupancy of Circle two, however, is evidently not typical of the position of other members of the cabinet. On the contrary, it is seen to be 'an exclusive relationship. In a curious way, it serves only to magnify the distance between Mr Blair and the cabinet bystanders'.[71] The scheme produced by Hennessy has a resonance with the list of those quoted by Derek Draper, in July 1998, as the 'seventeen people who count' in the

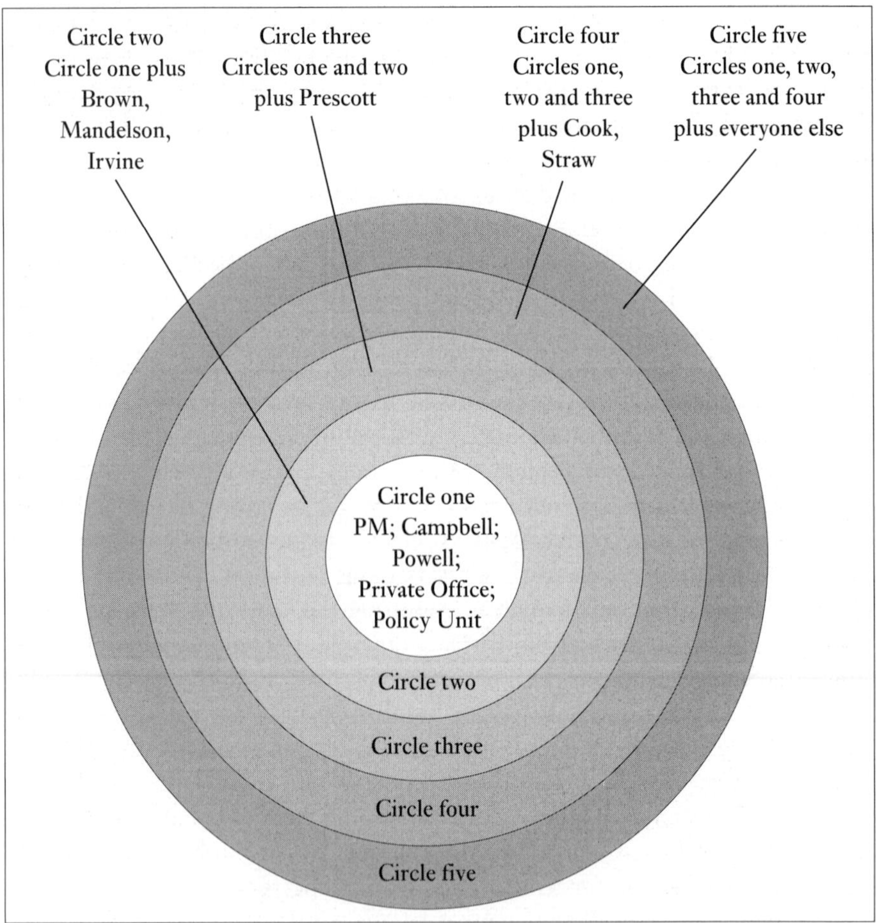

Figure 9.1 The concentric pattern of power at the 'Blair centre': version 1.

Source: Peter Hennessy, *The Blair Centre: A Question of Command and Control?* (London, Public Management Foundation, 1999), p. 10.

Note: Version 2 produced six months after Version 1, includes Peter Mandelson, Philip Gould and Lord Falconer in Circle one, reduces Lord Irvine to Circle four, and adds Sir Richard Wilson to Circle three. See Peter Hennessy, 'Lord Mayor's lecture', extracted in Peter Hennesy, 'Tony Blair, the Caesar of our times', *Daily Telegraph*, 13 July 1999.

Labour government.[72] In the 'cash for access' affair, the well-attuned senses of the New Labour lobbyist attributed pivotal positions to only six members of the cabinet other than Blair himself (i.e. Gordon Brown, Peter Mandelson, John Prescott, Jack Straw, Derry Irvine, Alistair Darling). The remaining ten figures were mostly accounted for by the prime minister's inner circle of aides and advisors (e.g. Alastair Campbell, David Miliband, Anji Hunter, Sally Morgan, Philip Gould, Jonathan Powell, Roger Liddle).

Hennessy has resisted using the term 'presidential', but others have had no such reservations.[73] The usage of presidential terminology in relation to the Blair administration has become an almost prosaic form of descriptive licence. The sense of radical departure and extraordinary authority has propelled commentators and analysts out of the customary frames of reference into what is taken to be an alien superlative. These types of observation and analysis can give substantial assistance to the claim of an emergent British presidency. Given the central significance of the cabinet in the British system, references to its demise and displacement are often taken as the decisive and climactic elements in the thesis of a *de facto* presidential element in British government. And yet it is precisely at this point of apparent prevalence that a strong note of caution is required.

It is important to note that the case for a presidential dimension is not reducible to the categories of executive decision making and institutional power distribution. On the contrary, by concentrating wholly upon these apparently pivotal areas for the clinching evidence of a presidential presence, the proposition of a Blair presidency is in fact placed at risk. Nevertheless, this is the ground upon which the presidential case is normally presented. By the same token, this is also the basis on which the proposition is customarily disputed, contested and rejected. The critical reaction to the presidential reputation of the Blair administration, like the initial response to *The Rise of the British Presidency*,[74] has almost without exception been centred upon the notion that the presidential proposition is an affront to the British system's traditional structures and processes and to the conventions of analysis that rest upon them. This has in turn provoked a series of counterarguments designed not merely to refute the claims of a presidential dimension but to refute them absolutely without qualification. In order to assess the validity of these arguments, and by extension the reliability and limits of the current proposition of a genuine presidential dimension, it is appropriate to explore the nature and force of these rebuttals. It is only by examining the conventional case against a British presidency that the case for the unconventional position can be placed in context and gauged accordingly.

The case against

There are essentially four discernible types of analytical argument against the claims of an emergent presidential element in the British system. The first is what can be described as a case of *deceptive appearances.* This position concedes that flamboyant prime ministers can distract and disorient the normal news coverage of politics to an extent where they can give the impression of personal hegemony. As the premier comes to dominate the lines of political communication, and as political issues become personalised in relation to the prime minister's interests and priorities, so the tendency is to extrapolate substance from the sheer scale of appearance. But, according to this line of argument, such an inductive leap is wholly unwarranted and completely unfounded. The centrality of the premiership is confined to the sphere of impressions and appearances. Presidential frames of reference may be useful in conveying the sensory dislocation and frisson of high leadership exposure in a predominantly corporate structure, but to draw any substantive conclusions from such dazzling superficialities is to confuse outward form with interior substance.

According to this perspective, allusions to a presidential dimension originate in, and are confined to, the level of individual style and personal affectation. While the latter can generate widespread public attention and can possess a political utility in its own right, political style cannot be equated with political structure. As a system, British government is reducible to a prevailing set of institutions and governing principles. While a prime minister may achieve high levels of public prominence, this does not, and cannot, neutralise the power of the great departments of state. It is these organisations that provide the constitutive basis of British government and invest ministers with immense resources and high levels of autonomy. In such a system, a prime minister finds it politically and administratively impossible to be a chief executive. Ultimately, he or she remains *primus interpares* in a framework that only functions according to a corporate ethos that combines the devices of ministerial accountability to parliament into an aggregate of cabinet collective responsibility. The Whitehall machine, and the political arrangements and doctrines that underwrite it, remain the undeviating substructure of the British system. Prime ministers may affect a presidential style but this is almost invariably a reaction to the weakness of the 'hollow centre' rather than an expression of executive strength. The political gains achieved by a publicity-seeking premier, therefore, will always be marginal in nature because of the material reality of the departments and their ministers.

Prime ministers and their ministerial colleagues co-exist in a dynamic relationship in which neither can ever be discounted. The two cannot be disconnected from one another. To concentrate on the prime minister at the expense of the cabinet will necessarily lead to distortions and misinterpretations. In the view of Jack Straw, Blair's Home Secretary, the system remains rooted in the palpable reality of departments, parliament, statute law, administration and ministerial accountability: 'The people who have to go to parliament and to make the propositions are not the prime minister on the whole but the Secretaries of State and their ministers ... It's always been very frustrating for prime ministers in terms of getting departments to take an initiative.'[75] Ministerial authority continues to be substantial because of this formal linkage to parliament as the source of legal enactment. The prime minister has no department and therefore is proportionally impoverished: 'One of the realities is that we live in a parliamentary democracy not in a system of presidential government ... For all the guff about presidential government, the prime minister is running cabinet government.'[76] Tony Blair may have gone to considerable lengths to accentuate the status of the premiership. Yet even he has had to concede that a hegemonic prime minister cannot escape the traditional constraints of the system: 'The Government is more collective than many people think',[77] he told reporters in September 1999.

Cabinet government may have become a misnomer, and even a fiction, because the cabinet with its committee system has become a much more complex and multidimensional entity. Nevertheless, the cabinet's decline as a corporate entity should not be equated with the onset of a British presidency. Indeed, there is every reason to be cautious over abandoning one simplicity in favour of an even greater simplicity. Any attempt, therefore, to put forward a case for changing the terminology, either to that of prime ministerial government or to a British presidency, can be dismissed on two grounds as an unbalanced proposition. First, its plausibility rests upon a capacity to ignore or to discount the evident gravitational force of the government departments and the cabinet. Second, the proposition can be criticised for being excessively dependent upon interpretation and construction for its effect and, as such, it raises as many questions over the validity of the technique as it does over the accuracy of the observations.

The *flash in the pan* response accounts for the second main argument against the claim of a British presidency. This perspective recognises that some premiers do indeed achieve extraordinary levels of prominence which diminish the status and authority of the cabinet and confound the traditions and conventions of the British constitution. A political leader with the appropriate conviction and skills can exploit a favourable set of circumstances to generate an exceptional reach within government and society. Such individuals can tilt the balance so far towards the premiership that the cabinet can appear moribund and lacking a viable political role. The caveat to this creative flux is that while the system permits the extraordinary, it does not allow it for long. The extraordinary only exists and is only conspicuous set against the prevailing expanse of the ordinary. According to this perspective, dominant prime ministers may punctuate the prosaic rhythms of British political life but they do not transform it into a different condition. Their means of pre-eminence remain idiosyncratic and peculiar to each of them. As a consequence, they form no pattern and generate no cumulative set of achievements that can approximate to a process of institutional development. On the contrary, the very personalisation of their premierships have ensured that their individual contributions have never been institutionalised into lasting achievements.

Commentators can be dismayed and perplexed over the penetration of presidential forms and over the extent to which the system can accommodate such apparently alien incursions for short periods of time. Peter Riddell, for example, has been surprised by the scale and reach of Blair's presidential style of government. To him, the level of centralisation has been a remarkable achievement and one that has allowed Blair largely to dispense with the cabinet, in favour of bilateral contacts between Number 10 and individual ministers. But Riddell strikes a note of caution. It is the very success that Blair has had in dominating the key decisions which would, in Riddell's view, inevitably provoke a comparable reaction against Number 10. Mr Blair might expect and demand collegiate support and collective responsibility, but his presidential style would undermine these attributes. This would inevitably leave him isolated at times when he would be most in need of assistance.

> Most decisions are taken on a bilateral basis between 10 Downing Street and affected ministers ... There is little collective discussion, virtually never in Cabinet and seldom in committee on key issues. So other ministers do not always feel committed to decisions in which they have had no say. 'Departmentalitis' is a direct result of a lack of collegiality.[78]

As there was 'little sense of collective decision-making', many ministers did 'not feel part of the team'.[79] Riddell concluded that Blair would 'need to involve his cabinet before long'.[80] There was no escape from the central dynamic, even for Tony Blair. 'The Prime Minister faces powerful departmental interests. They have to be managed and can seldom be commanded ... He can work only through his ministers.'[81]

Peter Hennessy shares the same sense of fatalism. While Blair would 'remain an issue of fascination and contention, ... the tension between Prime Minister and Cabinet [w]ould not be resolved'.[82] In such a context, 'there are no permanent victories'.[83] While Blair's attempts to create a 'command premiership' might allow the prime minister to prevail in several skirmishes, it was likely to be at the price of long-term weakness. Hennessy pointed out the need for Blair 'to go against all his instincts and be more collegial'.[84] This was not simply a matter of political prudence but of historical instruction:

> [A]ttention to the *longue duree* of British governance does induce a sense of and respect for the importance of being collective, both as a safeguard against overmightiness at the top and as an aid to careful, effective and durable policy making. Command models, Napoleonic or otherwise, have a habit of ending in tears.[85]

Another experienced observer concurred. To Michael White, Blair's impact upon government had been extraordinary but it had to be set against the inevitability of a very ordinary fate: '[W]hatever short-term gains Mr Blair's Praetorian Guard has made, the long-term trend is always against a sitting premier.'[86] His colleagues may be quiescent for some time but ultimately they will turn against him – 'in the end, they always do.'[87] In the final analysis, presidential prime ministers are unsustainable in a system predisposed to party politics and collective enterprises from elections designed to produce governments geared to mandates rather than to individual leadership.

Claims in support of an increasing presidential component in British politics are confronted by a third argument. This can be described as the *iron law of politics*, which embraces an altogether more fundamentalist approach than either of the arguments already cited. A presidency is largely defined by reference to a set of centralising and unifying properties that reflect and support a construction of executive supremacy. The normal condition and organisation of politics, on the other hand, relates strongly to division, conflict and challenge. In this dualistic perspective, any attempt to introduce a presidential dimension into a parliamentary democracy like that of Britain would not only entail some derogation of established political processes but would be doomed to failure because political dissent and argument will always undermine those efforts to suspend them. A presidency out of context may be able temporarily to reduce political activity for limited periods but in essence the position is one of artificial pre-eminence because it relies upon the fiction that politics can be taken out of politics. As this is ultimately an impossible managerial task, notional 'presidents' soon find that presidencies exist only as intellectual abstractions that are quite unable to withstand the material reality of power politics. The greatest danger to prime ministers in this respect is to believe the hype over their own *de facto* presidential status. Nothing could be less factual. The need for prime ministers to be released from the stratosphere of presidential pretensions and to refamiliarise themselves with the predatory nature of political appetites is typified by Andrew Marr's warning to Tony Blair: '[T]here are limits to the power of presidential politics inside a system of cabinet government ... However big the mandate and however dominant the prime minister, the acrid mix of ambition, vanity and ideology that comprises the internal combustion of cabinet-level politics eventually explodes, and explodes again, and again.'[88]

Although this line of argument is strongly influenced by general propositions over the reductionist nature of political behaviour, it does give particular weight to those political forms and institutions that can be seen to exist and to function. This positivist outlook is reflected in the way that the cabinet, parliament and political parties are seen as retaining their significance not least because of their status as having an objective existence. Greater analytical weight is given to that which is an empirical fact rather than to that which is not. The cabinet, for example, clearly exists and is still pivotal in the hierarchy of government, in the allocation of power and in the transmission of disputes. Cabinet reshuffles are still seen as being of critical importance to a prime minister and the government. The need to reshape the cabinet is central for a prime minister to build or to maintain authority. Rivals and future competitors for the leadership will emanate from the cabinet. Even though a figure like Peter Mandelson possessed formidable political resources outside the cabinet, he aspired to the power base of a ministry in order to give him the status and leverage to advance his political career.

By the same token, that which is not evident is seen as being just as significant. Notwithstanding the claims of a British presidency, there remains no structural separation between the prime minister and the cabinet, or between the prime minister and any other Member of Parliament. There is no prime minister's department. Even though it was thought that the Blair team wanted one, the proposal was effectively blocked. Again, there are no press conferences given by the prime minister's press secretary, as this would be seen as undermining the separate authority and collective responsibility of ministers. Conspicuous absences like these are taken as a reaffirmation of the permanence of established political forces. According to this line of argument, no institutional basis exists for the presidentialisation of British government. Richard Crossman's original assertions of prime ministerial/presidential government were made over thirty-five years ago. They remain mere assertions that are yet to be verified by substantive change that takes account of the realities of political behaviour. Prime ministers can neither be extracted from the corporate habitat of the cabinet, nor abstracted from the compulsive interplay of political competition.

A final argument which is more implicit than explicit, but which informs much of the three reactions mentioned above, can be referred to as the *problem of precision.* In political inquiry, as in all fields of human understanding, there remain limits to reliable knowledge. A case like this involves a profusion of political, institutional, situational, personal and psychological factors, compounded by a code of confidentiality and a framework of official secrecy. Given this level of complexity, it is a practical impossibility to elicit a sufficient amount of accurate information to achieve a level of understanding capable of supporting precise conclusions over 'cabinet government' or 'presidential government'. The number and variety of contingent variables are so extensive that generalisations will always remain indeterminate and crude estimations. The problematic nature of the enterprise precludes simple truths and final answers.

In such an analytical context, it is better to opt for the generalisation that has a higher probability of approximating to an underlying condition. Cabinet government may be a very loose generalisation in many respects, but nevertheless it rests upon a long tradition of observation and a solid history of possessing a material presence in the system of governance. The cabinet has been shown to be a mutable institution whose roles and significance have varied over the course of its development. Nevertheless, it is an objective entity and one that has been a central determinant of policy and power. For such a generalisation to be displaced by another generalisation based upon a presidential theme, it would be necessary to produce a greater body of evidence at higher levels of validity than the pre-existing, if flawed, construction. The burden of proof lies with the innovative perspective. Like any paradigm shift, a new way of looking at an old subject requires dramatic and conclusive forms of evidence that not only provide enhanced forms of explanation, but decisively subvert and delegitimise old forms of comprehension. Because notions of presidential government have so little historical or structural basis to rely upon, and so limited a level of analytical inquiry, they cannot hope to meet the criteria of a paradigmatic change in conception and understanding. Until such time that the presidential government paradigm has generated a body of evidence and a theoretical structure comparable to that of cabinet government, then it is better to err on the side of caution. Notions of presidential government, therefore, should be restricted to the sphere of metaphysics or epi-phenomena where, in the absence of a set of decisive observations and a clinching argument, they rightfully belong.

Arguing against the grain

Readers of this study will by now have become aware that the observations and arguments enumerated in the previous eight chapters are utterly out of synch with the standard charges against the existence of a British presidency. On the contrary, the analysis of spatial leadership, outsider politics, competitive populism, personal projection, media management, individuated party images, the 'permanent campaign', and the contractual and affective linkages between leaders and their public constituencies have controverted both the traditional methods and the normal conclusions of British political inquiry. This has not been deliberate, but it has been unavoidable. The extraordinary developments in leadership politics under Margaret Thatcher, John Major and Tony Blair have transcended the normal dynamics within and between institutions, parties and political organisations. Similarly, their premierships have superseded conventional forms of analysis and established constructions of the political process. These changes simply cannot be reduced as a matter of course to variations within the tolerance levels of a fundamentally static system. It is no longer a plausible position to claim that the prime minister's position is distinguished by 'an almost total lack of development'.[89] The changes are radical in nature and in many respects alien to the formal configuration and operating principles of the governmental system. Furthermore, they are cumulative in effect and constitute a developmental process that will lead to the premiership moving further and further away from the anchorages of the traditional conception of prime minister. The sheer level of exceptionalism associated with Blair's rise to power cannot, therefore, be dismissed as simply the result of a set of idiosyncrasies that are peculiar to Blair and to his milieu. On the contrary, the authority and development of his premiership are attributable more to the presence of a range of underlying forces that are continually increasing the pace and penetration of leadership politics within the British system.

The changes referred to in this study are not isolated and discrete in nature. Collectively, they account for a discernible trend-line of systemic change. This is exemplified by the transformation in the way that political leadership is cultivated and exerted in British political life. The existence of deep-set shifts in the nature of the political system has altered the standing and role of leadership in the dynamics of political relationships. These shifts have also allowed the personal nature of leadership to have a powerful bearing upon the wider fields of political perception, evaluation and discourse. These changes have been of an order and magnitude to make the comparison between the British prime minister's position and the American presidency far more pertinent now than it used to be. There is now more point to the comparison, as there are now more analogies that can be drawn between the interior dynamics of both offices. In effect, there are more characteristics that are palpably common to both in terms of pressures, constraints and contingencies.

This study has attempted to demonstrate that the developments and forces underlying the changes in the political position of the British prime minister are not merely similar to those experienced in the White House, but are illustrated most fully in their nature by the American presidency. The analytical and interpretive insights afforded by studies of the American presidency can, therefore, be exploited to great effect to increase further the understanding of contemporary developments in the British premiership and to illustrate the many political and social repercussions that flow from the intensification of these trends. This is not to underestimate the importance of the structural differences that exist between the two systems. But it is to draw attention to, and to recognise the significance of, the dramatic extent to which even within two such different contexts, certain profound similarities have arisen. In spite of the clear contrast in institutional superstructures, the underlying points of resemblance are so exceptional that there is now evidence to support the contention that the similarities between the two offices are more revealing than their differences. Furthermore, it can be contended that these similarities are increasing in scale and importance all the time.

The pressures and opportunities, the expectations and motivations, and the restraints and problems associated with the business of being, and remaining, a prime minister are now sufficiently analogous to the equivalent conditions faced by an American president to justify the term 'president' being applied to the occupant of Number 10. In fact, it would be no exaggeration to assert that what this country has witnessed over the last generation has been the growing emergence of a British presidency.

It is important to point out that such an assertion does not imply that the British premiership has become indistinguishable from the American presidency. But neither does it carry the implication that the two positions are continuing to follow divergent courses of political development. What is being suggested is that they have come to move along parallel paths. The comparability that has come to exist does so at a level that transcends the constitutional differences within the two systems. It relates to a commonality of experience. 'Changes in the conditions of governance have spawned a convergence of executive leadership in Anglo-American states that – to a degree – functions independently of structural factors'.[90] Their separation is still significant, but the changes in the politics of the British premiership have now had the effect of pulling the conditions and properties of British political leadership in the same direction as the contemporary evolution of the American presidency. These forces underlying the presidency's development are now so clearly evident in the British context that they provide compelling grounds for establishing the existence of what is to all intents and purposes a *de facto* British presidency.

Rubber bands, riddles and the species barrier

These assertions do not merely fly in the face of the customary depictions of British government. They confront and confound the standard methodologies of analysing the system. The arguments assembled in the 'case against' pivot upon an underlying assumption that the nature of the British executive is ineluctably inclined to a collective entity. This can be distracted and even temporarily subverted by the personal characteristics of a party leader but under no circumstances can it genuinely be compromised. It will always reassert itself irrespective of the forces ranged against it and irrespective of developments around it. The presumptive existence of collective cabinet rule, or even of some pure derivative of it, is taken as being axiomatic. It is the point of departure. It is also the inevitable destination. The cabinet may be modified, adapted and even diminished, but it never disappears. It remains the pole star of British government. Views of it may change, but it is always assumed to be there as an active force and as a working principle of government. Analyses of central administration and executive power are dominated by the presupposition of a competitive body of ministers, who always have political resources at their disposal and who always condition the prime minister's authority along the lines of a contingent and reversible level of political status.[91]

Margaret Thatcher, for example, is now seen as having stretched and strained the boundaries of cabinet government, but never to the point of rupturing them. In fact, she is even used to affirm and to vindicate the processes of British constitutional constraint. In passages that evoke the mechanical dynamics of America's checks and balances, commentators refer to Thatcher's decline as a consequence of an adventure in presidential deviancy that was predetermined to end in a revival of cabinet government. Mrs Thatcher is said to have 'certainly flouted the spirit of traditional cabinet government', even to the point of placing it 'temporarily on ice'.[92] What she could not do was to extinguish it. Moreover, she could not prevent the pendulum of power swinging back against her. In Ronald Butt's view, 'Mrs Thatcher's personal handicap had been her failure to see that she could not continue indefinitely to override and bypass her cabinet'.[93] Peter Hennessy agreed: 'The problems that had stored up under her style of Prime Ministerial leadership finally did come home to roost. An "over-mighty" premier had been unable to withstand them.'[94] And to Peter Madgwick, it was clear that 'Mrs Thatcher's fall from office showed the ultimate force of collective interest sorely tried, and striking back at arrogant prime ministerial power'.[95]

In refuting the possibility of a presidential dimension in British government, George Jones uses the analogy of an elastic band. It stretches to accommodate an activist prime minister and contracts with the arrival of a more quiescent chief executive. The more the rubber is stretched, the greater the force that is exerted upon the prime minister by the collective energies of the cabinet. Margaret Thatcher stretched the elastic but, in the end, she had to submit to its countervailing strength. It slipped effortlessly back into shape as she left Downing Street.[96] There are many contentious aspects to such an analogy. For example, it assumes that the prime minister's office and powers have an objectively defined and, thereby, 'normal' shape. It assumes that the authority and style of different prime ministers constitute nothing more than a series of variations upon a single overriding theme. That theme of cabinet government is so rubbery and amorphous, it is capable of embracing almost any configuration of government in the name of collective decision making and collegiate power sharing. To this extent, the rubber band idea approximates to a truism that government is about more than one person. Apart from the various tautological and self-validating aspects of such a notion, the elastic band analogy is significant in another and more fundamental respect. In spite of its deficiencies, or more likely because of them, Jones's elasticated device is a way not of explaining the relationship between prime ministerial power and the traditional norm of the cabinet, but of closing consideration of the issue down to an absolute and static minimum. To this extent, it is utterly symptomatic of the British constitution's aptitude for evading analysis and for suspending appraisal of its opaque interior. The elastic band only appears to explain everything by appearing to cover everything. But it hardly explains anything at all. It is rooted to an *a priori* position rather than to a sense of empirical curiosity.

Devices like that of the elastic band are thoroughly consistent with the British constitution's traditional code of swathing difficult issues in an upholstery of corporate negligence. Such a model epitomises those forces and habits that preclude any revision to the orthodox conception of the British executive, or any corrective to the British myopia over the complex and problematic issue of executive leadership. It excludes notions of prime ministerial access to exclusive sources of power. It rejects presidential analogies as self-evidently inapplicable and logically inadmissible. In their place, it relies upon the casuistry of an iron law of elastic indeterminacy governed by a fixed attachment to a pre-existing and absolute form of cabinet government. In this sense, cabinet government acts as the core condition, the gravitational field and the home base – i.e. an entity which does not require explanation or even verification, and which successfully distracts attention away from areas of constitutional sensitivity.

The present analysis takes issue with another characteristic property of the 'case against'. This relates to the supposition that if a case for a presidential element in British politics were to exist, it would not warrant serious consideration because it can only ever be a temporary phenomenon. At one stroke, the possibility of such a dimension is conceded and then dismissed. The implication of this position is that departures from the British norm are possible, but that they can only be accounted for as deviant cases. This disjunction can be described as the 'Riddell riddle'. Peter Riddell is one of the most experienced, respected and thoughtful observers of the British scene and one who has a forensic interest in the ebb and flow of power politics at the highest levels of British government. As a long-established Whitehall watcher with a highly developed sense of history, Riddell has noted the extent to which Blair has 'cultivat[ed] a presidential image ... He is the People's Tony above the partisan battle and the Prime Minister above the ministerial debate – with no nonsense about equals. This style has fostered ... record approval ratings'.[97] More significantly, it has had a material influence upon the operation of government. Riddell is not the only commentator to have alluded to the unprecedented reach of the Blair premiership, to the 'demise of the Cabinet as a central organ of government'[98] and to the transition from a 'collective to a centralised system directed by 10 Downing Street'.[99] Nevertheless, in spite of his experience and his reputation for careful analysis, Riddell does not see any case to be made to account for such radical departures from the norm.

Riddell exemplifies a genre that records the extraordinary reach of a prime minister but which offers no real explanation for the recorded phenomenon. The properties of Blair's premiership are recognised as being substantive rather than merely a matter of style or appearance. And yet the reasons for developments that are palpably inconsistent with the traditions and conventions of cabinet government are not part of the analytical agenda. The implicit explanation is that no explanation is necessary for something which is a temporary aberration in the historical sweep of British political institutions. Just as the customary patterns of political dynamics can be temporarily suspended, so the explanatory impulse can be similarly held in check during the hiatus. The only response required is one of prescriptive advice on the need to prepare for the time when normal service is resumed. After six months in office, Riddell issued a warning: 'Mr Blair can command now. But he will need to involve his Cabinet before long.'[100] Two months later, the advice was the same: 'Mr Blair will not achieve his main policy goals unless he alters his way of governing.'[101] After a year in office, Riddell detected that the Blair administration was 'growing up' and showing signs of maturity: 'Both the habits and personnel of Opposition are being discarded'.[102] He encouraged further efforts towards cabinet adulthood: 'It is time to be less informal and more serious about the procedures of Government.'[103]

However, Blair provided only partial relief. The prime minister continued to operate at a thoroughly unconventional level of detachment in the British system. This pre-eminence may have strained cognitive structures, but the response remained the same: 'A British prime minister is not a president. He or she has to operate not only through ministerial colleagues but also through Parliament. They need to be nurtured.'[104] In 1999, the disjunction still showed no sign of being resolved. Something strange had happened but whatever it was, it could not go on. While there remained little sense of collective decision making or genuine teamwork, the detached premiership of Tony Blair rolled on to the sound of Riddell's exhortation: 'You'll never walk alone, Mr Blair.'[105]

The 'Riddell riddle' rests upon a driving supposition at the heart of traditional analysis in this field. Cabinet government in all its various guises is a reductionist scheme of explanation. Anything that lies outside this sphere is therefore designated as a deviant phenomenon requiring no explanation. Abnormality can not only be defined by the greater mass of documented normality, but can be effectively disregarded as a meaningless mutation doomed to irrelevance. Even though change is observed, it is implicitly dismissed as a curiosity. It may divert attention from the dynamics of cabinet government but it cannot alter the timeless imperatives of a system that is necessarily collective in character. One of the key arguments which informs this study is that these presidential deformities have become too frequent in number and too extensive in time to be continually dispatched as aberrations. The peculiarities of Margaret Thatcher's pre-eminence, the external tribulations associated with John Major's efforts to meet the demands of personalised leadership and Tony Blair's exceptional disengagement from much of the political process are simply too extensive and significant to be pigeon-holed away in the lost letter department of cabinet government.

The 'iron law of politics' position further exacerbates the dearth of analysis. This is normally combined with cabinet government reductionism to produce a position that equates the restitution of normal cabinet dynamics with the resumption of normal political activity. This outlook is based upon a conception of a presidential office as being one of unqualified supremacy and unbridled power. The standard usage of presidential terminology is generally motivated by an impulse to give dramatic emphasis to the idea of a deviant prime minister. In Britain, the term 'presidential' is sufficiently alien and exotic to convey a level of deformity that places it at the opposite end of a spectrum to that occupied by cabinet government. Just as the notion of presidential government becomes an accumulation of negatives it develops into an antithesis of cabinet government and with it the definitive standard of British abnormality. The degree of central power, unified command and personal rule that is commonly attributed to a presidential status has on occasion been almost authoritarian in scale. It is true that the allocation of characteristics has been through default rather than through a process of precise definition but the net effect has remained the same – namely the acceptance of cabinet government and presidential government as two diametrically opposed models. The dysfunctional associations with the presidential model are often so severe that it is difficult to reconcile them with liberal democratic principles. On occasions, even this constraint gives way as Blair's presidential pretensions have led him to be compared to Cromwell, Napoleon and Mussolini.[106]

The problem with working to a duality like this is that it distorts and corrupts analysis. First, it degrades the content and usage of the analogy with the American presidency. The attribution of a monopolised power structure to the presidency owes more to the preoccupations of British commentators concerned over the cabinet's inherent pluralism being subverted by an overmighty prime minister. Within this simplified duality, the presidential comparison immediately becomes compromised as extreme and, therefore, inapplicable. The presidency is almost always employed in a facetious way. It is first turned into a bloated parody of itself and then deployed to affirm the absence of an implausibly autocratic form of central government in Britain. It is easily picked off as a gross and unjustifiable disfigurement. After alluding to the presidential comparison, therefore, it is customary to discard it.

It is clear that in many cases the presidential comparison is employed solely for the purpose of dismissing it and of vindicating the characteristics and the principles of traditional cabinet authority. In this light, the American presidency is regarded as a cautionary example – a repository of autocratic command thankfully absent in Britain. The American grotesque is then held up as the equivalent of what Britain's cabinet government would look like if its constitutional principles had been completely corrupted. The fact that the British prime minister cannot be equated with the American presidency is then taken as proof positive of the continued viability of cabinet government and of its interior capacity to prevent such American-style mutations.

The second problem with this duality is that it implies the existence of a single dimension of political arrangements and conditions. These may vary but only in relation to the same unilinear scale. When Peter Hennessy, for example, ruminates upon Margaret Thatcher's handling of the cabinet, he speculates on where she would be placed on a 'spectrum stretching from collective decision-making to "presidential" command'.[107] Apart from underwriting the idea of a zero-sum relationship between mutually exclusive cabinet and presidential models, a scale of this nature carries the implication that the presidency is an advanced progression of the prime minister's position. Just as the notion of prime ministerial power is, in many respects, taken to be a collective projection of the cabinet, references to a presidential form of power amount to a unitary conception of what is a store of pre-existing powers. As a consequence, to be presidential in Britain, therefore, usually means to be a prime minister in a condensed and highly potent form. By assuming the existence of such a continuum, the presidential analogy implies an extreme, rather than an alternative conception of executive power and leadership in the British system.

A final objection to the presidential–cabinet duality is that it confines the natural impulses and processes of politics to the disputatious context of cabinet decision making and collective action. British conceptions and attitudes towards the American presidency in this type of comparative exercise tend towards an 'end of politics' posture in which a president is protected by a suspension of normal political activity. If a prime minister becomes unusually dominant, then it is common for him or her to be given a presidential appellation to denote a curious suspension from conventional politics. But this is seen as a temporary condition before the artificiality of such an anomaly is stripped bare by the inevitable recurrence of political realism. Such a view is far from being realistic because it misunderstands the nature of the US presidency. As this study has sought to make clear, the presidency is not a model of command and control for the duration of a statutory period. It is a highly politicised position in which the office-holder continually has to deploy a range of political skills and resources to maximise the available opportunities for power. A president's authority and reach are permanently contingent upon a profusion of political variables. The reference points and the strategies, the arenas and the language may be different from the British system, but political disputes, conflicts and challenges flow as persistently through the system as they do through Westminster and Whitehall.

The 'case against' argument can also be contested on grounds of institutional change and development. The supposition at the heart of the British tradition of cabinet government is that the institution is a mutable entity capable of great variation within an outward form of continuity and permanence. In accordance with the principles of the British constitution, it is understood and accepted that the cabinet is an adaptive organisation whose role and function evolve over time. This common law perspective of principles elucidated by practice and successive adjustment has been a dominant theme in Britain's development into a parliamentary democracy. As the parliament was gradually woven into a democratic form, the crown prerogative powers were gradually transposed to the cabinet. A vast metamorphosis had occurred within a framework of apparent continuity. The mutability of the forms and processes of the executive has continued to be a characteristic feature of the British system. In fact, no sector of the British state has demonstrated a greater capacity to evolve into radically innovative structures of executive government, public administration and organisational management.

And yet in spite of this tradition of evolutionary development, the position of the 'case against' is one of a fundamentalist rejection of a presidential dimension on the grounds that it is necessarily dependent upon the presence of change. A British presidency is seen as an anathema because it is viewed as being unhistorical, or ahistorical or even anti-historical. In such a framework, any construction relating to a presidential element is contrary to the prevailing Whig view of history, which interprets Britain's parliamentary democracy as the point of culmination of a long historical process. To claim the existence of a British presidency, therefore, is tantamount to challenging Britain's national identity and to subverting the integrity of the historical process that has underwritten Britain's political exceptionalism as a liberal democracy brought into existence by spontaneous and incremental adjustment. Notions of a presidential element are challenging because they point to a discontinuity in the evolutionary scheme. Being a disjunction necessarily means that it cannot be reduced to an evolutionary frame of reference. Since the British constitution is an evolutionary system, it would be impossible for a president to emerge through such methods. It would be the equivalent of claiming that a species barrier had been crossed as a result of the very evolutionary processes that had originally generated the idiosyncratic British model.

Notwithstanding the argument that an evolutionary model is an open system capable of substantial and unpredictable change, the position of this study has always been one of giving recognition to a hybrid. It has never been claimed that the British presidency represents a crossing of a species barrier. It is true that it questions the existence of such a dichotomy and challenges the absolute perspectives associated with it. The view that the parliamentary/cabinet model and the presidential model are mutually exclusive and self-contained entities that are incapable of sharing individual characteristics is one which cannot be sustained. Likewise, the implication that it is necessary to demonstrate a total and complete process of 'presidentialisation' in order to substantiate a claim of a partial development is also rejected. But irrespective of the dispute over the levels of systemic autonomy between the respective models, the claim in this analysis has always been one of locating the presidential dimension in a British context.

British political leadership and the presidential dimension

The British presidency is derived from a series of general developments and underlying dynamics within the British system. It is an emanation of conditions that approximate to a form of uninhibited presidential politics. This is exemplified by Britain's increasing preoccupation with the nature and role of political leadership. The properties, requirements and expectations of leadership have generated an entire medium of political exchange, in which a specialised vocabulary and set of evaluative categories has grown up through which leaders are observed and appraised. Leaders still remain utterly dependent upon parties for their formal position and initial platform as well as their access to government. Yet it is also true to say that the leaders of the political parties in Britain increasingly occupy a world of their own.

This presidential dimension is dominated by the need for leaders to have leadership qualities, to have the opportunity to demonstrate them and to have them publicly appreciated. The net effect of all these imperatives is a uniform strategy adopted by leaders to maximise their chances of success by seeking an intimate *rapprochement* with the general public. Leadership is watched, tested and assessed for its public qualities by a public increasingly interested in, and even absorbed by, the public performance of leaders. Leadership has now become an established political issue in its own right. The issue is played out in public, not least because it is this arena in which the issue is most significant. It is the arena in which the varying conceptions of leadership, and the differing estimations of leaders in fulfilling those conceptions, are discussed and debated. Not only are leaders constantly on show in such an arena, but they have to be on permanent parade in order to remain leaders. To do this, they must acquire a high level of public visibility, continually advance the conception of a general public, and link their *raisons d'être* as leaders to that of the public's concerns and fears. Political leadership is now expected to be public leadership. It is no longer enough to be a political leader who merely appears in public. Leaders now have to possess the qualities to lead the public, or at least to make a plausible assertion to be able to lead the public. As a result, the competition for Number 10 is increasingly a public contest about public leadership by public leaders.

British political leaders now have to lay claim to a communion with the public interest by way of a physical attachment to the public itself. Leaders continually have to give the impression to mass audiences that they identify closely with them. These efforts to establish a visceral immediacy with the public can be so intense that they amount to an attempt to establish public leadership by leaders insinuating themselves into the public itself and becoming a constituent part of it. So great is the pressure to acquire and to maintain a condition of public engagement that leaders have cultivated outsider strategies, techniques of spatial leadership and spectacles of personalised interventions.

Responding to, and intensifying, the same pressures for public leadership, the press and electronic media help to stretch the leaders away from their parent party organisations and, where the prime minister is concerned, from the government itself. Through their news coverage, their unremitting usage of opinion polls and their leader-oriented analyses of political developments, the media encourage the shift of interest towards party leaders and their leadership performance. They assist in the generation of a leadership agenda, an aroused consciousness of leadership characteristics and a differentiation of leaders from their parties in respect to both image and substance. This sense of distinction supports the sense of leadership. It also allows a leader considerable licence to appeal across already weakening party lines, to divert criticism away from the party or the government, and to develop multiple points of personal access to the broader constituency of the general public. Such opportunities are particularly useful for a prime minister. If premiers are skilful enough, they can cultivate their personal prestige with the public and deploy their incumbency advantage for national leadership. By doing so, they both increase their negotiating leverage inside government, and enhance further their dominant position in the party and in the cabinet. But whether it is the prime minister or any other leader, they all seek to use their leadership positions to establish leadership as a political issue, as a separate criterion of political evaluation and, thereby, as a forum for personal advancement.

The onset of the British presidency has been accompanied by a critical change in attitudes towards leadership. Previously, party leaders occupied positions of formal leadership. They were seen in essence to assume, rather than to construct, a centre of influence. A party leader might, thereupon, seek to personalise the position and even succeed in closely associating the office with an overlay of selected individual characteristics. But there were always strict limits to this sort of convergence. The leader remained a prominent yet integral element in a highly structured corporate organisation. The leader was the projection of the party – its chief spokesperson and its senior representative tied to the party organisation by innumerable formal and informal cords. The leader was at the top only by being on top of the party's own hierarchy. The prime minister suffered from a double dose of institutionalisation insofar as he or she was a captive of both his or her party and of an office which was officially only first among equals. A prime minister was assumed to inherit the office rather than to fill it with him- or herself. 'The first priority of a prime minister' was to 'do what was expected of him'[108] – i.e. to perform functions, not to provide performances.[109]

The position now is not so restrictive. The old moorings of institutionalisation have been stretched in response to the new context of personalised public leadership. As leaders increasingly stake their claim to leadership positions on the basis of personal characteristics and of a personal rapport with the public, the leadership positions themselves have changed to accommodate the altered outlook and dynamics of political leadership. A prime minister is still supported by the infrastructure of party and cabinet, but to an ever increasing extent that support, and the executive authority derived from it, is clearly dependent upon his or her day-to-day performances as a personal leader of public stature operating in a presidential dimension. Today a prime ministership is increasingly sustained by the need both to attract public approval and to radiate it back to the populace. The public does not tend to demonstrate active approval for institutions or, at least, not in any sustained condition of agitation. But prime ministers and potential prime ministers are locked in a continual struggle for public approval and, as such, they personalise the contest for leadership as a public competition for personal leadership. The public is enticed and cajoled into giving or withdrawing approval from leaders on the basis not only of their public performance as leaders, but of the perceived relationship between their publicly revealed character traits and the provision of personal leadership. In this respect, it was utterly appropriate for Charles Kennedy to mark the new leadership of the Liberal Democrat party in 1999 by launching himself as a public personality. A 'bio-pic' video, screened at the outset of the party's conference in September 1999, featured Kennedy's family and background, and was accompanied by music from his father on violin and mother on piano.[110]

A leader's success is no longer measured solely by his or her instrumental efficiency in acting for the party. It is also assessed by the leader's ability to personify the party, even to the point of translating that personification into a guiding vision and operational identity for the party – i.e. melting the party into him- or herself at the leadership level. Political leaders in Britain today are distinctive from their predecessors in this important respect. In order to survive and to compete effectively in the highly exposed and hostile environment of competitive leadership politics, leaders have to radiate themselves, their character and their background in any way possible to gain tactical advantages over other leaders. By projecting him- or herself, a leader can not only look more like a leader in the singular individual sense. He or she can also assume the individual discretion (1) to match the presentation of personal properties to the public's changeable conceptions of his or her leadership and his or her party in particular; and (2) to respond to the public's more general expectations of political leadership in modern conditions.

What these developments have led to is a widening sense of differentiation between the leaders and their parties. Leaders now stand out to a greater extent than before for reasons that are different from before. They are conspicuous because they have to be. They have to cultivate prominence both to capture public attention and to sustain it on the basis of approval. Their parties expect nothing less. Leaders also stand apart from their parties because they are in essence fighting a different campaign. They are competing with other leaders on grounds of leadership, together with all the distinct criteria and categories associated with it, for the opportunity to become prime minister. Just as leadership has become a political issue in its own right, so leadership has also become accepted as an indispensable function of modern British government. As a consequence, the office of prime minister is now seen as a leadership role to be filled by individuals with proven credentials for leadership. Prime ministers, and aspiring prime ministers, are expected to be forceful personalities with demonstrable drive, independence, integrity and with 'big ideas' of their own.

A party leader is no longer simply a front organisation for a party. By the same token, leaders are no longer just party leaders. Leading a major party is a necessary, but not a sufficient, condition to meet the requirements of contemporary political leadership. To be a prime minister, a leader has to prove in a most direct and immediate way that he or she is worthy of popular consideration as a leader of the British public as well as a leader of the British nation. Within the constraints of what is still primarily a party competition for government, the contest between leaders for the occupancy of Number 10 has assumed an identity that is very much its own. It possesses its own rules of engagement, its own strategies and objectives, and its own standards of assessment. The efforts of leaders to impress the public with their personal leadership, and the emphasis given to the value of leadership in the process, have led to the emergence of a distinctly presidential dimension in British politics. This is not an alternative construction or perspective of the traditional framework of party politics and party government, which continues in much the same vein as it has in the past. The presidential dimension represents a separate and altogether different set of political dynamics.

The presidential dimension may have originated in the old party framework, but it has taken on such a momentum of its own that it has diverged away from the established patterns of political exchange and evaluation. In doing so, it has generated its own form and style of politics that have grown to a position of central importance in British government. Apart from explaining and promoting the popular interest in the substance and provision of political leadership, the presidential dimension fosters an ever closer convergence between connotations of the public and the nation on the one hand and the properties of individual leadership on the other. Britain's leadership specifications are becoming increasingly presidential in character. This means that party leaders are significant not only because they can profoundly affect public confidence in their parties' competence to govern, but also because they work to insinuate themselves into the public's view of itself and of the nation's conception of its distinctiveness.

William Hague and the imperative of the Blair model

The centrality of these leadership dynamics has been decisively affirmed by the recent reforms in the Conservative party. Far from offering the prospect of a future return to traditional forms of collective enterprise, the Conservatives reacted to New Labour's triumph in 1997 by accepting a series of sweeping initiatives designed to enhance the position of the leader in a more democratised party structure. William Hague's leadership was based at the very outset on the need to emulate Tony Blair's position in the Labour party and to engage in a modernisation process comparable to that achieved by New Labour. The compulsive drive to reinvent the party around the central investment in leadership, and the impetus that led to the most drastic changes in the Conservative party since the time of Disraeli, amounted to further proof of a progressive and cumulative development towards the institutionalisation of leadership politics in Britain.

After becoming leader through the traditional means of selection by Conservative MPs, Hague promptly launched a radical offensive against the established party structure, including the rules relating to leadership selection. Hague proposed the streamlining of the separate elements of the party into a single structure with a new constitution. A governing board of 14 members would replace the unwieldy 200-strong Conservative National Union. The board, which would have responsibility for overseeing the whole party, would keep in close contact with members and local associations and be responsive to grassroots sentiments. The declared ethos was one of expanding the scale and vitality of the membership, which would now be encouraged to see itself as 'owning' the party. With this in mind, there would be a national membership system to replace the fragmented and randomly organised format of local association memberships. Members would now be centrally registered and have the organisational capacity not only to engage in rolling policy reviews but also to be part of a new electoral college to select the leader on a 'one member, one vote' basis. Hague also proposed a recruitment drive to increase the membership to one million by 2000 and a set of initiatives to raise the number of women and young people entering the party. In an effort to eliminate the sleaze issue from the party, the new leader announced that the Conservatives would no longer accept foreign donations and would publish the names of major donors. Furthermore, new procedures would be put in place to suspend or expel members whose behaviour brings the party into disrepute.

Hague saw his role as one of reinventing the Conservative party by removing it from its past and challenging it to become at one and the same time an open organisation of participant members and a disciplined support system for the purposes of leadership projection. Hague had to show that he was in touch and could personally and symbolically reach out to the mass of voters who had become disenchanted with the Conservatives. Hague himself would be the instrument of reconnection: 'I want to change the nature of the party so that it is more involving, more democratic, more able to protect its integrity with a single united party constitution.'[111] The image of the Conservative party threatened the prospect of Hague developing a communion with the British public and, therefore, the chief priority was to confront his own party. Hague publicly acknowledged that his chief problem lay with the Conservative party itself: 'We were voted out of office because we lost the faith, the confidence, the goodwill of the electorate. Because we failed to communicate with the people and to show we understood their concerns.'[112] In a campaign similar to Blair's drive to change the status and wording of Clause Four, Hague placed all his political capital and his authority as leader on the need to confront the party's past and its present framework. It would be unacceptable for the party to distract attention from Hague's strategy of public outreach in the same way that it had subverted John Major's authority as prime minister. Accordingly, when Hague announced his plans on 23 July 1997, he made it clear that they were to be on a take-it-or-leave-it basis: 'Back me or sack me',[113] declared Hague. There could be no compromise on such a pivotal issue to his leadership.

The new leader toured Britain in the summer of 1997 in order both to publicise the reform plans and to disengage visibly from Westminster in order to begin to establish a Hague constituency. By the time of the 1997 Conservative party conference, Hague was assured that the party had endorsed his selection as leader and his reform programme. Upon being selected leader in May 1997 by Conservative MPs, Hague had insisted that the party membership should be given the opportunity to confirm or to reject his appointment. The authority of the parliamentary party was no longer sufficient. He wanted 'a mandate, and [he] would not continue as leader without it'.[114] As Tony Blair had done during the period of Labour modernisation,

William Hague linked party reform with the foundations of his leadership. The two issues were conspicuously fused on the ballot question and had the effect desired by Hague. At the 1997 Conservative party conference, it was announced that 81 per cent of those members returning ballots had given their approval to the question posed: 'Do you endorse William Hague as leader of the Conservative Party and support the principles of reform which he has outlined?'.[115]

With the endorsement of his leadership and of the party reforms now assured, Hague set about denouncing key party elites and confronting the prevailing image of the Conservatives following the debacle of the Major administration. Supported by vociferous elements in the rank and file, Hague gave expression to the frustration of the members over the behaviour of the parliamentary party during the previous administration. In attacking the indiscipline that had undermined his predecessor, Hague sought to prevent its repetition during the period of his leadership. The new leader acknowledged that the party in Westminster had become conceited and ingrown: 'People thought we had lost touch with those we always claimed to represent. Our parliamentary party came to be seen as divided, arrogant, selfish and conceited. Our party as a whole was regarded as out of touch and irrelevant.'[116] Humility and contrition were required, but more important was a need to revive the leadership's relationship with the rank and file. Hague promised unity and integrity: 'Never again will we have a divided organisation. Never again will the voice of our members go unheard and never again will we allow the good name of our party to be blackened by the greed and selfishness of a few.'[117] A palpably different party had to be brought into existence through a leadership that would empower the membership as it enhanced the position of the party leader. The new party chairman assured the membership that the party would now belong to its supporters: 'It is going to be your party – not Smith Square's poodle, not the preserve of the National Union, not the parliamentary party's plaything. The new single Conservative Party will belong to its members – all its members. We will all have a say. We will all have a part to play.'[118] Like Blair, Hague set out to forge a party that could be closely identified not just with a new leader but with a new ethos moulded to the organisational requirements and political imperatives of effective personalised leadership.

Further points of comparison were to follow. Hague sought to emulate Blair's successful campaign to reconnect the Labour party to the nation through public policy positions and personal style. Hague set out to distance the party not only from the Major administration but also from the strident tones of the Thatcher era. In 1998, he once again resorted to a ballot of the mass membership to resolve the issue of the party's stand on Britain's participation in the process of European Monetary Union. Hague also pioneered a movement to soften the party's reputation on social issues. He gave emphasis to the ideals of social compassion, community partnership and mutual tolerance. For example, he endorsed the principle of gay marriage and voted to reduce the age of consent for homosexual activity. The Conservative leader also made a point of recognising the value and role of multiculturalism in contemporary Britain. He used himself to give visible and symbolic expression to a leader reaching out to, and engaging in, a more diversified society. Hague's celebrated photo-opportunities of him wearing his baseball cap at Thorpe Park and sipping coconut cocktails at the Notting Hill Carnival were symptomatic of a genre designed to put the party back in touch with the rhythms of a changing Britain.

As part of a general strategy to become even more populist than New Labour, Hague launched his 'Listening To Britain' campaign in July 1998. It was planned to last for a year and was dedicated to eliciting the views, fears and demands of the British people. Under his leadership, the party would become whatever the people wished it to be. The 'Listening To Britain' venture consisted of over a thousand events and featured a series of 'town hall' meetings where any member of the public could attend and speak out to the leadership. During this period, Hague publicised the need for a 'kitchen table conservatism' that attended to those core domestic issues that the Labour government was not succeeding in effectively addressing. A party political broadcast launching the idea featured a young couple discussing education and health issues over their kitchen table. The soap-opera format 'was intended to epitomise ... Hague's determination to take politics out of Westminster and into the nation's kitchens'.[119] This process of listening and learning culminated in the 1999 Conservative party conference when Hague announced his plans for a 'Common Sense Revolution'. Again emulating Blair, the Conservative leader put forward five personal guarantees to the public to show that he understood their concerns and the level of their distrust. His 'common sense' pledges related to education, welfare, the family, national protection and a restoration of faith in politics that embraced not only a reduced bureaucracy, but also cuts in the number of MPs, ministers and political advisors. The latter was part of a general reaction to Labour's programme of constitutional reform that sought to present a more radical set of responses to the problems of government (e.g. greater open government, a Conservative primary for the party's candidate for Mayor of London, a democratically elected second chamber and a quasi-federal proposal for eliminating Scottish and Welsh MPs from parliamentary participation in English legislation).

William Hague has used New Labour's own methods to confront Tony

Blair and to try and establish a new leadership-centred identity for the Conservative party. For example, Hague has followed the Labour leader into the studios of soft format shows (e.g. *Des O'Connor Tonight*, *Parkinson*, *Woman's Hour*) in order to propagate his message. He has also instituted a 'war room' at Central Office with a twenty-four hour rebuttal and attack operation. In an effort to improve the imagery and projection of the leader and to enhance the professionalisation of research, publicity and propaganda at Central Office, Hague has drawn on the services of experienced journalists and broadcasters. Ceri Evans of Channel 4 was made Director of Presentation. Jonathan Holborow, the former editor of the *Mail on Sunday*, was appointed as a campaign consultant. Nicholas Wood left *The Times* to join the Conservatives' media team. The position of chief spin doctor went to Amanda Platell, who had been editor of both the *Sunday Mirror* and the *Sunday Express*. The leverage and status afforded to such individuals in the Hague teams reflected the priority given to leadership outreach and the need to compete with Tony Blair on New Labour's own criteria.

Between 1994 and 1997, Tony Blair had underlined the integrity of his personal vision with public displays of individual origins and family life. At the very outset of his leadership, Hague followed the same route. Just as his relationship with Ffion Jenkins served to exemplify the ideals and problems of a young married couple, so the significance of his past was accentuated for political effect. Hague's trustworthiness and beliefs came from inner experience:

> I didn't learn about enterprise from economics textbooks and the back pages of the Financial Times. I learnt about enterprise first hand, from my own family. My father ran a small business. Hague Soft Drinks ... We were never rich. But we were comfortable. I knew from an early age what that comfort depended on: diligence, enterprise and initiative. Sound business practice, dedication, hard work and long hours.[120]

Hague has also tried to turn Blair's own populism back on to the prime minister. Hague's brand of spatial leadership has not been confined to a dramatised separation from the previous Conservative administration or from the social prejudices of Tory traditionalists. Hague has sought to make a virtue out of the Conservatives' minority status by opening up space between his party and the Labour government on social and geographical grounds. Under Hague, the Conservatives are depicted as the 'outsiders' and Labour is portrayed as the governing establishment. Hague reminds his audiences that he is a Yorkshireman, that he did not attend a public school, and that he is not an urban sophisticate: 'I'm not one of those politicians who looks at the United Kingdom through a pair of binoculars from inside the M25.

I don't look at the world through the wrong end of an Islington drain pipe.'[121] With impeccable populist allusions, Hague has tried to distance himself and the Conservatives from their status as the governing party. In the 1999 Conservative party conference, for example, he rounded on Blair for having complained 'the establishment' was holding the country back: 'He's a 40-something, public school-educated barrister from Islington, with a 200-seat majority in the House of Commons. Who does he think is the Establishment?'[122]

In spite of considerable efforts to engage effectively in 'outsider' politics and to cultivate his own brand of spatial leadership, Hague has found it difficult to make a public impression. He may well find that he will be the leader to have laid the organisational foundations of a new party structure, but that he will not be the person to benefit from them. The investment in personalised public leadership is a two-edged instrument. By orienting the party in a systemic way to the pursuit of power through leadership, Hague has incurred the risk of being replaced by a figure better able to engage in the politics of public leadership. Under Hague, the Conservative party has given the ratchet of presidential politics a further turn by emulating New Labour and even at times surpassing Blair's process of modernisation. Hague and his party have shown that there is no plausible alternative other than to respond to the underlying dynamics of leadership stretch.

A very British presidency

It is important to reiterate that the entity under consideration is very much a British phenomenon. The presence of a *de facto* presidency in the British system has been occasioned by British circumstances and traditions. Just as there are several forces (e.g. spatial leadership, populist politics, public outreach, leadership projection, personal visions, 'contracts') contributing to a 'pull factor', so it is necessary to underline the existence of a strong 'push factor' in the development of this presidential dimension. Key institutional and organisational elements of the British system have not only condoned, but have been active participants in, the contribution of a highly potent and sophisticated politics of public leadership. Pressures from established features and central components of the British constitution have been instrumental in the progressive elongation of leadership stretch.

The political parties, for example, have come not only to sponsor the issue of leadership in political competition, but also to project their leaders as individual summations of public hopes, anxieties and ideals. The organisational impetus and evangelising discipline of Labour's modernising movement found their defining expression in Tony Blair's extraordinary licence to engage in the personalised medium of leadership projection. The discretion afforded by a party previously hostile to the prerogatives of leadership was unprecedented. The party pushed Blair into exaggerated prominence, either by explicit force or by suggestive acquiescence. He was in effect propelled to a level of leadership pre-eminence that was quickly marked by a conspicuous detachment from the party's traditional codes and priorities, and by Blair's almost uninhibited immersion in outsider politics and spatial leadership. So great was the need for electoral success that the party shared in the complicity to provide a leader in the mould of Margaret Thatcher. Blair redefined, relocated and re-branded his party from the top. He provided a necessary source of focus and unity. He also engineered a high level of central direction and co-ordination. Both contributions were based upon a wider organisational impulse to exploit Conservative weaknesses and to demonstrate Labour's competence as an alternative government. The managerial ethos of the Blairite project and the New Labour movement was exemplified by the leadership's ability to manage the party. This drive for professionalism and discipline in the increasingly public context of political engagement continued into government as the party was immediately mobilised into a leadership-centred campaign for a second term of office.

The power of collective self-interest in the dynamics of leadership promotion is also evident at the level of the cabinet. Cabinets – filled as they are with professional politicians who know what is required for governmental and electoral viability in modern conditions – underwrite prime ministerial prominence and leverage as the necessary instruments for remaining in office. Many of the prime minister's colleagues around the cabinet table will still aspire to his or her position, but their highest priority will be to remain in government. They will therefore condone and even encourage a prime minister to go out and cultivate a presidential status in the public battle to provide high profile popular leadership. This amounts to collective peer group pressure to a prime minister to breach the collective ethos of the cabinet and to assume both a public persona and an individual pre-eminence for the sake of the cabinet and the party as a whole.

In spite of the changes in leadership selection rules in both the main parties which now protect prime ministers from boardroom reshuffles, the cabinet continues to be the major constraint upon the prime minister and the main source of alternative leadership. The cabinet remains the structural expression of the system's corporate ethos of collective action and responsibility. The cabinet still provides a pool of senior figures from which potential leaders will emerge. Political security and individual advancement are the drives that generate the pack instincts of outward solidarity and mutual support in a cabinet context. And yet these self-same drives are also responsible for the cabinet underwriting the prime ministerial role of a personalised public leadership that will project the party's merits and provide a defence to the leadership claims of other parties. The imperatives of political competition that drive the cabinet to close ranks as a corporate entity, therefore, can also propel one of their number to break ranks continually and flamboyantly for the sake of the cabinet and the interests of the governing party. Not to allow or to encourage this maverick behaviour would be to risk repeating the cautionary experience of John Major's second administration, which collapsed into cabinet disarray and a leadership that became a public liability.

The presidential dimension is deeply situated in British conditions, traditions and structures. Its integral relationship to British forms and processes also means that the scale and penetration of this presidential development have been largely ignored. Indeed, its existence has been strenuously refuted. This in itself has been another very British feature of this presidential presence. Given the British political tradition of pragmatic adjustment within a continuity of forms, there has been little impulse to give recognition to an outcome that appears to contravene the evolutionary thrust of British political development. The unassimilable nature of this apparent discontinuity is further exacerbated by the characteristically empirical predisposition of British political analysis in this area. The tendency in this perspective is to see the British system as a summation of historical and contemporary experience, which is defined by generic characterisations such as parliamentary sovereignty, constitutional monarchy and cabinet government. Presidentialism has never received recognition in this tradition. Moreover, in many respects it has been depicted as a point of contrast that assists in the demarcation and identity of British forms in relation to others. In this respect, the presidential form has often been taken to be the polar opposite of a parliamentary form of government. The contrast is based upon empirical differences that can be discerned between two systems that are then assumed to be decisively distinct from one another. A dialectical element to the relationship can often be detected in the respective treatments given to the two forms. Thus the more presidential a system is perceived to be, the more divergent it is assumed to be from the British model of parliamentary democracy. Accordingly, prime ministers and cabinets have an identity that is often based upon a negative – i.e. they are not and cannot be constituent parts of a presidential system. To claim that a presidential dimension exists, therefore, represents a double affront. First, it is dependent upon using a frame of reference that is widely assumed to be historically and structurally alien to the British system. Second, the presidential analogy is assumed to rely upon a form of analysis that is oriented less to the traditions of empirical inquiry and more to conceptual abstractions and rational devices.

Normally, the study of the prime ministerial office is synonymous with the study of individual prime ministers. While analysis of American presidents is always linked to, and conditioned by, a conception of the presidency, prime ministers are examined as discrete episodes with no aggregate or developmental overlays. On the contrary, it is more likely that a prime minister will be seen as a derivative, or as an expression, of the cabinet. Prime ministers may be used to explain issues and decisions but not something as abstract as the premiership or the notion of its linear progression. In the United States, the presidency is the constitutional point of departure in examining the executive branch. Such a palpable and singular foundation to the political executive is absent in the British premiership. To regard the premiership as an originating and activating central agency of executive government, therefore, can seem highly contrived. It offends the empirical perspective because it seems as if the premiership has been created as an explanatory construct, or a historical progression where no material or institutional grounds exist to support such an abstraction. This piece of interpretive creation cannot easily be reconciled either with the segmented biographical approach of mainstream prime ministerial study, or with the conventions and protocols of an unwritten constitution that are designed to foreclose serious constitutional speculation. The legitimacy, and even existence, of the premiership, therefore, can be brought into question as an alien construct conceived through alien methods. Scepticism of this order renders the premiership an implausible basis for a presidential dimension in Britain.

This study acknowledges these perspectives and traditions but refuses to be bound by them in the face of an emergent hybrid that fuses presidential characteristics with the forms of parliamentary democracy and cabinet government. The position adopted by this analysis, on the basis of a variety of developments and trends, is one of a genuine British presidency that has grown, and is growing, incrementally into a permanent feature of the British system. The general difficulty in giving credence to such a development is entirely consistent with the dualistic outlook towards presidential and parliamentary government, which allocates mutually exclusive identities to two forms that are in fact capable of selective areas of convergence. Opponents of any reference to a presidency in British conditions claim that such heresies are ahistorical in nature and contrary to the evolutionary scheme of the British constitution. Nevertheless, adherents to the historical continuity of the cabinet can sometimes overlook the ahistorical properties of their own attachment to an institution that has demonstrated a variety of forms and functions.

More significantly, the rise of the British presidency is based not upon a sudden and temporary mutation but upon a series of extensive developments buried deep in the dynamics of British politics. The very evolutionary outlook that has facilitated the emergence of such a presidential entity has also induced a state of imperturbable myopia that cannot recognise the already assimilated innovation within its midst. The pragmatism that fosters the evolutionary outlook militates not only against the recognition of a British presidency, but also against the need to give any acknowledgement to a necessarily integrated feature within the overall system. It is necessary for this myopia to be corrected to the extent of underlining the existence of an authentic presidential dimension within the framework of British government. The purpose of this study has been to show that while forms can remain the same, substantive and far-reaching changes can occur within their interiors. In this case, a *de facto* British presidency has emerged within a *de jure* parliamentary–cabinet format.

Just as important as what is being claimed is what is not being asserted. By alluding to a British presidency, the aim is not to imply the presence of a process of 'presidentialisation'. The British presidency is a hybrid. It is not a transitional process from one pure form to another. It does not signify part of a metamorphosis that has an absolute and conclusive end point. The existence of a British presidency does not infer a progressive and enveloping set of dynamics that will culminate in a full presidential system. Moreover, the validity of the British presidency proposition does not depend upon evidence of a complete and final development towards a full presidential state of existence. On the contrary, the impulse to defer any recognition of a British presidential dimension until it can be shown that a full presidential system has emerged constitutes one of the chief problems in this field. In being seen as an either-all-or-nothing phenomenon, then the British presidency is nothing and will remain nothing. But the argument has never been couched as a total and comprehensive proposition.

The case advanced in this study for a presidential dimension in British politics is not the same as, and is not dependent upon, the case for the 'presidentialisation' of British government. In some respects, attempts to substantiate a presidential element in British politics as part of a wider 'presidentialisation' process serve to delay or to defer recognition of the existence of a presidential dimension. In following the British constitution's reductionist themes of singular motives and forces of political explanation, attempts to couple 'presidentialisation' with electoral behaviour and party choice, or with the formal configuration and resources of the core executive, can be a positive hindrance to reaching an understanding of the pluralist character of the British presidency.

This study does not take the term 'presidential' to mean a set of closed categories and absolute properties that are only relevant and applicable *in toto*. Presidential systems are as mutable, contingent and evolutionary as the British parliamentary system. What this analysis seeks to show is that an evolutionary ideal is two edged. It does not just underwrite continuity but incorporates the idea of an open-ended system that accommodates gradual change but which can also lead to the graduated production of radical change. In this case, the emphasis lies appropriately upon that area which is responsible for producing extensive change – namely the ramifying dynamics of the relationship between party leaders and public expectations, and upon the generation and assimilation of new, extended and transposed roles on the part of party leaders in general and prime ministers in particular. It is this synergy between the public and personal constituents of contemporary leadership that is reconfiguring the British premiership into a new identity.

Writing off presidential-style prime ministers as individual idiosyncrasies that denote no sense of underlying change is no longer satisfactory. The British prime minister has evolved, and is evolving, away from what a prime minister used to do and used to be. It is no longer acceptable simply to wait for Tony Blair's premiership to decline, in order to dismiss its extraordinary features as the ultimate depiction of the presidential fallacy. On the contrary, Blair's premiership represents another part of the clinching proof that British politics has accommodated and adjusted to a distinctive presidential dimension. Evolution, even political and constitutional evolution, cannot turn the clock back. It cannot reverse itself because time is a generative force in its own right. If evolution means never escaping from the inheritance of the past, it also means that it is impossible to return to the conditions of the past.

Britain has a reputation both of dependency upon benevolent political evolution and of denying the onset of change. But a point comes when the scale of change is so extensive that even the British have to acknowledge it. That point has now been reached with the premiership. The present position of the British prime minister may be derived from, and sustained by, the conventional anchorage points of the British constitution, but the nature of the office is no longer wholly reducible to them. The parallels drawn with the American presidency indicate that the contemporary strategies and roles that have become integral to the British premiership can no longer be satisfactorily accounted for by the conventional depictions of the prime ministerial office. British prime ministers and opposition leaders are now pushed and pulled and stretched into unparliamentary states of exaggerated prominence. These conditions require such a grasp of presidential skills and denote such a level of presidential penetration that the British premiership has become in essence a British presidency.

This study has attempted to draw attention to the existence of a presidential dimension in British politics and, in doing so, to convey something of the properties and dynamics of what is a rapidly evolving hybrid. However, an examination of this kind cannot answer all the questions nor resolve all the issues raised by such a development. The role and position of the premiership now have a greater sense of identity and definition than in the past. This in turn has led to a heightened awareness of a linkage between personality characteristics, leadership qualities and institutional requirements. Nevertheless, the implications of such an enhanced centre of personalised and publicised leadership cannot yet be discerned with any degree of precision or certainty. The rise of the British presidency denotes a movement into the unknown where future projections remain largely problematic.

While it is not possible to predict all the ramifications of the British presidency, on the balance of current probabilities some developments seem more likely to occur than others. It is probable, for example, that the decentralising drives associated with Scottish and Welsh devolution and the establishment of an elected London authority and mayor will prompt party leaders at the centre into various compensating strategies, designed to generate new gravitational fields of influence for their parties. The prime minister experienced a rapid reaction to Millbank's efforts to organise the Labour party's choice of leaders in Wales and London. In February 2000, Alun Michael was forced to stand down as the Welsh assembly's First Secretary and leader of the Welsh Labour party after being politically undermined by his position as Blair's preferred choice of leader. A month later, Ken Livingstone launched a campaign to delegitimise the party's selection process for the mayoral candidacy in London. He subsequently announced that he would stand as an independent, relying upon his political status and his personal claims to leadership, in order to generate the support and resources required for a viable campaign. The coalitional and openly negotiable basis of political movement occasioned by the plurality of domestic leaders in Cardiff, Edinburgh, Belfast and London will be further intensified if devolution spreads to the English regions and to other major cities. The pluralistic nature of political engagement will also be advanced if some element of proportional representation is introduced into the system of parliamentary elections. Tony Blair may have made constitutional reform a defining theme of his premiership, but even the chief patron of the British constitution's modernisation will be subject to the conditioning constraints of the new or revived features of the constitutional order.

The aggregate effect of the creation of new centres of power and the relative decline in influence of other centres is difficult to subject to precise measurement. But it seems likely that the changes in the infrastructure will complement the trends towards electoral volatility and party dealignment. As a consequence, the clustering of parties in the centre-ground will be intensified. In this context, each party leader will increasingly be expected to inject some form of personalised branding into the message of each party in order to differentiate it from the others. Contenders for the premiership will have no alternative other than to give emphasis to the language and imagery of consensus leadership if they are to maximise their opportunities for securing a winning electoral coalition. By the same token, the only substantive alternative to the displaced tradition of governments alternating between left and right would seem to lie in the individuated visions and policy nuances of the leaders competing for power in the centre-ground.

The imposition of new constitutional constraints (e.g. devolved assemblies, a reformed House of Lords, freedom of information and the incorporation of the European Convention on Human Rights), together with the contingent political properties of high profile leadership within a democratic polity, may well lead British premiers to gravitate increasingly to the refuge of the international dimension. It is probable that prime ministers, like American presidents, will come to value the enriched potential of foreign policy for developing the extra-constitutional properties of executive prerogatives and for enhancing leadership claims with the symbols and allusions of the national interest. Whether or not British prime ministers will extend the principle of a foreign policy premiership to the level that produced the 'two presidencies'[123] thesis in the United States is open to question. What seems certain, however, is that the British leader will need to be actively engaged in the development of the European Union and in the process to enhance the premiership as a centre of international leadership and national destiny. At the same time, British prime ministers will need to be sensitive to the populist potential of anti-Europeanism. Like an American president who has to guard against popular perceptions of excessive international distractions, the British premier will need to demonstrate a resolve to protect British interests and Britain's identity from the threat both of European integration and of domestic politicians laying claims to leadership on the basis of nationalist prejudices.

The conspicuously exposed position of a contemporary British premier as an alternative construction of popular sovereignty gives rise to another likely parallel with the American presidency. This relates to the processes of political decline. Parties now invest enormous resources in the selection, development and security of their leaders. None of the main parties are now able to replace damaged leaders quickly and painlessly through back-bench coups. Leadership contests are protracted and hugely expensive in financial, organisational and political costs. The decline of a party leader, and especially a premier, will, therefore, be a slow and debilitating experience. Just as presidents progressively lose authority behind the grandeur of appearance and formal power, so British premiers will also face a slow disintegration of both their visions and their personal reputations for competence, skill and decision making.

Furthermore, it would be wholly consistent with such individuated claims to leadership for British premiers to follow their American counterparts in becoming acutely vulnerable to the politics of scandal, in which authority is undermined through a succession of moral and ethical indictments of a leader's behaviour and judgement. Given the developing levels of constitutional consciousness derived from the reforms of the Blair administration, such scandals would be shaped and intensified by the usage of constitutional arguments and references to delegitimise a government through allegations of an abuse of power. This resort to constitutional redress may well be part of a larger movement to deploy the modernised constitution as a reference point for political opposition and policy challenge through allegations of executive excess. Given the enlarged opportunities for fomenting leadership crises, it is not inconceivable that a solution could be found in the form of a first minister from Wales or Scotland, or a London mayor, running on the basis of a model national or municipal administration and offering an antidote to the alleged sleaze of a Westminster-based government.

Such speculations may seem remote eventualities but even now they would not be regarded as inconceivable or implausible. On the contrary, they are consistent with current trends. The British system has already revealed itself to be amenable to a highly advanced and sophisticated politics of public leadership. The strategies, dynamics and vocabulary of such a politics have been shown to co-exist effectively with the parliamentary and cabinet structures of the British government. In many respects, the adversarial culture of British politics and British institutional design has been reformulated to accommodate a state of continual competition over the respective claims to political, national and even international leadership. Responses to profound social and political issues are increasingly subsumed under the rubric of new leadership. In contemporary British politics, policy prescriptions are almost invariably refracted through the agency of an enabling leadership. Solutions to problems that are reduced to problems of leadership are now habitually defined in terms of the need for alternative leadership. Political parties are permanently enthralled with the projected utility and leverage of their actual or potential leaders.

It is difficult to discern the limits of such a leadership-centred political culture. This is partly attributable to the sheer pace of change. But more significantly, it is also because there are no precise boundaries to what it is to be presidential. On the contrary, the essence of presidentialism is an enduring debate on the meaning and implications of its existence and on the potential and usage of its authority. The American system, in particular, demonstrates that an integral characteristic of a functioning presidential system is a highly self-conscious and articulate set of disputes over the rightful roles, powers and reach of executive leadership in a democratic system. Debates over competing interpretations of executive authority, and over the constituent requirements of contemporary leadership, already form part of the British political landscape. In doing so, they constitute further evidence of the onset of a British presidency. As this study and the responses to it will attest, the British presidency has become a live political issue because it is an active and open-ended political development.

Notes

1 Paul Whitley and Patrick Seyd, 'Blair's armchair support', *The Guardian*, 7 April 1998.
2 See Anthony Giddens, *The Third Way: The Renewal of Social Democracy* (Oxford, Polity, 1998).
3 Dominic Wring, 'From Mass Propaganda to Political Marketing: The Transformation of Labour Party Election Campaigning', in Colin Rallings, David M. Farrell, David Denver and David Broughton (eds), *British Parties and Elections Yearbook, 1995* (London, Frank Cass, 1996), pp. 105–24.
4 Richard Burden, 'Pause for thought', *The Guardian*, 11 August 1995.
5 Bob Marshall-Andrews, 'Don't push the Labour party too far, Mr Blair', *Sunday Times*, 11 January 1998.
6 Bob Marshall-Andrews, 'Let's make a bonfire of Labour's vanities', *Sunday Times*, 3 January 1999.
7 Ken Livingstone, 'When will we get democracy back in the Labour party?, *The Independent*, 23 September 1998.
8 Anne McElvoy, 'Paradox at Labour's heart', *Daily Telegraph*, 27 October 1997.
9 Siôn Simon, 'We are all control freaks', *Daily Telegraph*, 16 November 1998.
10 Hugo Young, 'Spin is the source of this trouble. It's not a big deal', *The Guardian*, 24 June 1999.
11 Young, 'Spin is the source of this trouble.
12 William Rees-Mogg, 'Remember the Bounty, Mr Blair', *The Times*, 16 November 1998.
13 Siôn Simon, 'Soothing the footsoldiers', *Daily Telegraph*, 24 May 1999.
14 See Maurice Winstone, 'Filtering out democracy', *Red Pepper*, October 1999.
15 Speech by the prime minister at the Birmingham International Convention Centre, 22 June 1999, http://www.number–10.gov.uk/public/info/ ... ches/Speech_display. asp? random+0&index=1.
16 Speech by the prime minister to the CBI at Birmingham International Convention Centre, 2 November 1999, http://www.number–10.gov.uk/public/news/index.html.
17 Speech by the prime minister to the CBI.
18 Speech by the prime minister to the CBI.
19 Andrew Rawnsley, 'Relax Prime Minister, it would be good for you and your Government to let the pager slaves go free', *The Observer*, 7 June 1998.

20 Rawnsley, 'Relax Prime Minister'.
21 Steve Richards, 'Why is Blair so worried by Labour's hard left?', *The Independent*, 17 August 1998.
22 Mark Austin and Zoe Brennan, 'Obey, obey … how Mandelson's men turn MPs into Daleks', *Sunday Times*, 29 March 1998.
23 Anne McElvoy, 'Tony has some little lambs, but they never bleat', *The Independent*, 2 April 1998.
24 Donald Macintye, 'Where will Blair find the critics in this parliament?', *The Independent*, 13 May 1997.
25 Cabinet Office press release, 9 May 1997.
26 Peter Mandelson and Roger Liddle, *The Blair Revolution: Can New Labour Deliver?* (London, Faber, 1996), p. 203.
27 *Labour Party Manifesto 1997*.
28 Robert Blake, 'The show ain't over yet', *Sunday Times*, 27 September 1998.
29 'Contempt for Parliament', *Daily Telegraph*, 12 July 1997.
30 'Contempt for Parliament'.
31 Peter Riddell, 'Does anybody listen to MPs?', *The Times*, 23 March 1998.
32 Riddell, 'Does anybody listen to MPs?'
33 Mandelson and Liddle, *The Blair Revolution*, pp. 237–8.
34 Mandelson and Liddle, *The Blair Revolution*, p. 238.
35 Mandelson and Liddle, *The Blair Revolution*, p. 238.
36 Mandelson and Liddle, *The Blair Revolution*, p. 236.
37 Mandelson and Liddle, *The Blair Revolution*, p. 237.
38 Mandelson and Liddle, *The Blair Revolution*, p. 240.
39 Tony Blair quoted in Peter Hennessy, *The Blair Centre: A Question of Command and Control?* (London, Public Management Foundation, 1999), p. 2.
40 Caroline Daniel, 'May the taskforce be with you', *New Statesman*, 1 August 1997.
41 Quoted in 'What's it all about?: frequently asked questions (FAQs)', Social Exclusion Unit Homepage, http://www.cabinet-office.gov.uk/seu/index.htm.
42 Quoted in 'What's it all about?
43 Quoted in John Lloyd, 'Holistic medicine for the excluded', *The Times*, 5 December 1997.
44 Lloyd, 'Holistic medicine for the excluded'.
45 Written statement by the prime minister on the Cabinet Office Review, http://open.gov.uk/co/review.htm.
46 Written statement by the prime minister on the Cabinet Office Review.
47 Written statement by the prime minister on the Cabinet Office Review.
48 Dennis Kavanagh and Anthony Seldon, *The Powers Behind the Prime Minister: The Hidden Influence of Number Ten* (London, HarperCollins, 1999), pp. 285–6.
49 Peter Riddell, 'We're missing you, Mr Blair', *The Times*, 8 June 1998.
50 Hennessy, *The Blair Centre*, p. 3.
51 Hugo Young, 'Labour is at peace: the lion lies down with the lamb. For the time being', *The Guardian*, 28 July 1998.
52 Young, 'Labour is at peace'.
53 Executive Summary, White Paper, Modernising Government, Cabinet Office Homepage http://www.cabinet-office.gov.uk/moderngov/1999/whitepaper/related/executive.htm, p. 2.
54 Hugo Young, 'Wilsonian shadows dwarf Tony Blair', *The Guardian*, 2 January 1997.
55 Young, 'Wilsonian shadows dwarf Tony Blair'.

56 Hugo Young, 'Amazingly good so far', *The Guardian*, 30 November 1997.
57 'Welcome to the cabinet', *The Economist*, 25 July 1998.
58 Kavanagh and Seldon, *The Powers Behind the Prime Minister*, p. 288.
59 Kavanagh and Seldon, *The Powers Behind the Prime Minister*, pp. 300–1.
60 Kavanagh and Seldon, *The Powers Behind the Prime Minister*, p. 300.
61 Peter Hennessy quoted in Michael Cockerell, 'The secret world of Tony Blair', *New Statesman*, 14 February 2000.
62 Quoted in Peter Hennessy, 'Tony Blair, the Caesar of our times', *Daily Telegraph*, 13 July 1999.
63 Quoted in Hennessy, *The Blair Centre*, p. 8.
64 Philip Stephens, 'Rule by lighthouse', *Financial Times*, 16 July 1999.
65 Quoted in Hennessy, 'Tony Blair, the Caesar of our times'.
66 Philip Stephens, 'Shuffling the pack', *Financial Times*, 27 July 1998.
67 Steve Richards, 'You got what you deserve', *New Statesman*, 1 May 1998.
68 Hennessy, *The Blair Centre*, p. 9.
69 Martin Burch and Ian Holliday, *The British Cabinet System* (Hemel Hempstead, Prentice Hall/Harvester Wheatsheaf, 1996), ch. 5.
70 Hennessy, 'Tony Blair, the Caesar of our times'.
71 Stephens, 'Rule by lighthouse'.
72 Quoted in Gregory Palast, 'There are 17 people who count. To say that I am intimate with every one of them is the understatement of the century', *The Observer*, 5 July 1998.
73 See pp. 12–19.
74 Michael Foley, *The Rise of the British Presidency* (Manchester, Manchester University Press, 1993); first edition of the present volume.
75 Quoted in *Matrix of Power: The Cabinet*, 8 October 1999.
76 *Matrix of Power*, BBC Radio 4.
77 Quoted in an interview with Peter Riddell and Philip Webster, *The Times*, 2 September 1999.
78 Peter Riddell, 'Blair needs a sharper team to focus on the big picture', *The Times*, 23 January 1998.
79 Peter Riddell, 'You'll never walk alone, Mr Blair', *The Times*, 22 February 1999.
80 Peter Riddell, 'Cracks in the Cabinet cement', *The Times*, 10 November 1997.
81 Riddell, 'You'll never walk alone'.
82 Hennessy, *The Blair Centre*, p. 17.
83 Hennessy, *The Blair Centre*, p. 17.
84 Quoted in Anthony Bevins, 'The Blair audit', *Independent on Sunday*, 17 April 1998.
85 Hennessy, *The Blair Centre* p. 18.
86 Michael White, 'Tiger Tony's hamsters', *The Guardian*, 21 January 1999.
87 White, 'Tiger Tony's hamsters'.
88 Andrew Marr, 'For Tony Blair, the real enemy is within the walls of the cabinet', *The Independent*, 23 December 1997.
89 Richard Hodder-Williams, 'The Prime Ministership, 1945–1955', in Donald Shell and Richard Hodder-Williams (eds), *Churchill to Major: The British Prime Ministership since 1945* (London, Hurst, 1995), p. 225.
90 Colin Campbell, *The U. S. Presidency in Crisis: A Comparative Perspective* (New York, Oxford University Press, 1998), p. 29.
91 For example, see Peter Hennessy, *The Hidden Wiring: Unearthing the British Constitution* (London, Victor Gollanz, 1995), ch. 4; Burch and Holliday, *The British Cabinet System*; Rodney Brazier, *Ministers of the Crown* (Oxford, Clarendon, 1997); Gerald Kaufman,

How to be a Minister (London, Faber, 1997); Graham Thomas, *Prime Minister and Cabinet Today* (Manchester, Manchester University Press, 1998), ch. 9; Martin J. Smith, *The Core Executive in Britain* (Basingstoke, Macmillan, 1999), ch. 4.

92 Peter Hennessy, *Cabinet* (Oxford, Basil Blackwell, 1986), p. 122.

93 Ronald Butt, 'A missionary in politics', *The Times*, 23 November 1990.

94 Peter Hennessy, 'How Much Room at the Top? Margaret Thatcher, the Cabinet and Power Sharing', in Philip Norton (ed.), *New Directions in British Politics? Essays on the Evolving Constitution* (Aldershot, Edward Elgar, 1991), p. 34.

95 Peter Madgwick, *British Government: The Central Executive Territory* (London, Philip Allan, 1991), p. 238.

96 George Jones, 'Prime Minister and Cabinet', *Wroxton Papers in Politics* (Wroxton College, 1990), p. 13.

97 Riddell, 'You'll never walk alone, Mr Blair'.

98 Peter Riddell, 'Cracks in the Cabinet cement'.

99 Riddell, 'Cracks in the Cabinet cement'.

100 Riddell, 'Cracks in the Cabinet cement'.

101 Peter Riddell, 'RIP, Cabinet government', *The Times*, 5 January 1998.

102 Peter Riddell, 'Blair's new look reveals growing signs of maturity', *The Times*, 29 July 1998.

103 Riddell, 'Blair's new look reveals growing signs of maturity'.

104 Riddell, 'We're missing you Mr Blair'.

105 Riddell, 'You'll never walk alone, Mr Blair'.

106 For example, see Hennessy, *The Blair Centre*, pp. 1–2; Ian Aitken, 'It's winners who change the course of history', *The Guardian*, 12 August 1999; Mike Diboll, 'The Duce of Downing Street', *The Times*, 6 August 1999.

107 Peter Hennessy, *Cabinet* (Oxford, Basil Blackwell, 1986), p. 121.

108 Richard Rose, 'British Government: The Job at the Top', in Richard Rose and Ezra N. Suleiman (eds), *Presidents and Prime Ministers* (Washington, DC, American Enterprise Institute, 1980), p. 44.

109 It should be pointed out that this remains the view held by most of the leading scholars in the field. Anthony King, for example, believes that the 'person who walks for the first time through the door of Number 10 as prime minister does not create or recreate the prime ministership: the job, to a considerable extent, already exists' (p. 31). Prime ministers, therefore, 'just acquire the job and do it' (p. 45). Consequently, scholars need to study, 'not the prime minister but prime ministerships' (p. 43). See Anthony King, 'The British Prime Ministership in the Age of the Career Politician', *West European Politics*, 14, no. 2 (April 1991), pp. 25–47. See also Peter Hennessy, 'Finding a job for the prime minister', *The Independent*, 8 July 1991.

110 Party political broadcast, 20 September 1999.

111 Quoted in Peter Stodhard, 'A chameleon on a sheet of glass', *The Times*, 6 October 1997.

112 Quoted in Michael White, 'Hague attacks Tory "legacy of sleaze"', *The Guardian*, 22 May 1997.

113 Quoted in Siân Clare, 'Hague plans biggest party reform since Disraeli', *Western Mail*, 24 July 1997.

114 Quoted in Philip Webster, 'Hague promises immediate vote for the grassroots', *The Times*, 17 May 1997.

115 Hague received the support of 80.78 per cent of those responding to the ballot. The number of ballots returned amounted to 44.84 per cent of the ballots distributed by the party.

116 Leader's speech to the Conservative party conference 1997, *The Times*, 8 October 1997.
117 Leader's speech to the Conservative Party Conference 1997, *The Times*, 11 October 1997.
118 Speech by the party chairman (Lord Parkinson) to the Conservative party conference 1997, *The Times*, 9 October 1997.
119 Lucy Ward, 'In true soap style, Hague's kitchen table couple stick the breadknife into Labour', *The Guardian*, 15 April 1999.
120 Leader's speech to the Conservative party conference 1997, *The Guardian*, 11 October 1997.
121 Leader's speech to the Conservative party conference 1997, *The Guardian*, 11 October 1997.
122 Leader's speech to the Conservative party conference 1999, *The Times*, 8 October 1999.
123 The classic statement on the 'two presidencies' thesis is provided by Aaron Wildavsky, 'The Two Presidencies', in Aaron Wildavsky, *The Beleaguered Presidency* (New Brunswick, Transaction, 1991), pp. 29–46.

Index